Unjust Deeds

Justice, Power, and Politics

The Justice, Power, and Politics series publishes new works in history that explore the myriad struggles for justice, battles for power, and shifts in politics that have shaped the United States over time. Through the lenses of justice, power, and politics, the series seeks to broaden scholarly debates about America's past as well as to inform public discussions about its future.

More information on the series, including a complete list of books published, is available at http://justicepowerandpolitics.com/.

Unjust Deeds

The Restrictive Covenant Cases
and the Making of the
Civil Rights Movement

Jeffrey D. Gonda

The University of North Carolina Press
CHAPEL HILL

This book was published with the assistance of the
Thornton H. Brooks Fund of the University of North Carolina Press.

Manufactured in the United States of America
Set in Charter and Museu Slab
by Westchester Publishing Services
The paper in this book meets the guidelines for permanence
and durability of the Committee on Production Guidelines for
Book Longevity of the Council on Library Resources.

The University of North Carolina Press has been a member
of the Green Press Initiative since 2003.

Cover illustration: House for sale at 6911 Eighth St. N.W., Washington, D.C.

Library of Congress Cataloging-in-Publication Data
Gonda, Jeffrey D., author.
Unjust deeds : the restrictive covenant cases and the making of the civil rights
movement / Jeffrey D. Gonda.
    pages cm. — (Justice, power, and politics)
Includes bibliographical references and index.
ISBN 978-1-4696-2545-4 (cloth : alk. paper) — ISBN 978-1-4696-2546-1 (ebook)
1. Shelley, J. D.—Trials, litigation, etc.   2. Kraemer, Louis—Trials, litigation, etc.
3. Discrimination in housing—Law and legislation—United States—Cases.   4. Real
covenants—United States—Cases.   5. African Americans—Legal status, laws, etc.—
United States—Cases.   I. Title.
    KF228.S53G66 2015
    344.73'0636351—dc23
                                                                2015010508

Portions of chapters 2, 3, and 4 appeared earlier in somewhat different
form in Jeffrey D. Gonda, "Litigating Racial Justice at the Grassroots: The
Shelley Family, Black Realtors, and *Shelley v. Kraemer* (1948)," *Journal of
Supreme Court History* 39, no. 3 (November 2014): 329–46.

For my grandmothers,
Maxine Moore Sehring and Elizabeth Chandler Gonda,
who taught me everything I know about strength,

and for Paul Gonda,
who was loved and left us too soon.

To the one who knocks, the door will be opened.
—Matthew 7:8

*I say to you today, the Negro stands on the porch
and knocks. He holds in his hands the bill for
nearly three centuries of unrequited toil. He knocks.
"Let me come in," he says. "Let me come in and sit by
the fire. I helped to build this house!"*
—George L. Vaughn,
attorney for J. D. and Ethel Lee Shelley

Contents

Acknowledgments

This project was long in the making and benefited at countless points from the generosity and effort of so many individuals and organizations. The combined support of Yale University, Syracuse University, and the Giles K. Whiting Foundation made possible much of the research and writing that has come together herein. Assistance from the American Historical Association's Littleton-Griswold Research Grant program underwrote key archival research as well.

I have been fortunate to work with an outstanding team at the University North Carolina Press as part of the Justice, Power, and Politics Series. Rhonda Williams and Heather Thompson have been supportive from the moment they laid eyes on the manuscript, and Brandon Proia has brought a deft touch, keen enthusiasm, and a whole lot of man-hours to these pages. The editors believed in this project from the start, and I am grateful for all of their hard work toward putting it into print. Two excellent readers, Rob Smith and Susan Carle, both helped transform this into a stronger book with their encouraging observations, and they have my profound thanks. I am especially indebted to Susan Carle for her extensive and thoughtful comments. She understood the mission of this work with a depth and clarity that was invigorating and that made the text better at every turn.

I owe additional thanks to the people who sustained, challenged, and shaped this work from its inception. At Princeton I benefited from the guidance of Kevin Kruse—who first introduced me to the covenant cases—Daphne Brooks, Valerie Smith, Eddie Glaude, and Noliwe Rooks. Saje Mathieu inspired me to pursue as a scholar the issues discussed in this book. At Yale I received guidance of a caliber for which I cannot sufficiently express my gratitude. The intellectual fingerprints of John Witt, Jennifer Klein, Jonathan Holloway, and Glenda Gilmore are everywhere in these pages. Jonathan and Glenda were tireless in their efforts to give my writing and my scholarship more nuance and impact. I am forever grateful for their investment in me and for the sterling examples they provided of the power of mentorship. Without them I would not be where I am today. Rick Brooks, Carol Rose, Rick Sander, and Nathan Connolly all shared their work with me along the way and provided illumination and encouragement. The advice and support of Elizabeth Alexander, Ed Rugemer, David Blight, Steve

ix

Pitti, Naomi Lamoreaux, Bill Rando, Kathleen Cleaver, Wendy Plotkin, Dan Sharfstein, and Randall Kennedy all made the journey smoother.

A great team of young scholars were intellectual partners as this book took shape, including Ryan Brasseaux, Erin Wood, Allison Gorsuch, Betsy Beasley, Caitlin Verboon, Julia Guarneri, Tafari Lumumba, Lerone Martin, and Chris Bonner. Delaina Price kept me going. Lauren Pearlman offered insight on D.C. and thought-provoking conversations. Sam Schaffer gave wise counsel. Katherine Mooney watched out for me at conferences and on a research trip to Lexington. I found a kindred spirit in Brandon Terry who lent his friendship, time, and expertise to this project for eight years. I have also been blessed with generous and supportive colleagues at Syracuse who have helped move this project along. My thanks go out to Carol Faulkner, Michael Ebner, Andrew Cohen, Keith Bybee, Tom Keck, Grant Reeher, Dave Van Slyke, Elisabeth Lasch-Quinn, Gladys McCormick, Norman Kutcher, Peggy Thompson, Drew Lipman, and a host of other folks who walk the halls here. The institutional support from the Maxwell School and Campbell Public Affairs Institute has been tremendous.

The research for this project took place at an array of institutions and with the help of a number of archivists. Special thanks are owed to Bill Frank of the Huntington Library, Seth Kronemer of the Howard University Law School Library, the staff of the Moorland-Spingarn Archives, Sam Rushay and Randy Sowell at the Truman Presidential Library, and Michelle McKinney at the Wright Museum in Detroit.

To my family, who have listened to me talk about restrictive covenants over dinners and holidays for nearly a decade, I owe more than I can put into words. Their support, love, and patience have been boundless. This work is a testament to the inspiration and encouragement they have provided throughout. Noma Ndlovu, Brandon Nicholson, Brandon Terry, and Jonathan Beauford have been a part of that family for years, and their generosity of spirit made this journey possible. Lastly, I could not have made it to this moment without my wife, Jedidah Isler, whose courage, brilliance, kindness, faith, and love have sustained me from start to finish and beyond. She kept me sane—which was no easy task—inspired me to reach further and brought joy to each day. You are more than I ever knew to ask for in life. I look forward to all that awaits.

Unjust Deeds

Introduction

Restrictive Covenants, Housing Rights, and the Civil Rights Movement

The white marbled halls leading to the U.S. Supreme Court's main chamber started filling early on a brisk January morning in 1948. For hours, eager onlookers lined the corridor hoping to obtain one of the few seats left available for the general public. Spectators packed the Court's gallery beyond capacity that afternoon as they listened to the arguments for what many in the audience called "our most important case to come before the Supreme Court in this generation." Editors of the country's major black newspapers took the seats usually occupied by their reporters and an assortment of other prominent African American officials filled out the rows behind them. The journalists joked that a number of lawyers had sought admission to the Supreme Court bar in recent weeks just to avail themselves of the extra seating reserved for members. A common refrain among black Washingtonians held that "any person who got himself in trouble" during the next two days would be out of luck. "All the lawyers in town," explained one observer, "were listening to the arguments in the covenant cases."[1]

For two days, a fight over the future of the American ghetto captivated the eager audience. The four cases on the docket, known collectively as *Shelley v. Kraemer,* had originated in the neighborhoods of Detroit, St. Louis, and Washington, D.C., several years earlier and together they struck at the heart of residential segregation in the nation's cities by challenging the legal legitimacy of instruments known as "racial restrictive covenants." For more than half a century, white homeowners and homebuilders had established contracts or inserted clauses into property deeds prohibiting the use or occupancy of designated homes by African Americans and members of other minority groups. By the end of World War II, restrictive covenants had become one of the most daunting obstacles to black postwar progress and had leapt to the front of many civil rights activists' sociopolitical agendas. Covenants were, in the words of W. E. B. Du Bois, "the most discouraging situation that faces us," among the panoply of indignities that characterized life in Jim Crow America. Countless experts and advocates agreed that these instruments had formed the foundational building block of the nation's rapidly deteriorating racial ghettos. In 1948, America's foremost civil rights attorneys came to Washington to break the stranglehold that covenants had placed on growing urban black communities across the country.[2]

At the heart of the cases stood six African American families who joined with local lawyers and the National Association for the Advancement of Colored People (NAACP or the Association) in a desperate fight to keep their homes. Their efforts carried with them the hopes of a generation of black Americans striving to lay claim to some piece of the prosperity and security promised by the end of war. Together they mounted a campaign that many at the time believed could forever change the destiny of the nation's cities and the pursuit of racial freedom. That dream of expunging the American ghetto, however, would prove far more elusive than any of them imagined.

Though the fight against restrictive covenants would culminate with a unanimous victory before the Supreme Court in May of 1948, it never became the triumph that its supporters hoped it might be. In the ensuing decades, residential segregation would remain perhaps the most intractable of the nation's color lines, enduring with a tenacity that has made *Shelley* seem almost foolhardy in its optimism. The case has haunted the margins of civil rights movement history ever since, a reminder in many respects of what the struggle for racial justice failed to achieve in its midcentury heyday. The racial ghetto looms large in America's history and in its present, casting a shadow that has engulfed the promise of *Shelley* and the anticovenant campaign. What remains obscured by that shadow, however, is a largely untold story about how the restrictive covenant cases helped to remake the civil rights movement in the postwar years.

The unfolding battle for housing access and integration transformed black legal activism. The men and women who built the anticovenant campaign forged new partnerships, developed innovative strategies, and nurtured a new urgency and boldness within courtroom struggles for racial freedom. A determined, if at times unwieldy, coalition of homeowners, scholars, activists, and attorneys left their mark on the struggle for racial justice in these cases. In the years after the decision, civil rights litigators would use the experiences, tactics, and alliances from *Shelley* to help pave the way for a triumph over the doctrine of "separate but equal." They, like so many others before and after them, dreamed of a more just world and fought tooth and nail to make it a reality.

The deeper history of this fight provides a remarkable window into the inner workings and the evolution of the struggle for civil rights in the nation's courts. Paradoxes littered the anticovenant campaign from its inception and help reveal the conflicts and unexpected turns that so often shaped the path toward reform. Indeed, despite its eventual success, the *Shelley* case itself was one that the NAACP hoped would never reach the Supreme Court and that they deeply doubted they could win. When *Shelley* first came to the NAACP's attention, it had been percolating through the Missouri courts for more than a year—driven forward by an enterprising coalition of black real estate brokers and a popular local attorney in the twilight of his long career who all thumbed their noses at the NAACP's plea to wait. By that time, the Association had spent years crafting a careful and deliberate strategy meant to reverse two decades of the Supreme Court's support for covenants. The NAACP did what they could to prevent *Shelley* from becoming a test case, assuming that it would keep them from scoring the landmark victory they so feverishly desired. Understanding how they managed to prevail before the Supreme Court in spite of their initial fears ultimately offers insight into the processes of legal protest and the role of law in social justice movements at midcentury.

Frustrating as these early tensions may have been, anticovenant activists faced their greatest challenges after the decision. In the wake of the cases, white homeowners and developers in the North and West stymied the desegregation of urban areas through staggeringly effective resistance. The ghetto only seemed to grow more entrenched in the aftermath of *Shelley*, confounding the hopes of civil rights litigators. The story of what the covenant cases failed to undo remains etched into America's neighborhoods to this very day. Yet in the face of this intransigent opposition, those who had worked to make victory possible now labored to seize whatever gains they could from the litigation and the energies that had fueled their campaign. They would fashion a meaning for the cases beyond their shortcomings, channeling the lessons they learned into a reinvigorated and newly powerful struggle against Jim Crow's legal foundations.

The rightful history of the *Shelley* campaign lies in these varied efforts and complex legacies. It is a profoundly human story fueled by desperation, resolve, innovation, and hope. It is the story of a dynamic and potent struggle to make a way when there often seemed to be none. It is a story that would reach into neighborhoods and courtrooms across the country and that would leave the resurgent crusade for civil rights and justice under the law forever transformed.

The Seeds of Conflict:
Restrictive Covenants and Escalating Urban Tensions

Americans emerged from the experiences of World War II wrestling in new ways with the future of race relations and indeed the future of the nation as a whole. The campaign against restrictive covenants rose to increasing prominence during the 1940s in no small part because of this atmosphere of turmoil and transition. Yet the battle that black communities and the NAACP waged against the practices of residential segregation stood rooted in more than three decades of legal protest.

The *Shelley* litigation, like the broader civil rights movement in which it took place, flowed from a long tradition of resistance. For thirty years, the NAACP's attorneys had battled an assortment of exclusionary tactics including municipal zoning ordinances, discrimination by federal agencies and private developers, and the early spread of restrictive covenants. The Association's national legal committee cut its teeth on the issue of housing within just a few years of its founding with a concerted foray against racially based zoning regulations. One of the more popular forms of residential discrimination in the years immediately preceding the First World War, zoning ordinances sprang up in cities across the South and in several border states. Voters and city councils had hastily enacted prohibitions against black and white residents occupying homes in the same city block. By 1913, the Association's attorneys were determined to challenge the spreading practice and soon selected Louisville, Kentucky, as a good location to develop a national test case.[3]

In Louisville, the NAACP's legal leadership manufactured their case from the ground up, creating a local chapter of the fledgling organization in the city and recruiting both the plaintiff and the defendant for the case. These local machinations eventually set the stage for a 1917 U.S. Supreme Court decision in *Buchanan v. Warley* where the Association's attorneys scored a significant victory. They convinced the Court that residential color lines established by law violated the Fourteenth Amendment's prohibition on discriminatory state action. While these ordinances would defiantly linger on in certain areas, the NAACP's success in *Buchanan* marked an important early curb on the practices of housing discrimination, one that came just as the first massive wave of black migrants began abandoning the rural South for cities across the country.[4]

This influx of black southerners fueled a growing urgency among white urban communities to keep residential color lines in place. As zoning lost its legitimacy and fell out of favor, white homeowners and homebuilders increasingly turned to racial restrictive covenants. Covenants seemed a ready-made solution in many respects. Though not generally extensive in their use prior to *Buchanan*, these instruments had often preceded zoning schemes in various cities by a decade or more and thus offered an already available tactic that white developers and residents could fairly easily adapt to new areas of the city. The familiarity of covenants thus made them a relatively convenient answer to the challenge that *Buchanan* posed for segregationists. Even in northern cities where municipal ordinances had never taken hold and covenants were rare prior to World War I, restrictive agreements quickly came into vogue as they were easily reproduced from other locales and steadily encouraged by the realty industry. Perhaps the chief advantage that covenants afforded, however, was that they relied upon private contractual agreements to discriminate rather than formal legislation or regulation, and thus appeared to avoid enlisting state action to ensure the neighborhood color line would hold. The covenanting craze that ensued proved frighteningly successful at helping to seal burgeoning black populations into relatively small and deteriorating sections of cities in the North and the South and provided a far more challenging target for black housing activists to assail.[5]

Still, the NAACP's attorneys quickly understood the dangers that covenants represented and challenged the legality of these agreements in short order. The Association's first anticovenant litigation emerged in Washington, D.C., in the mid-1920s and culminated with a 1926 decision by the U.S. Supreme Court. In *Corrigan v. Buckley*, the Court declared that it lacked jurisdiction to scrutinize private contracts such as racial restrictions and suggested that the NAACP's idea of applying constitutional scrutiny to these instruments was "plainly without color of merit and frivolous." The Constitution, a unanimous Court insisted, could not constrain "private individuals from entering into contracts respecting the control and disposition of their own property." Covenants now enjoyed a new legitimacy and *Corrigan* ignited an explosive spread of these agreements. Racial restrictions emerged for the first time in cities like Chicago. Two decades after the decision, a study of segregation in the Windy City concluded that 40 percent of all the covenants that had spread around the city's Southside had originated in the three years after *Corrigan*. Local civil rights lawyers and the NAACP's national office never gave up the fight in the wake of this setback, but as they labored to carve out new opportunities for black homeseekers their success would only be marginal at best.[6]

Indeed it would take nearly fifteen years after *Corrigan* for the Supreme Court to even consider arguments in another covenant case. That suit, *Hansberry v. Lee* (1940) from Chicago, overturned a single restriction on very limited technical grounds but left intact restrictive covenants' overall strength and effectiveness. Litigation accelerated thereafter but without any reliable successes. As late as 1945, the Supreme Court refused to budge from its position of nonintervention, declining to hear *Mays v. Burgess*, a District of Columbia case piloted by NAACP legal luminary William H. Hastie. Covenants thus remained a particularly intractable legal problem for the NAACP in the mid-1940s, one that rather desperately needed a solution.[7]

As World War II drew to a close, racial restrictions took center stage for civil rights advocates in the North and West. The stakes of the conflict seemed to rise higher with each passing month as a new influx of black migrants uprooted themselves and set off in search of opportunities beyond the clutches of the Jim Crow South. This groundswell of migration would quickly eclipse the flood of the previous three decades. At the same time, reinvigorated American industries shook off the Depression-era rust, throttled into the high gear of wartime production, and fed off the manpower of this exodus. Together these processes suddenly put whole cities and seemingly the entire nation in motion, presenting new challenges and opportunities at every turn. The demographic revolution taking hold marked the start of a profound, sustained, and exceedingly visible transformation throughout the urban North and West. Each new train arriving from points south seemed to carry with it the seeds of an impending reckoning over the future of America's metropolitan areas.[8]

All three of the cities at the heart of the postwar anticovenant cases— Detroit, Washington, and St. Louis—absorbed black migrants at record rates between 1940 and 1950. Detroit's black communities added some 50,000 new members by 1943 and another 100,000 by the decade's end, doubling the Motor City's black population in ten years. Washington's black neighborhoods housed nearly 100,000 new residents, with the vast majority arriving in the nation's capital before 1947. The allure of federal jobs sent the city's black population soaring from 187,000 to over 280,000. St. Louis was the slowest growing of the three, yet the Gateway City's black districts strained at the seams with a 40 percent increase over prewar numbers. Forty-five thousand new souls piled on top of each other along the city's segregated streets. This rapid growth, replicated across the country, exacerbated racial tensions as widespread discrimination choked off the possibilities of expansion and potential relief for increasingly overcrowded racial ghettos. White neighborhoods in turn faced mounting pressure from black homeseekers who desperately sought access to decent housing. These efforts to alleviate the burdens of residential exclusion sparked even more determined efforts among many white homeowners hoping to prevent African Americans' "encroachment." As a result, covenanting enjoyed a renaissance and flourished across broad swaths of the postwar urban landscape.[9]

Though numbers and demography would lend an inherent urgency to the housing fight, it was also fundamentally a question of rights. As black and white Americans began to debate and contest the destiny of America's ghettos, they offered competing claims rooted in a rights-based language that raised the stakes of this confrontation even higher. African Americans increasingly asserted that the ability to purchase a decent home free from discrimination was a vital civil and human right. For many black urban communities, there was no distinction to be made between the right to access decent homes and the right to have a meaningful future. White homeowners countered by insisting upon a set of property and contractual rights that entitled them to protect their homes and by extension the financial and social stability of the neighborhoods where they lived. Covenants and the systematic exclusion of minority groups, white residents maintained, safeguarded home values from the inevitable damage and deleterious influence that they attributed to black occupancy. Again and again, white property owners extolled their right as private citizens to choose whom they wished to associate with and to have as their neighbors. This "rights consciousness" permeated the debate over restrictive covenants on both sides of the color line.[10]

By the mid-1940s, these competing narratives about housing rights had taken on additional meaning as Americans of all races increasingly claimed the sanction of federal support for their contradictory goals. A decade earlier, a series of New Deal programs including the Home Owners' Loan Corporation (HOLC), Federal Housing Administration (FHA), and the Wagner Housing Act of 1937 had marked unprecedented federal efforts to provide and secure access to both public and private housing. President Franklin Roosevelt's administration reshaped housing markets and began to transform homeownership into a fundamental privilege of American citizenship. By 1944, Roosevelt had proclaimed "the right of every family to a decent home" as a foundational element of American prosperity and security. Black homeseekers immediately seized upon the egalitarianism of the president's rhetoric to bolster their claims for equality of access. White homeowners, on the other hand, justified continued exclusion by pointing instead to Roosevelt's promises of security and stability as well as the discriminatory practices that these new federal housing agencies employed. The HOLC, FHA, and Veterans Affairs would each condone and encourage racial segregation and restrictive covenants in particular. White Americans thus saw residential discrimination as an extension of the Roosevelt administration's guiding principles rather than a departure from them. Members of both races declared that the federal government unequivocally stood behind them and supported the rights to which they laid claim.[11]

The experiences of World War II helped to harden further these attitudes for many individuals. A number of white Americans believed that their wartime sacrifices in the military and on the home front had earned them the right to keep their neighborhoods segregated and "stable." African Americans instead looked to their own sacrifices and the ideological tenor of a war fought against fascist rule and under the banner of democracy to affirm their entitlement to the full privileges of American citizenship, including the right to purchase a home wherever their means allowed. In the wake of the war, the burgeoning rights consciousness of the 1940s increasingly transformed the restrictive covenant fight into a struggle over the contours of postwar democracy and the meaning of freedom in America. Anticovenant advocates fought the campaign against racial restrictions with an urgency, ingenuity, and sincerity that reflected this larger significance.[12]

Up from the Margins:
The Restrictive Covenant Cases and Civil Rights History

Despite the *Shelley* campaign's importance to contemporary activists, observers, and experts, the covenant cases have lingered at the margins of civil rights movement history over the past half century. *Shelley* has remained little more than a footnote in the narrative of African Americans' efforts for greater freedom since historian Clement Vose penned the last full-length treatment of the campaign in his 1959 work *Caucasians Only*. A deeper consideration of the postwar fight against racial restrictions, however, offers a unique vantage point from which to rethink the origins and priorities of America's civil rights movement and presents some unique contributions to emerging scholarly conversations about race and reform in the twentieth century.[13]

Over the last decade, historians of black protest have increasingly called for the development of a "Long Civil Rights Era" paradigm to highlight the longer traditions and trajectories of African Americans' organizing and resistance efforts. These scholars have expanded the temporal, geographic, and ideological boundaries of black freedom struggles by examining events from the decades before the landmark *Brown v. Board of Education* (1954) case and the 1955 Montgomery Bus Boycott, the significance of protest efforts outside of the Deep South, and the possibilities engendered by political radicalism that stretched across racial and national boundary lines. Historians of the civil rights struggle have built a growing body of evidence that these events and ideas constituted more than simple precursors to the movement of the 1950s and 1960s. Instead, these early campaigns represent a vibrant and vital part of a long-standing fight for racial equality and justice. The explosion of studies in this vein has enriched and broadened perspectives on the context, substance, and consequences of black protest efforts. Yet as a historiographical venture still relatively young in its development, much remains to be done.[14]

An examination of the restrictive covenant cases joins this wave of scholarship while filling in some of the critical gaps left in its wake. African Americans' struggle for housing access in the courtrooms of the 1940s highlights the significance of protest in the decade preceding *Brown* and beyond the borders of the Cotton Belt. The substance of the *Shelley* campaign points to the Second World War as a watershed moment in the history of black activism and highlights urban centers—especially those outside of the South—as sites that generated an energetic and innovative resistance to discrimination. Additionally, this lens captures an area of black protest that has remained relatively underexplored. While much of the recent thrust of Long Civil Rights Era scholarship has stressed labor organizing and attempts to form class-based interracial coalitions during the 1930s and 1940s, *Shelley* calls attention to a different strain of rights claims from Americans in the immediate postwar era. Housing access became an urgent concern that attracted the impassioned efforts of many of the most influential black activists and organizations in the country. In the aftermath of World War II, the fight against housing discrimination featured just as prominently as the struggles over segregation in education, labor, and public accommodations.[15]

Though campaigns against residential segregation took a variety of forms and targeted an array of practices in both public and private housing during this era, restrictive covenants stood at the center of activists' efforts to combat the tightening grip of America's racial ghettos. Leading historians of urban race relations have often painted covenants as a vestigial facet of Jim Crow that had become largely obsolete by the time of the *Shelley* decision in 1948. Yet to many urban civil rights advocates, there were few issues more urgently in need of a remedy. In both symbol and substance, racial restrictions posed a dire threat to African Americans' prospects for economic and social progress. The victory in *Shelley* inspired hope—albeit only briefly—that the ghetto would not become a permanent fixture in the nation's cities.[16]

While the lasting tenacity of residential segregation has kept *Shelley* on the margins of civil rights movement history, a detailed reconsideration of the cases points to *Shelley* as something much more than a hollow victory. Whatever the disappointment that ensued, civil rights activists and the black communities they represented ultimately fashioned a substantial and enduring legacy from the anticovenant campaign. Residential segregation may have held fast through the concerted efforts of white homeowners, homebuilders, realtors, and policy makers, but the fight for access to a greater number of homes—a related, but distinct goal within the campaign—proved more successful. Tens of thousands of black families found some material relief in the immediate wake of the decision. Just as importantly, the success of the litigation strategy that the NAACP adopted in *Shelley* would equip the organization with new tactics and alliances that facilitated additional legal victories in the ensuing years. The covenant cases would quickly come to play a central role in civil rights litigators' more far-reaching attacks on the legal foundations of Jim Crow. Better understanding the *Shelley* campaign thus offers valuable insights into the role of law in social justice movements and the anticovenant struggle's lasting impact on postwar civil rights litigation.

Indeed much of *Shelley*'s historical richness derives not from what happened after the Supreme Court's decision, but instead from how the campaign emerged and evolved in the mid-1940s. An account of the covenant cases that emphasizes their development at the grassroots builds upon legal historians' recent efforts to capture community-level perspectives on the practices of litigation and the significance of the law for local black activists. Reconsidering *Shelley* from the ground up ultimately reveals a great deal about how black communities wielded the law as an instrument of reform and how the larger courtroom campaign against Jim Crow took shape.[17]

The events of *Shelley* are particularly helpful in exposing the full array of activities and individuals that made litigation campaigns possible. Through fund-raising, social organizing, and political mobilization, local actors engaged with anticovenant lawyers and their litigation efforts, exerting considerable influence on the direction and pace of legal change. Recognizing these efforts suggests the need for a broader lens to encompass the ways in which African Americans interacted with the law and highlights the fact that telling the legal history of the civil rights movement need not leave out ordinary people and local communities. In fact, a detailed examination of the *Shelley* litigation reveals that consigning these individuals to the sidelines of that history disembodies the law from its impact in the daily lives of black Americans and discounts their contributions and connections to the processes of legal change. A more comprehensive look at individual cases and broader campaigns offers a truer sense of the people and the forces at work in effecting reform. This approach to the movement's legal history provides a valuable window into the interplay of individual determination, grassroots activism, national advocacy groups like the NAACP, and federal policies and institutions in shaping postwar race relations. The covenant cases thus help to bridge the gap between policy-oriented, top-down scholarship on racial reform and accounts that tout local organizing as the driving force of change in black freedom struggles.[18]

Additionally, a deeper look at anticovenant litigation sheds light on the contours and evolution of legal protest in the wake of World War II. The practice of litigating racial justice was never as well organized as those ostensibly in charge of the campaign had hoped it would be. Conflict and experimentation became defining features of the covenant cases as they progressed from the local to the national level. Ideological and personal tensions between the NAACP's legal team and local advocates—especially the black realtors in St. Louis who spearheaded their own case without the NAACP's assistance—took the fight for housing access in unexpected directions. Simultaneously, anticovenant lawyers' efforts to explore new tactics revealed legal activism as a process characterized by high degrees of innovation, dynamism, and uncertainty. The *Shelley* campaign also calls attention to the growth and importance of extensive collaborative networks between attorneys and a host of intellectuals, advocacy groups, and local leaders. These evolving relationships exerted a steady influence on the trajectory of the campaign and the effectiveness of legal protest in combatting segregation's various forms.[19]

Beyond these insights, *Shelley* offers a crucial window into the development of the coalitions and strategies that became hallmarks of successful civil rights litigation. Ultimately, three signal elements of the campaign would redefine the legal battle against Jim Crow. First, the cases marked a critical turning point in the NAACP's efforts to integrate into their legal briefs social scientific arguments about racial discrimination's negative consequences for American society. On an unparalleled scale in their long history of litigation, the NAACP's attorneys joined with a committed group of academics to harness a rising tide of antiracist scholarship in the courtroom and forged an enduring partnership. Complementing this tactical creativity, a second significant feature of the cases was that they brought together the largest coalition of civil rights advocacy groups assembled in the Supreme Court's history. The NAACP drew on newly strengthened alliances with an assortment of racial, religious, and labor groups to build an unprecedentedly broad set of multiracial partnerships that would soon become a staple of their courtroom endeavors. Finally, *Shelley* marked a substantial shift in the exercise of federal authority in support of African Americans' claims to equality. The Department of Justice (DOJ) intervened in the cases on the NAACP's behalf when they reached the Supreme Court. The federal government's intercession in a civil rights case between two private parties marked a significant departure from standard practice and fueled a new hopefulness among black activists. The attorney general and solicitor general of the United States ultimately aligned themselves with the demands of black homeseekers both inside and outside of the courtroom. Their efforts spurred forward a federal partnership with the NAACP that became an increasingly powerful tool as the Association expanded the horizons of its litigation and soon took aim at the long reach of *Plessy v. Ferguson* (1896). In the end, *Shelley* marked a turning point that set the NAACP on a collision course with "separate but equal" jurisprudence and helped reshape the tactics that would allow the Association's lawyers to strip that half-century-old burden from the nation's legal lexicon.

THE NARRATIVE THAT FOLLOWS charts the path of the restrictive covenant cases from their inception to their final adjudication by the U.S. Supreme Court and the decision's reception in neighborhoods across the country. Hewing to a roughly chronological arc, the chapters focus on the various groups of actors who shaped the meaning, trajectory, and outcome of the campaign. Chapter 1 introduces the litigants in the cases against the backdrop of the housing crisis that seized the nation during the 1940s. A widespread shortage of decent homes compounded the tensions wrought by mass migration and the intensifying rights-conscious debate over housing access. This chapter argues that the shortage of decent shelter forced the housing issue to the forefront of African Americans' civil rights concerns and that covenants stood at the center of the ensuing fight. Exploring the processes of covenant breaking and enforcement, the chapter also illustrates the impact that racial restrictions had in the lives of black homeseekers and what they meant to both black and white communities.

The second chapter moves from the neighborhoods into the local and appellate courts for each case, tracing the work of anticovenant lawyers who were the lifeblood of the fight for housing access. As these attorneys battled against covenants' proponents, their struggles evidenced the collaboration and exchange that helped to hone strategies for victory over the entrenched legal support that discriminatory customs enjoyed. Additionally, this chapter chronicles the efforts of black realtors and local communities who exerted their own influence on the cases, insistently pressing the issue forward. These grassroots-level theaters displayed perhaps more clearly than any other venue the energy and innovation that drove legal protest during the postwar era.

Chapter 3 captures the NAACP's efforts to coordinate a nationwide campaign against restrictive covenants. The discussion examines the Association's evolving strategies and coalition-building within the larger intellectual currents of the 1930s and 1940s as a way to understand the dynamics of reform litigation at the national level. Building upon the organization's rapid growth and a unique moment in American intellectual and political development, the NAACP legal team experimented with social scientific arguments against racial discrimination in new ways and cultivated a powerful network of sympathetic organizations in an effort to bolster their campaign.

The fourth chapter considers the Justice Department's intervention, the presentation of the cases before the Supreme Court, and the Court's decision in favor of the NAACP's clients. These events reveal the political pressures that helped to inaugurate a newly strengthened partnership between the Association and the federal government in the courts. The final chapter then contends with the cases' complex and paradoxical legacies for America's cities and the civil rights movement. The covenant cases returned from the Supreme Court chamber into the hands of the white and black communities who would determine their impact on the substance of American life. The ensuing struggle to define and control the meaning of the cases gave new contours to two contradictory forces in the postwar nation: the racial ghetto and the struggle for black freedom.

The story of *Shelley v. Kraemer* began in the neighborhoods of Detroit, St. Louis, and Washington, D.C., and wound its way through various courtrooms, the offices of the NAACP and the attorney general, and ultimately to the Supreme Court chambers on a cold morning in January 1948. The campaign was simultaneously national in scope, locally influenced, and profoundly personal in meaning. Along the way the cases bore the fingerprints of black families desperate to find decent homes, white homeowners fighting to hold on to a social order that defined so many aspects of their lives, a host of little-known attorneys who lent their voices to a burgeoning movement for racial equality, some of the best-known civil rights lawyers of the era, and a federal government that had only recently begun in earnest to offer its energies to the cause of racial justice. In the span of three tumultuous years, their struggles would transform the course of black legal activism and help to chart a path toward greater freedom for African Americans in the postwar world. The road they traveled toward that end, however, was almost never the one they expected.

ONE

Covenants

Race and Housing in the 1940s

Robert Harris Rowe had spent twenty-one years living in the nation's capital when he suddenly found his family facing eviction from their apartment on Florida Avenue in the early months of 1945. Rowe, a day laborer, clearly grasped the potential for disaster. He immediately left his job to look for new housing full time. Rowe understood that in wartime America, it could be a great deal easier to find a new job than a new place to live. Black families like the Rowes confronted particularly severe challenges in housing markets across the country, and despite his investment in this search after the first week Rowe had nothing to show for his efforts. His frustration and determination both began to mount as he promised his wife Isabella, a registered nurse in Washington's Freedmen's Hospital, "I won't work anymore until I do find something." Later that year, Rowe reflected on this moment: "I . . . kept going until I could find somewhere to move to, couldn't find nowhere for rent, neither to buy, so far. . . . I didn't give up though. I kept going."[1]

Over the following weeks, as the eviction date grew closer, Rowe visited five different real estate agencies, all with the same lack of results. Some simply had no vacancies. Others had their offerings snapped up before Rowe could even make a bid. Finally, after yet another unsuccessful day, the Rowes sat at their kitchen table combing the evening newspaper for possibilities and ultimately hung their hopes on the promises of Slaughter and Company. The next day, Rowe visited their offices and began touring some of what the city had available for those urgently in need of a place to live. The first stop was a collection of "two-room kitchenettes" that Rowe deemed far too small to live in comfortably, followed by another overly cozy apartment. The third option seemed better until he reached the kitchen and discovered that he "could see the stars and moon shine through the roof." As Rowe's hopes were rapidly fading, the real estate agent held out a final possibility on the 100 block of Bryant Street. Despite the overgrown yard and the loose bricks in the stairs and columns in front of the house, Rowe saw the promise of a home that he and his wife could make their own and they signed the contract to purchase it the very next evening. The Rowes moved to their new address at 118 Bryant on August 12, having successfully fought in municipal court to delay their eviction from Florida Avenue until then. Two months later, they were back in court again, this time fighting to hold on to the home they now owned.[2]

Robert and Isabella Rowe were among millions of Americans who struggled to find adequate shelter during the 1940s. The Rowes' difficulties bespoke the dire state of housing in America's cities where long-standing problems of quality and quantity—for both white and black alike—grew acute during World War II. The shortage of building resources, the sharp downturn in construction, and the massive migration that accompanied the war exacerbated conditions to a crisis state in many areas. Moreover, for those without adequate housing, the end of the war promised no better. The influx of millions of veterans in need of homes and the potential expiration of wartime rent controls would largely offset the immediate benefits of rising construction. By 1946, apprehensions about the nation's housing supply had risen to a fever pitch. At times this threatened to rend the seams of unity and domestic peace the war had ostensibly threaded together.

Beneath the physical shortages and inadequacies that made housing a fundamental concern for all Americans during the war years was a particular crisis within urban African American communities. Various overlapping strategies of racial discrimination in housing markets—including disparities in mortgage rates and availability, collusion among real estate brokers, mob violence, and restrictive covenants—created artificial shortages for black residents by severely limiting access to available homes and disproportionately pushing African Americans into the poorest-quality housing. Rapidly expanding urban black communities in the wartime and immediate postwar era found themselves with a stagnant, increasingly overcrowded, and deteriorating share of the nation's housing supply. As a result, African Americans' desperation in the search for homes exceeded that of whites, a state of affairs that inevitably led to confrontations as members of both races struggled for a share of a scarce and precious resource.

IN THE 1940S, these clashes frequently led to the litigation of restrictive covenants. Though white sellers and black buyers had disregarded and contested these agreements for several decades before World War II, the exigencies of wartime brought new urgency and insistence to these struggles. The breaking and subsequent enforcement of covenants became an especially controversial point in urban racial tensions of the immediate postwar era.

A better understanding of precisely how black homebuyers came to defy these agreements and how white homeowners implemented them to evict these purchasers offers insight into why covenants were an especially serious burden on those African Americans who sought adequate homes. In detailing how covenants operated on an individual level, the cases that culminated in *Shelley v. Kraemer* (1948) bring to life the struggle for housing access and demonstrate just how hard these restrictions made it for many black Americans who sought homes beyond the segregated boundaries of urban neighborhoods in the 1940s. As African Americans faced the harsh realities of confinement to worsening ghettos, wartime promises of freedom and progress for all quickly began to fade. The six families in the covenant cases and their supporters, however, chose not to let those hopes dissolve without a fight.

Housing America: The Crisis of the 1940s

The wartime and postwar housing crises that gripped America's cities materialized out of long-festering problems of adequacy and availability. Lower-income and marginalized populations in particular had faced deplorable housing conditions for decades. The widespread shortages of the 1940s highlighted long-standing issues in many urban areas and made the problems more apparent and more immediate for a larger segment of the population. By the time that massive internal migrations began in World War II, many cities already suffered from a decade-long shortage of both construction and maintenance. The nation's urban centers were wholly unequipped to absorb significant population growth and much of the existing housing supply had severely deteriorated.

After a homebuilding boom in the 1920s, production had slowed to a crawl in the Depression. In the 1930s, new private housing construction averaged only 265,000 starts (the number of dwelling units on which construction had begun) each year, just 38 percent of the previous decade's average and less than three-quarters of the rate at the turn of the century. About 65 percent of this building took place in America's urban areas. Additionally, a significant segment of the country's existing homes remained barely habitable. Housing expert Charles Abrams wrote that "two-fifths of our non-farm homes were known to be below civilized standards before the war began; two-thirds of our farm families were improperly sheltered." Other experts—using a more technical and narrow definition of habitability—found more than 27 percent of existing units in "substandard" condition by 1940. In that year, 167,000 families nationwide made their homes in "boats, tent, trailers," and other unconventional arrangements. St. Louis mayor Aloys Kaufmann described a "situation so chronic and of such long duration . . . [that] the advent of war caught us short. Overnight, vacancies disappeared and a critical shortage set in." Indeed the coming of war and the accompanying flood of new residents rapidly pulled cities like St. Louis into dire straits.[3]

The sudden expansion of urban populations across the country coincided with another collapse in construction rates in early 1942. Economic recovery had spurred increased housing production from 1939–41 at levels well above the Depression-decade average and nearing the rates of the 1920s. However, America's abrupt entry into World War II precipitated the largest single-year plunge ever recorded, more than halving the pace of construction. New private housing starts continued falling in dramatic fashion in 1943 and 1944, and reached lows that were worse than all but three years of the 1930s. The year 1945 brought a notable uptick in the rate, but still fell more than 20 percent below the Depression-era average. Though publicly funded war housing construction significantly mitigated this shortfall, building remained far below the needed pace.[4]

New construction also largely took place outside of major urban centers. During the four years of war, urban building constituted an even smaller percentage of housing starts than in the Depression decade—though the total numbers were slightly higher. Because homebuilding followed war industries to cities of all sizes and locations, these low overall construction numbers meant particularly paltry figures for major cities like Detroit, St. Louis, and Washington, D.C. Indeed, cities of more than 500,000 residents—like each of these three—saw less than 40,000 total public and private unit starts in each of the war years, just 12.2 percent of all wartime construction. Given that experts in Detroit insisted that the city would need 65,000 new homes in 1942 alone to accommodate population increases, the total wartime construction of less than 155,000 units in all of America's largest cities obviously fell far short of these major urban centers' needs. In places like Chicago and St. Louis, construction in the early 1940s barely outstripped and sometimes fell short of the pace of demolition.[5]

The combination of minimal construction and significant migration taxed the limits of the available housing stock across the country. One of the clearest indications of the housing shortfall proved to be vacancy rates. In ordinary times, most experts and the National Housing Agency (NHA) considered 5 percent as a "normal" vacancy rate that indicated a steady and healthy turnover in occupancy. During the war years, however, many cities fell far below this number, meaning that homeseekers found it exponentially more difficult to find accommodations of any sort. In the nation's capital, vacancies plummeted from a comfortable 5 percent in 1940 to only 2 percent in 1941 and less than 0.5 percent in 1947. By 1945, St. Louis had a rate of only 1 percent—which actually marked a slight improvement over the previous year's numbers. Unfilled homes were so rare in the Gateway City that Mayor Kaufmann remarked, "'Wanted to rent' almost displaced 'For rent' advertisements in the newspapers." In Manhattan, residential vacancies stood at less than 0.4 percent in 1944. San Francisco hovered at 1 percent and Detroit at even less than that in mid-1945.[6]

Even good news came with a cost during this period. Substantial increases in income led to a rising level of homeownership during the war, but the growth of owner-occupancy pushed many tenants out of their homes. Dispossessed renters like the Rowes suddenly found themselves at the mercy of the shrinking housing market. Though some renters succeeded in delaying their evictions through the courts, these efforts only postponed the inevitable.[7]

THE END OF WORLD WAR II brought reasons for both hope and further despair among homeseekers. The easing of wartime restrictions on construction and the increased focus of policy makers on resolving the nation's housing shortage indicated that rapid improvements might well be on the way. At the same time, veterans were returning far faster than new homes could be built, meaning that the housing situation stood poised to worsen in the immediate future. Already racked by scarcity and deficiency, millions of Americans faced mounting desperation and discomfort with little hope of relief. Some observers believed whole-heartedly that in postwar America, "*Shelter, one of life's essentials, has become a luxury.*"[8]

By 1945, experts pegged the total supply deficit somewhere between 8 and 12 million units. Most other calculations came to a similar conclusion. Estimates from the NHA identified an immediate need for more than 5 million units and an additional 7.5 million before 1955. Private construction accelerated considerably with the cessation of war, but building rates failed to reenergize fully until the end of the decade. Indeed, the numbers in 1946 still fell almost 100,000 short of the 1928 level and it took until 1949 before production surged past pre-Depression peaks. The availability of homes rapidly improved, but for those millions of Americans suffering without adequate shelter, the first few months or even years of peace brought little respite from the anxiety and misery that gripped them in the present day.[9]

Access to adequate housing proved difficult even for veterans, who enjoyed at least some potential advantages through the GI Bill and Veterans

Administration. The postwar construction boom could not keep pace with the rapid return of the country's armed forces from deployment overseas. Shortages became "particularly acute" for veterans within months and congressional inquiries soon discovered significant numbers of former servicemen living in "garages, trailers, barns, and even chicken coops" around the country. The St. Louis Veterans' Service Center could only find accommodations for about 40 percent of the applicants in 1947 and a local Veterans of Foreign Wars representative placed the number of veterans' families needing housing at 20,000. In 1945, commentators in Washington charged that "unquestionably, shelter is the toughest problem facing the returning veteran here. Not even the matter of making a livelihood is as imminent to the GI who's coming back." These fears proved prophetic. By 1948, more than 46,000 servicemen from the District had applied for assistance with housing and they received only 7,000 offerings. The local housing authority in the capital had a waitlist of more than 20,000 with at least 6,000 low-income veterans whose cases seemed almost hopeless in the face of high rents.[10]

Existing conditions for veterans and civilians alike ranged from the uncomfortable to the downright horrifying. Across the country, the shortage forced more than 2.5 million families to share accommodations with other relatives. This alternative seemed far preferable by comparison to the circumstances that hundreds of thousands of other families faced. Roving reporters for *Collier's* magazine labeled the postwar period the "Houseless Era." In Detroit, a city where industry had flourished throughout the war, a study found that in mid-1947, "3,600 families were living in shacks, trailers, sheds, barns, and other makeshift arrangements." Still others secured the use of stables, basements, attics, and fought off the cold in a former church. Even these accommodations might seem a blessing given that some families faced the prospect of spending the Michigan winter huddled in tents scattered around the city's parks. In 1947, Detroit's Housing Commission concluded that they would need immediate construction of no less than 25,000 units to resolve these shortfalls—more than ten times the number that builders started in the first half of that year.[11]

The Motor City's circumstances were no exception to conditions elsewhere. Los Angelenos took shelter in "old trolleys, abandoned busses, [sic] tents and in shacks built from surplus Army gliders." Around St. Louis, desperation led many to "most crude living in garages, basements without floors, attics, coal sheds, and stables." Advertisements for vacant apartments in the local paper would frequently elicit hundreds of responses and the situation seemed to be getting worse. "Rental property," testified one man, "is almost out of the question." For many St. Louisans, the place of last resort became "store-front homes" that had appeared throughout the city. Taking up residence in former offices and retail establishments, residents found "just a roofed room, no hot water, many cases no toilet and certainly no bath." An investigation of Chicago revealed that "house-hungry squatters tear down boards from condemned buildings, move in and take their chances with crumbling walls, rickety stairways, weakened roofs." "Today," *Collier's* reporter Lester Velie declared, "the shame of [America's] cities is their housing." His assessment echoed a long string of similar observations.[12]

Even when urban residents did not find themselves in the most desperate of circumstances, conditions often seemed unlivable. In St. Louis, a city commission determined that "one-half of the city's residential area is obsolete or blighted; fifty percent of our housing is in decay, or worse." Commentators put the number of substandard homes at approximately 25 percent in Chicago and 20 percent in Detroit and Washington. In city after city, inspectors and evaluators found tens of thousands of existing dwelling units poorly equipped, in disrepair, or worse. Desperation, discomfort, and discontent abounded among the millions of urban Americans without access to adequate shelter.[13]

The Double Barrier: African Americans and the Housing Shortage

While the housing crisis of the 1940s touched millions of Americans of all races, the nation's urban black communities often took the brunt of the impact. Entrenched and extensive racial discrimination strictly limited African Americans' access to decent homes and further exacerbated overcrowding. The resulting deterioration of existing dwellings and the heightened tensions and misery of black homeseekers put the nation's cities on edge and stood as one of the greatest obstacles to black Americans' postwar progress. The overall physical shortages and inadequacies combined with the artificial limitations of segregation to create a "double barrier" to housing access for nonwhites. The costs and consequences of these additional constraints defined the urban experience for millions of African Americans at midcentury and quickly became a focal point of black activists' wartime and postwar political agendas.

The forces that came to shape the racial divisions of America's neighborhoods proved abundant and deeply interconnected. Effective discrimination relied upon an array of actors and methods that reinforced one another and created an almost overwhelming atmosphere of support for residential segregation. Those responsible for creating and defending housing discrimination fell into four general groups—individuals, realtors, mortgage lenders, and the government—though networks of communication and collusion often blurred the boundaries of these categories.

These groups fed off of each other to create, promote, and sustain both the rationale and the means of residential exclusion. First were individuals, acting alone or in concert. Local residents confronted the prospect of racial integration in a variety of ways and became the most personal and most explosive element of white resistance. The next group included interested parties from the real estate industry. Professional organizations like the National Association of Real Estate Boards (NAREB), the Washington Real Estate Board, or the St. Louis Real Estate Exchange centralized and codified practices that upheld segregation as an industry standard. Additionally, financial institutions played a significant role by ensuring that lending followed racial boundary lines—making it difficult for African Americans to obtain loans in the first place and nearly impossible should a black family desire a home in an all-white area. The final set of actors consisted of government agencies at the national, state, and local levels. Nationally, the FHA literally underwrote the continued segregation of American neighborhoods through its official guidelines. State and local housing authorities played a complementary role by controlling the allocation and distribution of resources for building. These four groups of actors remained a formidable presence in residential discrimination efforts throughout the 1940s and worked diligently to ensure that housing segregation remained intact.[14]

Like the groups themselves, methods for encouraging and enforcing housing discrimination were myriad, overlapping, and exceedingly effective. The institutions, organizations, and individuals who ensured the success of residential segregation each limited African Americans' access to decent homes through varying means. These strategies ranged from the crudeness of overt violence to the sophistication and formality of mortgage insurance procedures. Whatever their form, the presence and persistence of these forces in the 1940s compounded the struggles of black citizens who grappled with far greater restrictions on their access to homes in the midst of a crippling shortage. When urban African Americans looked beyond the confines of existing slums and black enclaves for decent shelter, they encountered an array of obstacles designed to intimidate, isolate, and ultimately exclude them from most of the available housing supply. The imposing power of discriminatory custom and racial hostility met black homeseekers at every turn.

One of the most frightening and obvious tactics at the disposal of individuals who supported residential segregation proved to be violence. African Americans who sought homes outside of all-black areas constantly faced the prospect of violent reprisals from their neighbors and risked both their investments and their lives. The potential costs deterred many black home-seekers from a large portion of the available residences in America's cities. Historian Arnold Hirsch extensively documented the "pattern of chronic urban guerilla warfare" that sprang up in Chicago and repeated itself in numerous other cities following World War II. An NAACP study of violence in the Windy City uncovered fifty-nine attacks on black homeowners between 1944 and 1946 alone without a single conviction against any of the culprits. These bombings, arsons, and acts of vandalism built upon long-standing traditions of vigilantism and mob violence that had enforced neighborhoods' racial boundaries for decades. Just as it had in the wake of World War I, surging black population growth in the early 1940s contributed to escalating tensions and heightened levels of racial antipathy in the urban North and West. Hostilities over black housing access tore at the nation's hopes and images of unity during World War II and spawned a series of infamous confrontations.[15]

Two of the most notorious events occurred in Detroit, the nation's self-proclaimed "Arsenal of Democracy." In late 1941, a proposed public housing project for black war workers—and named for Sojourner Truth—drew the ire of the predominantly Eastern European residents in the Seven Mile–Fenelon neighborhood. The prospect of 200 homes for African Americans in the all-white region generated a storm of protests that led to a dizzying series of confrontations, policy reversals, and ultimately violence. By January of 1942 and under heavy pressure from an array of local and national politicians, Federal Works Agency (FWA) officials decided to open the project only to whites. Just two weeks later, counterprotests by local black residents and national civil rights organizations—eventually joined by the city political leadership—forced the FWA to backtrack and readopt their original plan for black occupancy.[16]

In late February, when African American workers attempted to move into the homes, a mob of several hundred white residents prevented their entry by conducting armed pickets. Within hours, the conflict degenerated into a series of verbal and physical skirmishes that continued over the course of the following week as more than 1,000 Detroiters of both races rushed to the scene to hold their respective lines. It would take two more months to muster the political will and police protection to allow black workers to start occupying the homes.[17]

The city exploded into even greater levels of violence in June of 1943. With tensions rubbed raw by the Sojourner Truth controversy and a second bitter clash over black war workers' housing in the suburb of Willow Run earlier in the year, anxieties and anger about housing conditions helped foment a brutal wartime riot. Thousands of Detroiters brawled in almost every corner of the city for three days and the situation deteriorated to the point that Mayor Edward J. Jeffries Jr. and Michigan governor Harry F. Kelly requested the intervention of federal troops to quell the racial violence. For a time, the nation's "Arsenal of Democracy" became occupied territory. Shortly thereafter, the fighting subsided and the city returned to an uneasy peace, the mourning of thirty-four dead, and the mending of millions in property damage. Though housing concerns did not directly cause the riot to boil over, Detroit's frequent tensions over race and residence brought the city to a simmer. The riot in the Motor City and other instances of unrest in wartime vividly reminded black homeseekers of the raw power of racial hatred and helped to harden racial boundary lines in housing markets.[18]

Even if African Americans considered braving the specter of mob violence, they often encountered considerable resistance from individuals and institutions in the real estate industry. For most white realtors, professional guidelines prohibited them from facilitating sales to black buyers in predominantly white areas. Brokers who helped transgress racial boundaries risked losing their license to operate and faced social and professional ostracism that could cost them their livelihoods. When the *Pittsburgh Courier* unearthed a set of NAREB guidelines titled "The Fundamentals of Real Estate Practice," it exposed some of the pressure that the organization placed on its constituent boards across the country. The NAREB functioned as the most powerful organization in the real estate industry's professional community and helped set the standards for local brokers in most major cities. In their discussion of broker's obligations, the group insisted that realtors must seek to prevent the "objectionable use" of decent homes, which included occupancy by "a bootlegger who would cause considerable annoyance to his neighbors, a 'madam' who had a number of 'Call Girls' on her string, a gangster who wants a screen for his activities by living in a better neighborhood, a colored man of means who was giving his children a college education and thought they were entitled to live among whites."[19]

The NAREB did not create this principle or the sentiment behind it on its own. These guidelines simply echoed the tone of existing local industry standards or formally expressed the unwritten rules of many realtors who operated within segregated local boards. The NAREB, however, officially sanctioned and promoted the ideas that residential integration constituted a form of "blight" and that realtors had an ethical obligation to prevent any African American homeseeker—regardless of their class or character—from purchasing homes in white communities. The organization helped ensure that brokers bought into the practice of housing discrimination as a necessary element of their professional responsibilities. Though the NAREB and its affiliated local boards were not always successful, they provided substantial pressure for realtors to inhibit the efforts of black homeseekers, further limiting African Americans' access to decent accommodations. The NAREB did this despite a widespread recognition among its members that better housing for African Americans constituted a "pressing need" in many of their local communities and a general acknowledgment that black renters and homebuyers proved to be responsible clients. As far as the organization was concerned, however, maintaining neighborhood segregation was of paramount importance.[20]

Governmental forces complemented the tactics of individuals and real estate interests and further hindered black Americans' prospects in the housing market. Indeed, many historians have suggested that federal agencies and local governments constituted the primary influence behind the deepening chasm of urban segregation and the curtailment of African Americans' residential options in the 1940s. Agencies like the FHA codified and implemented racially discriminatory standards in the lending and mortgage insurance industries at a national level. On a local scale, city housing authorities restricted the provision and location of publicly funded housing. Together, federal, state, and municipal government actors strengthened and expanded the reach of residential segregation throughout the 1940s and 1950s.[21]

RESTRICTIVE COVENANTS, however, tied together these four broad categories of actors more powerfully than any other single tactic and highlighted most profoundly the connections between these groups and the challenges that black homeseekers faced in the 1940s. Covenants simultaneously relied upon individual enforcement and enjoyed the sanction and promotion of the real estate industry and both federal and local housing agencies. To African Americans, these agreements demonstrated the strength and breadth of the interests arrayed against them and represented the greatest threat to black housing access in the immediate postwar era.

The fate of African Americans' chances to enjoy the prosperity and security augured by the end of war seemed to hinge in no small part upon whether or not restrictive covenants would continue to exist and expand in America's neighborhoods. Indeed, for most knowledgeable commentators at the time, these contracts represented one of the greatest obstacles to black progress and their continued strength and spread posed a tremendous threat to the economic and social advancement of urban black populations in the postwar years. Economist and housing expert Robert Weaver—one of the more prolific authors on urban segregation during this era—acknowledged that covenants were only one tool among many, but insisted throughout the 1940s that "of all the instruments that effect residential segregation, race restrictive covenants are the most dangerous." Housing expert and advocate Charles Abrams attributed similarly dire consequences to the spread of covenants, whose discriminatory terms had become "as routine a part of conveyancing language as the words 'to have and to hold.'" Their spread, he argued, meant that "the involuntary ghetto may soon be an unalterable American institution." NAACP officials charged that "such restrictive agreements represent the *core* of the housing problem of Negroes and other racial minorities," while the Truman administration's postwar Committee on Civil Rights reflected the broad consensus of experts and activists alike when it labeled the restrictions "the most effective modern method" for maintaining urban residential color lines.[22]

Covenants' importance to housing segregation in the 1940s stemmed from a number of different factors, but two of the most significant overarching themes were the wide base of support that the agreements enjoyed and the physical magnitude of their presence and propagation. These contracts benefited from a singularly broad and collaborative array of backers in the arsenal of discriminatory tactics. No other enforcement mechanism attained the same sheer level of collusion and cooperation between the various categories of actors. Covenants began as the product of individual or industrial action, originating with residential subdividers, local real estate boards, and neighborhood associations. Business interests predominated in the efforts to establish covenants. A detailed study in postwar Detroit determined that approximately 90 percent of existing restrictions in the city came from subdividers. In St. Louis, the local Real Estate Exchange drafted more than 85 percent of the covenants within city limits. Across America, homebuilders and the real estate industry proved to be the primary engine of covenants' growth throughout the first half of the twentieth century.[23]

Implementation of these restrictions, on the other hand, most often fell to individuals. If black homeseekers managed to break covenants, it became the duty of local property owners to enforce the restriction's terms—though they could often expect the aid of city real estate boards in their efforts. The energy, time, and financial resources that successful litigation might require encouraged individual residents to organize collectively into "homeowners' associations." These groups pooled community resources and policed the standards of their neighborhoods. Often the creation of these associations predated the existence of covenants and their responsibilities normally included more than maintaining segregation. However, by the time African Americans began migrating to urban centers en masse, racial exclusion had become the "controlling motive" of many of these groups and they served as the primary enforcers of restrictive covenants for decades. During World War II, Detroit had upward of fifty homeowners' associations in active operation around the city, nearly a third of which had come into existence after the start of the war. The roster of organizations included the Seven Mile–Fenelon Improvement Association that had spearheaded white resistance in the 1942 Sojourner Truth housing controversy. Chicago boasted nearly eighty groups and the most substantial associations in St. Louis included thousands of property owners.[24]

Covenants had helped spawn the expansion and the race consciousness of these organizations over preceding decades and homeowners' associations had become the epicenters of local resistance to integration. In cities like Washington and Chicago, neighborhood homeowners' organizations also began creating citywide "federations" in order to "produce the greatest possible strength in keeping Negroes within the iron band" of covenanted boundary lines. One contemporary study aptly described the associations in Washington as "the front-line shock troops. . . . Their job has been to hold the line and sound the alarm whenever 'danger' threatens." Groups like these facilitated mobilization against black homeseekers, provided intense social and political pressure to maintain residential color lines, and ensured the implementation of racial restrictions in the courts.[25]

While real estate interests helped establish covenants and individuals spearheaded the enforcement effort, federal agencies played an equally significant role by encouraging the spread and implementation of these agreements. The FHA's place in this process garnered particular scrutiny from organizations like the NAACP. The institution's underwriting guidelines helped reinforce public perceptions of covenants' validity and necessity while conferring financial benefits for areas where these restrictions were present. From 1938 to 1947, when the agency deleted explicit references to race from its manual, the official guidelines for underwriters condoned racial segregation and extolled the advantages of restrictive covenants. In the section on "Rating of Location," the FHA discussed the "social attractiveness" of communities as an important factor for appeal and stability. "Satisfaction, contentment, and comfort," it began, "result from association with persons of similar social attributes." Lest anyone mistake what these attributes might be, the manual offered clarification—informing readers that America's homeowners "enjoy social relationships with other families whose education, abilities, mode of living, and racial characteristics are similar to their own." Racial homogeneity meant as much to underwriters as a region's "natural physical charm," "architectural attractiveness," or the absence of nuisances.[26]

The FHA expanded on these views elsewhere in the manual. In their discussion of how to evaluate a neighborhood's "protection from adverse influences," the agency offered this: "Areas surrounding a location are investigated to determine whether incompatible racial and social groups are present, for the purpose of making a prediction regarding the probability of the location being invaded by such groups. If a neighborhood is to retain stability, it is necessary that properties shall continue to be occupied by the same social and racial classes." To guard against "invasions" of this type and other negative influences, the manual discussed the utility of restrictive covenants and advised not only their establishment, but also their consistent and vigilant enforcement. Because an area's level of "protection" counted as the second most important factor in determining that location's rating, the presence of covenants could go a long way toward assuring the eligibility of homes for FHA assistance. Indeed, the agency counseled its underwriters that "where little or no protection is provided . . . the Valuator must not hesitate to make a reject rating of this feature."[27]

Covenants, then, helped neighborhoods secure the more generous financing and repayment terms that the FHA's mortgage insurance could provide. These guidelines encouraged the growth and enforcement of residential restrictions across the country during the 1940s. By the end of the decade, federal agencies would guarantee fully half of all new mortgages, indicating just how widespread this encouragement proved to be. The FHA's policies toward racial integration and the implementation of covenants only served to stimulate and incentivize the ongoing activities of real estate interests and white homeowners.[28]

Covenants granted the force and protections of law to discriminatory custom and wedded private interests with public support. Restrictive agreements provided a thread that tied the strength of individual resistance to the resources of private industry and the sanction of federal authority. In this achievement, covenants uniquely embodied and enjoyed the broad base of power arrayed against black homeseekers and signified the futility of urban African Americans' prospects for advancement in the postwar era. Eschewing the ferocity of mob violence or the invisibility of realtors' "gentlemen's agreements," these restrictions offered a respectable, publicly accepted, and legal means of exclusion that received approval and support from every one of the major forces that promoted residential segregation. To the extent that they covered America's homes then, they represented one of the most daunting obstacles to progress that African Americans confronted during the 1940s.[29]

Not surprisingly, restrictive agreements maintained a relatively extensive presence across America by the end of World War II and stood poised to increase their reach and effect. Though no overarching national study has determined just how prevalent these covenants were, the bulk of the available evidence from case studies and anecdotal accounts suggests that these restrictions occurred with great frequency. In Detroit, the general understanding in the early postwar years held that over 80 percent of residences outside of the inner Grand Boulevard area and the oldest areas of the city were covenanted. The local black press lamented that "today there is hardly an acre of unrestricted land in Wayne County." A detailed investigation of more than 10,000 subdivision deeds confirmed these estimates in 1947.[30]

Covenants in the Motor City proved more widespread than in other locations, but the numbers were still substantial elsewhere. A 1948 study of residential developments in the counties surrounding New York City determined that approximately 56 percent of all homes had race restrictions and that larger subdivisions had more than 80 percent coverage. In Kansas City, each of the four metropolitan counties had no less than 60 percent of subdivisions under covenant, and most had substantially more. Unofficial surveys in Washington, D.C., concluded that at least half of the city's residential areas were restricted. Numbers approaching and exceeding 50 percent coverage seemed the norm.[31]

An even more disturbing trend suggested that as new housing construction began to accelerate in the postwar years, covenants stood poised to grow just as rapidly. In major hubs of black migration like Detroit, "new restrictive agreements [came] into force almost daily." By 1945, one Wayne County civil servant remarked that new covenants sprang up at an average of ten or twenty each month. An extensive case study in the Motor City saw a 30 percent jump in the rate that subdividers enacted covenants over the course of the war. "Since 1940," the author noted, "not a single new subdivision has been established without a race restriction." A sampling of covenants in Chicago found that more than half of the agreements originated in the 1940s, with 1946 as a banner year for their establishment. Chicago NAACP branch president Oscar Brown warned of "unusual activity on the part of the whites to put into effect more and better restrictive covenants. Our backs are to the wall." Washington, D.C., saw more than 200 new covenants registered during the war and its immediate aftermath. In St. Louis, the Urban League— who played a key role in the broader social and political thrust of the anti-covenant movement—determined that only thirty-five newly constructed homes in the metropolitan area were open to African Americans out of the nearly 70,000 that builders offered between 1947 and 1952. By 1947, knowledgeable observers nationwide had expressed concern about the "alarming rate" of covenant growth and the "continued and intensified effort" to expand their reach. "Nobody really knows how much land is covered by covenants," declared *U.S. News & World Report* in 1948, "but all students of it agree that the practice is widespread and growing fast."[32]

For countless experts and observers then, covenants seemed the key to the enduring and increasing success of residential segregation efforts in the 1940s. Though many of these individuals overestimated the impact that negating restrictions would have on the future of black housing access, they had every reason to believe that covenants posed a significant ongoing threat to urban black communities. Housing discrimination remained a complex and heavily supported practice in the postwar years and restrictive covenants played a central role in that process. The combined effect of the myriad methods and layers of discriminatory action had stark consequences for black homeseekers across America's urban landscape.

By the end of World War II, whites' efforts to keep neighborhoods segregated had denied African Americans access to newly constructed homes for decades. Because homebuilders and subdividers played such an active part in housing discrimination, black residents rarely had opportunities to purchase recently built homes before the 1940s. Even when the pent-up demand and some federal prodding forced open the doors of wartime private building, black buyers still received a miniscule proportion of these homes. In Los Angeles, attorney Loren Miller claimed that although black Americans represented one-seventh of the migrant workforce during wartime, restrictive covenants barred them from over 95 percent of private construction for defense industry laborers. Nationwide the numbers proved even worse. An NHA analyst determined that during four years of war just 2.8 percent of private dwellings were available to African Americans. This amounted to only 15,000 homes, with 3,000 of these in one city alone. Numbers from the early postwar period maintained these distributions. In early 1947, St. Louis designated only 2.5 percent of its housing starts for black homeseekers, Washington assigned just over 3 percent, and Detroit made none of its 2,300 new units available to African Americans during that time.[33]

The inaccessibility of new building for urban black communities compounded issues of overcrowding in existing homes. In city after city, African Americans occupied significantly smaller percentages of the housing supply than their proportion of the population indicated were necessary. For Detroit, before the war began African Americans made up 9.2 percent of the population and held 8.2 percent of available dwelling units. By 1947, black residents constituted 13 percent of the city and held just 11 percent of the homes. For Washington, postwar data showed that black Americans made up 24 percent of the population and held only 20 percent of the homes. Cities like Baltimore, Chicago, and Cincinnati showed similar gaps.[34]

Inevitably, their disproportionately low share of the existing housing stock left African Americans more vulnerable to overcrowding. Black communities saw even smaller vacancy rates than their white counterparts. Cincinnati provided one of the most egregious examples, with the white vacancies hovering above 2 percent while the rate for African Americans stood at 0.5 percent. Because the overall numbers were small to begin with, gaps for other areas including Atlanta and St. Louis proved slighter, but still relevant. For Washington, more than one in five black families lived "doubled up" in 1947, while only 7 percent of white families suffered the same problem. Within the District, 12 percent of African Americans lived in homes with more than 1.5 occupants per room compared with 4 percent for whites. In St. Louis, almost a quarter of the city's black population lived with similar levels of crowding, compared to just 5 percent for local whites.[35]

THE COMBINED EFFECT of deeply restricted access to new homes and heightened levels of overcrowding forced African Americans into the oldest and most inadequate segments of America's urban housing stock and greatly overtaxed the capacities of those homes. Discrimination in the newest residential areas compelled black homeseekers to find shelter in already decaying and rapidly worsening regions of a city. In 1940, even before wartime migration accelerated fully, an NHA analyst concluded from a survey of forty-two cities that African Americans occupied substandard homes at three times the rate that whites did, with nearly 60 percent of urban black residents living in inadequate accommodations. By 1947, the disparities seemed worse. Under the most severe measure of adequacy—the need for "major repairs"—black communities suffered to a far greater degree than white areas. In Washington, just under 20 percent of black homes had major structural deficiencies compared to just 2 percent of white units. Detroit's black residents found one in four dwellings needing major repairs while only 3 percent of white homes fell to that level. St. Louis had almost one-third of black units in need of repair compared to 9 percent for whites.[36]

By nearly every other measure African Americans found their portion of the housing stock at a disadvantage to that of whites. More than 40 percent of black Detroiters and 70 percent of black St. Louisans spent their winters without central heating. One of every nine units that African Americans occupied in St. Louis and Washington was without running water. Before the end of World War II, engineers declared more than half of the units in Detroit's black communities substandard while the proportion for whites was only 14 percent. After the war, the proportion of substandard black homes approached 90 percent in the heavily populated Black Bottom and Paradise Valley regions.[37]

A tongue-in-cheek advertisement in *American City* magazine presented the realities of black housing options in a different way. Reginald Johnson of the National Urban League penned an offering that listed a "Ten room house" for rent. A description followed: "At least sixty years of age, badly in need of repair and redecoration. House is cold in winter and hot in summer. Conveniently located near smoky factories, noisy railroad yards, and receives frequent fragrance from nearby stockyards. The neighborhood is highly deteriorated and is well supplied with all the factors that encourage crime and delinquency. Heavy truck traffic in area, no nearby playgrounds, and firetrap school-house within walking distance. Best thing available for nice Negro family at exorbitant rent." The satirical tone of Johnson's glimpse at the classifieds captured the frustration and discomfort that segregation forced upon black urban populations. Even where African Americans could gain access to homes, much of what these cities had to offer them proved wholly inadequate. [38]

By the mid-1940s, overcrowding and its resultant strains on the physical infrastructure in black communities seemed unlikely to subside in the near future. African American homeseekers confronted an intense nationwide housing shortage and even more extreme limitations because of rampant discrimination. Restrictive covenants, white resistance, and pressure from the real estate industry and housing agencies choked off urban black districts from the breathing space that unimpeded access in residential markets might provide. African American communities continued to grow while their share of the existing housing supply failed to expand and deteriorated further, leaving black homeseekers with impossible choices to make. For black purchasers in cities across the country, the gloomy assessment of St. Louis businessman Fred Jones rang true when he declared that "there is [*sic*] only two ways for the Negro to go in quest of relief and they are to the attics or the basements." Realtor James T. Bush had even less optimism, remarking that the only way for black St. Louisans to obtain housing "would be if someone should die, leave the City or be evicted."[39]

Reluctant Pioneers: Breaking Restrictive Covenants

Despite the note of truth that Fred Jones and James T. Bush sounded in their portrayals of black residents' housing options, small numbers of African Americans found their way into covenanted homes and confounded efforts to keep them out. The initial process of covenant-breaking was often an ugly affair built upon a mixture of desperation, deception, risk, and greed. The six families at the heart of the covenant cases did not set out to defy the customs and strictures of residential segregation; they only sought to purchase homes of their own and provide themselves with a decent place to live. Yet, when confronted with the housing shortage, each of these families fell at the mercy of both a market that held few adequate options apart from covenanted homes and realtors whose motives were unclear at best and outright exploitative at worst. Indeed, several of the families had no idea about the existence of the covenants they violated until they received an attorney's letter or papers from a U.S. Marshal. How these families became the exemplars of covenant-breaking revealed some of the weaknesses in the barriers that enforced residential segregation, but also illustrated the complexity, uncertainty, and risk that black homeseekers faced.

Transferring covenanted homes relied, at its most basic level, upon the availability of eager black buyers and willing sellers. The former were quite obviously in abundant supply. The sheer desperation of the housing situation in most cities compelled many African Americans to consider taking up residence on previously all-white blocks—though typically only in districts that bordered existing black enclaves. Sellers proved far less numerous and distinctly uncooperative. Most homeowners who were party to a covenant and chose to sell either believed in the validity of the restrictions or feared the potential social and legal repercussions of violating them and thus refrained from selling to black purchasers.

The onus of covenant-breaking then typically fell to realtors of both races as the most active agents in the process. These men saw opportunities for considerable profit and facilitated many of the transactions by whatever means they could, often leaving either the seller or the buyer—and occasionally both—unaware of the fact that they were violating the agreement. Breaching covenants therefore rarely began as a political act. These were instead the efforts of individual families to claim some measure of security and comfort amidst trying conditions. Their struggles spoke to the desperation, desires, and dignity of African Americans who fought to own a decent home and in the process came to fight for their right to do so.[40]

J. D. and Ethel Lee Shelley made their way to St. Louis from rural Mississippi in the years leading up to World War II, chasing the lure of employment opportunities in the urban Midwest and fleeing the brutality of Jim Crow in the Magnolia State. J. D. Shelley resolved to leave his home near Starkville in 1939 shortly after the vicious beating by local police of a young domestic worker and a friend of the Shelley family. Mr. Shelley, a proud and protective family man and father of six, later admitted that he headed for St. Louis because he worried that "if they beat my kids like that, these white folks [would] have to *lynch* me down here." Like many other southern migrants, Mr. Shelley left on his own with a promise to send for Ethel Lee and their six children as quickly as he could. The rapid blossoming of wartime industry reunited the Shelleys some months later in 1940.[41]

During the war, Mrs. Shelley found work in a child-care service while her husband secured a new job as a mechanic at the Small Arms bullet factory. The Small Arms plant was a hotbed of protest and racial contention throughout the early 1940s. The sharply segregated facility experienced "hate strikes" by white employees who objected to black mechanics like Mr. Shelley tending to machinery that white women operated. Simultaneously, local civil rights organizations targeted the factory, demanding greater access to jobs and better working conditions for African Americans. The Shelley family, then, was reminded on a daily basis not only of the hardships and indignities that faced them in Jim Crow America—but of the capacity of resolve and community strength to foment change.[42]

Urban living with such a large family, however, proved decidedly uncomfortable. For nearly five years the Shelleys, like so many others, made do with limited space in a series of small apartments that struggled to fit them all. Having young children made it all the more difficult for the Shelleys to find places for rent and made each time they had to search for a new apartment a risky endeavor. Still, the family saved diligently and by the time the war began drawing to a close, the prospect of owning their own home for the first time in their lives seemed—at least financially—within reach. After debating and worrying for some time about whether or not they could truly afford the burden of a mortgage, Mrs. Shelley won her husband over to the idea of reaching out to a real estate agent when their daughter Leatha narrowly escaped an assault on her way home to the family's apartment one afternoon. In July of 1945, Ethel Shelley approached Robert Bishop, her pastor at the Church of God in Christ and a part-time real estate dealer, for help in their search.[43]

Bishop, a Gateway City resident for more than four decades, worked for prominent black realtor E. M. Bowers and quickly began showing the Shelleys the limited potential options from Bowers's listings. Bishop's initial efforts failed to impress the couple and they reached out to a representative from another real estate company, but shortly thereafter Bishop brought them to an understated brick home at 4600 Labadie Avenue. The Shelleys could only afford to occupy the four rooms on the lower floor and Mrs. Shelley later remarked that "of course it ain't enough for my family," but it did represent a considerable improvement over their current apartment's space and security. Bishop informed them that the flat currently belonged to "a widow lady" who was eager to sell. In fact, he had arranged for a white "straw-party" named Josephine Fitzgerald to purchase the house on his behalf from the previous owners.[44]

Straw-party sales served as a common way to facilitate covenant breaking by having a white purchaser acquire the property from a willing white seller and immediately resell or transfer the title to black buyers. Bishop himself admitted using the tactic in previous transactions and it remained one of the simplest methods of undermining covenants. Ultimately, the strategy of using straw purchasers served several purposes. Having a white purchasing party allowed realtors to circumvent discrimination by both sellers and financial institutions. White homeowners who avowedly upheld race restrictions were usually unable to know if the purchaser intended to resell. Indeed, in the case of the Labadie property, Bishop negotiated the sale with a white realtor who stated "that she preferred to sell it [the home] to a white." Only when Bishop assured her that Ms. Fitzgerald was white could the sale proceed.[45]

Perhaps just as important, lenders also eased their restrictions when faced with white buyers. As Bishop put it, "using a white straw party has been an advantage to me in financing . . . [it is] easier to finance through [a] white. That's common knowledge." The straw purchaser could "secure larger loans, better loans," leaving the person who assumed the subsequent transfer with a lower interest rate and more manageable payments. Brokers in St. Louis knew that African American borrowers typically found mortgage rates that were fully one-third more than whites' and tended to receive shorter terms for repayment.[46]

As this particular case would demonstrate, however, the straw party served an additional purpose. Bishop purchased the home on Labadie through Josephine Fitzgerald for $4,650. The following day, he resold the property to the Shelleys for $5,760—a 24 percent profit. Though Bishop insisted that his selling price remained a bargain for his clients, that he had originally negotiated the purchase in order to live in the home himself, and that his actual net profits on the deal were far less than the price difference made them seem, his most telling rationalization was perhaps unintentionally revealing. Under intense questioning from St. Louis County Circuit Court judge William K. Koerner, Bishop claimed that "that's some of the practice of the . . . real estate business; your Honor." Straw purchasers, especially when acting on behalf of—or in concert with—realtors, allowed for significant price markups and profit taking.[47]

In the end, not only had Bishop forced the Shelleys to overpay for their home, he left them completely unaware that their purchase violated the neighborhood's restrictive covenant. Though Bishop later protested that he himself had been ignorant of the covenant's existence, it seemed far more likely that he willfully chose to ignore the agreement. For their part, J. D. and Ethel Shelley simply believed that the neighborhood would be receptive to their presence because the block on Labadie had actually been integrated for decades prior to their arrival. When they viewed the house for the first time, the couple saw black children playing in the street and perhaps noticed one of the four black-owned homes along the avenue—which included the house next door.[48]

As Ethel Shelley later testified, "I [had] see[n] other colored people on the street, that's why I bought it. If I hadn't a-seen them I never would." Her statement revealed two frequent themes from the process of covenant-breaking. First, many black homeseekers did not actively wish to violate covenants or enter into solidly white neighborhoods. The fact that the Shelleys saw other African Americans on the block likely assuaged concerns about the potential for legal action or violent physical reprisals against them. They had been in the city long enough to know that lone black entrants into all-white regions made easy targets for vandals, mobs, and vigilantes, and presumably for that reason sought the relative safety of an already-integrated block. As with many black residents in search of wartime or postwar housing it was quality and safety that were of primary importance, with integration as an afterthought or even a discouraging factor in their decision making. Moving in alongside whites ultimately had few benefits and even less appeal if the neighborhood might terrorize or evict them.[49]

Second, Mrs. Shelley's statement called attention to how confusing and uncertain the process of changing neighborhoods and seeking adequate housing could be. The covenant that she violated covered a patchwork of parcels rather than the entire block and left intact a multiracial neighborhood whose first black residents had been in place since the 1880s. Restrictive agreements that sprang up in zones that had already experienced some degree of integration were rare and sought to protect white majorities rather than white exclusivity. The Shelleys' neighbors had hoped to minimize the potential impact and growth of an African American presence. These contracts subsequently frustrated black homebuyers who attempted to avoid integrating all-white regions by seeking out neighborhoods with an existing black population. The result was that even in some integrated areas of the city, black families had to fight house by house and spend years in courtrooms to gain access to properties right next door to other African Americans.[50]

Some 450 miles north of St. Louis, in the winter of 1944, a soft-spoken black couple had moved from their residence on Detroit's Ironwood Avenue to a new home at 4626 Seebaldt Street. Though Orsel and Minnie McGhee moved only five blocks, they found themselves in markedly different surroundings. Orsel "Mac" McGhee had come to Detroit from Eutaw, Alabama, with his family as part of the Great Migration. He had married his first wife, a fellow Alabaman and schoolteacher named Dora Diffay, in 1925 and found work in the Motor City as a janitor and then an elevator operator while providing for their two sons. As a mixed-race man of fair complexion, Mr. McGhee later "passed" as white in order to secure a new custodial job at the *Detroit Free Press* in the midst of the Depression. Tragedy visited the McGhee family, however, when Dora died in 1937 and Mac found himself raising the boys alone. Not long after, he met a charming and quiet young woman named Minnie who was a recent migrant from Elberton, Georgia, and who had found a job working nights at the local post office. Mac and Minnie married in 1939 and they soon began thinking about buying a home of their own.[51]

By the summer of 1944, the hardworking couple had put together enough money to try their luck in the city's dismal housing market. For years they had taken long Sunday walks together, but always with an eye out for a home they might one day own. Their long-standing search had amounted to nothing until one October evening Mr. McGhee strolled north of Tireman Avenue—a dividing line between the races in that section of town. Just a few blocks north of their current home, he found a four-bedroom bungalow with a "for sale" sign out front that seemed to suit all the family's needs. He met briefly with the owner, a German-born baker named Walter Joachim who was desperate to move his two sick children to a more forgiving climate. Mr. McGhee asked if Joachim would be willing to sell to a black buyer and when Joachim informed him that he would, the McGhees quickly placed a down payment on the property. Two days after Christmas, the family received the keys to their new home.[52]

Choosing a home in an all-white neighborhood was a calculated risk. The unassuming couple knew that they faced the prospect of both legal and physical intimidation. As the purchase proceeded, Mr. McGhee apparently consulted with a lawyer who informed him that the family would likely encounter some trouble with covenants. Mac declared that he was willing to take the chance. Mrs. McGhee would later explain that "he had worked among white people all his life and he felt that he knew them very well, in fact he felt he knew them better than he did his own people. He just felt there was nothing to their talk . . . that it would blow over." With at least a decade spent passing as white in his professional life, Mr. McGhee believed that their new neighbors would come to accept the family. If they could weather the initial bluster of threats, he reasoned, the controversy would eventually dissipate. Pride also played a role. In the end, Mr. McGhee "saw the house that he liked of his choice and he wasn't going to give it up." Even in the face of Detroit's long and notorious history of violence against pioneering black homeowners, he simply refused to be afraid.[53]

Whatever their initial expectations, the McGhees immediately set about being model neighbors in their new surroundings. Reporters described the family as "neat, likeable people" who had quietly worked their way into Detroit's black middle class. Minnie spent her weekends as part of a local black women's bridge club and she and Mac put a good deal of effort into keeping their new home in the best condition. As one observer put it, they "conform[ed] very closely to the popular conception of the average American family." The McGhees kept to themselves, however—a product of the frosty reception from the neighborhood and the fact that despite Mac's familiarity with white people, the family "didn't move over here to associate with them. We just were looking for a home." Their sense of resolve to brave whatever storms might come, though, only strengthened when their sons enlisted in the U.S. Army in the spring of 1945. The home suddenly meant something even more to them. It became a symbol of the freedom for which their sons now risked their lives in service to their country.[54]

Halfway across America, in Northwest Washington, D.C., a handful of black homebuyers found themselves in a situation remarkably similar to the Shelleys and McGhees. Robert and Isabella Rowe were one of four couples that all took up residence within a matter of months along a single block of Bryant Street. Much like the area along Labadie in St. Louis, the homes surrounding this block had experienced a significant degree of integration over the preceding years—including the residences along Adams Street directly in back of Bryant and several of the houses further up the street that already belonged to black renters or owners. By 1944, what remained of the previously all-white neighborhood was a row of twenty houses that faced the park between First and Second Streets. White homeowners had already successfully rebuffed several previous attempts by African Americans to rent some of the dwellings, but found their covenant faltering in the late years of the war.

The first African Americans to land on that stretch of Bryant Street were James and Mary Hurd, who purchased the home at 116 Bryant in May of 1944. Mr. Hurd had been born in North Carolina and had grown up in Knoxville, Tennessee—the son of a stone mason and a laundress. Through most of his adolescence, Mr. Hurd and his family had lived in a white neighborhood. Listed in the Census as a "mulatto," Mr. Hurd perhaps dubiously insisted that he was a Mohawk Indian and had no "negro blood." When he left home in search of work as a teenager, he passed as white for some time and eventually secured a job in the whites-only Boilermakers Union as a steam engine mechanic during World War I. After the war, Mr. Hurd met his future wife in New Jersey where she too was living in a white neighborhood. She was a soft-spoken Catholic and single mother who had grown up as an orphan in Washington, D.C., knowing nothing about her parents or their racial identity. When they married in 1928, they moved back to Washington where Mr. Hurd found work as a welder and they raised their son—who in 1944 was serving as a first class seaman in the U.S. Navy and had spent the previous two years overseas in that capacity.[55]

During the war, the Hurds had searched for decent housing on and off for three years and had been unable to acquire a suitable place at their desired price. Finally, one day in the spring of 1944, Mr. Hurd had driven down Bryant Street and noticed the empty house at 116. When he asked the real estate agent about its availability, he was pleasantly surprised to find a willing seller and the couple closed their purchase in early May and moved in the following week. The Hurds had actually checked for the presence of a covenant on the home and realized its existence, but as Mr. Hurd later maintained, "I didn't know I was of negro blood." The complexities of racial identity quickly became a centerpiece of the NAACP's initial postwar attack on restrictive covenants precisely because of cases like the McGhees' and Hurds' that called attention to the challenges and absurdities inherent in America's system of racial categorization.[56]

Just under a year later, in March of 1945, Robert and Isabella Rowe moved into 118 Bryant, next to the Hurds. Shortly thereafter, Pauline Stewart and her family moved into 150 Bryant at the opposite end of the block. Stewart, along with her eighty-three-year-old father, her sister, her brother-in-law, and her fourteen-year-old nephew, had suddenly found themselves without a home in March of 1945 when they received an eviction notice at their previous apartment on Thirteenth Street. Stewart, a lifetime resident of the District and a federal employee at the Bureau of Engraving and Printing, had hastily and desperately searched for somewhere to house the family—and especially her father—in comfort and decency. The pressure and immediacy of her need brought her to Bryant Street, where the real estate agent refused to allow her even to look inside the building before making an offer. The realtor informed her of the covenant on the property and advised her that she would be "taking a chance" if she chose to occupy the house. But her present situation required that she take the risk and her family moved in shortly thereafter.[57]

At the end of that summer, Herbert and Georgia Savage joined the Hurds, Rowes, and Stewarts by purchasing the residence at 134 Bryant. Like the Rowes and Stewarts, the Savages had faced eviction from their previous apartment and sought out a number of options before finding their way to Bryant. Mr. Savage, a fifty-two-year-old employee of the Treasury Department, knew about the covenant that covered the property when he bought the home, but the exigencies of his predicament compelled him to take the same chance that the Stewarts had.

The Rowes, Stewarts, and Savages had all obtained their homes from the same seller, an Italian immigrant, former high school teacher, and now a real estate lawyer named Raphael Urciolo. Urciolo had become deeply involved in covenant-breaking during the war years and was soon infamous among local white homeowners and realtors for his disregard of racially discriminatory agreements. As one observer put it, "we have a very distinguished gentleman who causes most of the trouble in the community." In 1942, he facilitated the desegregation of previously covenanted homes on Adams Street directly behind the 100 block of Bryant and owned numerous other properties throughout the city. By the time he completed the sale to the Savages, he had already personally financed several legal cases to protect black covenant-breakers—and himself as a seller—and had an array of suits pending against him for his efforts to integrate neighborhoods.[58]

Urciolo's motivations in his real estate business were complex. He freely admitted that he was first and foremost interested in "making as much money as you can possibly make" on his property investments. In the case of the Bryant Street homes, he had purchased the residences for around $6,000 each and resold them two years later for over $9,000. Given that average sales prices in the District increased approximately 40 percent between 1940 and 1945, Urciolo marked-up the prices for these units more than the typical realtor did during this time. He was able to reap such dramatic profits in part because of the desperation of African American buyers like the Stewarts.[59]

Yet, Urciolo's statements and actions also revealed a deeper sense of egalitarianism and some level of concern for black homeseekers. For instance, Urciolo had quickly come to the aid of a black woman named Clara Mays who faced eviction after two failed appeals to prevent the enforcement of a covenant two blocks away from Bryant on First Street. Mays had reached out to Urciolo who promptly "bought a house and moved Mrs. Mays in it, so that the fight against covenants might keep on at full blast." When asked why he so often chose to ignore restrictive covenants, he answered that he simply did not believe in discrimination "against any race or nationality." "I have no interest whatsoever in a man's color; only what he is," he added. In addition to this basic principle against prejudice, Urciolo expressed a particular sympathy toward disadvantaged groups in the housing market. "I have an added reason," he said of his penchant for covenant-breaking. "Since it is about five times as hard for colored people and foreigners to get houses . . . if I had a choice between selling to a colored man or a foreigner, and another—I would prefer to sell to the colored man because he has [a] much harder time getting a house than the other person."[60]

Regardless of his true motivations, Urciolo stood more prominently and resolutely against racial restrictive covenants than any other white realtor in the country. Indeed, it was resolve—more than perhaps anything else— that determined the success of covenant-breaking. When black families were able to circumvent covenants either intentionally or unintentionally, they often found themselves at the start of what could easily become a protracted, costly, humiliating, and ultimately futile legal battle. Perhaps none of the six families understood this as well as Herbert and Georgia Savage, who began moving their belongings into the house on Bryant Street the same day that the trial to evict them began.[61]

Holding the Line: Enforcing Restrictive Covenants

What the Savages and other covenant-breaking black families quickly learned was that even when covenants initially failed to preserve residential segregation, local homeowners could still implement the agreements to evict their new black neighbors. Although covenants could break down on the level of individual enforcement, part of what made the agreements powerful was that they provided a legally legitimate means of removing black homeowners even after they had broken the restriction's original barrier. The collective will of the community, or some element thereof, could reclaim the prerogative of racial exclusion that a single seller might choose to relinquish.

Because the process of covenant enforcement was a relatively simple legal procedure that could obviate the need for violence and the uglier methods of residential exclusion, it left white homeowners with an instrument that normalized and sanitized housing discrimination. The legitimacy that court enforcement conferred upon segregation and the racialized beliefs that underpinned covenants had an impact that extended beyond the boundaries of the agreements themselves. Contemporary observers saw restrictive covenants as pernicious despite the limitations on their enforceability and actual coverage in part because they gave sanction and respectability to underlying white assumptions about the undesirability of black homeownership and mixed-race neighborhoods. Those beliefs and the attitudes and behaviors they engendered had a reach that affected areas that never bothered to create covenants. This in turn rationalized more overtly confrontational and destructive responses and the rights-based language of racial exclusion that pervaded American cities and reified housing segregation regardless of the presence of restrictive agreements. Covenants reinforced the racial fears of white homeowners and gave those concerns a readily available, legitimate, and peaceful outlet.[62]

Still, enforcement required organization, time, and money on the part of white communities. Once black buyers had broken covenants, local whites had to rally to implement the restrictions. For the six families involved in the *Shelley* cases, the process unfolded in much the same way each time. A formal notification from a local attorney or an organized group of homeowners about the covenant's terms and the intent to implement them marked the opening salvo and tried to frighten off African American homebuyers with the threat of enforcement. This initial attempt at intimidation sought to secure the removal of these black neighbors without the expense and time of a legal proceeding. When this failed, local whites moved ahead and served the black residents with a summons to appear in court. Black homeowners sought out legal advice and clarification from their realtors and local attorneys as they determined what their next step should be.

As white residents saw it, a broken covenant meant a serious threat to each homeowner's financial security and to the racial and social "character" of a neighborhood that many whites had called home for decades. Organization and mobilization were therefore the first steps in removing black newcomers. In Detroit, St. Louis, and Washington white residents used existing networks of local property owners to coordinate their respective actions and present a united front to each black family. These targeted expressions of resistance to integration put collective pressure on individual African American purchasers in an effort to remove them quickly and quietly from the neighborhood. Groups in each city sought to make it unmistakably clear that new black residents were not welcome and that it would be in their best interests to pick up and leave immediately.

In Detroit, local white resistance began with a meeting of property owners from the Northwest Civic Association (NCA), including the McGhees' next-door neighbors Benjamin and Anna Sipes. Mr. Sipes and his family had come to Detroit from northern Pennsylvania and had lived at 4634 Seebaldt Street since 1927. He found a series of jobs over the next decade, ultimately joining the ranks of blue-collar auto factory workers during the 1930s. The children of Russian and German immigrants, Mr. and Mrs. Sipes found comfort in their new neighborhood that sported a mixture of native-born and immigrant residents and a blend of blue- and white-collar workers, lending at least the perception of comfort and upward mobility. By 1934, however, the Depression brought the Sipes family to the brink of foreclosure until the HOLC helped them save their home. The following year—perhaps more sensitive than ever to the risks that homeownership entailed—they joined their neighbors in signing a restrictive covenant and assisting the NCA's efforts.[63]

When the McGhees moved in, the NCA chose Mr. Sipes to head the campaign for the newcomers' removal. As the first step, Mr. Sipes recounted, "a committee of taxpayers in the neighborhood got together and I composed this letter, and asked them if it was satisfactory to everybody concerned in this group and they said it was." On January 7, 1945, he then led ten of his longtime neighbors to the McGhees' home and asked to speak to them inside. Mr. and Mrs. McGhee, reasonably assured that the situation was not poised to devolve into violence, welcomed Mr. Sipes in. As he sauntered through the door he announced that "we are a group of taxpayers in the neighborhood, who are representing the Civic Association . . . and we are asking you to kindly vacate the property." "We also wish to inform you," he continued, "that . . . unless you move out, the Civic Association will take you to court."[64]

Duly warned of his neighbors' intentions, Mr. McGhee asked if the NCA wished to buy the property from him. The McGhees appeared willing to avoid the potential legal confrontation and face the harsh realities of the housing market once again. Mr. McGhee's bravado that had led him to risk purchasing the home in the first place momentarily faltered as they faced the prospect of losing their investment. For black covenant-breakers, one of the most daunting consequences of litigation was the possibility that they could be left without a legal claim to their property and without a means to recoup their financial outlays—which often represented a significant portion of their life savings. Mrs. McGhee in particular feared that the family might never reclaim their money from Walter Joachim, the seller who had escaped the wrath of his neighbors by fleeing to California just two weeks after agreeing to the sale. Volunteering to resell the property immediately, then, might have at least saved the McGhees from dire economic vulnerability. In response to this offer, however, Sipes only replied, "That isn't for us to decide." Apparently the leadership of the homeowners' group had only empowered him to go so far in his efforts to remove the new neighbors. The NCA felt that the threat of legal action would provide sufficient motivation.[65]

Faced with an array of unpleasant options, Mr. McGhee stood his ground. He had not initially thought of his decision to purchase the house on Seebaldt as a political act, but he clearly understood the implications of what it would mean to stay and fight. When one of the ten angry neighbors standing in the doorway of his home demanded to know why he had moved onto their block and why they could not "find any other place to move rather than over here," Mr. McGhee shot back that he "could find another place . . . but how about the other fourteen million black Americans that have no place to live but in the ghetto or doubling up?" The odds were high that they would lose in court, especially since they lacked enough money to afford an attorney. Yet the McGhees recognized that their struggle represented a much larger yearning in the black community south of Tireman Avenue and others like it across the country. Moments earlier they had been willing to forgo the court battle that awaited them. Now they defiantly faced the hostile crowd gathered in their home and invited them to leave. Not long after, Sipes and the NCA made good on their promise and filed a bill of complaint in the Wayne County Circuit Court to start the covenant enforcement process.[66]

Legal intimidation, however, would not be the only tactic the neighborhood relied on to drive the couple out. Almost immediately after filing with the court, white residents began a concerted effort to harass and frighten the McGhees. Threatening phone calls, verbal abuse and epithets shouted out in the streets, even a blazing cross on the front lawn made the ensuing months deeply unsettling. A concerned neighbor secretly confided to Mrs. McGhee one afternoon that a group of men in the area had recently discussed the idea of burning the home to the ground. The stress of this nearly constant coercion ultimately drove Mrs. McGhee to seek medical treatment for nervous exhaustion. Through it all, though, the family remained resolute and steadily set about the work of building a better life for themselves in the midst of incredibly trying conditions.[67]

IN ST. LOUIS, the local homeowners' group targeted the sellers of 4600 Labadie Avenue for intimidation before the Shelleys had even seen the property. Representing over 2,000 members at its peak and around forty homeowners on Labadie's 4600 block, the Marcus Avenue Improvement Association (MAIA) presented formidable opposition to potential covenant-breakers. As soon as black prospective buyers began viewing the home, the MAIA's chairman—a baker named Emil Koob—sprang into action, repeatedly calling the seller's agent. Koob initially obtained the assurances of the realtor "that he wouldn't entertain the idea [of selling to black purchasers] under no circumstances, because of his membership in the [St. Louis Real Estate] exchange." Koob attempted to draw on the power of the exchange's racial mandates by either implicitly or explicitly reminding the agent of his ethical obligations. Soon Koob found the man no longer accepted his calls. The MAIA then sent a different representative to the realtor's office hoping that an unfamiliar name might get them in the door, but to no avail.[68]

After these months of wrangling, it came as no surprise when the Shelleys obtained the house on Labadie. By that time, Koob's organization had resigned itself to evicting any black family that occupied the premises rather than vainly protesting to the realtor. The MAIA wasted no time in fulfilling its promise to enforce the covenant. Just hours after the Shelleys had finished unloading their belongings into their new home, Ethel Shelley received a summons for the eviction proceedings. Koob and his colleagues chose long-time residents Fern and Louis Kraemer to serve as their plaintiffs in the proceedings. Mrs. Kraemer had inherited her residence at 4532 Labadie after the death of her father and together the Kraemers had moved back to the largely blue-collar neighborhood of her youth in the 1930s. Though the MAIA's leadership spearheaded the case against the Shelleys, the Kraemers were close acquaintances of Koob's and remained deeply invested throughout the proceedings.[69]

It was the cases from Washington, however, that revealed the covenant enforcement process in the greatest detail. On Bryant Street, white homeowners were without an official organization to coordinate their efforts and most of the legwork in implementing the covenant fell to a local real estate lawyer named Henry Gilligan and a zealous resident named Lena Hodge. Mrs. Hodge and her husband Frederic had moved to Washington from the Northeast and bought their home at 136 Bryant Street in 1909 shortly after its construction. The newly built, white-collar neighborhood had the added appeal of racial and ethnic homogeneity, as nearly all of the local residents were native-born whites and at least second- or third-generation Americans. The Hodges admitted that they selected the property in part because of the racial restriction against African Americans written into the deed. Though the neighborhood would lose its ethnic uniformity in the 1930s to a rapid influx of Italian and "Assyrian" immigrants, Lena and Frederic Hodge proved far more welcoming to these newcomers than to the black homeseekers that took an interest in the homes along Bryant Street.[70]

In the decades after the Hodges first arrived, the couple—and especially Mrs. Hodge—actively sought to defend and extend the block's racial regulations. When African Americans began purchasing the uncovenanted homes at the very end of the block, Mrs. Hodge led an ultimately unsuccessful effort to establish a homeowners' committee to create and enforce a new covenant for those residences. As she told it, "when we first took this up . . . I was practically the only one concerned in it." After that time, she slowly became the nucleus of an organized effort to ensure that the Bryant Street covenant remained intact.[71]

While she failed to restrict additional homes, Mrs. Hodge fared much better implementing the deed restrictions on the twenty houses that already had them. Over the years, some property owners had attempted to rent out their homes to black tenants on various occasions, and in each instance

Mrs. Hodge helped discourage the prospective renters from ever taking occupancy. Then, early in 1944 and not long before the Hurds moved in, a black family purchased the home at 152 Bryant. Mrs. Hodge immediately consulted local attorney Henry Gilligan and organized a meeting of the block's white homeowners. With some concerted pressure from Gilligan, "they gave up ownership of the house without any trouble whatever."[72]

When asked how she became the leader of the neighborhood's exclusionary efforts, Mrs. Hodge remarked, "I don't know, it is just one of those things. I got into it, I guess, and . . . as soon as they [the neighbors] would hear or know of a colored person moving, they always called me and I just simply assumed the responsibility, I guess, because they wanted me to." Mrs. Hodge took on the role of organizer in rather haphazard circumstances, but embraced the responsibility with gusto. By the mid-1940s, she had fought covenant battles along her block for nearly two decades, becoming—as one local attorney called her—the "big chief" of the neighborhood.[73]

Like many local property owners fighting for racial exclusion, however, she actually retained a narrow sense of her obligations. When African Americans began purchasing the Adams Street homes on the block directly behind hers, she felt no need to engage since, she said, "Those people over there could do their own fighting; I was fighting for my own street and home. . . . I felt that I had enough to think about and fight for on my own street." Though she would fiercely defend the covenant on her block, the energy and time that organization and enforcement required led her to limit the extent of her concerns in the area. Indeed her attitude was a common one, for apart from national professional organizations like the NAREB, those individuals and groups who defended covenants usually had limited ranges of interest that rarely extended beyond the neighborhood or at most the city in which they operated. For Mrs. Hodge, protecting the restrictions on the stretch of twenty houses remained her only real interest. While she reached out to "people in the community, citizens associations, or [an] executive committee of owners" for help in preserving the racial exclusion on her own block, she refused to lend her support to efforts beyond the cross-streets.[74]

On the day the Hurds moved in to 116 Bryant in May of 1944, Mrs. Hodge engaged in an informal interrogation of the new residents, approaching James Hurd as he brought his belongings into the house. After conversing briefly with Mr. Hurd, Mrs. Hodge apparently informed him that, "It is just too bad, because this may be a case of your having to move out . . . because some other ones [black residents] have moved out that have gone in to these houses." She later recounted a rather lengthy conversation in which she admonished Mr. Hurd that there were "lots of people along here who are elderly people and they will have to move probably if the colored come in, it will force them out. . . . I don't want anything to force me out of my home. . . . That is probably what you are going to do here." Despite Hurd's assurances that the neighborhood would "find out that we will be as clean as a lot of white ones will," Mrs. Hodge insisted, "That isn't the issue. The covenant has been violated and that is the thing we don't want to happen." When she returned home, she immediately called her collaborator in covenant enforcement for nearly twenty years: Henry Gilligan.[75]

Gilligan had been and remained an ardent advocate of racial property restrictions and served the Hodge family and the Bryant Street community since the 1920s. When the Hurds purchased their new residence, Gilligan—at the urging of Mrs. Hodge—took swift action. He first placed a call to Mr. Hurd to inform him of the covenant situation and the neighborhood's intent to evict him unless he complied with the terms of the agreement. James Hurd recounted that the call itself was so laced with contempt and condescension that "you talked like you was talking to a dog and therefore, I didn't care about talking to you, and lots of things you said I didn't pay attention to."[76]

When the call failed to intimidate the Hurds, Gilligan sent them a registered letter in June to threaten legal action again. "It has been my hope," he claimed, "that we might have this matter adjudicated, but I am now putting you on notice that we must bring the question to an immediate conclusion." He delivered an ultimatum that within a week's time the Hurds officially needed to state their intent to move and show that they had secured new lodgings—a Herculean task given that it typically took weeks, if not months, of searching to find adequate housing in the city. Should they fail to satisfy this request, "I shall prepare and file . . . an injunction suit and will make every effort to have the Court grant a preliminary injunction requiring you to move. It is my earnest hope that this suit may not be necessary, but I assure you it will be brought if I do not have definite assurance." By way of conclusion, Gilligan highlighted his two latest covenant case victories from recent weeks in order to remind the Hurds that his threats were by no means idle.[77]

In this instance, however, Gilligan backed down and turned his attention to other matters after assurances from the Hurds' realtor that he was actively scouring the city for a new home for the couple. Several months later, in November of 1944, the attorney found the Hurds had still not moved so he and

Mrs. Hodge called a neighborhood meeting together at the Hodges' residence to sign a formal complaint for court action. It was unclear whether Gilligan and Mrs. Hodge even explained to everyone exactly what they were signing and since a number of the local residents were recent Italian immigrants with only partial English literacy, some dispute lingered about their understanding of what they had agreed to. But the duo was apparently convincing enough—with or without an explanation—to get the signatures and to collect an $85 retaining fee from the gathering.[78]

Because of delays in the court's processing of the complaint, the other black families who broke the Bryant Street covenant began arriving while the action against the Hurds stalled. Mrs. Hodge discovered that Gilligan was out of town when the new couples appeared on Bryant and took it upon herself to collect the signatures for a new complaint, going house by house down the block. Mrs. Hodge used a combination of familiarity and intimidation to obtain the coplaintiffs she wanted. Because she maintained cordial visiting relationships with most of her white neighbors and because she served as the "big chief" of the neighborhood's racial issues, Mrs. Hodge had a network of personal relationships with the women along the block that facilitated her mobilization efforts. In her haste and self-certainty, however, she also relied upon her status and the relative unawareness of her neighbors to cajole and bully them into cooperation without explanation. In one deposition, Victoria DeRita of 128 Bryant Street remarked that she was unable to read or write English and that when Mrs. Hodge showed up at her door, "she say I have to sign. That is all. I am supposed to sign," which Mrs. DeRita did. Because she had joined the earlier complaint against the Hurds, she likely would have had some understanding of the circumstances for the second petition, but Mrs. Hodge—who did not speak Italian—apparently failed to offer any explanation and simply insisted upon her signature. Though Mrs. DeRita and her husband remained committed participants in the case as it proceeded, they were also prime examples of how a single individual could manufacture broader support for covenant enforcement. Social pressures operated alongside genuine support for racial exclusion to create a neighborhood consensus and a united front against black homeowners.[79]

The black families at the center of these eviction efforts, however, hardly played a passive role. Confronted by a determined and well-organized opposition, each family ultimately chose to stand and fight against their neighbors and the courts. Though none of them knew just how far their litigation would take them, they all resolved to push back against the pressure and intimidation they faced. This process was certainly not without misgivings. After all, the McGhees had offered to sell their home to the NCA on the spot, Ethel Lee Shelley remarked that she never would have chosen the home had she known of the covenant, and James Hurd strongly considered moving out in the wake of Gilligan's threats. However, a combination of factors encouraged the families to oppose the eviction efforts. The dire pressure of the housing situation in each city stood as a strong deterrent to leaving and individual resolve played an important role. Additionally, when each family found local attorneys to represent them, these lawyers provided an external pressure to remain in the fight with an eye toward using the clients as test cases in a broader effort against covenants as a whole. The combination of factors helped ensure that covenant enforcement was not an easy or uncontested process for white homeowners.

Part of the basic struggle for some families was to understand exactly what the threats and legal actions meant. Many urban black homeseekers simply did not know what covenants were or where they existed. Despite the attempts of newspapers and organizations like the NAACP to explain what restrictive covenants did, families like the Shelleys were sometimes unfamiliar with how they worked. Mrs. Shelley's first reaction to the summons she received from the MAIA was to immediately contact her realtor, Robert Bishop. "I just didn't understand it . . . I didn't know what it was," she explained, "I just wanted to know whether the property was our property . . . I just wanted him [Bishop] to explain to me what it was." The fact that the neighborhood was already integrated only compounded Mrs. Shelley's confusion, because "I thought when they place a restriction, wouldn't be no colored in the block at all." In fact, perhaps the only thing that was clear to the Shelleys was the attitude behind the eviction efforts. When asked if she understood the lawsuit pending against her, Mrs. Shelley simply replied, "I just understand the white people don't want me back."[80]

The Hurds also turned to their realtor, a white man named Richardson, when Lena Hodge and Henry Gilligan confronted them. Though James Hurd insisted that he knew about the covenant before purchasing the Bryant Street home and that his racial identity would not disqualify him from living on the premises, Gilligan's letter apparently rattled him badly. Because he was only partially literate, Mr. Hurd had some difficulties understanding what the covenant and the legal threats meant, so he consulted his realtor for clarification. An admittedly "very nervous and highstrung" man, Mr. Hurd apparently required several weeks of convalescence after receiving the explanation. As a result of this incapacitation, the realtor composed a reply letter on the Hurds' behalf and brought it by Mr. Hurd's workplace for a signature three weeks later without explaining what was in the response.[81]

The letter, which Gilligan presumed was from Mr. Hurd himself, was a string of apologies and assurances that the family would vacate the premises as soon as they could. The realtor went so far as to promise that the Hurds would leave "even if it means a financial loss," a guarantee that the family certainly did not approve. He ended the letter with a plea for "a little human kindness by at least giving us sufficient time within which to comply with your mandate." It was unclear whether the realtor actually intended to move the Hurds or if he hoped to buy enough time for more African Americans to purchase homes in the neighborhood and perhaps break the will of the covenant's enforcers.[82]

In the end, it was Mary Hurd who convinced her husband to fight for their home on Bryant Street and to seek legal help. When her husband initially suggested his willingness to move out, she went to him and insisted that "she liked the place and wasn't going to move anywheres [sic]." Her resolve emboldened her husband and together they turned to the local NAACP for assistance. Their decision proved fortunate indeed, because the branch office passed their case along to renowned attorney Charles Hamilton Houston, perhaps the foremost civil rights lawyer in the country.[83]

In Detroit, the McGhees also looked to their local branch of the NAACP when they decided to fight to retain their property. The Association's conspicuous activity in covenant litigation and housing desegregation efforts around the city made them the logical place to turn when challenging the white homeowner's association. Mac and Minnie McGhee contacted the branch's Legal Redress Committee to ascertain whether one of the affiliated attorneys could assist with their case. Two local veterans in the fight against covenants, including the committee chairman himself, volunteered their services. Willis Graves and Francis Dent represented as formidable a team as one could find in the city.

Families like the McGhees and Hurds who chose to fight back against covenant enforcement relied upon the local NAACP or their realtors for help in their efforts. Since most covenant-breaking black buyers were not attorneys and found themselves up against a larger, experienced, and organized opposition, they sought out institutions within black communities that were equally—or even better—organized and practiced advocates. For most major urban centers the most recognizable and best resourced option was the local NAACP branch where memberships and legal efforts were riding a wave of wartime and postwar political urgency and mobilization. An additional factor was that most individual families who confronted covenants had just sunk the bulk or the entirety of their life savings into the homes they now needed to defend. They had to rely upon organizations with the willingness and financial capacity to fight on their behalf without demanding legal fees.

The NAACP was not, however, the only place for these families to turn. Indeed for the Shelleys in St. Louis and three of the families in Washington, realtors helped secure and fund their attorneys. When the Shelleys went to Robert Bishop to better understand what the eviction efforts meant, Bishop eventually steered them to the offices of local attorney and politician George L. Vaughn, who took to their defense. By the end of 1946, when their case had moved to the Missouri State Supreme Court, the Shelleys' legal efforts had a new benefactor in the recently formed Real Estate Brokers' Association (REBA)—a collective of local black realtors whose first order of business became the financial support of the *Shelley* case. The Shelleys' original backers joined with an array of other agents in St. Louis to coordinate the case's advancement. Bishop, who had facilitated the family's covenant battle from day one, served as the secretary of the new organization.[84]

Bishop's and REBA's interests in the covenant cases stemmed from both fiscal and political concerns. As they saw it, restrictive covenants stood between black realtors and a flood of potential profits given the demand for housing among their clientele. Though the group had some political motivation, the pecuniary interests weighed heavily in their decision to form an independent organization and to fund the Shelleys' defense.

In Washington, attorney Raphael Urciolo's motives were noticeably similar to Bishop's and REBA's. Urciolo, who sold covenanted homes to the Rowes, Stewarts, and Savages, also provided their courtroom defense, working pro bono to protect his sales. Since Urciolo stood to lose more than $10,000 in profits if the court voided the transactions, he took a very active interest in supporting each of the families. As Henry Gilligan pointed out to him at trial, "It pays to go into court and let yourself be sued . . . trying to defeat the covenant; look at the money you make." Whether their objectives were financial or political, individuals like Urciolo and Bishop and organizations like the NAACP and REBA provided the resources and support that made it possible for covenant-breaking families to defend themselves in court.[85]

Family Matters: Restrictive Covenants
and the Postwar Moment

Despite the best efforts of their advocates, the six families in the covenant cases quickly came to realize that they faced the very real chance of losing their homes. Though some challenges to restrictive agreements had started to enjoy success in other parts of the country, they knew when they entered the courtrooms in St. Louis, Detroit, and Washington that the law looked to be against them. Whether they took the risk of purchasing a covenanted home knowingly or not, each of these individuals found themselves clutching the dream of postwar comfort, security, and prosperity that their neighbors were threatening to rip from them. Though their struggles would come to symbolize African Americans' prospects for progress to a broader audience of civil rights supporters, for the Shelleys, McGhees, Hurds, Rowes, Stewarts, and Savages these homes had additional meaning. The house on Labadie offered added room and a safer place for the Shelleys' children to grow and play. For Pauline Stewart, Bryant Street meant that her aging father might live out the rest of his life in the comfort and dignity he deserved. The Rowes knew that their home meant the difference between a peaceful night's sleep and years of restless anxiety about when the next eviction might come or what to do about the holes in the kitchen ceiling.[86]

Faced with the resistance of their neighbors and the uncertain future that litigation promised, each of these families—like many others across the country—summoned the courage and resolve to fight back. They declared to their neighbors and ultimately the nation that they had "as much right to live in a house as anybody." Perhaps the McGhees' and Hurds' thoughts lingered on the service of their sons in the military and how they might make a better future for their boys when they returned. Herbert and Georgia Savage might simply have looked around at the not-yet-unpacked moving boxes in their home and shuddered at the memory of week after week of uncertainty about where they might be forced to sleep the following night. J. D. and Ethel Lee Shelley's minds undoubtedly returned to the day their daughter arrived home in hysterics having narrowly escaped unspeakable brutality. Whatever their reasons, these six families clung to the hopes that they could forge a new and better life in the years following World War II. For them, that dream began at home.[87]

Still, resolve alone would only take them so far. As the cases emerged in 1945, these individuals discovered an array of supporters who offered the resources to carry their cause into the courts. Assistance from NAACP branch offices and interested parties in the real estate industry remained a vital part of covenant litigation in the 1940s and continued a long-standing but newly reenergized effort to undermine restrictive agreements at the local level. While urban whites organized to prevent black encroachment and expel African American property owners, local civil rights attorneys fought back against covenants in the same way: block by block.

TWO

Courtrooms

Local Lawyers and Legal Activism

It must have been an odd sight for passersby—the judge marching down the block while the dueling attorneys trailed close behind, interjecting their thoughts as they saw fit. Judge Thurmond Clarke, the son of a prominent local attorney, strode with the power that had shattered the state's sprinting records as a youth, pausing only to inspect the condition of the houses along Oxford Avenue and Harvard Boulevard. A political conservative, he bore the confidence of wealth and of a man who had held his post on the Los Angeles Superior Court since his appointment a decade earlier at the age of thirty-two.[1]

One of the attorneys matching his pace on that December morning in 1945 had grown up under quite different circumstances. Born in the hamlet of Pender, Nebraska, in 1904, Loren Miller had been raised on the Kansas plains—trapping ground squirrels and indulging his passion for books in the town where his grandparents had fled after their emancipation. As a boy, Miller had wanted to become president of the United States, exhibiting the ambition and precocity that fueled his later career as an activist, attorney, and entrepreneur in California's City of Angels. His parents and siblings had joined together to put him through the University of Kansas. It was there that he first confronted the daily indignities of segregation. In those years, Miller later recounted, "I dug into my text books and written large between the lines was the lesson that the Negro had a place, a subordinate place, in America. I was, in turn, hurt, then stunned, then angry, then driven to sullen acceptance. I went to college an American. I emerged a Negro." His collegiate experience burned into his mind the desire for change. In the ensuing decades, Miller would hungrily pursue the prospect of racial reform, exploring a variety of political commitments and undergoing a dramatic professional evolution. By the mid-1940s, his legal work had made him into California's premiere civil rights advocate.[2]

It was, in the end, Miller's advocacy that brought these two men together that day. Judge Clarke had agreed to inspect the integrated neighborhood that black Angelenos called "Sugar Hill" in order to assess the claims of Miller's courtroom opponent that African American homeowners devalued and ruined healthy properties. At Miller's urging, Clarke walked the streets of the West Adams Heights district to see for himself the products of racial housing integration. The case at hand, involving some fifty black property owners in the area, drew nationwide attention due to the high profile of Miller's clients. The individuals who faced eviction from the old colonial mansions that lined the streets included Academy Award–winning actress Hattie McDaniel, renowned blues singer Ethel Waters, and an assortment of other prominent African American entertainers. They had chosen Miller to represent them because by that time he was one of the nation's most experienced and successful anticovenant litigators. Their decision paid quick dividends as Miller became one of the handful of local attorneys to score an unlikely victory against racial restrictions.[3]

Within eighteen months Miller would go from representing movie stars and other members of Los Angeles' black elite to fighting in the U.S. Supreme Court on behalf of Orsel McGhee, an otherwise anonymous custodian half a nation away in a city Miller hardly knew. Indeed, for the McGhees in Detroit and the families in St. Louis and Washington, D.C., those Sugar Hill mansions and the celebrities that owned them seemed worlds away from the modest homes and stretched budgets that would send them to their own court battles. Yet the fighting connected them. Regardless of their status, black covenant-breakers took to local courtrooms to assert their rights as citizens and homeowners. In doing so, they entrusted their fates to attorneys like Loren Miller, Charles Hamilton Houston in Washington, or a host of lesser-known lawyers in cities around the country who could navigate the arduous process of civil rights litigation.

AS LEGAL BATTLES over covenants took shape in the 1940s, they provided an important perspective on the contours of litigating racial justice at the grassroots. At the heart of these efforts was a dynamic brand of "collaborative legal activism" that helped to guide and sustain attorneys in cities across the country. The work of anticovenant lawyers and the progression of the *Shelley v. Kraemer* (1948) cases through the courts in Missouri, Michigan, and the District of Columbia revealed that although local courtrooms played a critical role in shaping the development of civil rights campaigns, legal activism rarely stopped at the courthouse door. Five central themes characterized the structure of this style of litigation. Taken together these themes offer insight into the strategies that drove the legal battle for civil rights forward and speak to the relationship between legal advocacy and the broader cause of black freedom at midcentury.[4]

First—and most obviously—collaborative legal activism relied on the law to defend the rights of African Americans and to effect change in local and national patterns of racial discrimination. Legal activists believed in the importance of the judicial system as a forum to articulate black Americans' demands for the full privileges of citizenship and to guard against infringements of existing rights. They sustained this belief in spite of the fact that in the past the law had often facilitated the subjugation of African Americans. Legal activists looked beyond this discouraging history and evinced an underlying faith that the law was a necessary and at times uniquely powerful tool to fulfill the promises of equal treatment and the protection of life and liberty. Wielded skillfully, the law could be an engine of remarkable change.[5]

Second, this brand of activism challenged the law's institutional fixity. Black advocates well understood the legal system's imbrication with the popular customs of segregation and white supremacy and the deference to precedent that bolstered the nation's racial status quo. In order to challenge the courts' relative stasis, legal activists advanced new theories about jurists' duties in adjudicating cases. Attorneys in anticovenant litigation integrated statistics, social scientific observations, and moral appeals into their cases and asked judges to consider the full consequences of their decisions and to acknowledge the affirmative roles that they played in sustaining patterns of inequality. These advocates challenged the courts to look beyond the settled principles of law in order to achieve justice and they framed their arguments in ways that could encourage and allow for a departure from the judicial orthodoxies of decades past.[6]

Collaborative legal activism also relied upon intellectual creativity and courtroom experimentation. This third characteristic grew unavoidably from the difficulties of fighting against the solid bulwark of Jim Crow's legal legitimacy. Veteran attorneys like Houston and Miller constantly probed the defenses of American segregation with new strategies and claims as they searched for breaking points. Local courts simultaneously became battlegrounds and proving grounds—theaters and laboratories—where legal activists sought out the right combination of evidence and argument to achieve a victory.

This innovation and dynamism sprang in no small part from collaborative legal activism's fourth feature: national networks of communication between civil rights litigators. A vigorous exchange of ideas between attorneys from across the country brought local struggles into dialogue through a nationwide community of legal activists. Through correspondence and professional societies, lawyers traded tactics and shared their experiences as they refined various methods of attack in their respective cities. Local attorneys still exercised a considerable amount of independence in their decisions, but most engaged frequently with their peers as they pursued their cases. This collaborative approach promoted experimentation, provided intellectual and professional support, and helped disseminate successful strategies. While local particularities always profoundly shaped individual cases, in many respects civil rights lawyering was never strictly a local process.

The final characteristic of this activism was that it closely linked the efforts of attorneys with the energies of the communities in which they worked. These individuals, often themselves local leaders, tapped into the resources and support of black professional, social, and religious networks in their cities as they pursued litigation at the grassroots. Some of those same interests exerted their own influence on the litigation process, as did St. Louis's black realtors when they helped to bankroll and guide the *Shelley* case. Though the process was not always pleasant, the interaction of legal activists and the communities they served was both a formative and essential part of the campaign against segregation in the courts.

As the *Shelley* cases moved from the neighborhood streets in Washington, Detroit, and St. Louis into courtrooms, they revealed the complexity and importance of local legal activism. The work of attorneys like Miller, Houston, and the other men who fought against covenants in the 1940s exemplified the local contests that ultimately formed the foundation of broader national campaigns that would receive far greater public attention and recognition. Fighting within and against a legal system that offered little promise of change, these attorneys pitched battles that held in the balance not only the fate of the litigants, but their own ambitions, the desires of businessmen, and the concerns of entire communities.[7]

Profits: Black Realtors and Neighborhood Integration in St. Louis

When J. D. and Ethel Shelley discovered that they might lose their new home on St. Louis's Labadie Avenue in October of 1945, they had turned to Robert Bishop, the man doubling as their pastor and realtor, for guidance. Bishop immediately took the matter up with his employer, E. M. Bowers, and the two men joined with James T. Bush, another prominent black realtor, to secure legal representation for the family and began to fund the Shelleys' defense.[8] Bishop and Bowers were part of an informal coalition of black real estate men in the Gateway City who were spearheading the local fight against restrictive covenants.

Across the country, in crowded postwar conditions, realtors who catered to an African American clientele recognized that supporting the legal challenge against residential restrictions could pay significant dividends. Breaking open a new housing market for black homeseekers meant the prospect of major financial windfalls. After all, Bishop had resold the Labadie residence to the Shelleys for a one-day profit of more than $1,100 and he later suggested that he could have charged up to $750 more given the state of the city's housing conditions. Progress stood to be lucrative.[9]

Undoubtedly genuine political concern played a role as well in the decision of black St. Louis realtors to underwrite the Shelleys' defense, but the potential for profits was always part of the equation. For these men, the litigation in *Shelley* was as much about commercial opportunity—their right to sell homes where they pleased—as it was about the Shelleys' right to purchase property wherever their means allowed. The situation in St. Louis reflected the impact that black professionals who were not lawyers could have in grassroots legal activism. While the conflation of black business interests with the pursuit of civil rights litigation was nothing new, this case offered a stark reminder that among the forces that drove the legal fight for racial justice, altruism and moral righteousness occasionally had less noble companions.[10]

Regardless of their motivations, the sincere desire of Bishop, Bowers, and Bush to defeat restrictive covenants dictated their choice of counsel for the Shelleys. Attorney George L. Vaughn had earned a reputation as one of the city's most ardent civil rights advocates in his forty-year career as a lawyer and politician in St. Louis. The grandson of Louisiana slaves, Vaughn was born in Kentucky in 1880 and worked his way through college and law school in Kentucky and Tennessee before heading west to Missouri. In 1905, Vaughn passed the Missouri bar "at the head of a class of which he was the only colored member," and began serving the black community in the Gateway City. He was an avid student of history, a skilled writer and orator, an ambitious leader, and always maintained a certain flair for the dramatic. An acquaintance once remarked that "he could thrill an audience at any time with his eloquence . . . he was the only local Negro who could fill the gymnasium of the Pine Street Y.M.C.A with people to hear him, as they would hear W.E.B. DuBoix, [*sic*] Carter G. Woodson, or Mordecai Johnson, distinguished national leaders." His friends also knew him as a man who cared far more for serving his fellow black citizens than for the monetary rewards that could accrue from his legal and political offices.[11]

For four decades, Vaughn carved out a place at the heart of St. Louis's black community. He cofounded the *St. Louis Argus*—the lifeblood of the city's black press—and the Mound City Bar Association where he led the fight to include black St. Louisans as jurors in the state's local and federal courts. He held leadership roles in numerous black fraternal organizations including the Masons, Elks, and the Omega Psi Phi Fraternity, Inc. He served as lead counsel for the city's NAACP chapter in its early years and helped spearhead the branch's efforts to defeat a 1916 ballot initiative that imposed racial zoning restrictions in the city's neighborhoods.[12]

As World War I approached, the thirty-seven year-old Vaughn enlisted in the U.S. Army and ultimately became a first lieutenant. His experiences with discrimination at southern training bases and in America's Jim Crow military during his two years of service further solidified his commitment to civil rights advocacy. He referred to these encounters as "a blessing in disguise," a crushing reminder of the depth of the nation's prejudices and the inequities of the color line that gave him—and tens of thousands of other "New Negroes"—a renewed sense of purpose and urgency.[13]

Following the war, Vaughn expanded his legal endeavors and political aspirations. He became a prominent Democratic Party official in the 1930s and 1940s, standing at the vanguard of the party's effort to rehabilitate its image among African Americans. After an unsuccessful run for Congress, Vaughn served briefly as a justice of the peace in the city's Fourth District and as an assistant attorney general for the state throughout the 1940s. Vaughn also took a turn as the chairman of the St. Louis NAACP's Executive Committee and played a part in founding the local chapter of the March on Washington Movement.[14]

Vaughn's litigation efforts during this time focused on conditions in and around the main black residential district known as "the Ville." He led a series of legal protests to secure better school facilities and educational access for the area's children, sued Washington University to end its policies of exclusion, and increasingly began to work in the arena of covenant litigation. In the mid-1940s, Vaughn may not have been the city's most accomplished civil rights attorney, but it was not for lack of effort.[15]

When Robert Bishop and James T. Bush approached Vaughn with the Shelleys' case late in 1945, the veteran lawyer had been steadily building a record of fighting restrictive agreements. Vaughn's advocacy on housing matters had begun when he helped lead the local charge against legislative residential segregation in 1916, but by the 1930s he had started attacking covenants in earnest. Vaughn had at least six different covenant cases under his purview in the months after World War II's end and had won at least one other suit in previous years. Though it was unclear how many of these cases he took at the behest of the city's black realtors, he and Bush had likely crossed paths in Vaughn's earliest anticovenant work. The attorney had earned his stripes in the battle against racial restrictions by successfully defeating a covenant on Page Avenue. Bush himself moved there following Vaughn's victory and he had been one of the most active brokers on the street. Regardless of the nature of their prior relationship, the two men became fast friends. Bush's daughter described them as "soul brothers" after they joined forces behind the Shelleys' case.[16]

Though Bishop and Bowers were the agents most directly involved with the disputed property, it was Bush who became Vaughn's primary benefactor in the ensuing legal fight. Only a generation removed from Texas cotton plantations, Bush had come to the Gateway City working in the railway mail service before taking an interest in real estate. His ambition and business acumen sparked a rapid ascent in the 1920s. The onset of the Great Depression, however, wiped out his financial holdings and forced him to abandon his company and take work as a foreman in the city's garbage collection division. By 1935, however, Bush had reopened his doors and developed a penchant for covenant-breaking as a means of generating business. To succeed in this endeavor, Bush cultivated a cadre of straw-party purchasers made up of fair-skinned black St. Louisans who could pass for white during the initial transactions. Before long, Bush rebuilt his wealth and developed a particular interest in seeing restrictive covenants laid to waste in America's courtrooms.[17]

WHEN GEORGE VAUGHN ENTERED the St. Louis City Circuit Court in October of 1945, then, he served at the behest of two clients. While J. D. and Ethel Shelley's interests were the focus of his efforts, Vaughn also understood that the realtors paying for his services had certain expectations of their own. Ultimately both clients sought the same practical results—namely that the Shelleys be allowed to keep their new home. The realtors funding the case, however, had the additional demand that Vaughn defend their business practices should the need arise.[18]

The hearings began on October 18 in the courtroom of Judge William Kinney Koerner. Vaughn offered a barrage of written and oral arguments against the covenant in question and the use of racial restrictions as a whole.

At the center of his claims were four main points. First, Vaughn argued that the agreement covering the property at 4600 Labadie was invalid due to defects in the instrument itself. Here, he adopted the wisdom of a young anti-covenant lawyer from Virginia named Spottswood Robinson who had pointed out a legal conference a few months earlier that "more attention could be paid to the matter of execution of restrictive agreements. In probably 10 or 15 percent of the cases, you are apt to find that the restriction is not valid to start with."[19] The most obvious problem for the white homeowners in the current case was the fact that the Shelleys' home was in a neighborhood that had been integrated for several decades. Vaughn insisted that the neighborhood's long-standing acceptance of other black property owners—including those in the home next door to the Shelleys—rendered the intentions of the agreement void. A restriction whose sole purpose was the exclusion of African Americans from the area only served an unfairly punitive function if enforced against individuals after the region was already integrated.[20]

Vaughn's second chain of arguments dealt with constitutional and statutory violations. Covenants, Vaughn reasoned, abridged black homeowners' rights by preventing African American purchasers from making contracts with willing sellers and by denying them access to the use of properties because of their race. Such efforts clearly infringed upon the protections guaranteed by the Fourteenth Amendment and the Civil Rights Act of 1866 that provided all citizens "of every race and color" with the right "to make and enforce contracts . . . to inherit, purchase, lease, sell, hold, and convey real and personal property." This set of arguments, however, left Judge Koerner unconvinced because the courts presumed that these protections only addressed discrimination by agents of the state and not the actions of individuals.[21]

Koerner similarly rejected Vaughn's third argument that emerged in his cross-examination of the Shelleys' white neighbors. Through his questioning Vaughn attempted to strip those defending the Labadie covenant of the facade that their only concern was for their property rights. Vaughn believed that if he could expose the prejudices at the root of this effort to evict his clients the court might be more inclined to see the case as a flagrant denial of the Shelleys' rights because of their race than as a simple contractual dispute between homeowners. To that end, he probed various witnesses' participation in prior local segregation efforts outside of the housing arena. He questioned several Labadie residents about their roles in the protests against opening a local school to black enrollment. He interrogated a white business proprietor about whether he accepted black customers at his establishments. He pounced when an elderly witness stated that he joined the covenant enforcement effort "simply to keep up the standards of the neighborhood" and to "keep away slaughter houses, junk shops, anything that was objectionable." When Vaughn seized upon this last statement and tried to coax the witness into an outright admission that he saw African American homeowners to be as offensive to his sensibilities as the stench of a killing floor, Judge Koerner intervened. "We don't want to get in such discussions as that, comparing colored people to slaughterhouses," the judge insisted. "We want to keep all such things as that out of the case. I am sure he has no such idea in his mind." Vaughn was considerably less certain that this was true, but before he could press any further Koerner made his stance clear. He stated flatly from the bench that the "only question in the case" that he was willing to consider was "whether or not they [the Shelleys] violated the contract . . . and of course your constitutional questions." Vaughn moved on.[22]

The fourth series of claims that the attorney offered seemed to strike Judge Koerner more. Vaughn's witnesses, including James T. Bush, offered compelling evidence of the overcrowding and resulting struggles of St. Louis's black communities. Vaughn highlighted the rapid growth of the Gateway City's black population from approximately 40,000 residents in 1910 to nearly triple that number by the end of World War II. At the same time, he insisted, "the portions of this City . . . occupied by Negroes have been narrowed, surrounded and circumscribed almost completely" by the growth of covenants and "by increasing business areas and the condemnation of lands . . . for the purposes of widening streets and beautifying the city and building public institutions." Vaughn pointed to the social consequences of these trends as evidence of restrictive covenants' inhumanity and injustice. The veteran attorney made his case to the court and hoped that moral as well as legal arguments would sway the judge.[23]

For an important portion of the trial, however, Judge Koerner seemed far more interested in an injustice of another sort. During the testimony of the Shelleys' realtor Robert Bishop, Koerner took a particular interest in the practices of the city's black real estate agents and offered at times a cross-examination more strident than that of Vaughn's opposing counsel. Koerner seemed genuinely appalled by Bishop's overzealous profit taking. "Don't you know," he demanded of the realtor, "that an agent owes loyalty to his clients and is not supposed to buy property in his own name and then turn it over to his clients at a profit?" Bishop's rather weak defense of his actions amounted to his insistence that "that's some of the practice of the . . . real estate business; your Honor, I didn't make much, not considerable, but that's what I did." As Koerner and the opposing counsel, Gerald Seegers, both hammered away at the unapologetic businessman, Vaughn scrambled to protect his benefactors, doing his best to shut down the line of questioning with objections. If the Shelleys' attorney felt any compunction about vigorously maintaining Bishop's blamelessness for having exploited his clients, he never showed it either inside or outside of the courtroom. Vaughn doggedly worked to counter Koerner's distaste for Bishop's actions, insisting that the realtor's profit was not nearly as much as it seemed and that Bishop had simply followed the practices of other members of his profession—both black and white. "They do it all over town, your Honor," Vaughn pleaded. If anything this only frustrated the judge more.[24]

Ethel Shelley, who was likely better acquainted with the predatory realities of the real estate industry for African Americans, took the courtroom revelation of Bishop's profit taking in stride. While she admitted that she had not known that her pastor and realtor had drastically marked-up the price of her home, she made no comment regarding her feelings about this discovery and exhibited considerably less resentment than Judge Koerner. Still, it must have been difficult for her to watch her own attorney defend the man who had abused her family's trust and vulnerability. It must have been even harder to know that her only chance of keeping the home depended on this man's willingness to continue financing her case. She was no doubt keenly aware at that moment of her relative powerlessness in the face of hostile neighbors who wished to force her out of her home, a court that held the authority to do so, and financiers whose interests—while temporarily aligned with hers—were not focused on the welfare of her family. Yet it was her resolve in the witness chair that began slowly to win over the judge.[25]

Coming on the heels of Bishop's testimony, Judge Koerner appeared roundly unmoved by the Shelleys' case before Ethel Shelley took the stand. Gradually over the course of her testimony, however, Koerner seemed to express measures of admiration and sympathy for this strong and beleaguered woman. As Mrs. Shelley explained her family's circumstances, their struggles with finding a home, and her interactions with her realtor, Koerner found himself vocalizing his empathy for her plight. When she expressed her bewilderment at the fact that she could be evicted from her home despite the fact that she lived on a block with several other black families, Koerner assured her, "You have the sympathy of the Court; I will tell you that." Koerner's interactions with Mrs. Shelley later earned a rebuke from the opposing counsel, who insisted that, "the Court . . . was overly kindly, courteous and condescending" to her and other witnesses during the trial.[26]

Judge Koerner ultimately ruled in favor of Vaughn and the Shelleys in mid-November of 1945. In his decision, the judge relied on his belief that the restriction covering 4600 Labadie was invalid because the original signers had never fulfilled the intent of the agreement. By leaving almost 20 percent of the properties unrestricted, and several of those in the hands of African American homeowners, Koerner argued "the agreement [was] not signed by a sufficient number of landowners to accomplish its purpose." Koerner—moved by the testimony he had heard—also took judicial notice of Vaughn's moral and demographic claims regarding the state of overcrowding in St. Louis's black neighborhoods. The judge dealt Vaughn's constitutional and statutory arguments a blow when he curtly dismissed them all, but the balance of his findings supported the Shelleys. The family would keep their home. Moreover, Koerner also ordered the plaintiffs Fern and Louis Kraemer to pay more than $700 in court costs to Vaughn and the city. Though the looming appeals would threaten this hard-won victory, the Shelleys could breathe a little easier for the time being.[27]

WHILE MOST of the real estate men backing the Shelleys' case were thrilled by this outcome, Robert Bishop likely had some misgivings. Despite Vaughn's efforts to soften the judge's distaste for the man, Bishop ultimately found himself facing an official complaint that Judge Koerner personally filed with the Missouri Real Estate Commission. The judge's opinion also singled out what he saw as Bishop's abuse of Vaughn's clients, describing the realtor's "antagonistic" interests and leaving no doubt about who he believed to be at fault for the entire situation. The Kraemers might have been on the wrong side of the law in this case, but in the court's eyes it was the realtor who had crossed the line both ethically and morally.[28]

Koerner was certainly not the only one to have qualms about the role of black realtors in the business of covenant-breaking. For anticovenant advocates, black realtors were complicated partners in the effort to secure better housing access for African Americans' urban communities. Litigators and activists across the country faced the question of whether or not to embrace and defend the potentially unseemly practices of covenant-breaking realtors. This somewhat reluctant partnership extended beyond instances like that of the Shelleys, where real estate men directly funded the defenses of particular clients. In the summer of 1945, just months before J. D. and Ethel

Shelley purchased the house on Labadie Avenue, the legal leadership of the NAACP addressed this issue at a conference of lawyers engaged in covenant cases. During the gathering, the St. Louis NAACP's director David Grant had asked the conferees what to do about "some intrepid, energetic real estate operator who to make money will go out . . . and buy up in the names of straw parties 3 or 4 houses. Then he will get a Negro buyer and move him in there and sit back and wait to see what happens. . . . To what extent should we go to the aid of these real estate brokers?" Charles Hamilton Houston, the man leading the campaign against residential restrictions in Washington, D.C., immediately exclaimed, "You should go completely to their aid." The prospect made Grant somewhat uneasy.[29]

As the lawyers discussed the appropriate course of action in such a case, they largely dismissed popular concerns about realtors' professional practices. Though Grant insisted that there was "a lot of community disapproval on profiteering," and suggested that an ardent defense of black real estate men might harm the popular appeal or fund-raising ability of local litigation campaigns, the other attorneys quickly dispensed with the issue. One participant stated flatly, "I don't see how we can expect to break the agreements if we don't have these law breakers." NAACP special counsel Thurgood Marshall even justified the excessive profit taking that occurred by maintaining that "this is not an ordinary service. You can't expect to break into a neighborhood at the regular rates." The lawyers, however, were not oblivious to the importance of perception in both the arena of public opinion and in the courtrooms themselves. As such, Houston advocated that the speculating realtor "should also try to cover his hand and divorce himself from the matter so that it will look like a natural development of sales." The methods were dubious enough that this partnership was better if kept out of the public eye. With only minor hesitations the NAACP and legal activists across the country welcomed the mingling of financial and political interests in postwar covenant cases.[30]

Still, the whole practice often reeked of exploitation. These members of the city's black professional elite—part of the upper crust of their community's income earners—had built their business in part on the desperation of their peers and of blue-collar families like the Shelleys. The realtors did not create the distressed conditions of these populations or the problems that black homeseekers faced; those were the fault of the housing shortage and discriminatory practices by white homeowners and real estate men. Still, individuals like Robert Bishop, E. M. Bowers, and James T. Bush made the decision to profit off of these circumstances. Though these men risked their careers to provide much-needed housing to members of their communities, the rewards they reaped came primarily at the expense of their African American clientele. Indeed, Bishop stood to lose his license as much for his profiteering in the Shelleys' case as for his willful disregard of a discriminatory instrument. The service these men provided was a necessary one. The way in which they provided it, however, left a bitter taste in the mouths of many observers.

What made the *Shelley* case and St. Louis unique was how prominently the professional community of African American realtors figured in the drive to move the cases forward. While black real estate men in cities across the country stood to benefit from—and therefore lent their support to—covenant-breaking litigation, Bush, Bishop, and other realtors in the Gateway City took this participation to new heights. As *Shelley* moved through the appeals process, Bush and Bishop began formalizing the unofficial network of businessmen that had coalesced around the case. In December of 1946, a little more than a year after the suit first entered Missouri's courtrooms, Bush created the Real Estate Brokers Association (REBA) of St. Louis. Comprised of most of the city's black realtors and several salesmen, these men rejected Houston's admonition from the previous year and chose not to play silent partners to the civil rights lawyers in the city.[31]

The group quickly announced its formation on the front page of the *St. Louis Argus* and began publicly issuing appeals for donations. Though their first order of business was to generate financial support for the *Shelley* litigation, they articulated a broader social and political purpose. They hoped to lead the way "in the protection of homes and investments in real estate" for the Gateway City's black community by lobbying for reforms in property assessments and taxation, ensuring appropriate municipal services and facilities for African American districts, and pursuing neighborhood beautification campaigns. One goal had particular resonance for the realtors as the men sought to "improve and expand certain neighborhoods."[32]

The REBA's formation and day-to-day operation was truly Bush's brainchild. Though Bishop would take a prominent role in the organization, serving as its second-in-command and using his office on Finney Avenue as the association's headquarters, Bush was its undisputed leader. Bush acted as the group's president and he stocked the other key leadership positions with his close allies. He chose as treasurer Dr. Charles T. Herriot—a prominent physician and landlord who had long served as one of Bush's straw-party buyers. As his public relations officer, he selected his protégé, a realtor named P. T. Robinson. Together Bush and his colleagues constructed a very public and prominent role for the city's black real estate men in the fight for improved housing conditions. Their support would prove tremendously effective, especially in their first major campaign to bolster the *Shelley* litigation.[33]

In the fight to sustain this case on appeal, however, Bush also recognized the limitations that an advocacy group based solely upon realtors would face. Given the level of popular mistrust or distaste for some of their professional practices, soliciting contributions to meet their $5,000 fund-raising goal could prove difficult. To combat this issue and to defray successfully the financial burdens and organizational responsibilities of the campaign, Bush created an offshoot outfit in early 1947 that incorporated a range of community leaders and activists. Called the "Citizens Committee," the group remained closely tied to the REBA. They shared the same headquarters, Bishop and Robinson served as officers in both organizations, and other key REBA members like Bush, Herriot, and Bishop's employer E. M. Bowers were significant forces on the committee.[34]

While the real estate men retained enough of a presence to steer the new group, they populated the committee's large advisory board with an array of black middle-class St. Louisans. Apart from the realtors the sixty-six board members included a dozen reverends, eight attorneys, seven doctors, a handful of newspapermen, and a healthy collection of business owners. The group also featured ten prominent women including the president of the St. Louis County Teachers Association and members of the executive boards of the local NAACP and the Association of Colored Women's Clubs. The committee's acting chairman was Herman Dreer, a well-respected author and faculty member at Sumner High School.[35]

Despite the legion of legal and political activists who lent their names to the Citizens Committee, the group functioned almost exclusively as the fundraising arm of the REBA. The organization successfully tapped into the broader African American business community of St. Louis and many of the city's key religious, social, and political institutions to amass donations totaling more than $4,000 during a period of economic retrenchment for many black St. Louisans. Members of the REBA would add close to $3,000 more of their own contributions to the case by the end of 1947. The Gateway City's black realtors had stirred a community desperate for change and yearning for progress in an uncertain postwar climate.[36]

Shelley highlights some of the ways that class dynamics and tensions within local black communities affected the trajectory of legal activism. The collision of professional, political, and class interests that restrictive covenants generated was in some respects uniquely situated in the continuum of civil rights causes. Litigators had worked shoulder-to-shoulder with black middle-class and professional groups like teachers and railway workers on other issues, but rarely had the triangular relationships between clients, attorneys, and "constituents"—those benefactors to whom the attorneys owed some part of their allegiance—been so complex.[37]

In *Shelley*, black realtors were able to use covenant litigation to refocus popular distaste for their practices on an external target while simultaneously strengthening their businesses. These cases and the actions that precipitated them therefore represented a form of investment in the growth and success of local real estate companies, one where an assortment of other middle- and working-class black Americans—including a blue-collar migrant family on the tenuous dividing line of class status—bore the risks and costs of litigation most substantially. The realtors who promoted *Shelley* and other covenant cases around the country had much more to gain and less to lose than individuals like the Shelleys who they sometimes callously shoved onto the frontlines of urban America's battle over residential segregation.

At the same time, these realtors were also the men who enabled and sustained a campaign against restrictive covenants at times and in places when local political advocacy groups could not. In St. Louis they helped to generate the kind of capital and popular support that fueled the costly process of litigation. The larger fight against covenants and individual cases like *Shelley* could not have endured without this. Legal and political activists in the immediate postwar years were spoiling for a renewed attack on residential restrictions and the participation of realtors in a campaign that intended to move forward with or without them helped to defray the financial and organizational burdens of the movement. *Shelley* galvanized broad swaths of the city's black population and served as a reminder that litigation was rarely the province of only one group or individual. Instead, legal activism on behalf of civil rights often became the product of various forms of broad-based community participation, with all of the benefits, pitfalls, tensions, and partnerships that entailed.

Local Lawyers? Professional Networks and Covenant Litigation

Covenant-breaking homebuyers could not always count on the support of their realtors when the time came to go to court. Many families thus found themselves at the mercy of local civil rights organizations or, if they could afford it, hired an attorney on their own. James and Mary Hurd in Washington, D.C., and Mac and Minnie McGhee in Detroit—already straining to meet the burdens of their mortgage payments—sought the assistance of their local NAACP branches. They were not alone. Branch offices became clearinghouses for the onslaught of covenant litigation that arose in the 1940s. To handle the volume of casework, branches tapped the reserves of local legal talent, often finding men willing to volunteer their time and services at little to no cost. Attorneys like Charles Hamilton Houston in Washington, Willis Graves and Francis Dent in Detroit, and Loren Miller in Los Angeles opened their offices to families like the McGhees and Hurds and took up their struggles.[38]

These legal activists fueled local campaigns against restrictive covenants. City courtrooms served as sites of protest and innovation where civil rights lawyers could use their professional expertise to erode the legitimacy of racial restrictions. Attorneys experimented with tactics and legal arguments as they sought to generate enough traction to win cases at the local level and build broader national momentum that might force the U.S. Supreme Court to revisit the issue of covenants' constitutionality. In the twenty years since *Corrigan v. Buckley* (1926), when the Supreme Court had ruled that neither the Fifth, Thirteenth, nor Fourteenth Amendments "prohibited private individuals from entering into contracts respecting the control and disposition of their own property," the Court had allowed only one covenant case appeal to reach its chamber. Anticovenant lawyers had therefore recognized that they advocated within and spoke to a legal system that took many of its cues from the national level. Because the vast majority of covenant cases would never pass beyond local and state courts for adjudication, civil rights advocates increasingly understood that a string of individual efforts would ultimately prove far less successful than a collaborative approach that allowed their courtroom experiments to work in concert.[39]

By sharing their experiences and ideas through national communication networks legal activists built local campaigns rooted in the particular struggles of their communities while sharing the wisdom earned by a battery of their colleagues locked in similar struggles around the country. Anticovenant attorneys from coast to coast explored and exchanged strategies designed to achieve success in their cases locally while eyeing the larger goal of forcing a reconsideration by the U.S. Supreme Court. Covenant lawyering relied upon individual ingenuity and resolve to fight unfavorable precedents through city and state courtrooms, but the task was rarely ever a truly local or solitary endeavor.

WHEN THE MCGHEES TURNED to the Detroit branch of the NAACP for legal assistance early in 1945, they found a pair of experienced, capable, and creative advocates in Willis Graves and Francis Dent. Graves and Dent had each migrated to the Motor City in 1919 to pursue careers in law and though they maintained separate practices after an initial partnership in the 1920s, by the end of World War II their commitment to the local NAACP's Legal Redress Committee had again turned them into a formidable team. By the time they took the McGhees' case they had become Detroit's point men in the fight against restrictive covenants.

Willis Graves had begun his life in Raleigh, North Carolina, remaining in the city from his birth in 1890 until he completed college at Shaw University. Not long after graduation, Graves found his way to Howard University School of Law in Washington, D.C., where he received his degree in 1919. Enticed by the opportunities of a growing black community in Detroit, Graves left for Michigan and quickly discovered the direness of the Motor City's housing problems. A close friend of Ossian Sweet, a Detroit physician and fellow Howard graduate, Graves watched the 1925 prosecution of the Sweet family for the murder of a member of a violent mob that had attempted to drive the Sweets out of their new home in a white neighborhood. The events surrounding the case instilled a sense of outrage and resolve in the young attorney and he vowed to help break the barriers of residential segregation in the city.[40]

Graves developed into a significant community leader in the interwar period, becoming active in the business and political life of Detroit. A lifelong Republican, the stoic and "refined" attorney never held office himself, but instead organized and campaigned on behalf of others. By the 1940s, Graves had also received his license as a real estate broker and assumed the office of chairman of the board of directors at the Morison Investment and Realty Company—the state's self-proclaimed "fastest growing realty corporation." It was unclear whether the Morison Company participated in covenant-breaking and Graves's anticovenant crusade certainly never enjoyed the same financial backing from the real estate community that his counterpart George Vaughn had received in St. Louis. Yet there was undoubtedly some link between Graves's entrepreneurial and legal activities. His financial stake in opening the housing market may well have played some role in his enthusiasm for fighting covenants.[41]

It was in Detroit's courtrooms, however, that Graves made his most enduring impressions. In addition to his law practice, Graves became the official counsel for the local NAACP and served on the Association's National Legal Committee. As the leader of the Detroit branch's legal activism from 1939 to 1949, the respected attorney "handled, without remuneration, the greatest number of legal cases initiated by [the] branch for a period of ten years." Graves understood the law as a potent instrument of change in a community that so desperately needed it. He worked himself to the point of exhaustion on various occasions, paid out of his own pocket to keep underfunded cases alive, and fought the daily cruelties of prejudice and segregation with an elegant tenacity.[42]

Housing access became the central cause of Graves's legal career in the 1940s. Driven by the sheer necessity attendant with the issue in Detroit and his own determination, Graves fought case after case in the hope of prying loose the grip of residential segregation. He worked alongside Thurgood Marshall in a 1944 suit protesting the NHA's exclusion of African Americans from public residential projects for war workers in nearby Willow Run. He also handled—often with his colleague Francis Dent—as many as ten covenant cases at a time in the months following the war. In the process he became something of an evangelist for the anticovenant cause. At one point, when community spirit behind the litigation appeared to be flagging, Graves addressed a gathering at a local church to reenergize the campaign. "It was a passive audience," observed one of the attendees, "until Willis M. Graves recalled the German invasion of Czechoslovakia." Invoking the specter of Nazism, Graves maintained that only when "the world came out of its state of apathy and decided to match steel with steel," did the threat give way. "This we must do in the covenant fight," he continued. "Plan to lose on all levels until we reach the Supreme Court—there with our legal forays . . . expect to win. You have then matched steel with steel!" His impassioned speech apparently convinced his audience, who gave him a standing ovation and "a substantial amount of money" to support the ongoing cases. Graves remained utterly convinced that the right combination of arguments could bring down residential color lines. He was certain that he could change the prevailing winds of the nation's legal attitudes.[43]

Graves's partner in the McGhees' case had followed a somewhat similar path to that defense table in 1945. Francis Dent, known as "Freckles" or "Freck" to his friends in the legal community, was another southern transplant to the Midwest. Born in Rome, Georgia, in 1894, his parents were college-educated members of the state's black elite. Like Graves, he spent several years in Washington upon leaving the South when his father, an attorney and later a government clerk, moved the family shortly after the turn of the century. Dent graduated from the prestigious M Street High School in the same class as fellow civil rights litigators Charles Hamilton Houston and George E. C. Hayes and went on to attend Amherst College where he graduated in 1916. Shortly thereafter, he enlisted in the U.S. Army along with his brother. He went on to attain the rank of first lieutenant and was subsequently wounded in military action in the Argonne Forest in 1918. That same fighting spirit would serve him well after the war.[44]

Following the completion of his service, Dent decided to pursue a new profession in a new city. He entered Detroit College of Law at the same time that Graves began his preparation for the Michigan bar and soon embarked on a long and successful legal career. He also flirted with politics in a failed campaign for the Michigan State Senate in 1930 and remained politically active afterward. He lobbied against the creation of segregated dormitories for women at the University of Michigan and fought to stop the screening of D. W. Griffith's paean to white supremacy, *Birth of a Nation*, when theaters sought to bring a revival of the film to Detroit in 1931. As early as 1929, Dent identified restrictive covenants as "the most dangerous blow toward the colored race since the acts of disfranchisement in the South," and he subsequently dedicated his energies to the campaigns of local and national advocacy groups like the NAACP, National Lawyers Guild (NLG), National Bar Association (NBA), and the Wolverine Bar Association, which he and Graves helped to found. At one point during the height of his anticovenant battles in the 1940s, Dent was serving on the legal committees of eight separate organizations and used his position in each of them to push resources toward the fight for housing access.[45]

When Graves and Dent brought the *McGhee* case before Judge Guy A. Miller in the Wayne County Circuit Court, they arrived eager to experiment with whatever tactics might work. At trial they emphasized four points. First was the claim that Seebaldt Street's white residents had improperly executed the covenant. The attorneys challenged the validity of a number of individual signatures and argued that the notaries for the original agreement had failed to provide enough detail in their certification of the contract. The court largely ignored these technical claims as insufficient to render the covenant void.[46]

Their second contention alleged that the covenant violated the "public policy" of the state of Michigan and the United States. The public policy argument gave attorneys some added maneuverability in their courtroom claims by focusing on specific issues of law in a broader legal and political context. By insisting that residential restrictions violated the rather broad concept of "public policy," Graves and Dent suggested to the court that even if covenants did not breach the exact letter of the law they certainly violated the spirit of it. Because states like Michigan had prohibited racial discrimination in other arenas and the federal government had embraced more racially egalitarian policies and rhetoric during wartime, the attorneys argued that continued housing discrimination would undermine the thrust and intent of these efforts. The larger aim of the state and nation, the public policy argument contended, was to limit the extent of racial exclusion. Therefore even if the ongoing support of restrictive covenants in the courts was in keeping with judicial precedent, it would subvert the interests of local and national government and should be discontinued.[47]

Their third claim maintained that both the racial restriction and the court's enforcement of the contract would violate the Fourteenth Amendment. The argument that covenants themselves were unconstitutional was nothing new, but their second contention—that judicial enforcement would contravene the strictures of the amendment—stood at the cutting-edge of anticovenant litigation tactics. The idea that attorneys could challenge the constitutional right of a court to implement the terms of a restrictive agreement had only started to gain traction in the months before the *McGhee* case went to trial. Two lawyers in Chicago and California had taken a simultaneous interest in the issues surrounding the explosion of covenant cases during World War II. Harold Kahen and University of California law professor D. O. McGovney published law review articles in February and March of 1945, respectively, touting the argument that courts should consider the judicial enforcement of restrictive covenants as discriminatory state action and therefore an act proscribed by the Fourteenth Amendment.[48]

McGovney's lengthier and more technically specific article laid out a strategy to circumvent the roadblock that the U.S. Supreme Court had established with its 1926 decision in *Corrigan v. Buckley*. The Court overreached in that case, he argued, by discussing the applicability of the Fourteenth Amendment to covenants in a suit from the District of Columbia, which was under federal and not state authority. Lower courts and anticovenant advocates, therefore, could not simply accept the Supreme Court's pronouncements on that particular issue. The Fourteenth Amendment still provided ample ground from which to stage an attack on racial restrictions. The key to making covenants appear to be a matter of state concern rather than simply a private arrangement between individuals, however, was to ask courts to consider their own role in the process of enforcement. By choosing to implement the terms of these contracts, McGovney insisted, "the state through one of its organs is aiding, abetting, enforcing the discrimination." Calling attention to the way that judicial rulings effected racial exclusion and lent the authority of the state to those acts might force courts to reevaluate constitutional leeway that they had thus far accorded to covenants. Graves and Dent hoped that process might start in the Wayne County Circuit Court.[49]

For their final argument at trial, Graves and Dent moved even farther out onto the frontier of innovative tactics. Because Mr. McGhee had been fair-skinned enough to pass as white for more than a decade and his wife also had a light complexion, Graves and Dent decided that they would try to force the plaintiffs and their attorney to prove that the McGhees were in fact African Americans. This was a tactic they had employed at least once before in another restrictive covenant case just months earlier. The only two witnesses they offered at trial were not their clients, but instead two social scientists from nearby Wayne University.[50]

During the testimony of Dr. Norman Humphrey, a professor of sociology and anthropology, Graves and Dent asked what it would take to determine an individual's racial identity with accuracy. "In order to approach knowing what racial derivative a person possesses," Humphrey began to expound, "one would proceed to measure a number of known points by means of calibers and develop their relation . . . to certain averages which have been worked out." When Judge Miller asked for clarification, the professor elaborated that the measurements would include "structural features such as the eyefold, degree of freeness in the upper lid . . . the shape of the nose and that sort of thing." Here, the attorneys flirted dangerously with endorsing a style of physical classification that had eerie similarities to those employed by white supremacist sociopolitical orders in Nazi Germany, South Africa, and Australia that gave the patina of scientific legitimacy to the identification and isolation of racial "others." Their purpose here, however, was to harness that scientific authority for a different end.[51]

Graves and Dent quickly turned the focus onto the issue of who was qualified to determine an individual's race. The men sought to challenge plaintiff Benjamin Sipes's authority to label the McGhees as African Americans in the courtroom. Graves and Dent struck at the idea that Sipes's only basis for his conclusions was the observation that "I have seen Mr. McGhee and he appears to have colored features. They are more darker than mine." The reality that the court would accept this simple and superficial evaluation as legal fact disturbed the two men. They used Dr. Humphrey's testimony to address this point in particular by asking whether or not "the average layman could look at a person and tell what . . . racial classification they should be put under?" Humphrey answered no and again insisted that only "scientific determination" could establish the "racial stock" to which someone belonged. This legal strategy pushed back against decades of judicial deference to the popular wisdom of the white "common man" concerning who did and did not qualify as white under the law. One's right to keep their home, Graves and Dent implied, ought to hinge on something more substantial than the opinion that his or her features were "more darker" than his neighbors.[52]

When the attorneys finished their arguments, Judge Miller deliberated for almost three months before rendering his decision in August of 1945. Despite the lengthy wait, however, the judge's decree rejected all of Graves and Dent's claims. Miller dispensed with the technical and constitutional questions hurriedly, declaring that the homeowners had properly executed the covenant and that state and federal precedents had thoroughly established the legitimacy of private residential restrictions. He ignored the public policy arguments in their entirety and was only slightly less dismissive of the attorneys' claims respecting the racial identity of their clients. His opinion simply stated without explanation that the McGhees were "not of the Caucasian race but . . . of the colored or Negro race." He gave the family ninety days to vacate the premises.[53]

Judge Miller's rejection of Graves and Dent's challenge to the system and authority of racial classification in America, however, came too late to discourage the dissemination of the tactic to other anticovenant advocates. Within weeks of Graves and Dent's initial experiment, the national community of anticovenant lawyers was abuzz about the potential benefits of disputing racial categories in their cases. When the NAACP's National Legal Committee sponsored a meeting in July of 1945 to discuss the future of covenant litigation, it was Dent's associate from high school and college, Charles Hamilton Houston, who extolled the virtues of this strategy. "We must," he exhorted his colleagues, "make it just as difficult as possible for the plaintiffs. . . . The first thing I recommend is to deny that the plaintiffs are white and the defendants are Negroes." He had refined the original argument somewhat, turning away from supporting rigid scientific determinations of racial categories and instead encouraging lawyers to focus on the murkiness of popular definitions of race and the haziness of biological boundary lines.[54] He described the purpose of the tactic by pointing out that "in denying that your defendants are Negroes, you go to the question of the standards of race. There are many people who cannot give any reason why they are white. They don't have any standards about Negroes either. The more you shake them, the better off you are. If they make a definition—you can't do it on color or hair, make them admit it will not hold."[55]

The rapid diffusion and adaptation of this tactic to different local courtrooms and covenant fights bespoke the importance of this network as a tool of legal activism. Communication and connections between civil rights attorneys were largely the products of social acquaintance—as in the case of Dent and Houston—as well as the marginalization of African American attorneys within a predominantly white legal system and the exhausting demands of legal and political activism. National organizations involved in legal advocacy like the NAACP and the National Bar Association also provided forums and formalized spaces for interaction and exchange like the July anticovenant conference. The networks these advocates established became a market for the best strategies to uproot the pillars of de jure segregation and innovation was the currency that fueled it. Graves and Dent's experiment quickly took hold in the professional network of anticovenant attorneys and by the end of the year a handful of cases across the country had field-tested their own versions of the argument. Among the attorneys who put this tactic into practice was Dent's friend in Washington, Charles Hamilton Houston.[56]

IT WAS IN HOUSTON'S very capable hands that James and Mary Hurd placed their trust in the summer of 1944 when they reached out to Washington's local NAACP branch. The man who would serve as their counsel stood as perhaps the most renowned civil rights attorney in the nation and was an avid opponent of restrictive covenants. By the 1940s, Houston had played an especially influential role in the process of refining anticovenant litigation tactics. In taking the Hurds' case, Houston brought a national profile to the local stage of Washington's district court, where he returned after leading the NAACP's national legal office from 1935–39.

Born in Washington in 1895 to a prominent local attorney, Houston's intellect and precocity took him to Amherst College where he was Phi Beta Kappa and graduated magna cum laude before the age of twenty. Houston, like his elder St. Louis counterpart George Vaughn and his friend Francis Dent, enlisted in the U.S. Army during World War I and served as a second lieutenant for a field artillery unit. Houston's experiences with racial hostility and discrimination in the war shook him from the relative shelter and privilege he had thus far enjoyed in life and helped spur his ambitions for reform. After completing his service to his country he enrolled at Harvard

Law School in 1919 and quickly became the first African American elected to the editorial board of the prestigious *Harvard Law Review*. Houston later won a fellowship to continue his legal studies in Spain and traveled the European continent before returning to Washington to join his father's practice.[57]

The late 1920s witnessed Houston's emergence at the forefront of African American legal work. He assumed a leadership role at Howard University School of Law and spearheaded its rapid transformation into the nation's principal training ground for black attorneys. In 1935 he took over the office of special counsel for the NAACP's national office and crafted the Association's civil rights litigation agenda for the next five years before relinquishing the position to his protégé, Thurgood Marshall, and resuming a less taxing role on the organization's National Legal Committee. On his return to Washington, Houston took over teaching Howard's newly established course in civil rights law, served on President Franklin D. Roosevelt's Fair Employment Practices Committee investigating instances of labor discrimination, and expanded his local legal pursuits—taking on a variety of cases in his private practice and on behalf of the local NAACP.[58]

As the wartime housing shortage forced the issue of restrictive covenants toward center stage in civil rights litigation during the 1940s, Houston's anticovenant efforts quickly blossomed. His caseload grew to the point that he engaged the services of attorney Spottswood Robinson, who had taken a particular interest in the covenant issue. The two men spent long hours hunched over their desks going line by line through briefs and appeals that they hoped would break open the barriers to better housing for their fellow black Washingtonians.[59]

Houston's efforts gave him considerable familiarity with the Bryant Street neighborhood that James and Mary Hurd attempted to enter in 1944. Before the Hurds' case arrived at his desk, Houston had navigated a series of courtroom confrontations in 1941 and 1942 against restrictions including some on Adams Street in Northwest—the block directly behind the Hurds' home on Bryant. Though his arguments in these earlier cases had lost at trial, his persistence and tactics of delay allowed the Adams Street residences to remain in the hands of black purchasers long enough that the white plaintiffs abandoned their enforcement efforts and ultimately the neighborhood.[60]

Houston's work in the Adams Street cases illuminated his commitment to the issue of housing discrimination. He clearly felt a deep sense of personal resolve in his crusade against restrictive agreements and this determination fueled his cases. When he met a setback in the first of the Adams Street suits, he wrote a letter to every other African American living on the block promising them that "the fight goes on and that we intend to appeal . . . and to make Mr. Bishopp and Miss Musson [the white plaintiffs] fight every inch of the way for every single house in the block." That defeat sparked Houston's moral outrage and piqued his well-known appetite for victory. Those who sought to keep Washington's restrictive covenants in place, he warned, were on the wrong side of morality and liberty. "This fighting," he wrote, was for nothing less than to "establish some democracy here at home."[61]

By the time Houston took the Hurds' case to trial in October of 1945, just nine days before the Shelleys' entered their courtroom in St. Louis, he had cultivated a reputation as a resilient and ardent anticovenant activist. Through a combination of delaying tactics and slow movement by the district court in Washington, Houston's suit had taken more than a year to go to trial. When it did, the court joined his case with those of Raphael Urciolo—the white realtor who had recently sold three other homes to black purchasers on the Bryant Street block.[62]

As Houston formulated his strategy in the *Hurd* case, he experimented with a number of arguments. Finding the key to a successful courtroom challenge, he believed, would involve putting forward an array of claims in the hopes that one—or the sum total of all of them—might convince the court to rule in his favor. Houston had extolled the virtues of this strategy at the gathering of anticovenant attorneys in Chicago during July of 1945. Those who defended covenants at trial, he pointed out, always sought "to narrow the issues as much as possible" by arguing that the case revolved around nothing more than the rights of individuals to make private contracts as they wished. Anticovenant advocates, therefore, "should broaden the issues just as much as possible on every single base, taking nothing for granted." Three months later, when *Hurd* went to the courtroom of Judge F. Dickinson Letts, Houston sought to do just that.[63]

He began by challenging even the most basic of assumptions underlying the case. Houston put into practice a modified version of the tactic that his colleagues Graves and Dent had pioneered in Detroit. He insisted throughout the trial that his clients were not African American and that the covenant prohibiting use or occupancy by "any Negro or colored person" did not apply to the Hurds. In the *McGhee* case, Graves and Dent had kept their clients off the stand and had only disputed the right of a layman to determine the McGhees' race rather than explicitly claiming that they were not African Americans. Houston's clients, on the other hand, were more specific in their denials. James Hurd maintained that he was in fact Native American and Mary Hurd, an orphan who had lived among white people for much of her life, claimed not to know the racial identity of her parents. Houston demanded that the plaintiffs in the case prove that his clients were in fact black, an exercise he knew would expose the illogic and inconsistencies of the popular wisdom about what made "race."[64]

Because the Hurds' physical appearances—like the McGhees—put them in the poorly defined margins of standard racial categories, Houston tried to use the ambiguities of racial identity to his advantage. When questioning Frederic Hodge, the husband of the primary plaintiff, Houston went so far as to call James Hurd up from the gallery and have him sit in the jury box as the witness made a frank appraisal of the physical markers of his race. "What," Houston asked, "is a negro [sic] about Mr. Hurd's features?" Hodge strained forward slightly to inspect his neighbor, taking in the detail of his face and weighing his reply. "I would say the nose for one thing . . . the nostrils, the lower part of the nose." In the end, Hodge concluded that it was only his neighbor's "nose and his skin" that marked him as African American.[65]

Houston, however, went beyond contesting the racial identity of only his clients. Throughout the trial, he also attempted to force the plaintiffs to prove their whiteness for the court. His purpose in doing so, he had once explained, was that "every time you drag these plaintiffs in and deny that they are white, you begin to make them think about it. That is the beginning of education on the subject. . . . There are many people who cannot give any reason why they are white." The privilege of calling oneself white in the United States at that time came with a certitude that often seemed unshakeable—and indeed likely had to remain so for the system of classification to work. Houston took that self-certainty to task. In a particularly tense exchange with the primary plaintiff Lena Hodge, Houston asked how the witness knew that she was white and continued to press her on the subject until Hodge finally snapped, "How do you know you are a Negro?" Houston quickly shot back, "I know that, because you all say I am." Eager to get the final word on the subject, Hodge could only muster, "I know that you are and I know that I am white." The frustration and assuredness that Lena Hodge and her husband showed in their exchanges on this subject laid bare the kinds of assertions that passed for legal fact on the issue of race. The Hodges' whiteness gave them the prerogative to police the boundaries of racial categories and to claim the right to determine exclusion and belonging in the "common wisdom" of American racial identity.[66]

Houston and his cocounsel pushed this line of argument even further by calling in a pair of expert witnesses from local universities to testify about the ambiguities of racial categories. Monsignor John M. Cooper, head of the Department of Anthropology at Catholic University and editor of the *Review on Anthropology*, confirmed under questioning that visible physical traits were often unreliable indicators of a person's race and that his field was undecided as to whether a "pure white race" actually existed. He agreed that social concepts "enter very largely into the problem" of what was meant by the term "white," but he stopped well short of completely rejecting a physical basis for categorization or endorsing a purely social understanding of race.[67]

Houston's experimentation with this strategy in *Hurd* also bespoke a larger purpose than simply winning the case at hand. Previous chroniclers of the restrictive covenant cases have either ignored or dismissed these claims regarding race as little more than a desperate tactic designed to prolong litigation or manufacture technical grounds for a dismissal of the case. Houston undoubtedly proposed the idea in part as a strategy to frustrate his opponents—to "have them up a tree," as he put it—and to multiply the arguments available to potentially sympathetic judges. Yet, he always maintained that the act of questioning what made someone white was "the beginning of education on the subject." Houston hoped to use the district court trial as a forum to expose and interrogate the flimsiness of racial categories. Because one's access to full citizenship rights depended upon these perceived physical differences, Houston struck at the issues of how individuals made these distinctions and who had the authority to do so. It seemed indefensible that the right to live in a given home could hinge on a man's testimony about the shape of his neighbor's nostrils and the uncertain hue of his skin. In the immediate wake of World War II, when many Americans became more attuned to the dire potential consequences of a social and political order premised on a discourse of racial difference and superiority, Houston seemed to sense a moment of particular vulnerability for popular wisdom about race.[68]

The rest of Houston's tactics in the *Hurd* case were more straightforward. Beyond his assertions regarding the ambiguities of racial identity, Houston relied primarily upon an argument regarding the changing demographics of the neighborhoods surrounding the Bryant Street address. "The 100 block of Bryant Street, Northwest," Houston charged, "was not . . . a so called 'white' neighborhood . . . and could not be made such by any action of this Court." He elaborated that since the establishment of the covenant in 1906, the "neighborhood, square and surrounding area have completely changed in character . . . and that the purposes which called forth said covenants, if any, cannot now be accomplished." Pointing to the close proximity of black families on Adams Street immediately behind the Bryant properties and further down the same block of Bryant, Houston asserted that continued enforcement of the covenant could not possibly achieve the results its creators had intended.[69]

His criticism of the restriction's futility continued during the testimony of Howard University sociologist E. Franklin Frazier. Calling Frazier as an expert on urban demography and the process of racial succession, Houston laid out the facts for the court bluntly. "Would you consider the neighborhood in the 100 block of Bryant Street," he began, "where out of 31 houses, 11 houses were occupied by negroes, and . . . five or more houses were occupied by Italians and Assyrians, would you consider that a white neighborhood?" Frazier replied that he would not. Houston hoped the court would see those facts the same way.[70]

At the district court stage of the *Hurd* case, Houston declined to offer any constitutional or statutory points in favor of his clients' right to keep the home, arguing instead about the weaknesses of the particular covenant at issue. Houston relentlessly attacked the logic underlying the agreement— namely that African Americans' presence in the area would devalue the homes and upset the neighborhood's social dynamics—to show that enforcement was unnecessary. Houston extracted concessions from the neighborhood's white residents that the black families on the block had maintained their properties well and in several cases had improved them. Testimony from local realtors and a member of the city's Rent Control Board documented the fact that property values actually increased substantially when African American homebuyers entered new neighborhoods. Because black homeseekers would pay a premium to obtain decent residences, the covenants themselves hindered the appreciation of value by turning restricted homes into what one witness called "white elephants." "The whites don't want them," he explained, "the negroes can't have them."[71]

Houston, however, cautiously pushed back against the implication that white residents' only option was to sell to African American purchasers and leave the area. He attempted to show that integration had not adversely affected the social character of the neighborhood or provided white property owners with any legitimate reason to abandon the Bryant Street block. Houston challenged the insistence of the lead plaintiffs that black residents' presence had diminished the "sociability of the neighborhood." These same witnesses admitted under questioning that they had never had any problems or been disturbed by African American homeowners in and around the area, but that they simply "want[ed] to live with people [our] own color." When Houston pressed for specific answers or examples regarding how the block's "sociability" had changed since the Hurds' purchase, the witnesses offered vague assertions that failed to amount to anything more than a gut feeling. Houston had made his point. If black homeownership along Bryant Street had increased property values, improved the physical appearance of the neighborhood, and created only an ambiguous sense of social discomfort, his reasoning suggested, the covenant's only real function was to indulge the whims of a few prejudiced residents and unjustly punish desperate and responsible black homebuyers. The judge, however, proved unsympathetic to this logic.[72]

Houston gambled on one other maneuver midway through the proceedings. Frustrated by Judge Letts's lack of receptiveness to his defense, Houston sought for grounds to cast doubt upon his impartiality and perhaps have him removed from the case. Four days into the trial, Houston discovered that Letts was living in a rented property covered by a restrictive agreement and filed a motion alleging a personal bias against the interests of the Hurds and requesting Letts's recusal from the case. Houston politely—but firmly—insisted that when his clients had finished testifying the previous day, "they felt your Honor had his mind made up against them." Letts quickly overruled the motion while stating for the record that he did not own the property and was unaware of any covenants affecting its use. Houston could hardly have expected Letts to consider his allegation seriously, but the decision to press forward anyway testified to both his thoroughness and his commitment to a strategy of forcing the court to address as many issues as possible. The veteran attorney would try whatever he could to find a way to delay or defeat the enforcement of the Bryant Street covenant.[73]

Despite these efforts, Judge Letts eventually ruled in December of 1945 against the Hurds. He dispensed with each of Houston's arguments curtly. On the issue of racial identity, he found no cause to doubt the whiteness of the plaintiffs or the blackness of the defendants and dismissed James Hurd's testimony about his ancestry without comment. Houston's contention that the racial composition of the area surrounding the neighborhood had changed to such a degree that the covenant could no longer serve its stated purpose met a similarly blunt end. Letts construed the boundaries of the Bryant Street neighborhood narrowly, limiting it to the twenty houses that had remained under covenant and white ownership until the Hurds' purchase. "There has been no constant or substantial penetration of negroes into the area," the judge insisted, "sufficient to show that the purpose of the covenant . . . has been frustrated or that the result of enforcing it would depreciate rather than enhance the value of the property involved." With that, Letts voided the purchases of the Hurds, Rowes, Stewarts, and Savages and ordered the families "to remove themselves and all of their personal belongings from the land and premises now occupied by them within 60 days." They had always known their evictions were possible, perhaps even likely. Now, however, they suddenly faced the harsh reality that they would soon be at the mercy of either the appellate court or Washington's streets.[74]

ON THE WEST COAST, but in the center of a national network of anticovenant advocates, stood Houston, Graves, and Dent's future colleague in the *McGhee* case, Loren Miller. In the covenant litigation hotbed of Los Angeles, Miller had quickly built a reputation as one of the most experienced, innovative, and accomplished advocates for greater housing access. His work on the Sugar Hill cases in December of 1945 won him national recognition for his legal exploits.

Before taking up the fight against restrictive covenants in Southern California, Miller had been part of a cohort of young, radical activists that sharply criticized the NAACP and its reliance on litigation as a means of reform. Through most of the 1930s, Miller was an especially outspoken detractor of the Association's legal campaigns and of Houston's leadership as Special Counsel. Not long after he began his anticovenant practice in 1939, however, Miller found himself as a central figure in the professional networks whose efforts he had often disparaged. By 1944, he served as the chairman of the Los Angeles NAACP's Legal Committee and as his covenant work blossomed, so did his connections to the national office of the NAACP.[75]

In his first eight years of fighting covenants, Miller took up more than 100 local cases. None, however, won him more public recognition and acclaim than the Sugar Hill suits in 1945. In the months leading up to the Sugar Hill trial that December, Miller had grown particularly enamored with the "state action" theory that Harold Kahen and Professor D. O. McGovney had detailed earlier in the year and that Graves and Dent had wielded unsuccessfully in the *McGhee* case. The idea of challenging courts' enforcement of covenants rather than the constitutionality of the specific instruments, however, struck Miller as the key to unlocking the U.S. Supreme Court's closed book on the issue. He spent the rest of the year waiting for the perfect opportunity to build a case around the argument.[76]

Miller searched for a way to make state action claims the central issue in the cases. Earlier efforts by Graves, Dent, and George Vaughn had all included the enforcement argument in their respective cases and had been either ignored or dismissed without any substantive comment. The challenge Miller faced was how to get a court to rule specifically on the issue. His ability to do so depended upon finding a judge willing to take the claim seriously and some ingenuity in presenting his case. As the Sugar Hill suits readied for court, Miller streamlined his argument and made the decision to focus on only one issue at trial. "We did not file any briefs in the case," he later wrote, "and our authority as furnished to the court was contained in [Kahen and McGovney's] Chicago and California Law Review Articles." Miller then made a "motion to deny the introduction of evidence" and objected "to the introduction of testimony" by the plaintiffs in the case, asking Judge Thurmond Clarke to decide strictly on the state action argument that Miller put forth. At a time when the prevailing wisdom of anticovenant litigation called for attorneys to lob at local courts just as many arguments and pieces of evidence as they could, Miller's strategy was certainly unusual. He also had little reason to expect Judge Clarke to comply with his motions. Clarke would only have to overrule Miller's objection to force the attorney to pursue a more conventional line of argument. Miller offered no real indication of why he chose to pursue such an approach in this instance when success seemed so unlikely. Yet, Clarke—in a move that stunned nearly every participant and observer—granted Miller's motion and quickly ruled in favor of his clients.[77]

Clarke's motivations for this ruling remain unclear. Perhaps the celebrity of Miller's clients and the public scrutiny that would invariably ensue encouraged him. Perhaps it was what he had seen with his own eyes in the West Adams Heights district where they lived. The day before his ruling, he had chosen to walk with the attorneys through the streets of the neighborhood in question and inspect firsthand the conditions of black-owned homes and an integrated block. For nearly a decade, black and white residents had lived alongside each other on these avenues and the neighborhood hardly seemed on the brink of the destruction that was supposed to ensue. Or perhaps Clarke's decision in the case sprang from nobler principles. The text of his ruling suggested a personal conviction that the continued enforcement of restrictive covenants violated the essence of freedom promised by the Constitution and defended at tremendous cost in the recent war. He declared, "This court is of the opinion that it is time that members of the Negro race are accorded, without reservations and evasions, the full rights guaranteed them under the 14th Amendment. . . . Certainly there was no discrimination against the Negro race when it came to calling upon its members to die on the battlefields in defense of this country in the war just ended."[78]

Judge Clarke was not alone among his colleagues in finding fault with restrictive agreements, yet he was unique in his decision to rest his decision solely upon the state action argument. His intention in doing so was to provoke the U.S. Supreme Court into granting a new hearing on the issue of covenants. "Judges," he wrote, "have been avoiding the real issue for too long." Clarke's stunning and lonely act of judicial audacity evidenced the fact that local civil rights litigation could often hinge on an individual judge's principle, politics, or personality.[79]

In fact, a handful of jurists across the country had begun to take aim at the legitimacy of restrictive covenants. Most of the judges who took the strongest stands appeared to act out of genuine concern over the conditions for black urban communities in the postwar moment. Moral indignation at the injustice of America's racial ghettos fed anxieties about the public policy implications of deteriorating and overcrowded slums. Local judges like Clarke and William Kinney Koerner in St. Louis each noted the problems caused by racial housing restrictions in their decisions against covenants. Clarke in particular had bucked his fairly conservative judicial leanings to embrace Miller's state action claims, a fact that seemed attributable primarily to the urgency of the moral questions at stake in the issue. Other more progressive jurists like Justice Roger Traynor of the California Supreme Court or Judge Henry Edgerton of the Federal Circuit Court of Appeals in Washington, D.C., had also focused intently on the consequences of overcrowding as an exigent public policy concern in their opinions against restrictive agreements. Even those jurists who felt constrained by precedent to uphold covenants sometimes pointed to the evils that they helped create. Chief Justice Robert E. Crowe of the Cook County Superior Court in Illinois, for example, enforced a Chicago covenant even as he decried "those in our midst who would sabotage unity and break down our spiritual defenses by denying to certain minorities the rights which our Constitution guarantees to all citizens. Those who would continue old restrictive covenants and attempt to establish new ones are in this un-American group. They would do violence to American laws and traditions." Others were less strident in their reflections on the growth of housing segregation, but nonetheless urged legislatures to address the issue since they considered their hands tied by precedent. Miller's strategy in the Sugar Hill cases had tapped into this deep uneasiness within the nation's judiciary and, with a bit of luck, had succeeded in shaking something loose.[80]

News of Miller's victory elicited a mixture of shock and excitement among civil rights attorneys' national networks. Within days, praise poured in for

Miller's tactical maneuvers. "The newspaper quote suggests that the judge placed the decision squarely on the 14th Amendment," exclaimed attorney Pauli Murray—who had personally endured the process of covenant enforcement the previous year. "Is that true?" she asked. "If so, congratulations twice." Another colleague of Miller's wrote, "I needn't tell you how surprised I was to learn that . . . Clarke of all judges did what the liberal judges of Los Angeles haven't had the courage to do. . . . If there is to be an appeal, please let me help on it." Even Miller himself privately professed some surprise at the outcome when he claimed to a friend that he had "succeeded in pulling a rabbit out of the hat" in the case. With a hint of pride—and an appreciation of the good fortune involved—in his triumph, Miller confided that "this was a rather neat trick in view of the numerous holdings to the contrary by both state and federal courts." Miller had found the right jurist and the right strategy to stoke the zeal of anticovenant lawyers around the country. As NAACP special counsel Thurgood Marshall put it in a congratulatory letter to Miller the week of the ruling, attorneys everywhere began to feel that "maybe this is it."[81]

The California Supreme Court would ultimately derail the Sugar Hill cases' opportunity to reach the nation's highest court by refusing to issue a decision on the appeal for almost two years, but the state court could not obstruct the energy and ideas that Miller infused into local struggles in other cities. The conversations that Sugar Hill generated among anticovenant attorneys revealed the extent and power of the professional networks that would help to carry other cases forward. Letters flooded into Miller's office in Los Angeles for months from New York, Washington, D. C., Chicago, Detroit, and nearly every other covenant litigation hotbed. Lawyers fighting restrictions in each of these cities solicited advice, offered assistance, asked for copies of the case record and the state action law review articles, and briefly shared stories of their individual struggles against the prevailing tide of judicial support for enforcement.[82]

Miller wrote back, sharing whatever counsel and encouragement he could. A Chicago attorney seeking guidance on the latest arguments available in the covenant fight received a response that "urgently recommended" he read McGovney's article. "I would be glad to send you a copy," Miller offered, "but I have just sent my last one to Willis Graves in Michigan." As part of his correspondence on a single, particularly busy day, Miller commiserated with a Washington anticovenant attorney who lamented the volume of cases his office was forced to handle, shared details of his strategy with housing expert Robert Weaver at the American Council on Race Relations, discussed the tactics for an appeal with Howard Law School dean William Hastie, and advised a colleague in New York to try and generate "much more public discussion" regarding covenants to lay the groundwork for review by the U.S. Supreme Court. Miller also eventually corresponded extensively with each of the attorneys whose cases would reach the high court in 1948. He exchanged case records and regularly conferred with Charles Hamilton Houston and Willis Graves in the wake of the *Hurd* and *McGhee* rulings and received a $100 fee from George Vaughn for consulting on *Shelley* as it readied for appeal.[83]

Sugar Hill moved Miller to the intellectual center of the anticovenant legal crusade. The extensive professional network that Miller's activities revealed, however, indicated that successful civil rights litigation in a legal system generally hostile to change relied upon collaboration and the sharing of resources and ideas on a national level as much as it depended upon the tactical ingenuity and intellectual creativity of individual attorneys. As lawyers like Houston, Miller, Graves, Dent, and Vaughn battled the varied forms of racial segregation and discrimination in local communities across the country, they could feel the strength of a nationwide coalition of their colleagues at their backs. It was a strength they would need as they faced a dogged opposition in court.

Resistance: The Legal Defense of Restrictive Covenants

Across the aisle from the nation's anticovenant attorneys stood other local advocates fiercely committed to defending residential restrictions and white homeowners' claims. The opposing lawyers in the *Shelley* cases and the legal defense they mustered gave voice to white communities that had increasingly come to see their desire for racial exclusion as a matter of principle and property rights rather than prejudice. These attorneys—like the neighborhood associations and homeowners they represented—were deeply rooted in both discriminatory custom and segregated communities and felt a personal investment in the continuity of both. They were active local leaders and competent, if unremarkable, lawyers who adhered to a sort of legal orthodoxy that was fast dissolving around them. They fought adamantly to withstand the evolving challenges of civil rights advocates and sustain the legal legitimacy of their desire to exclude African Americans from white neighborhoods. Ultimately, the efforts and motives of restrictive covenants' courtroom defenders offered insight into the challenges that civil rights litigators faced and the reasons for the creativity that characterized the fight against segregation's various forms.[84]

In St. Louis, white residents of the Labadie Avenue area and members of the MAIA turned to a young, newly minted attorney to pursue the case against the Shelleys. Thirty-six-year-old Gateway City native Gerald Seegers had grown up in a blue-collar Catholic family and initially trained for priesthood at a local seminary before moving on to a legal education at both St. Louis University and Washington University. Graduating in 1943, one of his first clients was the MAIA, whose veteran covenant defender D. Calhoun Jones he replaced. Seegers came to the organization through his uncle, Martin Seegers—a founding member of the MAIA and its first president—and quickly became thoroughly involved in its operations. Though he still took nominal fees for his legal services, he extended his participation beyond the sphere of litigation, regularly attending meetings and taking on some leadership responsibilities. The young attorney, whether through his family ties to the area and the MAIA or through a personal conviction about the issues of residential segregation and property rights, soon found himself deeply invested in protecting racial restrictions. Lawyers like Seegers came to see the neighborhoods they fought on behalf of not as clients but as causes and their legal expertise and community leadership were a crucial part of the successful functioning of homeowners groups like the MAIA. Civil rights litigators often found themselves up against opponents as ardently committed and willing to work with minimal compensation as themselves.[85]

The man who battled Willis Graves and Francis Dent in Detroit, Lloyd Chockley, left a clearer sense of his personal beliefs on the issue of residential integration than his St. Louis counterpart. Born in 1889, Chockley grew up on a Colorado farm before abandoning the agrarian life and migrating to Detroit with his younger brother just before the First World War. Their first residence in the Motor City was on Seebaldt Street, the same street that Chockley would fight to keep restricted almost thirty years later. By the 1940s, he had moved just five blocks away and remained deeply tied to the white neighborhood north of Tireman Avenue. When the Northwest Civic Association retained Chockley's services on behalf of Benjamin Sipes in 1945 and began the process of evicting the McGhee family, they placed their interests in the hands of a man with no particular reputation, but with a fierce devotion to housing segregation and an acerbic temperament. Both of these qualities were on display in his briefs to the Michigan Supreme Court late in 1946.[86]

More than many of his peers, Chockley gave insight into his personal attitudes and motivations in his legal writings. He evinced a disdain for those "protagonists of the intermixture of the races" who wished to violate covenants and repeated the loaded term "intermixture" when characterizing the objectives of his opponents—echoing the implicitly sexualized threat of racial proximity that earlier protests against housing integration in the city had used. Chockley saw himself as a defender of the "right" of white Detroiters "to live and rear their families in white neighborhoods" and it was this steadfast determination that drove his advocacy for the exclusion of black home-buyers like the McGhees. Though Chockley would die suddenly in 1947 before the final appeals in the case, his work in Detroit, like that of Seegers in St. Louis, again spoke to procovenant attorneys' personal commitment to enforcing the racial boundaries of the nation's cities. Legal activists like Graves and Dent rarely faced off against men who were simply hired guns. Seegers, Chockley, and residential segregation's other courtroom defenders played the part of crusaders rather than mercenaries in that their efforts grew from an allegiance to some combination of custom and prejudice over an interest in financial gain.[87]

Like Chockley, Washington attorney Henry Gilligan—Houston's opponent in the *Hurd* case—felt an added personal incentive and urgency in his cause. Gilligan lived at 2304 First Street, Northwest, just around the corner from the homes along Bryant that he was fighting to keep out of the hands of African Americans. The sixty-two-year-old attorney had grown up in Baltimore before moving to his First Street residence around the time of World War I. Unlike his counterparts in St. Louis and Detroit, Gilligan brought an immediate profile to the cases and a reputation he had cultivated through nearly two decades of community leadership in the District of Columbia. He had held a seat for eleven years on Washington's Board of Education, was elected as a director of the District Building and Loan Association in the 1930s, served as master of his Masonic lodge, and as choir director, organist, lay leader, and chairman of the board at his Methodist church. Gilligan's neighbors also elected him president of the North Capitol Citizens Association (NCCA), a local homeowners' group where he provided both legal and organizational leadership.[88]

Gilligan's attitudes on racial and residential integration betrayed a man deeply unsettled by the prospect and pace of change in the bustling metropolis where he lived. In his occasional letters to the editor at the *Washington Post* and in some private correspondence, Gilligan pronounced himself a fair-minded friend of the District's black population. "The many movements now under way to encourage economic opportunities and independence for our Negro citizens," he once wrote, "are most commendable and right-minded citizens of all colors must approve." Yet through decades of political and legal activities, Gilligan consistently showed a reluctance to accept any form of integration as a feasible means of black advancement. In the early 1930s, he provided a vocal dissenting opinion on the Board of Education when faced with opening a new facility for African American pupils that he believed was "forcing on a white community a colored school."[89]

Two years after he left the board, he publicly objected to Howard University's efforts to hold a concert by Marian Anderson at a local white high school. Claiming to speak on behalf of the overwhelming majority of Washington's citizens—both black and white—Gilligan voiced his belief that such a gross violation of the city's Jim Crow ethics would only lead to "unrest and acrimonious discussion." "I have no racial prejudice whatever," he maintained perhaps a bit too vigorously. "The question with me is one of law, rules, and the best interests of our colored and white people." Gilligan captured with these words a pervasive sentiment that racial progress, if it came, should never take place at the expense of upsetting the lopsided comfort and civility of the status quo. For him, as for so many others of the era, the preservation of custom mattered far more than any agenda or immediate demands of those who sought greater rights for African Americans.[90]

Gilligan was especially adamant on the issue of segregated neighborhoods. Like Lloyd Chockley in Detroit, he articulated a belief in the right of "fine white people in our community to live their lives among people of the white race—in their homes, their schools and their churches," and some years later insisted that "there is no way that I know of to do this except through covenants." Ignoring the conditions that forced black homeseekers to obtain covenanted homes, Gilligan laid the blame for the increased agitation over racial restrictions at the feet of unscrupulous realtors and political antagonists who had "no compunctions of any kind" and were bent on the "destruction of white communities." He portrayed himself as a defender of a social and moral order that had its roots deep in the traditions of Jim Crow segregation. Restrictive covenants, he seemed to suggest, were one of the key pieces holding it all together.[91]

Gilligan's partner in the fight to preserve residential restrictions, James A. Crooks, seemed destined to follow in his mentor's footsteps as a community leader and proponent of racial exclusion. The attorneys lived next door to each other and as colleagues fought to enforce covenants for more than a decade. Crooks was nearly thirty years younger than his associate, but the two men recognized something familiar in each other—an ambition for leadership and a commitment to the mores of a segregated society. Though a native New Yorker, Crooks had grown up in the District, graduated from George Washington University, and attended law school at National University. He devoted his time to a series of organizations including the Americanization School Association and the NCCA, where he was secretary-treasurer and served alongside Gilligan. At the age of thirty, he became the NCCA's delegate to the Federation of Citizens Associations, an umbrella organization for the sixty-five homeowners' groups in the city, and helped lead the Law and Legislation Committee for a number of years. Late in 1942, Crooks accepted a position at the District Rent Control Office and quickly worked his way up to the job of chief counsel. Because of these additional responsibilities, Crooks did not participate in Gilligan's *Hurd* case until later in the appellate process, but he undoubtedly played a role and provided support to his colleague in these early stages through the NCCA.[92]

The experiences and attitudes of the four attorneys who fought to enforce covenants in the *Shelley* cases revealed the nature of the legal resistance that civil rights litigators faced. The lives of Seegers, Chockley, Gilligan, and Crooks exposed how community ties, local leaders, and the law interacted to create a formidable opposition to change. Men like Gilligan and Crooks floated between roles in the courts, neighborhood associations, and city governance—blending the boundaries of legal, political, and community opposition. Covenant cases were never just abstract principles being debated and decided by outsiders; rather they required the mobilization of entire communities to defend the customs and perceived rights that had kept their neighborhoods white. Procovenant attorneys, by virtue of their skill set and their commitment to the cause of exclusion, became influential in shaping the architecture of white resistance to residential integration.

IN THE COURTROOMS THEMSELVES, however, the legal defense of restrictive agreements looked positively mundane compared to the dynamism and intellectual ingenuity of anticovenant litigators. All of the procovenant attorneys in the *Shelley* cases followed a simple pattern during the first phase of the trials. Their only goals were to establish for the courts that a valid restrictive covenant existed for the property in question, that the restriction served an important purpose, and that the defendants had violated the terms of the covenant. The lawyers kept the matter as direct as possible, using strikingly similar formulations in each of their respective cases. The similarities extended to the specific language of what was at stake for their clients. When

discussing the consequences of violating the neighborhood's racial proscriptions, for example, St. Louis attorney Gerald Seegers insisted that his
clients would "suffer irreparable injury and irremediable damages to their
property." Lloyd Chockley of Detroit had argued at two separate points
that "continued violation of said restriction will cause irreparable injury to
these plaintiffs and all other owners in the vicinity." Likewise, in Washington,
Henry Gilligan maintained that "the continued occupancy and/or ownership
by the defendants . . . will constitute a continuing wrong and injury that is
irreparable, and is incapable of ascertainment and compensation in damages." The nearly identical patterns of argument and the close resemblance
of the language in each case exemplified how customary courts' enforcement
of racial covenants had become. All of these individuals—despite the fact
that they had no contact with one another—effectively worked off of the
same script that had emerged from decades of successful pleadings around
the country.[93]

Attorneys in the *Shelley* cases shared this method for good reason. The U.S.
Supreme Court decision in *Corrigan v. Buckley* (1926) and the local precedents that echoed that finding provided procovenant attorneys with a
straightforward and available source for a winning strategy that needed
little, if any, adaptation. As a result, these lawyers could ignore constitutional
and statutory arguments entirely in this initial stage of the case. The only
challenge they faced at trial was to try and limit the impact of any new arguments from anticovenant attorneys. By offering extensive objections to the
introduction of testimony respecting the growth and poor housing conditions of African American communities or by simply ignoring their opponents' constitutional claims altogether, procovenant lawyers tried to keep the
courts' focus on the narrow issue of whether black homebuyers had violated
properly executed private contracts. For the most part, judges obliged by only
addressing and upholding the validity of individual agreements.[94]

Even on appeal to the Michigan and Missouri Supreme Courts or the Federal Circuit Court of Appeals in Washington, D.C., the attorneys defending
covenants found their work comparatively easy to that of their colleagues
across the aisle. The short briefs to these courts were pointed restatements
of the U.S. Supreme Court's findings in *Corrigan* and the argument that the
Fourteenth Amendment was never intended to apply to the private actions
of individuals. In Washington, Henry Gilligan answered Charles Hamilton
Houston's nearly 100-page brief to the court of appeals with just ten pages.
Citing existing precedents, he stood firm on the presumption that the changing conditions of black urban life and the intellectual acrobatics of his

opponent would fail to shake the jurists out of their established custom of enforcement.

Lloyd Chockley followed the same playbook in the Michigan Supreme Court against Willis Graves and Francis Dent. The court, Chockley insisted, only needed to read the decision in *Corrigan* and not the "reams of arguments" that Graves and Dent had put forth in order to settle the matter. Chockley even took a swipe at one of the key architects of the new "state action" theory, offering the sneering suggestion that Professor D. O. McGovney's arguments were so wildly out of step with the existing legal orthodoxy that he could "hardly be trusted either as to his judgment or his intellectual integrity." Despite the occasional editorialized remarks, none of the procovenant attorneys in the *Shelley* cases felt it necessary to offer extensive rebuttals to their opponents. They never strayed far from the central strategy that had served the interests of clients like theirs so effectively.[95]

This strategy and its simplicity, its uniformity, and its presumption of success served as a reminder of the enormous challenge that anticovenant litigators like Vaughn, Houston, Graves, and Dent faced. In the courts, the status quo generally prevailed and white attorneys simply had to fend off the salvos of those who sought to change it. The creativity and collaboration—both local and national—that characterized anticovenant litigation in the 1940s thus sprang largely out of necessity. Facing formidable challenges, legal activists operated within an institution built upon the rule of precedent and an orthodoxy that had long favored the white majority's desires over black Americans' claims.

Though these legal conventions had weakened somewhat in the preceding decade, civil rights litigators increasingly recognized that they had to challenge fundamental jurisprudential traditions in order to attack segregation. Procovenant attorneys could turn back African Americans' attempts to secure decent housing with relative ease not necessarily because they were right about constitutional principles, but because precedent mandated a victory in all but the most narrow of circumstances. Black litigators recognized the need for a strategy that would put proponents of Jim Crow on the defensive by forcing them to justify a system of discrimination that wrought deep suffering in black communities. Precedent would always have a place, but it could not supplant justice. The dynamism and ingenuity of midcentury legal activism sprang in part from this dual effort to undermine not only specific methods of exclusion, but also the overarching philosophies that gave the defenders of white supremacy the benefit of the doubt.

The cracks of light that opened when procovenant attorneys met defeat showed the way forward. Yet even after victories like those of George Vaughn and Loren Miller, the appellate process quickly reminded civil rights litigators in the *Shelley* cases of the great hurdle they faced. One by one their cases foundered against discrimination's sturdy legal bulwark.

Appeals: The Cases and the Appellate Courts

In Detroit, Washington, and St. Louis, the losing attorneys all filed appeals in their respective suits. For the anticovenant advocates, it was a chance to hone their arguments and elaborate on the need for change as they prepared what might be possible auditions for the U.S. Supreme Court. They knew that the stakes rose on appeal and every loss made future litigation more difficult. Despite their efforts, however, the Missouri and Michigan Supreme Courts and the Federal Circuit Court of Appeals in Washington, D.C., all upheld the validity and legitimacy of residential restrictions and scorned the experimental arguments. As defeat after defeat rolled in, anticovenant litigators' frustration mounted. Yet the courts' decisions also further galvanized legal activists and the local communities that supported them.[96]

As Vaughn, Houston, Graves, and Dent readied their cases for these appeals, they could not help but feel a tinge of optimism. Armed with bold new arguments—and in Vaughn's case, a victory already in hand—they began to rally additional community support and to expand upon their claims regarding covenants' social and moral costs. The impact of the recent war featured prominently in several of the new briefs. Houston's simmering indignation seeped through: "No wonder the morale of most Negro troops in the war was low: when they realize that alien enemies, prisoners of war . . . and even unnaturalized foreigners all had superior rights, privileges and acceptance in this country over them, regardless what sacrifices they might be called upon to make." Himself a veteran of a different war, Houston called the mobilization of white communities to impose residential restrictions against black GIs and other African Americans "divisive maneuvering at its lowest and worst." Surely the service to their nation of so many would not be rewarded with their exclusion from decent homes.[97]

In Michigan, Graves and Dent argued that the war itself gave the court reason to repudiate covenants. They focused on the egalitarian rhetoric of freedom and democracy that American leaders had espoused to argue that the war heralded a new direction in public policy that deemed racial discrimination unfitting for the world's self-proclaimed beacon of liberty. Moreover, the United States had signed the 1945 United Nations Charter, a treaty that committed its signatories to "promot[e] and encourag[e] respect for human rights and for fundamental freedoms for all without distinction as to race." They insisted that it would be unconscionable for America's courts to continue to sanction the existence of minority ghettos and the tools that helped make and sustain them. Here, Graves and Dent innovated again as they reframed their public policy argument to include the pressures of international law and the nation's growing role as a global arbiter of justice.[98]

Not content simply to bolster their arguments for this new venue, Graves and Dent also enlisted the aid of Detroit's broader political community as they prepared the appeal. Signaling a growing popular support for black housing rights, the two attorneys found a series of organizations willing to lend their names and complementary briefs to the cause. Six groups ultimately filed arguments on behalf of the McGhees. Among them were the NAACP—where the national office had increasingly begun to lend legal support to local covenant fights—the American Jewish Congress, and a handful of legal advocacy groups including the National Lawyers Guild, the National Bar Association, and the Wolverine Bar Association. Graves and Dent also won the support of the United Automobile Workers union, which lent its voice to the plight of black homeseekers in the interests of promoting cohesion and fairness for its racially diverse membership. Several of the briefs stressed the injustice of restrictive covenants by drawing on recent surveys of black urban conditions and social-scientific scholarship to highlight the social consequences that emanated from residential discrimination. Following Vaughn in the St. Louis Circuit Court, Graves and Dent's coalition put forth a set of claims that used African Americans' dire housing situation to arouse the court's sense of justice.[99]

Each of the appellate courts answered with little sympathy for anticovenant advocates' arguments. In Missouri, the first of the three appeals to return a decision, early December of 1946 brought word that the state supreme court had overturned Vaughn's triumph. A unanimous decision found fault with Judge Koerner's reasoning that black residents' long-standing presence in the Labadie neighborhood meant that preventing further integration amounted to a futile and punitive effort that the court could not enforce in good conscience. The Missouri Supreme Court instead inferred that the homeowners must have known what they were doing when they created such an odd arrangement. "Obviously," the decision declared, "it could not have been the intention of the parties to prevent any negro occupancy at all because that already existed. It must have been their intention to prevent greatly increased occupancy by negroes. And their plan has succeeded." Regardless of how erratically the homeowners had thrown up the boundaries of this covenant, the court seemed to say, the desire of those individuals to prevent further integration was enough to justify this unusual solution. The court then added a hasty rejection of Vaughn's constitutional claims, pointing to the suffocating words of *Corrigan v. Buckley* to snuff out each of his arguments.[100]

The Missouri court did, however, take the opportunity to editorialize on the need for some remedy to the distressing urban conditions that African Americans increasingly faced. Citing the rapid growth of St. Louis's black population and the overcrowding shown in the case record, the court remarked that "such living conditions bring deep concern to everyone and present a grave and acute problem to the entire community. Their correction should strikingly challenge both governmental and private leadership." Adding that it was "tragic that such conditions seem to have worsened," the court then explained that solutions stood beyond its purview as it forced yet another African American family out of their new home and back into those same circumstances it had just decried.[101]

Initially the news of the decision disheartened some of *Shelley*'s key backers. James T. Bush's daughter described his reaction as "probably the only time I saw him look discouraged." At the urging of his wife, he quickly rallied. That night he vowed to found the St. Louis REBA in order to orchestrate an appeal to the U.S. Supreme Court. The ruling equally inflamed George Vaughn who declared in a series of editorials for the *St. Louis Argus* that he intended to make the court's mistake "an epoch-making event in the history of the Negro's struggle for the attainment of full citizenship rights." His office was flooded with "letters of inquiry from places as far away as New York and Los Angeles," convincing Vaughn now more than ever that "there is no backing down. This thing must be settled once and for all." The fight would go on, he insisted. Vaughn then took advantage of his reputation as one of the Gateway City's most influential black leaders and wrote that "naturally, I expect to receive the backing of the Negro people and their friends in this fight. It should rally them as nothing has done in many years."[102]

More bad news followed in January of 1947 when the Michigan Supreme Court upheld the covenant in *McGhee*. Like its counterpart in Missouri, the court quickly dispensed with Graves and Dent's constitutional arguments as thoroughly settled by precedent. Then the decision made short work of the two attorneys' claims regarding the McGhees' racial identity. After laying out the testimony regarding Benjamin Sipes's observation that Mr. McGhee "appears to have colored features. They are more darker than mine," the court declared that Sipes had provided information "sufficient to sustain this [lower court's] finding." The court justified this move with a reference to *People v. Dean*, an 1866 Michigan voting rights case that had maintained, "there is not a court in the United States which holds that a 'colored person,' in the popular acceptation . . . can be called white, without doing violence to language." Under this logic, denying a white individual's ability to make a commonsense observation of who was and was not white risked upsetting the entire language and popular conception of whiteness, rendering race less effective as a legal category of division. Because of the enduring relevance of race in the state and national legal systems, the Michigan court found this alternative unpalatable.[103]

The court elaborated most thoroughly on Graves and Dent's public policy argument. The concept of public policy, the ruling argued, was difficult to define and often carried multiple meanings. "In substance, it may be said to be the community common sense and common conscience," the court wrote. "Sometimes such public policy is declared by Constitution, sometimes by statute. . . . More often, however, it abides only in the customs and conventions of the people—in their clear consciousness and conviction of what is naturally and inherently just." Once again deferring to the traditions of the majority, the court effectively held that public policy was whatever the white mainstream desired. Despite some well-established areas where Michigan law prohibited racial discrimination, residential restrictions were not yet on the wrong side of public opinion. "These rules of property," the court concluded, "should not be brushed aside in the absence of strong and cogent reasons."[104]

For those anticovenant advocates who cited the suffering of black communities and the interests of social justice as compelling enough, the court had a ready answer. In the contest between arguments "predicated upon a plea for justice" and those that sought "the application of the settled principles of established law," a court's responsibility was to precedent and not to notions of justice. To emphasize this point, the opinion cited at length from an 1861 Texas Supreme Court case that amounted to an extended meditation on the respective merits of justice and the law in the American legal system. Though the Michigan court likely hoped to lessen the controversy of the ruling with this inclusion, the fact that the court took its lessons on justice from a pre–Civil War case in a slaveholding state infuriated black activists.[105]

Indignation at the court's decision swept Detroit's black communities. The local NAACP branch sponsored a rapid succession of public meetings to shore up popular support for the cause, particularly since the *McGhee* case was only the first of nine covenant cases the Legal Redress Committee had before the Michigan Supreme Court. One outraged editorial noted that the decision's parsing of justice from the law effectively vindicated the McGhees' cause even as the court ordered their eviction. The justices, the author opined, "make this decision with their tongues in their cheeks. . . . [They] abandoned right, and sought the greasy teat of spurious legalism." He continued, "Certainly no self-respecting Negro citizen of this state can allow this decision by our State Supreme Court to go unchallenged." As the public furor mounted over the ruling and weekly fund-raising meetings began to gather a war chest for another appeal, one speaker bellowed a clarion call: "We are starting an avalanche that will not stop until we are at the doors of the United States Supreme Court." The Michigan court had provoked a massive infusion of popular energy into the anticovenant fight.[106]

A little over four months later, the last of the three appellate courts reached its decision in Washington. Though Houston's efforts in *Hurd* still failed in the Federal Circuit Court of Appeals in May of 1947, a powerful dissent from one of the three judges on the panel gave anticovenant advocates across the country reason to hope. The majority's opinion had rested squarely on the numerous precedents upholding the applicability of covenants in the District and varied little from recent rulings on the subject. After their brief affirmation of the covenant's validity, however, Judge Henry Edgerton wrote a scathing repudiation of his colleagues' reasoning. Building upon a pair of earlier dissents he authored when the court of appeals had heard—and then reheard—the case of *Mays v. Burgess* (1945), Edgerton offered a lucid and impassioned analysis of the faults in the continued juridical support of covenant enforcement.[107]

Edgerton began by attacking the prevailing interpretation of *Corrigan v. Buckley*, the keystone of judicial resistance to anticovenant efforts. The U.S. Supreme Court, he insisted, had neither declared racial restrictions valid nor had they ruled on courts' authority to enforce these agreements. While *Corrigan* had established that the Constitution did not explicitly prohibit private racial covenants, the Court had left open the questions of their legitimacy with respect to public policy and the propriety of their enforcement by lower courts. Instead of engaging these issues on their respective merits, the federal circuit court had simply assumed the Supreme Court had answered them and had skipped over a substantive debate of the legal arguments. Rather than relying on the law, Edgerton argued, "this court's present decision . . . rests only on our own past decisions to like effect." The solid pillar of precedent that had held covenants up as nearly sacrosanct was in fact hollow.[108]

The judge then took on the two central issues. He first dealt with the subject of enforcement. "Restrictive covenants," he reminded his colleagues, "are not self-executing." Enforcement of the agreements with injunctions demanded the participation and intervention of the state. Because "arbitrary and unreasonable" restrictions imposed by state actors on citizens infringed upon individuals' ability to enjoy the full spectrum of rights accorded to them by the Constitution, Edgerton argued that the judicial defense of harmful contracts that were based on little more than blind prejudice had no justification under the law. "The right to buy and use anything that whites may buy and use is conferred upon Negroes implicitly by the due process clauses of the Fifth and Fourteenth Amendments and explicitly by the Civil Rights Act [of 1866]," Edgerton maintained. "Of the civil rights so conferred, none is clearer and few are more vital than the right to buy a home and live in it." Despite *Corrigan*, he concluded, the courts were under no obligation to abet or abide the "denial and destruction of the right of Negroes to acquire property."[109]

Edgerton then moved to the subject of restrictive covenants' relationship to public policy. Unlike the Michigan court in *McGhee*, Edgerton delved into the substance of white homeowners' justifications for residential exclusion. Simply accepting the wishes and property rights claims of white homeowners as the clearest expression of public policy, as the Michigan court had done, seemed unjust to the judge. "If the satisfaction which many . . . whites . . . derive from excluding Negroes is to be given weight," he wrote, "it must be weighed against the dissatisfaction which Negroes may feel at being excluded." Citing extensively from Swedish social scientist Gunnar Myrdal's *American Dilemma*—a detailed examination of American race relations and the state of black communities published in 1944—the judge contended that restrictive covenants failed to provide any financial benefits to white homeowners and actually increased the likelihood of racial conflict in the nation's cities. Edgerton insisted that courts must take into account these observations and the added knowledge of the crippling housing shortage and the costs of overcrowding in black neighborhoods. Indeed, much of Edgerton's passion in his arguments against covenants seemed to stem from these social consequences. At various instances in both *Hurd* and the earlier *Mays* case, Edgerton appeared viscerally aghast at the state of housing for

African Americans in the capital and it fed a moral outrage that fueled his dissents.[110]

Perhaps more than any of his colleagues on the bench, Edgerton also took seriously America's recent treaties and the words of its leaders as evidence of an evolving public policy in the wake of World War II. In contrast to a Michigan court that found the egalitarianism of these pronouncements quaint and "merely indicative of a desirable social trend," Edgerton argued that the United Nations Charter "and our American desire for international good will and cooperation cannot be neglected" when evaluating the obligations of the courts on racial issues. Quoting from the charter, General Dwight Eisenhower, and President Harry Truman on the importance of domestic justice and peace for the future of democracy in the world, Edgerton solemnly proclaimed that "suits like these, and the ghetto system they enforce, are among our conspicuous failures to live together in peace." Both the soundness of moral and legal judgment as well as the political objectives of the postwar nation demanded an end to the enforcement of racial restrictions.[111]

Legal activists hailed Edgerton's dissent as the clearest and most forceful argument in favor of the rights of black homeowners to date. One Chicago litigator acclaimed it as the new "model for the presentation of [a] direct attack" on residential restrictions and Loren Miller gleefully wrote to Charles Hamilton Houston that "Edgerton's dissent is one of the best things that has been done in this field." Phineas Indritz, a young white attorney in President Truman's Department of the Interior was so moved by the force of Edgerton's argument that he immediately called Houston to offer his assistance on any further appeal of the case. Perhaps this was the moment they had been waiting for.[112]

Looking Ahead: Test Cases and a U.S. Supreme Court Appeal

Legal activists felt glimmers of optimism, but if history served as precedent the appellate courts' evictions of the black litigants should have brought the cases to an end. Only two covenant suits in more than twenty years had gone beyond the state supreme courts or federal circuit court of appeals. Despite the bold proclamations of many of the *Shelley* cases' supporters, the decision on whether or not the U.S. Supreme Court would intervene did not rest with them.

Yet now more than ever, black communities and litigators in St. Louis, Detroit, and Washington saw the moment as their best chance and determined to fight as far as they could. The networks of legal activists and the creativity of local advocates had yielded some intriguing new arguments about the role of courts as agents of the state, the legal definitions of race, and the place of covenants in postwar public policy. Some of these new claims might well convince the Supreme Court to take another look at the covenant issue. It was at this moment—in the limbo between the story of a local failure and the seeds of a national campaign—that the eyes of many black homeowners and attorneys turned to the national office of the NAACP. The organization had been present throughout each of these cases to varying degrees, having only minimal connections to the *Shelley* suit and a more substantial role in *McGhee* and *Hurd*. Indeed, the NAACP's legal offices had sought to energize and facilitate a widespread campaign against covenants since the summer of 1945. As the public calls now rose for the Association to make a test case out of one or more of these suits, the NAACP's attorneys faced a crucial decision. The consequences of choosing the wrong case with which to appeal could set their cause back another two decades, but the fight against covenants could not remain locally oriented much longer. The time for a truly national campaign had come.

THREE

The NAACP

National Leadership and Housing Desegregation

With bated breath, the NAACP legal team looked to the U.S. Supreme Court in June of 1945. As the days rolled on, they waited eagerly for a decision on the fate of *Mays v. Burgess*. The office was abuzz with the prospect that the Supreme Court might grant a hearing in the case and anticovenant lawyers across the country understood exactly what hung in the balance. Since *Corrigan v. Buckley* (1926), the Court had refused to address directly the question of covenants' validity under the Constitution. That earlier decision had sparked an explosion of new restrictions and had ensured the sanctity of court-enforced housing discrimination for two decades. But *Mays* now held out the tantalizing possibility of a shift in that stance. Howard University Law School dean and longtime NAACP official William H. Hastie considered *Mays* "the best restrictive covenant case we have ever had in the District of Columbia." If any suit might force the justices to take a fresh look at covenants and perhaps weaken the scourge of urban segregation, this looked to be the one.[1]

Regardless of the Court's decision with respect to hearing the case, however, the NAACP legal team believed that now was the time to bring national leadership to the struggle against racial restrictions. In the second week of June, Thurgood Marshall called upon the nation's foremost civil rights attorneys, inviting them to gather in Chicago in order to determine how they might surmount "the foremost problem confronting Negroes today." The NAACP's National Legal Committee was a veritable powerhouse of jurisprudential intellect and Marshall sought to muster as much of that as he could. The coming fight would be difficult, he warned, and only the "pooling of our legal resources" would be able to assure the "best possible chance of success." One month later, the committee would convene in the Windy City to consolidate and coordinate the efforts of local anticovenant fighters and legal experts from around the country. For two days in July some of the best minds in the NAACP's legal arsenal would hammer out a strategy designed to overcome decades of entrenched support for covenants.[2]

Marshall's invitations had only just arrived when the Court knocked the wind out of the surging voice of those demanding change. On June 18, the justices denied a hearing to the *Mays* case and cast new doubt on whether or not the NAACP would ever be able to shake the Court's indifference toward restrictive agreements. Unwilling to let this latest setback stand, however, Marshall pushed ahead with his plans for the conference in the hopes that he could prevent the anticovenant campaign's momentum from stalling. His persistence paid off. The meeting in Chicago that summer became arguably one of the most significant gatherings of civil rights legal talent to that point in the Association's history. What transpired on those two sweltering days would define the NAACP's early postwar urban agenda and reignite the drive for a national reckoning on the issue of covenants.

The Chicago conference in 1945 launched the NAACP headlong into a renewed battle against housing discrimination, one that summoned the full measure of the Association's energy and resources. The attorneys now faced the daunting task of forcing the Supreme Court, in short order, to reverse its stance on twenty years worth of covenant enforcement—a stance the justices had reaffirmed just weeks earlier. To do this, the Association's legal staff hoped to establish the national office as a clearinghouse for the best arguments, most innovative tactics, and strongest test cases that emerged from local activists' struggles against individual restrictions. With *Mays* further weighing down the scales against them, they knew that there was virtually no room for error at the national level. They could not afford another rejection or another defeat in the Supreme Court.[3]

Something remarkable began to take shape at that conference, the seeds of a strategy that would grow and strengthen in the coming years. The Association remained hopeful about the prospects of their anticovenant fight in the wake of the Chicago gathering and strove to cultivate the best possible suits it could anywhere in the country. Yet it was not one of their carefully planned test cases that jolted the campaign forward, but instead the renegade actions of George Vaughn and his St. Louis real estate industry backers that flung the Association—much to their displeasure—back toward the Supreme Court years before the legal team felt they would be ready. The ensuing chaos born of Vaughn's uncontrollable zeal and the Association's frantic responses produced an unexpectedly sudden yield. In the summer of 1947, just two years after the failure in *Mays*, the Court granted a hearing to the *Shelley* and *McGhee* cases.

In parallel with this rather awkward leap forward, the NAACP found itself evolving dramatically in the immediate postwar period. By 1947, the Association was awash with record levels of popular support. The organization's size and political influence grew rapidly after the war, buoyed by the renewed urgency of black protest and an expansion of African Americans' voting power in the 1940s. At the same time, public opinion had grown increasingly receptive to arguments against racial discrimination. The anticovenant campaign took shape in a nation saturated by the language of freedom and democracy and newly responsive to the dangerous extremes of racial and ethnic discrimination. Because the issue of adequate housing deeply affected Americans of all races, covenant litigation fostered a tremendously broad coalition of activists, attorneys, scholars, and organizations as the cases moved through the courts.[4]

During this moment of unique opportunity, the NAACP brilliantly and effectively tapped into not only the popular backlash against America's traditions of racial inequality, but also into an evolving intellectual discourse about the social consequences of racial prejudice. Building on the influential work of antiracist social scientists who fought to reshape the contours of scholarly and popular thinking about race, the Association's lawyers fashioned a legal strategy in the covenant cases that relied upon a new body of socioeconomic research into the costs of segregation. Once the Supreme Court agreed to hear the cases, the attorneys used this emerging scholarship in an attempt both to sway the justices and to educate the broader public about the needs and nature of African American homeowners as the ghetto sought to tighten its grip on urban black communities.

How the NAACP crafted its postwar covenant campaign and how its lawyers prepared for the Supreme Court revealed a great deal about the organization's institutional priorities in the mid-1940s and the ways that World War II shaped civil rights protest in the aftermath of the conflict. Despite their initial caution, as *Shelley* and *McGhee* headed to the court the national legal staff enthusiastically embraced innovative tactics and brought together an unprecedented combination of allies as they readied for a court battle that very few of them were confident they would win.

A Cautious Campaign:
The Chicago Conference and the Seeds of Strategy

If the NAACP's Chicago meeting had marked a moment of unparalleled collaboration in the struggle against covenants, the gathering itself was largely the product of one man's efforts. Thurgood Marshall, the Association's special counsel, spearheaded the drive for a national conference and an organized campaign against restrictive agreements that put the NAACP legal staff squarely in the center of the fight. For at least a year prior to the July meeting, Marshall had publicly maintained his desire to have the Association "establish procedure which will lead to an all-out legal attack on restrictive covenants." "Residential segregation," he wrote elsewhere, "should be attacked at the earliest possible moment." While he and the legal staff of the NAACP had pursued this goal in house, Marshall refrained from consulting broadly with other attorneys or taking any real control over the course of pending litigation. Still, his insistence that a full-scale assault on housing segregation could only take shape "after careful planning" led him to seek greater influence over the myriad efforts stretched across the country. Marshall used both the promise and the disappointment of the *Mays* case to bring local covenant lawyers, housing experts, the National Legal Committee, and his own staff together in the hopes of developing a national strategy.[5]

Though Marshall would elect not to chair the conference and was not an especially vocal participant, the whole affair showcased his strengths as an organizer. As one of his biographers would later describe it, "This was Marshall in full flower, for the first time acknowledged by senior black leaders as one of their own." Marshall had by this time already made a name for himself in black legal and political circles as a prominent civil rights advocate; just the previous year he had argued successfully before the Supreme Court for the elimination of the white primary in *Smith v. Allwright*. The Chicago conference, however, signaled Marshall's emergence as a national leader and agenda setter in new ways. Here he grabbed the reins of complex and wide-ranging local efforts in an attempt to create and impose some overarching structure. Another biographer explains that this moment represented Marshall's "first major attempt to organize the nation's civil rights attorneys to play from the same sheet of music." Marshall designed the daily agendas, handpicked the leaders of each session, and even arranged for the Monday night dinner where the attendees and prominent Association officials met with the press.[6]

Apart from establishing the Association's lead role in the anticovenant campaign, the conference also tried to determine the best path for a new Supreme Court test case. The gathering had to focus on how and when to make another attempt at getting before the highest court. As Marshall sketched out the daily schedules, he ensured that each of the conference's four sessions pushed forward in this regard. Two meetings on Monday examined the present state of covenant litigation and some of the best tactics in use locally. The following day centered on how best to promote public awareness on the issue and how to select appropriate cases for appeal to the Supreme Court. The conferees would have a plan of action by the time they adjourned on Tuesday evening.

First, William H. Hastie presided over an initial postmortem of the *Mays* case. He insisted that *Mays* held out some hope. The attorneys in the case had fought the restriction thoroughly, "raising every possible ground" in an attempt to convince the Supreme Court to grant a hearing on the issue. The problem, he seemed to suggest, was not the strength or weakness of the case itself, but that the Court was reticent to entertain any serious challenge to the validity of these contracts. Hastie and his colleagues, however, believed that the justices were slowly warming to the prospect of reexamining covenants' place in American jurisprudence. Indeed, *Mays* had fallen just two votes shy of receiving a hearing before the Court.[7]

With his optimism for future test cases thus established, Hastie yielded the floor to a series of local covenant attorneys from around the country. Loren Miller of Los Angeles, Willis Graves of Detroit, George Vaughn of St. Louis, and Theodore Spaulding of Philadelphia all described the state of pending cases in their respective cities. Their opinions about the future chances of covenant litigation in local courts ranged from stark pessimism to guarded confidence. Miller, whose victory in the Sugar Hill cases was still six months away, addressed the nearly twenty suits presently in Los Angeles courts. While he noted that the "expenses of constant litigation [were] militating against" the enforcement of restrictions, he firmly believed that the "District Court of Appeals' decisions [were] increasingly reactionary, and I believe hopeless." On the prospects of five pending cases from Michigan, Graves reserved his judgment in anticipation of the Wayne County Circuit Court judge's forthcoming ruling in *McGhee*—which he and Francis Dent would lose some weeks later. Vaughn, on the other hand, evinced more hope than his colleagues. Speaking just weeks before the Shelleys would purchase their home on Labadie Avenue and become his clients, the St. Louis attorney highlighted a handful of recent victories in the Gateway City's courts. He attributed this latest, albeit small, rash of success to the political pressure on judges who faced elections and were thus increasingly conscious of alienating the city's growing black electorate. Covenants, it seemed, might have a political solution if not a legal one.[8]

After bringing the assembled attorneys up to speed on where the anticovenant campaign stood, the discussion turned to the issue of potential tactics. Charles Hamilton Houston, ever the eager strategist, steered the conferees toward a set of arguments called the "change of neighborhood doctrine." This tactic focused on the proximity of existing black-owned homes to restricted white neighborhoods and mirrored many of the claims he would use in the *Hurd* case. The basic premise of the argument held that when white and black homeowners already occupied areas that bordered one another, the purpose of the covenant—namely to prevent property owners of different races from being in the same neighborhood—had already failed. Any further enforcement of the agreement's terms, therefore, would be both fruitless and unnecessarily punitive. Houston had already been successful at least once before in pursuing this line of reasoning, winning a 1942 case before the Federal Circuit Court of Appeals in Washington, D.C., on the strength of this argument.[9]

The "change of neighborhood" claims relied in part upon social scientific assessments of cities' shifting racial compositions and on sociological arguments about the effects of integration in cycles of neighborhood development. Houston contended that evidence in Washington and other cities had shown that as older white neighborhoods deteriorated physically and became dependent upon renters rather than owners, African Americans' entrance into these areas actually rejuvenated the physical and social character of the region by promoting homeownership and better maintenance standards. By characterizing the entry of black homeowners into an area as "the orderly trend of development in a city," Houston confronted white residents and the courts with the idea that restrictive agreements impeded—rather than protected—the peaceful improvement of urban areas. Houston, however, recognized that the change of neighborhood doctrine could only apply to specific areas of cities where substantial numbers of black and white homeowners already lived in close proximity. Thus, the tactic had the potential to invalidate only individual covenants in cases that met these preconditions and could not provide courts with the grounds to reject all residential restrictions. Anticovenant experts understood this as primarily a "haphazard remedy." Still, Houston embraced this idiosyncratic approach to covenant-fighting, though he also believed in the merits of pursuing constitutional and statutory claims that would challenge these agreements collectively.[10]

The two most recent national test cases indicated that idiosyncratic arguments about the validity of specific covenants had a greater immediate chance of success than an approach on constitutional grounds. While the 1945 *Mays* case failed to win a Supreme Court hearing despite the attorneys' varied constitutional and statutory claims, the 1940 Chicago case *Hansberry v. Lee* had enjoyed a different reception. The Court had not only agreed to accept *Hansberry* for review, the justices also overturned the restrictive covenant at the center of the suit. The attorneys in *Hansberry* had originally relied upon the argument that the white homeowners had improperly executed the paperwork establishing the property restriction and that the courts could not consider this agreement valid due to these technical defects. The covenant's language had stipulated that the terms would become binding only after 95 percent of property owners in the area signed the restriction. Only slightly more than half of the residents had joined the agreement, however. The Supreme Court ultimately sided with the black homeowners in the case, but had only agreed to review the case because of questions surrounding class action litigation procedures. The decision relied on these narrow procedural grounds that had virtually nothing to do with the larger question of covenants' validity. Still, the justices reversed the state court's enforcement order and the white homeowners abandoned their efforts to relitigate the case, recognizing that they could not overcome the covenant's technical deficiencies.[11]

The *Hansberry* victory, limited as it was, marked the most significant national progress in almost two decades of covenant litigation. The case's success alongside the disappointment of *Mays* indicated that idiosyncratic claims might serve more appropriately the interests of local lawyers concerned with the immediate fate of their individual clients. In the larger picture, however, the precedent set in *Hansberry* proved extremely narrow and relatively easy for white homeowners to circumvent. Indeed, the case sparked a flurry of efforts to strengthen and solidify the technical elements of individual covenants.[12]

In spite of the limitations inherent in any idiosyncratic approach, the change of neighborhood doctrine seemed particularly promising in the postwar moment for Houston and his colleagues. The argument rested on facts that white property owners could not evade by refashioning their restrictions. One could not simply tighten legal language or gather new signatures to negate the reality that some white communities already existed in close proximity—often just one street away—from black neighborhoods. While Houston believed that constitutional claims would ultimately have the greatest effect on the broader pattern of residential restrictions, he did not feel that the pursuit of a total victory should come at the expense of immediate gains. As his peers clamored for national test cases on constitutional grounds, Houston reminded the conferees, "I don't think that in the interim . . . we should neglect making any progress we can." His insistence on the "potentialities" of the doctrine found a healthy reception. Indeed, William H. Hastie's only criticism of the *Mays* case record was that it had not relied more heavily on "change of neighborhood" claims. Houston's determination to refine and combine the idiosyncratic and constitutional approaches to covenant litigation gave the assembled attorneys a look at the cutting edge of available tactics.[13]

The strategy, however, had its critics. As the lawyers yielded the floor to some of the consultants that had chosen to attend, housing expert Robert Weaver spearheaded the early conversation. Weaver, a Harvard-trained economist, had played a prominent role on President Franklin D. Roosevelt's "Black Cabinet" in the 1930s and was presently serving on the Chicago-based American Council on Race Relations (ACRR). Weaver immediately challenged the suitability of Houston's change of neighborhood doctrine for the root problems that black homeseekers faced. Houston had argued that "we all oppose the question of ghettos. One of the ways of knocking them down is to broaden them." Weaver strongly disagreed. He cautioned against settling—even in the short term—for only the growth of present slums. "Expanding existing Negro areas," he insisted, "simply creates new islands and ghettos. The bands around these do not give way quickly enough to relieve congestion." Because the change of neighborhood doctrine required a lengthy challenge to each individual covenant and could only apply in the areas immediately adjacent to established concentrations of black homeowners, even this "broadening" of the ghetto that Houston advocated would proceed too slowly and too narrowly to provide any real relief. Attorneys could not resign themselves to arguing for "bigger and better ghettos," Weaver warned. Only a concerted and coordinated campaign for the outright dissolution of all racial covenants' strength could put black urban communities on the path toward progress and equality.[14]

Weaver and Houston agreed wholeheartedly, however, on the need for a program of public education about the consequences of covenants. Weaver recommended attacking residential restrictions in a campaign that combined litigation, legislation, public information, political pressure, and "economic action." While the courts would be an important theater of battle, he saw opportunities for state legislatures to enact anticovenant laws and for experts like himself to familiarize the public with the fallacies that justified covenants' use and the problems that these agreements engendered. Through widespread use of media, Weaver wanted to "present the economic and social problems incident to race restrictive covenants" and use this knowledge to undermine their popular support. Houston saw a similar need for public awareness and encouraged the conferees to "use the Court as a forum for the purpose of educating the public." Others at the conference felt that the NAACP was in the best position to disseminate information and at least one participant vigorously urged the Association to offset the propaganda that demonized black homeseekers, arguing that they should "go everywhere and educate people." Those supporting the campaign against covenants would have to fight intensely on many fronts. The courts alone would not offer the solution.[15]

As the conference drew to a close, the attendees sensed real progress. In their final meeting, the attorneys and consultants hammered out a plan to assemble the best test case moving forward. They focused most intently on constitutional and statutory tactics, looking for the arguments that would win over the Supreme Court when the time came. The attorneys paid particular attention to the recently developed theory that they could mount a constitutional challenge to courts' enforcement of restrictions in addition to contesting the validity of covenants themselves. Building upon the law review articles published earlier in 1945 by attorney Harold Kahen and University of California law professor D. O. McGovney, the conferees decided to argue that judicial enforcement of covenants constituted discriminatory state action as prohibited by the Fourteenth Amendment. Because the Supreme Court had begun to appear more disposed "to recognize as state action activities formerly deemed to be only of private concern" in other questions of law, the attorneys believed this line of attack would be essential to any future test cases.[16]

The second key to the constitutional approach, as Hastie saw it, was to "show that the courts, to the extent that they uphold the covenants, are acting contrary to the highest manifestation of public policy." He advocated that any test case "bring in just as many statutory and constitutional provisions as possible" to demonstrate the ways in which state court enforcement of residential restrictions directly contravened the intentions of the Constitution and the U.S. Code. Again, the focus rested on juridical support for covenants and an approach that would undermine the effects of all discriminatory homeowners agreements at once. The conferees wanted a coup de grâce.[17]

To that end, Hastie pressed his colleagues to specify what the ideal test case should look like. "What do we want," Hastie asked, "that we haven't had in previous cases?" The group decided on at least three key features. First, they wanted a case from an area with extensive covenant coverage throughout the city. They also insisted that the case come from a metropolitan area in the North or West. Finally, they agreed that testimony and social scientific data on "overcrowding, high rent costs, [and] social things" needed to be part of the case record. Coming from a major urban hub outside the South, the NAACP's ideal test case would revolve primarily around claims that judicial enforcement of covenants constituted discriminatory action by the state that denied African Americans equal protection under the law and greatly harmed their quality of life. The NAACP looked to take this fight to a national stage and its objectives were bold. Not only would the attorneys argue for a radical expansion of the Fourteenth Amendment's reach, they would also transform the way that they justified these claims—relying on social scientific data in their courtroom arguments more than ever before.[18]

With the plan in place, Thurgood Marshall sprang into action. He began to design a "campaign of publicity . . . against the evils of segregation and racial restrictive covenants for circulation throughout the country." For this, Marshall and the Association turned to Robert Weaver. Weaver's efforts resulted in the publication of an educational pamphlet on covenants later that year in which he consolidated the litany of social and economic arguments against covenants for public consumption. Marshall also wanted to shore up the strength of his legal team and add "a full time staff member to do nothing but work on housing" as a sign of the NAACP's commitment to the covenant fight. In December of 1945, he hired thirty-year-old Marian Wynn Perry of the NLG to handle the national office's housing cases.[19]

Marshall and Perry had met while lobbying on behalf of their respective organizations for state fair employment legislation in New York. Perry was a lifelong New Yorker and the daughter of Canadian immigrants who had grown up in a white-collar neighborhood in Queens. She graduated from Brooklyn Law School in 1943 and earned a master's degree in public administration from New York University (NYU). During the war, Perry took a job with the U.S. Department of Labor and began serving as the secretary of the New York NLG's Constitutional Liberties Committee. Perry's experience with lobbying and litigation and her connections to other local advocacy groups made her an appealing ally as the NAACP sought to expand its courtroom efforts and its cooperation with like-minded organizations. Over the next eighteen months, Marshall and Perry kept a watchful eye on the progress of dozens of local covenant suits, waiting patiently for the one that would make the perfect appeal.[20]

Marshall had wanted the NAACP at the forefront of the covenant campaign in part to ensure that his legal team would have control when that appeal came. After the 1945 conference, the Association's legal team left much of the work of developing cases in the hands of local legal activists who experimented with the best methods to undermine racial restrictions while adhering to the broad strokes of the strategy laid out in Chicago. At the national level, however, the Association exercised an abundance of caution in their preparations and wanted a methodical and deliberate approach to the Supreme Court, even at the risk of protracting the fight. Franklin Williams, one of the attorneys working with Marshall at the NAACP during this time—who later became particularly critical of his former boss—suggested that the legal team's leader was "very reluctant . . . to push the restrictive covenant cases." This wariness, Williams suggested, was not unique to the housing issue. Marshall supposedly "had to be convinced beyond a reasonable doubt of victory" in order to throw the full weight of the office into petitioning for a Supreme Court review. Perry later commented that "it was a deliberate strategy not to take chances" with litigation. "We expected to win," she said, "because our cases had to be so compelling to be brought in the first place." The Association was undoubtedly committed to moving forward on the matter of covenants, but the attorneys believed that careful and unhurried preparation was the only prudent course of action.[21]

The consequences of this more methodical approach were not insignificant. Waiting for the ideal case meant abandoning families like the Shelleys, McGhees, and others who hoped for another day in court. It also meant leaving adrift the campaigns that local communities had formed around these petitioners. Local branches and supporters invested considerable energy in individual suits from their respective cities. They raised money, sponsored public protest meetings, and galvanized popular outrage at the state of urban housing conditions. Turning away these cases as inadequate threatened to weaken morale and deflate communities' organizing efforts, making subsequent campaigns potentially more difficult.

Still, a losing test case might do even greater damage to the fight against racial restrictions. If the Supreme Court built up a lengthier precedent of denying hearings for covenant cases, the NAACP might never even get the issue before the Court. Moreover, a loss in the Supreme Court—one that upheld the rights of white homeowners over those of black homeseekers—might take decades of new litigation to unravel. Rushing ahead with a case that the lawyers had doubts about seemed not only unwise, but also dangerous. Additionally, the legal staff harbored concerns about their own reputation and resources. Perry explained that her colleagues "had to be cautious to build momentum and [a] sense of victory. . . . A loss could have been politically blown out of all proportion." Wins and losses mattered both practically and symbolically and by the end of World War II the Association knew that it needed victories to propel the civil rights struggle forward. Supreme Court decisions that rejected African Americans' claims to equality in the postwar moment might well become a new "separate but equal" doctrine, giving renewed courage and added strength to segregated institutions and the forces of racial discrimination. At the same time, Supreme Court losses would overtax the financial resources of the NAACP—which were considerable, but still limited. Marshall and the others recognized that only noteworthy victories could sustain the energy and fiscal viability of the Association's entire civil rights litigation agenda. The attorneys knew what was at stake for countless African American families desperate for decent homes. They also knew that a failure might cause much greater harm than a delay. Both the families and the organization stood to suffer severely if the campaign flopped and so the attorneys proceeded with caution to protect both their chances of success and the Association's future strength. Indeed, by 1946, the NAACP had more than ever to lose in this fight.[22]

Gathering Strength: The Postwar NAACP

The NAACP's carefully orchestrated postwar covenant campaign came in the midst of an incredible period of growth and activity for the Association. World War II had helped to spawn a wave of black political activism that energized and emboldened the organization and the postwar years yielded new levels of strength. The 1940s marked a transformative phase of the struggle for civil rights and the Association rode at the forefront. Infused with urgency and resources, the NAACP expanded its agenda and generated a degree of political access and influence that it had never before experienced. This vibrant moment of protest showed the NAACP at its most dynamic and most powerful.[23]

The Association's growth was nothing short of explosive. Membership skyrocketed from just over 50,000 in 1940 to nearly 450,000 just six years later. Wartime prosperity and dedicated organizing took the NAACP from some 350 branch offices at the start of the decade to more than 1,000 in the aftermath of the war. The years 1946 and 1947 marked a peak in the Association's strength and influence within African American communities, with the latter yielding "the greatest year of growth in the number of branches, youth councils and college chapters of the Association's existence. A total of 234 new units were organized." A greater emphasis on local leadership training accompanied the proliferation of branches and the expansion of the membership. By the end of the year, NAACP executive secretary Walter White would boast to the Association's board members that "we have built the greatest civil rights organization which has ever been created." Fueled by the rising tide of black activism and the ever-increasing demands for change, the Association mobilized and rode a tidal wave of support into the immediate postwar period.[24]

Income from membership fees mushroomed and the NAACP's operating budget grew and became markedly less dependent upon philanthropic contributions. In the 1930s, the budget had hovered near $55,000 with less than $10,000 of that for the legal department. As late as 1941, the lawyers at the national office ran their litigation campaigns with just a $14,000 allotment. By 1947, however, the Association was spending nearly $320,000 annually and the legal team had budgeted more than $20,000 for covenant litigation alone. The NAACP put its financial windfall to work.[25]

Flush with resources and followers as never before, the Association accelerated and emboldened its efforts in both litigation and political mobilization. In the legal arena, the influx of African Americans into wartime industry sparked a wave of labor cases under the NAACP's guidance. These determined efforts to protect workers' rights built upon—and helped to further—the growth of the Association's working-class membership that had reached unprecedented levels by the mid-1940s. The attention paid to workplace issues also laid the groundwork for an improving relationship with labor unions and helped bolster the Association's political clout and connections.[26]

NAACP attorneys found equally fertile fields for litigation in a range of other areas. Rampant discrimination and prejudice in the armed services prompted the hiring of a new attorney to help handle the legal team's expanded workload on this issue and in 1946 Thurgood Marshall helped bring *Morgan v. Virginia* to the Supreme Court, where he scored another important victory that struck down segregation in interstate transportation. NAACP lawyers also quickly reentered the fight against educational discrimination, taking up several cases in the postwar years.[27]

These litigation efforts also stretched into the critical arena of voting rights. In the 1940s, the NAACP's leaders, lawyers, and activists rallied around the cause of political mobilization and empowerment with newfound vigor. *Smith v. Allwright* (1944), the case that disallowed the exclusion of black voters from primary elections, had weakened one of the South's key instruments of disfranchisement and helped launch a large-scale voter registration movement. The decision had reinvigorated the efforts of organizers and made African American communities more cognizant of their rights and the potential power of their ballots. As a result, registrations rose dramatically across the Deep South, a place where the NAACP had historically tread with relative caution. Though the Association's estimates were some-what unreliable and registration numbers alone overstated African Americans' actual impact at the polls due to the varied methods of intimidation and exclusion on election day, the NAACP's mobilization of black voters proved promising. Even in light of the physical and economic repercussions doled out by white supremacists for the most basic of political activities, the NAACP claimed to have helped register nearly 700,000 new African American voters in the Deep South by 1948. Coupled with an additional 700,000 black Americans who had left the South and its voting restrictions during wartime and the hundreds of thousands that would follow over the remainder of the decade, the black electorate looked to exercise more influence than ever in the late 1940s. As the largest and most powerful African American interest group in the country, the NAACP suddenly found itself with a new level of access and influence in national politics.[28]

BY THE END of 1946, the Association had amassed an impressive record. A string of significant Supreme Court victories, the voter registration campaigns underway—even in the South—increased media attention and popular support, and staggering organizational growth all helped build the NAACP's momentum. The momentum promised to continue. Association officials and outside observers speculated that the group's size would surpass 500,000 or even 600,000 members. The scope of the organization's activities mattered just as much as its size. Indeed, the Association derived part of its strength and reputation in these years from the fact that it could balance—and often succeed in—so many simultaneous endeavors. Few savvy politicians doubted the influence that the NAACP might wield among an increasingly relevant black electorate. The growing size and strength of an African American voting bloc in the North and West promised that black ballots could matter more than ever before in postwar elections.[29]

The Association used its organizing triumphs in the years following World War II to reach political decision makers. Insistent lobbying and repeated reminders about the significant role that African Americans' votes would have in upcoming elections became staple tactics for the NAACP. In the eighteen months leading up to the 1948 election, Association officials made no secret of their intention to influence black voters. Walter White relished the opportunity to deploy constant references to the Association's numerical and mobilizing strength when he addressed political leaders. It was clear that the NAACP leadership wanted to sit atop the rising tide of black electoral power and use the increasing import of African American votes to advance a strong civil rights agenda.[30]

The NAACP's momentum soon generated a degree of political access that only further served to enhance the Association's strength. As President Harry S. Truman looked toward the electoral landscape in 1948, it seemed apparent that the NAACP could very well play a deciding part in the outcome. Within a month of assuming office following the death of Franklin D. Roosevelt in 1945, Truman arranged a private meeting with White where they discussed the problems of colonialism and international human rights. Two weeks later, White and Truman exchanged letters regarding discrimination in federal housing insurance and the need for better protections against racial prejudice in hiring practices. This correspondence proved encouraging for the Association's leadership. Over the next three years their lobbying efforts and attempts to build a closer relationship with the administration intensified.[31]

In September of 1946, White led a delegation of six men into a meeting with the president to discuss some of the lynchings and actions of "hate organizations" that had occurred in previous months. Of the half-dozen delegates that sat in the Oval Office that afternoon, three—including White— were NAACP officers, testifying to the prominent role the Association would play in civil rights lobbying efforts. Though White apparently entered the meeting with doubts that any real changes would result, a sustained discussion with the president buoyed his spirits. By the end of the day, Truman had agreed to establish a committee "to investigate the entire subject of violation of civil liberties and to recommend a program of corrective action." Most importantly, the president decided to circumvent any congressional filibusters or impediments by using an executive order to create the commission. He requested the advice of White's delegation regarding the committee's composition and White essentially handpicked the chairman and at least one other member of the fourteen-person body. Ten weeks later, the president made the committee a reality.[32]

On December 5, Truman's Executive Order 9808 created the President's Committee on Civil Rights (PCCR). A little less than a year later, in October of 1947, the PCCR's members announced their findings to the president and subsequently the nation. Named *To Secure These Rights*, the committee's final report offered what Walter White proclaimed was "without doubt the most courageous and specific" assessment of the nation's racial problems and potential remedies ever created. Reproduced in mass quantities by the

Government Printing Office—and later a trade press—Truman implored the American public to read what he deemed "an American charter of human freedom." In their proposed remedies, the PCCR articulated forty recommendations that would provide greater protections for civil rights, individual safety, the privileges of citizenship, the right to "freedom of conscience and expression," and equal opportunity. *To Secure These Rights* advocated—among many things—the creation of a civil rights section in the Federal Bureau of Investigation, national statutes directed against lynching and police brutality, the abolition of the poll tax, an extended program of civil rights education, and steps to eliminate residential segregation by weakening governmental support for restrictive covenants. The sweeping recommendations of the report seemed nothing short of revolutionary in a nation that still offered safe haven to Jim Crow and the "separate but equal" doctrine of the late nineteenth century.[33]

Even before the release of the PCCR's report, however, the Truman administration had made two significant demonstrations of its support for the NAACP and the Association's agenda. In the spring of 1947, administration officials dusted off a three-year-old plea from the NAACP leadership regarding discriminatory practices in FHA underwriting policies. The Association had strongly protested the FHA's endorsement and encouragement of racial restrictive covenants, especially in the manual for underwriters. After repeated complaints, the agency finally made some concessions to the NAACP by adjusting references to the desirability of residential segregation in the 1947 edition of the manual. Though the FHA continued to insure mortgages on covenanted property and declined to condemn racial restrictions in spite of the NAACP's objections on both of these matters, the changes to the *Underwriting Manual* signaled that the Association's lobbying was having a positive impact on the Truman administration's racial policies.[34]

In the wake of the manual's publication in May of 1947, housing officials in the administration circulated copies of the FHA's changes to prominent anticovenant attorneys. "It should be noted," one of the accompanying letters maintained, "that positive steps taken since Raymond Foley became commissioner of [the] FHA . . . together with the revisions in the *Underwriting Manual*, fulfill almost completely the four recommendations contained in the NAACP Memorandum of October 1944." The letter emphasized the agency's attentiveness to the NAACP's specific concerns and the willingness of Truman appointees like Foley to act on some of the Association's demands. While NAACP officials would continue to protest FHA activities that condoned discrimination, the agency's recognition of their appeal for change was certainly promising.[35]

Within weeks of the FHA's actions, President Truman himself made a bold and public demonstration of his support for the NAACP and the Association's agenda. Late in April of 1947, at the urging of Walter White, the president had promised to address the NAACP's annual convention in Washington, D.C., during that summer. Thus, Truman became the first president to address the NAACP in the Association's nearly forty-year existence. Standing on the steps of the Lincoln Memorial—where Martin Luther King Jr. would share his dream for America sixteen years later—Truman announced a vision of his own. Ignoring the counsel of one of his closest advisers to limit his discussion of civil rights to a minute-long paragraph, the president spoke at some length on the issue, adding an explicit message to the implicit symbolism of his appearance.[36]

The scope, urgency, and unbridled egalitarianism of the address proved remarkable. Truman's message reached not only the 10,000 convention delegates the NAACP had assembled, but also a national and international radio audience. The president's address promised a greater role for the federal government in the provision and protection of African Americans' rights. "The extension of civil rights today," Truman announced, "means not protection of the people against the government, but protection of the people by the government." The nation could not afford to wait for equality to take root and segregation to wither. Powerful, immediate, and decisive federal action had to lead the way. "We cannot wait another decade or another generation" to bring about the end of Jim Crow and its attendant evils, he argued. America urgently needed an end to racial injustice. As Truman concluded the address he took his seat next to White, leaned over, and affirmed to the secretary, "I said what I did because I mean every word of it—and I am going to prove that I do mean it."[37]

Skepticism lingered, however. White, recalling the event in his autobiography a year later, remarked that "the applause when he [Truman] finished was hearty but not overwhelming." Promises were just that until African Americans' social, political, and material conditions actually changed. Still, the speech confirmed to the NAACP's national leadership that they had Truman's ear. For the first time, an American president had publicly championed the Association's needs, its hopes, and its demands. Truman's address symbolized how far the organization had come and how much it might yet accomplish.[38]

The year 1947 marked the pinnacle of the NAACP's influence and strength during the first half of the twentieth century. Thurgood Marshall would call it "the busiest legal year in the history of the NAACP." The Association had amassed for itself an enormous following, a broad agenda, and unprecedented political influence that translated into a wave of institutional momentum. Through dedicated organizing, persistent lobbying, and carefully crafted campaigns like the attack on restrictive covenants, the NAACP looked as though it might achieve any and all of its goals. Still, the Association's officials knew that their string of successes and the rising tide of their power might falter at any moment. An attitude of caution and measured steps forward thus prevailed. The fight against residential restrictions—which constituted the centerpiece of the Association's agenda for that year—offered a perfect example of this approach. Time and again, the pervasive sense of urgency and opportunity in the postwar moment clashed with the NAACP's calculated line of attack. As the Association worked to transform their covenant campaign into another major victory, the attorneys suddenly found themselves at odds with advocates who had quickly grown tired of the caution and deliberation. Just as the NAACP embarked on what would soon become its most triumphant year to date, a key part of the careful planning that had brought the organization to that point looked ready to crumble at the hands of those frustrated by the pace of change. For some, any further delay on the issue of covenants proved unbearable.[39]

Caps over the Wall: Preparations for the Supreme Court

George Vaughn of St. Louis numbered among those restless souls determined not to wait a moment longer. Perhaps the urgency of the cause drove him. Perhaps it was a sense that this case might be the capstone to his career of advocacy for black St. Louisans. Perhaps the real estate brokers underwriting his efforts exerted some pressure. Or perhaps he simply felt compelled by his clients' struggles. Whatever the reasons, Vaughn entered the early months of 1947 in dogged pursuit of a hearing before the Supreme Court. Despite the NAACP legal staff's urgings for him to slow down or stop the Shelleys' case and coordinate his efforts with theirs, Vaughn drove relentlessly forward. He forced the Association's hand by applying for certiorari in April. That move dashed the NAACP's hopes for a carefully planned approach to the Supreme Court that would revolve around a perfectly crafted test case.

By petitioning the Court, Vaughn compelled the Association to decide whether to risk another denial of certiorari while waiting for one of their preferred cases to plod through the appellate courts, or to throw their energy into making the best possible case out of the less desirable suits their branch offices had available. The haphazardness of these events and the NAACP's efforts to respond to them reveal the practical complexities of civil rights litigation and highlight the Association's ability to mobilize its legal resources to react to changing circumstances. Order and chaos could simultaneously shape the course of civil rights cases.[40]

The St. Louis case would remain a thorn in the NAACP's side for the entirety of the litigation process. The organization's attorneys clashed with Vaughn and his real estate industry backers throughout the year—both publicly and privately. Decades after the conclusion of the cases, Thurgood Marshall still shuddered at the memories of Vaughn's involvement, insisting to his biographer that the St. Louis attorney was a "blunderbuss" and disparaging his colleague's performance before the Supreme Court by unjustly portraying him as a doddering and borderline incompetent showboater.[41]

The tensions first flared in late December of 1946, shortly after the Shelleys' loss in the Missouri Supreme Court. Loren Miller, who kept a watchful eye on developments in restrictive covenant litigation across the country, fired off an anxious letter to the national office about a troubling newspaper story out of St. Louis regarding Vaughn—whom he had met at the Chicago conference in 1945. "I notice that he [Vaughn] is saying that he will seek Supreme Court review," Miller wrote. "I think you will agree with me," he continued, "that any attempt to get Supreme Court review should be thoroughly discussed by those who are interested . . . my information is that the record in his case is not altogether satisfactory." Miller pointed out for the attorneys, who likely needed no reminder, that "our failure to get review from [the] Supreme Court at this time will probably result in another long delay." Miller urged them to restrain Vaughn because the consequences of presenting a weak case to the nation's highest court might short-circuit the potential impact of a handful of promising test cases working their way through the appeals process. These suits included Miller's Sugar Hill case that was presently stalled in the California Supreme Court, but had become a particular darling of the NAACP's legal staff.[42]

Thurgood Marshall immediately cautioned Vaughn against moving forward by himself. "You will recall that at our meeting in Chicago year before last," he prodded, "we all agreed that the best way to break restrictive covenants was by a full exchange of information and by acting only after consultation among all the different attorneys working on restrictive covenants all over the country." He reminded Vaughn that the Association was not simply sitting on its hands. Branch attorneys around the country were awaiting decisions on cases that could be coordinated for a petition to the Supreme Court.[43]

Vaughn was unbowed and unapologetic. He promptly notified Marshall that in spite of the Association's plea for patience, he intended to appeal the Shelleys' case. The veteran attorney seemed both resolute and positively giddy at times about seizing the chance to argue his case to the Court. He charged ahead with little regard for the Association's legal advice or for its preferred strategy. Vaughn's determination confronted the NAACP with the dilemma of how best to proceed in light of this upcoming effort.[44]

The Association's first step was to take stock of the cases their affiliated attorneys currently had in process. Unfortunately, the immediate options were severely limited. In fact, the McGhee case in Detroit looked like the only suit far enough along in the appellate process to go before the Supreme Court in time. In January of 1947, Marshall and the NAACP legal staff began writing to a select group of covenant experts from around the country, asking them to read the McGhee case record and to render their opinions on whether the suit represented an acceptable test case.

As the responses trickled in over the following weeks, it became clear that the Association's consultants were deeply divided over McGhee's fitness for appeal. Half of the respondents felt strongly that the case was simply not up to the task of winning either a hearing from the Supreme Court or a victory. Those who did think the case merited an appeal typically had reservations. New York anticovenant attorney Andrew Weinberger, for example, felt the NAACP should push forward on appeal primarily because he saw "great harm permitting to rest unchallenged an adverse holding by a state court of last resort." He had no particular faith in the chances of the case, but felt it would set a dangerous precedent not to pursue these suits to the fullest extent possible. Chicagoan William R. Ming also felt that the case itself was not very strong, but that the Michigan court's decision might be outrageous enough to warrant a committed challenge.[45]

Sensing only lukewarm support, Marshall decided to convene an urgent meeting of the national anticovenant leaders and hold an extended conversation. On Sunday January 26, the attorneys gathered on the campus of Howard University to discuss the case more fully and further assess the prospects for appeal to the U.S. Supreme Court. While most of the major figures in the fight against restrictive agreements were in attendance, George Vaughn was noticeably absent. There would be no opportunity to convince him that the time was not right for a coordinated push forward.

The Association's legal staff had to make the best of the difficult situation Vaughn had put them in. The two lead attorneys in the Michigan case, Willis Graves and Francis Dent, expressed a good deal of optimism about the issues raised by the state supreme court's decision in *McGhee*. The fact that they had secured a direct ruling on the matter of whether court enforcement of covenants constituted state action under the Fourteenth Amendment made the case particularly promising. The Michigan court's explicit rejection of the state action argument seemed ripe for adjudication by the Supreme Court. Dent also emphasized his belief that "in the present state of international relations, the Supreme Court of the United States would be most loath to uphold and enforce restrictive covenants since it would be embarrassing to the American position in foreign policy in which we purport to be the leader of the democratic forces." The time was right and the issues were compelling, he insisted. His arguments won several of the attendees over to his view.[46]

Indeed, the *McGhee* case met several of the criteria the attorneys had established at the Chicago conference. The suit came from a northern city, from an area with particularly extensive residential restrictions, and raised Fourteenth Amendment grounds in a clear and direct manner. Yet the case had powerful detractors in the room. Thurgood Marshall and William H. Hastie both expressed doubts about the strength of the suit and covenant expert Spottswood Robinson felt that because the case record had no sociological testimony or data the NAACP might not be able to introduce that material on appeal. The dearth of socioeconomic evidence and relatively thin case record proved especially disconcerting to the national office's legal team and several of the consultants. Still, given that Vaughn's petition looked as though it would move ahead regardless of their reservations, the assembled lawyers wanted to give the *McGhee* case a fair hearing among themselves and take a hard look at its chances of winning certiorari.[47]

As the conferees laid out the bare logistics of an appeal, they speculated that Justices Frank Murphy and Wiley B. Rutledge might vote to grant certiorari—as they had in *Mays*—and that Justice Harold Burton certainly would not. If the pattern from *Mays* held true to form, they could also expect Justices Robert Jackson and Stanley Reed to abstain from voting, meaning they needed only two additional votes for a majority. However, the remainder of the Court seemingly "did not want to touch restrictive covenant cases at this time." Just as with Hastie's assessment of *Mays* eighteen months earlier, however, this opposition appeared to the attorneys as reluctance rather than hostility. What the campaign needed, the lawyers argued, was a case that was strong enough to "provide Justices Murphy and Rutledge with leverage with which to bring two more Justices to their side in order to grant us certiorari." In that light, *McGhee* seemed inadequate for the task. The meeting therefore adjourned with the understanding that "there may be Michigan cases coming up before the court better than the Sipes [v. McGhee] case on which to appeal, and that therefore we would not file a petition for certiorari until the very last moment." The short-term prospects for the NAACP's restriction cases looked uncertain at best.[48]

The Association's legal staff held out hope for more time to develop a handful of promising cases that conformed better to the standards that the attorneys had laid out in 1945. The national office had kept its eye on two cases in particular, one of Loren Miller's in Los Angeles and one of Loring Moore's in Chicago. Miller had emerged from the 1945 conference committed to the NAACP's plan for developing ideal test cases and with a full caseload of restriction suits. His Los Angeles Superior Court victory in Sugar Hill had won a great deal of acclaim nationally and seemed perfectly poised for adjudication by the U.S. Supreme Court. Here, the NAACP seemed willing to overlook the lack of socioeconomic evidence in the case record in part because of its high-profile petitioners and partly because of Miller's eagerness to work with the national legal team. Miller was so hopeful about these suits that while he waited for the opposing counsel to petition the California Supreme Court for a rehearing, he confided to Hastie that "it would be downright dirty if the plaintiffs refused to appeal." The plaintiffs did eventually challenge the superior court's ruling and Miller's hearing before California's high court came in the summer of 1946. All that was then left to do was wait for a decision and prepare another appeal. The California Supreme Court, however, was in no hurry to dispense with the issue and Miller waited with dwindling patience as month after month passed without word on his case. In the summer of 1947, Miller privately seethed to Charles Hamilton Houston about the delay, fuming that despite the yearlong interval, "no decision is in sight yet." As Miller's test case languished in limbo, the NAACP's legal staff remained hopeful, knowing that a decision would inevitably come at some point. Still, they increasingly kept an eye out for other promising litigation.[49]

By the end of 1946, a new favorite case was emerging in Chicago under the direction of veteran anticovenant attorney Loring Moore. Moore unabashedly touted his *Tovey v. Levy* case as the best existing hope for the fight against racial restrictions and key NAACP legal staffers and other interested observers concurred. In mid-December, Marian Wynn Perry wrote a detailed memorandum on the *Levy* case for Thurgood Marshall, explaining Moore's strategy. Moore's approach to covenant litigation involved creating a comprehensive case record—a process that pursued the twin goals of thoroughness and delay, stretching the will and resources of covenant defenders as far as possible while developing every conceivable legal ground for appeal. The Chicago attorney began his case by filing "lengthy motions to dismiss . . . in which every possible objection was raised from . . . technicalities . . . to such substantial defenses as the constitutional and public policy ones." When this failed, Moore responded with lengthy answers on each point. Perry noted that these motions pushed the timing of a potential review by the Illinois Supreme Court into the spring of 1948, some fifteen or sixteen months in the future.[50]

What made the *Levy* case seem particularly worth the wait was in part the emphasis Moore had placed on social scientific evidence in his arguments. Moore made the most out of the plethora of Chicago scholars studying race relations and urban conditions for African Americans, calling upon the talents of renowned urban scholars Robert Weaver, Horace Cayton, and St. Clair Drake for both testimony and help in the preparation of written briefs. Their efforts made up an important part of the "more than fifteen hundred pages of testimony and more than one hundred exhibits in the record" that Moore's thoroughness had yielded by January of 1947. In working closely with some of the best-known experts on black urban life and the issue of race in housing, Moore generated the kind of case record steeped in social scientific testimony that the NAACP had sought since the Chicago conference. Weaver's involvement with the case was particularly heartening for the Association's attorneys as he had been the leading voice in the sociological attack against covenants and had been supportive of the NAACP's campaign from its inception.[51]

The national office, however, continued to feel the mounting pressure from Vaughn's unwillingness to cooperate and from the increasingly plaintive cries of the Detroit branch office—the Association's largest local chapter—that urged the legal staff to move forward with *McGhee*. After corresponding regularly with the national office for several weeks, Edward Swan and Robert Bradby of the Detroit branch finally received the NAACP's determination about *McGhee*'s immediate future. "Our legal staff will bear in mind the time limit for further action," the national office promised, "but will assist in no action until the very last moment in the hope that a better case will appear than the Sipes [v. McGhee] case."[52]

As the ninety-day window for an appeal steadily elapsed, the Association held out hope that it could wrest control of the covenant campaign away from

Vaughn. The NAACP's legal team had a great deal more faith in Miller's and Moore's legal skills, intentions, and ability to work as a part of a team. They lacked any real confidence in Vaughn and the *Shelley* case, not to mention their own existing options for appeal. *McGhee*, the Association's best available test case, had the National Legal Committee deeply divided over its adequacy and chances for success. Many of the top anticovenant attorneys in the country and most of the NAACP leadership hoped to wait for one of the more carefully crafted test cases in the litigation pipeline to make its way through the appeals process before they agreed to pursue a Supreme Court review. Their hopes, however, mattered little if they could not persuade Vaughn to stop the Shelleys' case.

The Association's legal staff began applying what pressure it could to dissuade Vaughn and disrupt his momentum. In early February of 1947, Marshall again wrote to Vaughn and pleaded for what he deemed a more careful approach. "We hope that you will cooperate with us in withholding any future action on your case," he urged, "until we can all get together on it because we are more than anxious to work together." Marshall hoped to arrange another meeting of the nation's anticovenant attorneys to stall Vaughn's action and put him under the direct pressure and scrutiny of his peers. Vaughn, however, filed for a stay of the Missouri court's ruling just days after Marshall's letter—the first step in his preparations to seek certiorari.[53]

When these gentler attempts failed, the NAACP's attorneys quietly began working behind the scenes to disrupt Vaughn's case before he could file his final petition. Vaughn chose to wait another two months before officially submitting his case to the Supreme Court in order to line up supporters for the litigation. The NAACP's lawyers sensed an opportunity. While the Association had little influence over Vaughn directly, the attorneys maintained strong ties with some of the organizations that Vaughn reached out to for help. Perhaps by isolating the St. Louis lawyer from additional assistance, the Association might induce Vaughn to back down and thus regain control over the fate and direction of the covenant campaign.[54]

NAACP lawyers convinced at least one potential ally to reject Vaughn's request for aid. When Clifford Forster, the acting director of the American Civil Liberties Union (ACLU), contacted the national legal office for guidance on how to approach Vaughn's plea for support, Marian Wynn Perry warned Forster off in no uncertain terms. Perry informed him that in the Association's opinion *Shelley* was a "weak case" and that it would be "unwise to apply for certiorari at this time." Forster soon replied, "I have written to our St. Louis committee outlining to them exactly what you discussed with me. I told them that . . . it would be futile and perhaps dangerous to take the case to the Supreme Court." In a follow-up letter to the ACLU's St. Louis director, Forster echoed the NAACP's tone regarding Vaughn's fitness to lead the charge against covenants. "The issues raised should," he insisted, "be handled by experts in the field. The cases must be meticulously prepared and require a wealth of knowledge and expert handling. . . . Rather than build a record of rejected cases . . . we believe that we should wait until an opportune time presents itself." Perry's actions in this instance evidenced the limitations of the NAACP's willingness to support the efforts of local civil rights attorneys. A lawyer who threatened the Association's planning and control—who disrupted the order of that careful campaign—might well find himself on the wrong side of the NAACP's growing influence.[55]

Vaughn again remained undeterred. Though the Association's pressure slowed his march to the Supreme Court, in April of 1947 he finally submitted his petition for certiorari. The NAACP's cautious planning descended into temporary chaos. The only options at hand were to proceed with the *McGhee* case or to let Vaughn go it alone. If the Association failed to match or even to support Vaughn's effort, then the national office risked losing its leadership on the issue entirely or could face a now-strengthened precedent of the Supreme Court's refusal to review covenant suits. Yet *McGhee*'s complete lack of socioeconomic data and thin case record appeared nearly as daunting an obstacle for the campaign's future. The prospect of having to wait another two years or more developing a new set of test cases, or of losing control over the covenant issue entirely proved even less palatable to the national legal staff than proceeding with a case that provoked more anxiety than approbation. The Association finally bowed to pressure from the Detroit branch and directed Graves and Dent to file for certiorari in the *McGhee* case in mid-April, hitching the immediate fate of their cautious campaign to Vaughn's insurgent crusade.

IN LATE JUNE of 1947, Willis Graves and George Vaughn received a succinct message from Supreme Court clerk Charles Elmore Cropley. The U.S. Supreme Court, Cropley informed the attorneys, had agreed to hear the two cases in the fall term. Vaughn's gamble had unexpectedly paid off. NAACP legal staffer Constance Baker Motley later revealed that there had been "little hope [among Association officials] that the petition would be granted." When it was, she reflected, "we realized that the Supreme Court had offered us the opportunity to draw up our battle line for a last ditch fight against this form of residential segregation." Vaughn's seemingly reckless shove into the spotlight had suddenly given the anticovenant cause its opportunity for a command performance. The fight was on.[56]

By granting a review of *Shelley* and *McGhee*, the Court raised the stakes immeasurably for the campaign. A loss before the Court would do a great deal more damage to the cause than a denial of certiorari might have. The Court's decision escalated the consequences of what transpired within the NAACP's offices and between Association attorneys and George Vaughn over the remaining summer months. Despite the successful petition for certiorari, the NAACP still looked upon Vaughn as a dangerous wildcard. Their fears had at least some merit. Vaughn's go-it-alone approach and lack of experience with the exigencies of Supreme Court litigation posed some substantial risks right when the costs of any mistakes were higher than ever. Though he had exposed the Association's plan as an overly cautious one, Vaughn's independence now proved a legitimate liability. Indeed, it soon became clear that he was less prepared than his colleagues at the NAACP for the intense scrutiny that awaited. The future of black Americans' access to decent homes hinged on how quickly the lawyers could restore cooperation and organization amidst the chaos that had ensued earlier that year. With thirty years of fighting residential discrimination behind them, the NAACP now had less than six months to perfect what might be their last real chance to stave off the permanent entrenchment of segregation in America's neighborhoods.

Immediately, the Association set about making the *McGhee* suit appear as similar as possible to one of the test cases they had wanted to pursue in its place. The first step was to put lawyers more closely affiliated with the national office in charge of the appeal. Within days of the Court's decision to hear *Shelley* and *McGhee*, Thurgood Marshall asked Willis Graves and Francis Dent in Detroit to step down as lead counsel. Marshall wrote that "we should make every effort to have the arguments made by Charlie Houston and Loren Miller," two of the men most closely tied to the NAACP's national anticovenant campaign and exceptional fighters against restrictions. Houston was eager to participate because his cases in Washington did not appear as though they would pass through the appellate process quickly enough to join the Michigan and Missouri suits. Marshall's request of Graves and Dent was truly that; he had no authority to remove them or force them to relinquish their role. "I am making this merely as a suggestion," he wrote, "in the interest of getting complete harmony in the matter and would appreciate your reaction." In subsequent conversations, however, Marshall apparently gave the attorneys the impression that Miller was a veteran practitioner before the U.S. Supreme Court and thus better suited for the task, despite the reality that Miller had no prior experience at the Supreme Court bar. The two Detroit attorneys quickly agreed to the substitution—in part because Graves had been in poor health—and handed over their place in history for what they saw as the good of the case and their race. Even when this bit of misdirection about Miller's experience soon came to light, the two men apparently harbored no bitterness over Marshall's desire to push them aside. "I was not interested in personal credit," Dent later reflected, "so much as having the principle established. I think we adopted the right course."[57]

With the NAACP's handpicked duo now at the helm, the Association set about the work of clarifying and orchestrating their strategy for the rest of the summer. The legal team's next order of business was to schedule another strategy conference with every available expert and lawyer who had collectively helped shape the covenant campaign up to that point. Two weeks after the Supreme Court's notification, Marian Wynn Perry fired off a letter notifying interested parties that "in order that we may present every issue as clearly as possible, and cover all conceivable arguments which might be presented to the court, we are calling a conference of lawyers who have worked on these cases with us." The legal staff set the meeting date for September 6—roughly halfway through the time allotted for preparing the cases. Unlike the two previous convocations at neutral sites in Chicago and Washington, the NAACP scheduled this meeting at the Association's headquarters in New York, leaving no doubt about who was in charge.[58]

Despite the NAACP's strong push forward, doubts lingered about the strength of the *McGhee* and *Shelley* cases. To bolster the Association's chances, Charles Hamilton Houston filed a new petition seeking certiorari for the Washington cases. The Federal Circuit Court of Appeals in Washington, D. C., had denied Houston and Raphael Urciolo's motion for rehearing on the same day in June that the U.S. Supreme Court had agreed to review *McGhee* and *Shelley*. Houston believed his cases were so strong that for the first time in his long career "I actually hoped [the court of appeals] would decide against me and was afraid I might win." He had pursued a rehearing, he admitted, only out of concern for the immediate best interests of his clients and had secretly hoped to fail "lest it might be granted and spoil my chances of applying to the U.S. Supreme Court." Because the court of appeals declined to reopen his cases, Houston was now free to file for certiorari in time to join the *Shelley* and *McGhee* suits. "This time," he sighed, "thank Heaven—the court would not see it my way." The attorneys now raced to bring the cases of the Hurds, Rowes, Stewarts, and Savages into the fold.[59]

Houston and a small cadre of lawyers including civil rights advocates Spottswood Robinson and Phineas Indritz now worked frenetically to refine a petition for certiorari in the Washington suits. They filed in mid-August and for two months, amid the NAACP's intensive preparation of the *McGhee* suit, Houston and his colleagues anxiously awaited word. Houston approached George Vaughn with the idea of asking the Court for a postponement of *Shelley* until after a decision on certiorari in the *Hurd* case. Vaughn apparently gave some consideration to the idea, but wavered in offering a definitive answer because of his desire to avoid any further delays in his appeal. In late October the Court agreed to hear Houston's collection of cases immediately following the presentation for *McGhee*. The Washington attorneys would have only a few weeks to prepare their arguments.[60]

While Houston, Urciolo, and their clients had waited for the Court's decision about their companion suits, the national legal staff had continued to ready the *McGhee* case. The NAACP's New York covenant strategy conference in September 1947 provided the Association with a chance to reassert control and establish an overarching structure for the potentially complex litigation ahead. The gathering served two important functions for the NAACP lawyers. First, it offered a chance to wrestle Vaughn into line with the Association's approach to arguing the cases before the Court. Second, it presented the assembled attorneys and experts with a valuable forum to debate ideas and air concerns about specific legal arguments while obtaining immediate feedback from a wide array of their colleagues. By challenging one another and laying out all the tactics and options available, they might just map out a feasible path to victory.

Even if the Association's legal team had forgiven Vaughn for ignoring their pleas for caution and patience when applying for certiorari—and it was by no means clear that they had—serious doubts lingered about the specific statutory and constitutional grounds that Vaughn had decided to argue before the U.S. Supreme Court. While the NAACP's arguments in *McGhee* revolved primarily around the central claim that judicial enforcement of covenants constituted discriminatory state action under the Fourteenth Amendment, Vaughn elected to ground his arguments primarily in the Thirteenth Amendment—which prohibited slavery and involuntary servitude—and the Civil Rights Act of 1866. The main concern of many of the strategists in September was to corral what they saw as an overly ambitious, idealistic, or simply foolhardy set of contentions from their Gateway City colleague. Vaughn, who was now set to argue first before the Court, threatened to undercut the legitimacy of the NAACP's entire set of arguments by framing the issue on Thirteenth Amendment grounds that the justices would view very unfavorably. His colleagues at the Association were not shy about telling him so.[61]

The NAACP's pressure on Vaughn to drop these claims and join the Association's line of argument came in two waves. First, the NAACP used its financial resources to coerce Vaughn into cooperating. The monetary burdens of litigating the *Shelley* case accumulated quickly for the REBA in the Gateway City. In the summer of 1947, as they prepared to fund Vaughn's U.S. Supreme Court challenge, the brokers initiated a local fund-raising campaign that reached out to the St. Louis branch of the NAACP. When branch president David Grant wrote to Thurgood Marshall soliciting support from the national office for a potential donation, Marshall responded that while the Association had been happy to support local anticovenant efforts that collaborated with the NAACP's campaign, "we have not had that type of cooperation concerning the case of Shelley vs. Kraemer." Rather than flatly denying the appeal for assistance and perhaps to ensure that Vaughn and his backers actually attended the September meeting, Marshall raised the possibility of revisiting the issue at the conference.[62]

When September came, NAACP attorneys used the proceedings to expose publicly the weaknesses in Vaughn's arguments and challenged him to defend his claims on each possible point. Vaughn found himself on the defensive throughout the conference, facing extensive and occasionally harsh questioning and criticism from a significant portion of the assembled experts. Much of the worry focused on Vaughn's decision to argue from the Thirteenth Amendment. Legal expert Robert Lee Hale had some particularly choice words regarding Vaughn's approach. If Vaughn proceeded with his current argument, Hale insisted, "the Court would not listen. . . . Prohibition to buy property shown as slavery would not be a good point. The Court would think you had a weak case if you relied on the Thirteenth Amendment." A handful of other participants repeatedly tried to convince the St. Louis attorney that Fourteenth Amendment grounds would better suit his arguments. At one point, Vaughn's exasperation led him to exclaim that it was "not necessary to discuss this point at the present time," though the conference's stenographer noted that "there were many who wished to continue the discussion."[63]

Even after Vaughn pushed through the strongest of the challenges to his claims, he found himself on the defensive yet again. At times, the questioning resembled a mock trial—something that would have seemed less confrontational at a legal conference had Vaughn not been the only one subjected to the high level of scrutiny. The assembled attorneys probed Vaughn's arguments for weaknesses, lobbing two or three questions and citations at a time toward the beleaguered lawyer. They pressed Vaughn on how he might defend the state action concept of the Fourteenth Amendment. When his frustrated answer proved unsatisfactory for his colleagues, Charles Hamilton Houston chastised him and warned that "you will be questioned further than that [by the Court]." At the end of the day, the group had turned so far against him that the NAACP record keepers purged from the official transcript the only positive words that Vaughn had received from his peers. Though Houston had expressed his belief that Vaughn should "be congratulated on being the first to go for certiorari in a case of this type," someone quickly struck through even this begrudging praise with an unforgiving line of ink.[64]

Marshall also resumed his financial maneuvers at the New York summit. When Vaughn arrived at the gathering with his friend and principal supporter, James T. Bush, Marshall negotiated with Bush in the hopes of using financial pressure to coerce Vaughn into a closer partnership with the Association's attorneys. Some days later, Marshall wrote to David Grant disclosing the agreement's details. "The Executive Committee of our Board of Directors has agreed to contribute a total of $1,000 . . . toward the expenses of the restrictive covenant case," Marshall wrote. He then revealed that the funds were "conditioned upon an agreement with Mr. Vaughn to work in close cooperation with the National Legal Committee and the staff of the NAACP under the direction of Charles H. Houston." Furthermore, he continued, "it is also conditioned upon the agreement that Mr. Vaughn will . . . work with the other lawyers who are handling similar restrictive covenant cases." The NAACP was understandably wary about funding Vaughn's rogue endeavor without any preconditions so they decided to withhold any disbursal of funds until after they appeared before the Supreme Court. Still the legal staff hoped that the shrewd proffering of the Association's resources might finally restrain their colleague in St. Louis. Their offer of $1,000 represented a substantial investment—though they had already provided a much larger sum for Loring Moore's *Levy* case in Chicago—especially as the national office assumed complete financial responsibility for the *McGhee* case.[65]

For the remainder of the month of September, however, Marshall and Bush exchanged a volley of confrontational letters disputing what the Association should expect from Vaughn in exchange for the promise of assistance. Two weeks after the conference Bush apparently came to believe that the Association wanted Vaughn removed from the case completely, something that he adamantly refused to consider. In his reply, Marshall seemed both baffled and indignant at Bush's tone. "I told you personally, and the record will show," Marshall insisted, "that this Association has never forced a lawyer to step aside in his own case." Marshall reminded Bush that the issue "is bigger than Vaughn, you, me or anyone else. . . . There is no question of glory involved in these cases. It is a question of getting a job done and the only way to really get a job done is for everyone to roll up his sleeves and work with everyone else in a spirit of cooperation." Marshall would later confide privately to David Grant that most observers generally agreed that the St. Louis case was in serious disarray and that the REBA was simply looking to lay the blame for this on the national office. "For the life of me," an increasingly bewildered Marshall wrote, "I cannot understand what is behind these moves of Mr. Bush, and I can only hope that we will some time down the line be able to work with them." The relationship between the REBA and the national office would only continue to deteriorate as the court date grew closer.[66]

Though the disputes lingered well into the middle of 1948, the final straw came for Marshall when a related group of St. Louis anticovenant advocates wrote to him late in 1947. In a letter on behalf of the REBA's Citizens Committee, chairman Herman Dreer berated the NAACP's legal staff. Concerned St. Louisans, Dreer wrote, "do not at all like the manner in which you have responded to our appeals for assistance from the national organization . . . your attitude is one of indifference or neglect . . . to our regret you have failed us." Marshall took exception to the entire tone and content of the letter and attempted to set the record straight with a stern rebuttal. Reminding Dreer of the NAACP's belief in the importance of all the cases at hand, Marshall detailed the utter lack of consultation that Vaughn had sought in the preceding months. Marshall's statements made clear that the NAACP would never be content to reduce its role to that of simply a philanthropic or lending institution for civil rights litigants, distributing money without any other involvement in what transpired. The whole premise and success of the Association's legal advocacy depended upon collaboration, exchange, and support between local activists and the national office.[67]

Through its nationwide networks of communication and organization, the NAACP saw itself as bringing the benefits of structure as well as financial assistance to the individual struggles of civil rights advocates. The two assets came hand in hand. Lawyers who sought the Association's backing to take their local issues to the national level could not expect to receive funds while refusing to coordinate their efforts with the NAACP's veteran cadre of legal experts.

THE NEW YORK CONFERENCE, of course, did not revolve completely around George Vaughn. The Association made its preparations for the *McGhee* case as well. Two significant conversations focused on how best to argue the scope of judicial state action and whether to frame the impact of restrictive covenants in terms of the collective effects of widespread agreements or the detrimental results of individual restrictions. The concern over the state action argument revolved around how the attorneys could advance the idea that judicial decisions constituted an exercise of state authority. William H. Hastie first raised the point out of pragmatic concerns. "I believe," he warned his colleagues, "that the Supreme Court is afraid of opening up a broad field of new situations in which it will be in the position of reviewing action of state courts." If every state court decision amounted to an exercise of state power rather than a presumably impartial adjudication of disputes, then the U.S. Supreme Court would radically extend the parameters of its jurisdiction. The Supreme Court, Hastie and others in attendance felt, would reject any universal attempt to cast lower courts as state agents rather than arbiters of state law. The NAACP risked having a Supreme Court that was "emotionally set against" them or "frightening" the Court into a negative ruling unless they narrowly defined the type of state action they sought to classify as discriminatory. In asking the Supreme Court to break new ground, the Association did not want to present the justices with too big a legal weapon for fear that they would hesitate to use it.[68]

Thus the attorneys tried to define what constituted impermissible state action by local courts in these cases. Hastie proposed an argument that would ask the Court "to go no further than to say that the [lower] Court shall not do under the Fourteenth Amendment anything the legislature cannot do under the [same]." Others present held fast to their belief that "every action by a state court is state action," but maintained that the discrimination at issue in these cases was unique in its legal form. Ultimately the lawyers and consultants came to a general agreement that Hastie's definition would best serve their interests in this case. Because the Supreme Court had found legislative racial zoning to be unconstitutional in *Buchanan v. Warley* (1917), the argument held, local courts should not be permitted to enforce contracts that accomplished the same results. "Private" zoning, enforced by the courts, should receive the same constitutional scrutiny as city-mandated residential segregation. This line of reasoning borrowed from the language and concerns of housing experts like Charles Abrams who had warned that "it is now possible that the use of restrictive covenants could blanket a whole community and a whole town if enforced by the court."[69]

Still, even this consensus fomented some additional legal debate. Loren Miller, for one, was concerned about arguing solely against the aggregate effects of restrictions in urban areas. He did not want the assembled lawyers—or more importantly the Supreme Court—to lose sight of the fact that even "if there were only one [covenant], you are dealing with a question of high public importance." As a result, he cautioned his colleagues not to rely completely on the concept of private zoning, but to emphasize additionally the harm, injustice, and significance of every single restrictive agreement in place in America's cities. While a handful of the conferees urged Miller not to try and "win too much at one time," his point resonated with the many in the group. This argument evinced a boldness and determination that wanted to settle for nothing less than a full acknowledgment by the Supreme Court that these contracts in and of themselves were unjust and immoral instruments of fear, hatred, and inequity.[70]

At the New York conference's conclusion, the advocates emerged with a reinvigorated sense of resolve. Only ten weeks remained before the attorneys in these cases would submit their briefs to the Court. The meeting had successfully imposed some structure and direction as preparations moved ahead. Out of the confusion and worry that George Vaughn created in the spring with his unwelcome, but successful, shove forward, the NAACP had marshaled its resources and restored as much of its original plan as it could under the circumstances. As the Association remade *McGhee* into the best possible test case, however, one crucial step remained.

Social Science and Segregation: The NAACP's "Brandeis Brief"

Throughout all of their jousting with Vaughn and the frantic preparations that ensued, the NAACP legal staff never lost sight of the nagging fact that the *McGhee* case record failed to include any social scientific arguments about the consequences of discrimination. This presented a significant problem for the team taking charge of the case. A centerpiece of the Association's postwar campaign against covenants had been the desire to integrate a burgeoning body of scholarship about housing segregation into its attorneys' legal arguments. For at least a decade the NAACP's lawyers had experimented with social scientific material as a part of their briefs, but in the aftermath of World War II they became markedly more determined in their desire to bring sociology, psychology, and economics into the courtroom. Their efforts in the covenant cases would serve as a turning point in their use of the social sciences as tactical instruments within litigation campaigns.

Though the explicit use of socioeconomic data in its legal work was a process that took until the 1930s to develop in earnest, the Association had deep ties with social scientists that dated back to the organization's founding. Indeed, the NAACP's multifaceted activism—in which litigation, lobbying efforts, and public relations campaigns frequently overlapped in complementary ways—had ensured that the Association's attorneys long understood the potential value of arguments rooted in social facts as a strategy for shaping the outcome of cases. Their litigation had always developed alongside broader institutional commitments that emphasized the need to study racial prejudice's impact on society and extolled the importance of disseminating that information widely. There was, in other words, never a stark dividing line between the NAACP's legal work and its efforts to educate Americans about race and racial inequality. What would change over the first half of the twentieth century was the form that relationship took.[71]

Just as important as the Association's long-standing ties to social scientists were the legal department's significant imbrications with the early twentieth-century evolution of sociolegal thought. Attorneys affiliated with the NAACP, including Charles Hamilton Houston, Albert Pillsbury, Karl Llewellyn, and Robert Lee Hale had all been eager practitioners—and in some instances, leaders—of emerging jurisprudential trends that saw great value in the use of data and nonlegal scholarship. Each of these individuals brought these progressive sensibilities to bear on their work with the Association and in turn helped to shape the organization's litigation strategies. As the legal battle against Jim Crow took shape, the attorneys embraced a gradual transition toward increasingly substantial uses of social scientific material in the courtroom.[72]

Despite these extensive connections, the Association's lawyers had generally refrained from deploying socioeconomic data in their legal briefs for the first two decades of their legal work. The NAACP's two early housing cases, *Buchanan v. Warley* (1917) and *Corrigan v. Buckley* (1926), offered an example of this reticence. As badly as they may have wished for the Court to understand the practical consequences of housing discrimination, not a single nonlegal citation informed their arguments. Instead, it was the Association's opponents in *Corrigan* who deployed the prevailing public scholarship of the day. Attorneys for the white homeowners in the case linked the propriety of residential segregation to prohibitions against racial intermarriage by citing a handful of popular tracts decrying the "amalgamation . . . of the races" as the "most dangerous" threat to the continued vitality of American civilization. The prevalence of such beliefs within social scientific scholarship at the time had contributed significantly to the NAACP's reluctance to offer sociological arguments in their written pleas. It would be another decade before the Association's attorneys began to dabble with social scientific data and statistics as a part of their briefs.[73]

By the late 1930s, as the NAACP's legal team trained their focus on the disparities in segregated education, the shift began to take shape. In the landmark *Gaines v. Canada* (1938) case contesting Missouri's discriminatory practices in postgraduate education, the Association's brief included a two-page statistical appendix highlighting school enrollments, literacy rates, and the distribution of higher education funding along racial lines. The attorneys used this data to demonstrate the inequalities of Jim Crow schooling in the state, but this proved a rather tepid experiment that would not become a regular practice in the ensuing years. While Charles Hamilton Houston, in his capacity as an NAACP attorney, would urge other lawyers to pursue sociologically oriented legal arguments during the late 1930s, the litigators at the NAACP's national office would only use nonlegal citations in amicus curiae briefs in educational and labor cases where they were not directly involved in the litigation at hand. They still hesitated to build their own cases on a record steeped in social scientific material.[74]

In the briefs for *McGhee* and *Hurd*, however, the NAACP would employ socioeconomic data as it never had before. By introducing legal arguments imbued with social scientific scholarship—a practice known in legal circles as a "Brandeis brief"—the NAACP now wholeheartedly embraced a tactic that had first appeared four decades earlier. In 1908, a young Jewish labor reformer and activist named Josephine Goldmark along with her brother-in-law, future Supreme Court justice Louis Brandeis, had pioneered the use of nonlegal information in this fashion. The NAACP would steadily turn toward this strategy in the interwar period and reach a decisive turning point in the covenant cases. Though the Association's attorneys would still rely primarily on constitutional claims, their choice to emphasize the social consequences of segregation more than ever before reveals a great deal about the opportunities that civil rights advocates felt they could seize in the wake of World War II. It seemed possible in the postwar moment to challenge fundamentally the rationalizations and supposed propriety of racial discrimination as a social norm or a social good.[75]

As the NAACP legal team worked feverishly throughout the summer and fall of 1947 to inject socioeconomic material into their briefs for the Supreme Court, their efforts highlighted both the importance the Association assigned to these arguments and the growing impact of the social sciences on the process of civil rights litigation. In *McGhee* and *Hurd*, the Association's attorneys would ask the Court more directly than ever whether American society could truly afford to accept racial intolerance in one of its most costly forms. The struggle was how best to pose the question.[76]

GRAPPLING WITH WHAT SOON became their accidental test case in *McGhee*, the Association's attorneys and consultants had devoted considerable discussion to the absence of any detailed sociological claims. As Willis Graves would later reflect, he and Francis Dent had never intended to "attempt any sociological defense" in the case. This had proven to be perhaps the greatest sticking point for the national legal team throughout the first half of 1947. Indeed, immediately after Loren Miller took the reins of *McGhee's* litigation in July, he set about preparing social scientific material for his arguments to remedy this omission.[77]

Since 1946, Miller had tied the future success of the anticovenant fight to the use of "the sociological data at our command." Now with his own Supreme Court test case in which to experiment, Miller quickly wrote to Thurgood Marshall to express his conviction that "extensive 'sociological briefs' should be filed." Simultaneously in Washington, Charles Hamilton Houston insisted on consulting "a panel of anthropologists, economists and sociologists" as the Hurds' case moved forward. Houston's verve for sociological arguments on appeal was unsurprising given his long-standing interest in the practice and his enthusiastic use of Howard University's social science faculty—including E. Franklin Frazier—in his local cases like *Hurd*. Both Miller and Houston were determined to make social scientific material a central point of contention in their pleas.[78]

Houston's own commitment to using socioeconomic scholarship found an equally adamant partner in Phineas Indritz, his new colleague on the *Hurd* appeal. Several times over the summer, Indritz wrote to prominent social scientists and housing experts soliciting their opinions and scholarly contributions for the Washington cases. In each request he plainly stated his belief that "the attack in the Supreme Court . . . must be supported by a full sociological presentation. Legal arguments, standing alone, may find a less fertile field for acceptance in this controversy which has so frequently been dominated by unspoken emotional preconceptions and misconceptions."

Again and again the attorneys in the covenant cases showed a remarkable insistence and urgency as they prepared their social scientific arguments.[79]

One of the NAACP's clearest indications of support for combining socio-economic and legal claims came in the form of financial allocations. When the legal staff drew up a proposed budget for the cases as they approached the Supreme Court, they set aside more than 40 percent of the funds for the research and preparation of socioeconomic data. Coupled with the national office's projected investment of anywhere from $8,500 to $12,000 in Loring Moore's *Tovey v. Levy* test case in Chicago—which won the NAACP's backing primarily due to the strength of its social scientific presentations—this meant that the Association was ready to commit an astonishingly large amount of its litigation money to chasing the strongest possible Brandeis brief.[80]

What made the legal team's dedication to this tactic all the more startling was that nearly all of their previous experiments with socioeconomic arguments in the courtroom had been fairly restrained. In an organization known for its general attitude of caution in civil rights litigation, the NAACP's lawyers now enthusiastically launched themselves headlong into waters in which they had only gently waded prior to that point. The relative ease and certainty with which the Association proceeded on this track testified to the urgency and innovation that postwar attacks on segregation increasingly cultivated. The moment and the issue demanded a new boldness—even if couched in the NAACP's highly organized and initially slow-developing campaign. Throughout the pursuit and preparation of their covenant test case, then, the organization seemed to harbor no doubts about the necessity and utility of a substantial Brandeis brief.

This unflinching confidence stemmed from a transformative movement within the social science disciplines and in American intellectual culture called scientific antiracism. Taking hold in the interwar period and flourishing in the postwar years, scientific antiracism strove to uproot the beliefs and practices of previous generations and had a profound influence on the NAACP's leadership. The Association relied heavily upon this emerging body of scholarship as it forged a growing alliance between activists and academics that quickly solidified the shift in its litigation tactics during the postwar era. Because the NAACP's legal team generally lacked the resources and personnel to generate original research on its own, the success of the Brandeis brief in the covenant cases would hinge upon the legal team's ability to mobilize a group of scholars who had begun to challenge the conventional academic wisdom about race in America.

In the first decades of the twentieth century, most of the available social scientific work about race had supported popular stereotypes asserting the innate inferiority of African Americans and the appropriateness of segregation as a natural order for society. Early scholarship in the social sciences typically defended the concept of an inherently superior white race and presented racial discrimination and the subordination of black Americans as the only reasonable solution in a racially diverse nation. For these intellectuals, the condition of African Americans and their place as second-class citizens was the inevitable result of natural deficiencies in their character. While this canon of "scientific racism" had helped provide an academic rationale for segregation, an antiracist intellectual counteroffensive took shape in the interwar period and slowly began to win out.[81]

Scientific antiracism, especially in the fields of anthropology, sociology, and psychology, gradually promoted an evolution in scholarly thinking. The interwar decades witnessed a shift away from Social Darwinist and sociobiological conflations of race, character, and caste. Over time, conventional thought in these disciplines gave way to a new stance that interpreted the conditions for African Americans in the United States as the product of white racial prejudice rather than biology. This understanding cast Jim Crow segregation as a problem and an impediment to progress rather than a sensible approach to social organization. In place of the intellectual authority that had strengthened racial prejudice for the first quarter of the century, a growing number of scholars began to portray this intolerance as irrational, harmful, and without a basis in scientific reality. As social scientists rejected theories of black biological inferiority, racial inequality came to represent a potentially solvable problem rather than an acceptable feature of American life.[82]

When the nation plunged once again into international warfare in the 1940s, scientific antiracism and the authority of antiracist scholars as social analysts gained increasing credibility. This new wave of social scientific thought had struggled to gain a large following during the 1930s, but the events of World War II focused national scrutiny on the problems that segregation caused while simultaneously building public confidence in social scientists as interpreters of societal conditions. The war solidified and expanded the popular legitimacy that these disciplines had steadily achieved in the quarter century prior to Pearl Harbor. America's wartime government invested unprecedented levels of trust and resources in social scientists' research, turning to these scholars—and especially social psychologists—for a variety of tasks including the assessment of national morale, the analysis and development of propaganda, and the evaluation of racial tensions on the home front. These opportunities provided scholars with extraordinary access and governmental support and helped reify the national public's faith in these disciplines as accurate and useful methods of social analysis.[83]

More importantly, the specter of Nazi Germany's racial ideologies forced many Americans to take a long, hard look at race relations in the United States. Within the social sciences, American scholars witnessed the potential consequences of theories that zealously exalted the biological superiority of one race over another as the physical and intellectual atrocities of their enemy unfolded. This sobering recognition of the extremes that scientific racism could promote and defend gave renewed purpose to the activism of antiracist scholars in the 1940s. Increasingly, the NAACP found at its disposal a multiracial network of social scientists who energetically championed civil rights causes and eagerly lent their expertise to the Association's courtroom efforts.[84]

At the same time, the war also influenced public perceptions of scientific antiracism—expanding both the public receptiveness and the size of the audience that these scholars enjoyed. As World War II came to represent a struggle between democratic freedom and Nazi totalitarianism, the gap between America's egalitarian promises and the stark realities of racial injustice garnered increasing national and international scrutiny. The vitality of Jim Crow and race prejudice forced many Americans to realize that the difference between their country's racial ideologies and those of their Nazi adversaries were at times paper-thin. This unsettling awareness led a growing number of Americans to embrace the sort of racially egalitarian ideas that the nation's social scientists had begun promoting in even greater earnest. Though scientific racism's legacy and proponents would linger long after the war's conclusion, by the late 1940s social science disciplines had largely overcome many of their early opinions about racial difference and discrimination.[85]

A high point of this rapidly culminating shift came with the publication of Swedish social scientist Gunnar Myrdal's *An American Dilemma: The Negro Problem and Modern Democracy* in 1944. When it appeared in the midst of World War II, Myrdal's work captured and epitomized the spirit of scientific antiracism and the changing intellectual consensus about racial subjugation in America. Myrdal and the legion of scholars who prepared the massive study offered a comprehensive interdisciplinary look at the problems confronting African Americans and the prejudices that undergirded inequality. The tome helped to consolidate an extensive body of interwar social scientific work on race and distill the message of racial egalitarianism for broad popular consumption. *American Dilemma* received overwhelmingly positive scholarly acclaim and remarkable public recognition. The NAACP's attorneys took notice and soon began preparations for their most expansive Brandeis brief yet.[86]

THE CAMPAIGN AGAINST housing discrimination offered an ideal issue around which to build a set of socioeconomic arguments. Few developments sparked more intensive social scientific scrutiny in the 1940s than the growth of America's racial ghettos. Antiracist scholars trained their considerable expertise on the nation's cities and produced an array of studies that would become pillars of the NAACP's arguments in the covenant cases. By 1946, this scholarship and the burgeoning intellectual networks between academics and activists had convinced the Association's legal team that a robust sociological presentation could and would aid the organization's campaign against residential segregation. Exactly what would constitute success, however, remained somewhat unclear.[87]

For all of its potential, the Brandeis brief represented a tool of litigation whose effects were largely hypothetical. In theory the social scientific material would show that racial discrimination caused the severe hardships that African American communities endured and this would somehow influence the Court's decision making. Loren Miller was particularly adamant that sociological data would help strengthen the argument that covenants worked contrary to public policy. Yet all of the NAACP's lawyers understood that direct causation was something extraordinarily difficult to prove through scattered psychological, public health, economic, and sociological studies. Furthermore, the Court could easily choose to ignore the data entirely as irrelevant to the constitutional issues at stake. As a result, one of the key challenges for the NAACP in crafting their Brandeis brief was how to make the theoretical potential of this strategy speak to the practical needs and difficulties both of black urban communities and the Association's agenda.[88]

This tension led the NAACP to establish a dual purpose for their foray into social scientific arguments in the covenant cases. The primary objective remained an attempt to convince the Supreme Court of the severity of the burdens and the extent of the consequences that flowed from housing discrimination. The brief's secondary function, however, was as a tool for educating the public regarding the costs of residential segregation. Indeed, the Association's legal staff ultimately wanted their Brandeis brief for the covenant cases to provide a nearly comprehensive survey "of all of the sociological studies that have been made on the question of restrictive covenants and housing." Though the NAACP's penchant for wide-ranging surveys was nothing new, the use of a legal brief to present and disseminate such extensive findings was. Whether or not the arguments prevailed before the Court, the NAACP planned in advance "to reprint this material for general distribution to all colleges and organizations in order to build wholesome support for the fight against restrictive covenants." The potential to use the brief as both a legal and an educational instrument ensured that even if the NAACP had misjudged the Court's willingness to entertain social scientific data, the attorneys' efforts would still serve to advance the anticovenant cause. If, on the other hand, the Court did acknowledge and accept the sociological arguments, then the Association would have a ready-made study to help counter public resistance and ease the decision's implementation.[89]

With this agenda in mind, the NAACP's legal team still confronted the basic difficulty of determining how to assemble the massive volume of data they would need in order to write the brief. Part of what made the covenant cases a turning point in the Association's experimentation with this tactic was the legal department's appointment of their first-ever "socioeconomic analyst" just as the litigation accelerated toward the Supreme Court. In 1947, Thurgood Marshall hired a recent graduate from NYU's Sociology Department—a young Jewish woman by the name of Annette Peyser. Over the coming year, Peyser served as a crucial liaison between the NAACP's national office and the cadre of social scientists working feverishly to compile the Brandeis brief. Her hiring marked an important shift in how the Association's litigators would approach the use of social scientific arguments.[90]

Annette Peyser had grown up in a white-collar immigrant neighborhood near Fordham University in the Bronx, the daughter of a successful accountant. She followed her father's footsteps to NYU, where she studied sociology and worked closely with renowned political scientist Harold Lasswell. It was Lasswell's influence and his strong letter of recommendation that ultimately secured Peyser a temporary job with the NAACP as a "press content analyst" in autumn of 1946. Her academic training, idealism, and work ethic earned her a quick series of promotions within the organization. After a few months, her work had come to the attention of the legal team.[91]

Peyser's talents caught Marshall's eye after she compiled a study on the "inequities in educational opportunity between negroes and whites in the South" at the request of the legal department. Her report came on the heels of the NAACP's most recent experiment with a Brandeis brief late in 1946. The Association had filed an amicus brief in support of *Mendez v. Westminster*, an educational discrimination case regarding the segregation of Mexican and Mexican American students in Southern California schools. Because the suit was not affiliated with any NAACP branches and the Association's only involvement with the case came late in the appellate process—just as it reached the Ninth Circuit Court of Appeals—it offered an ideal opportunity for the legal staff to continue their dabbling with the kind of social scientific arguments they soon hoped to use in one of their own cases. Amicus filings allowed the NAACP to conduct dry runs with the tactic without any real risks or costs in the event that a case lost. The resulting brief, authored primarily by attorney Robert Carter, had drawn from a handful of the leading sociological texts of the day including Myrdal's *American Dilemma*. Carter dedicated a substantial portion of the brief to an argument rooted in both statistical data and a larger claim about the social costs of racial discrimination. *Westminster* proved to be an important experiment, but was still tremendously restrained in scope and scale compared to what the NAACP's lawyers would undertake with Peyser's help less than a year later in *McGhee*.[92]

When Peyser joined the legal staff full time in early 1947, her primary responsibility was to prepare for the Association's next attempt at a Brandeis brief when an opportunity arose. Over the following months, she often labored alongside attorney Marian Wynn Perry and served as an important conduit between the national office and the network of scholars eager to aid in the NAACP's litigation efforts. She would work almost exclusively on the restrictive covenant cases once the Supreme Court granted certiorari that summer. Marshall described Peyser's duties as the legal team's first and only socioeconomic analyst, explaining that she provided "research in all extralegal fields connected with our work," "preparation of memoranda and sections of briefs on such extra-legal matters," and the "answering of correspondence and requests for information on such . . . matters." The attorneys increasingly relied upon Peyser to survey and distill the findings of any relevant scholarship regarding the consequences of racial discrimination across an array of academic disciplines. And they needed it done quickly.[93]

Peyser, thankfully, received a good deal of help in the buildup to the covenant cases. Knowing that a task of this size and importance would be too much for any one person to handle, especially considering the fact that Peyser was neither a lawyer nor a formally trained academic, the attorneys left the initial work of compiling the relevant data to a committee of consultants. At the September covenant conference in New York, the assembled delegates selected a team of ten individuals including urban scholars Robert Weaver and Louis Wirth along with attorneys Loring Moore, William R. Ming, Byron Miller, and Ruth Weyand to spearhead the preparations. Peyser's inclusion on the committee only further evidenced her significance in the national office's objectives.[94]

It was scholar/activist Louis Wirth, however, who had laid much of the groundwork for the new committee's hurried efforts. Since May of 1947—months before the Supreme Court had agreed to hear the covenant cases—Wirth had used his position as president of the ACRR to direct resources toward "the development of a model brief in which the scientific evidence, where now available and obtainable, can be brought to bear upon judicial decisions" in restrictive covenant litigation. The ACRR's board unanimously viewed their support of the NAACP's research as being of "singular importance" and allocated thousands of dollars toward the project. As a result Wirth could step readily into his role as chairman of the Brandeis brief committee and put the full resources of the ACRR at its disposal.[95]

Under the direction of Wirth, Weaver, and Miller, the group swiftly amassed a comprehensive sixteen-chapter study, which they released to the conferees three weeks later. The speed with which the team assembled the data resulted in part from the early legwork that both Peyser and the ACRR had done, from Weaver's efforts following the 1945 Chicago conference, and from the pragmatic decision to gather existing research rather than attempt to conduct any original work in the limited time available. The final document examined a wide range of issues from the current state of housing conditions for urban black residents to the effects of discrimination and isolation on black communities. Chapters covered the connections between segregation and health, "Crime, Delinquency, Vice and Family Disorganization," "the Quality of Public Services," "Access to Economic Opportunities," and "Public Peace and Order." Another chapter promised to illuminate the "Psychological Effects of Segregation and Its Relationship to a Democratic Order." The committee made sure to bring the full weight and breadth of scientific antiracist scholarship to bear in pronouncing the evils of covenants.[96]

The task then became one of translating this specially commissioned study into an effective legal brief. Accordingly, Peyser took on added responsibilities as the preparations proceeded. Throughout the month of October, Peyser and Perry sorted through the data and pored over the arguments and citations in Wirth and Weaver's report. As they traveled back and forth between New York and Washington, coordinating with both teams of attorneys arguing the *McGhee* and *Hurd* cases, they carried well-worn copies of some of the key texts on race and housing. In the end, their efforts yielded an astonishingly thorough presentation of social scientific claims in the briefs. Their reliance on this nonlegal data far surpassed anything the Association had done before.[97]

Indeed, each of the NAACP's previous attempts at a Brandeis brief had proven fairly limited in their scope. Even in the amicus filings from recent years, where the Association's lawyers had explored the use of social scientific data more freely, the legal team had never cited more than eighteen nonlegal sources in a single case. They matched that number in one of their own suits for the first time in an Oklahoma law school desegregation case, *Sipuel v. Board of Regents*, which arrived at the Supreme Court within a week of *McGhee* and *Hurd*. The NAACP's sociological arguments in *Sipuel*, submitted within a few days of the covenant case briefs, spanned fifteen pages of the document and doubled the number of extralegal citations from *Westminster* the previous year. This was a substantial escalation that demonstrated the NAACP's growing use of the Brandeis brief tactic. But even *Sipuel's* social scientific elements would pale in comparison to those in the covenant cases.[98]

For *McGhee* and *Hurd*, the legal team pulled out all the stops. In the Detroit case, they cited eighty-three different social science texts, government agency publications, journal and magazine articles, and NAACP pamphlets. Socioeconomic research filled more than forty pages of the document. The scale of the effort was staggering. Not to be outdone, Charles Hamilton Houston's arguments in *Hurd* relied upon 140 different nonlegal citations and occupied over sixty pages of text. With an additional fourteen pages of maps and tables in an appendix, social scientific material comprised just under half of the entire Washington case brief. Marian Wynn Perry later reflected that it was at this moment when "sociology was used for the first time in a major way" by the legal team. These filings in the covenant cases marked an unprecedented shift in the NAACP's reliance upon social scientific data in the courtroom. Now there could be no mistaking the legal team's commitment to the tactic or their sincere belief in its potential power.[99]

ALL OF THIS DATA in the covenant cases focused around two key objectives. First, the Brandeis briefs imparted the extent and the consequences of the hardships that black communities faced due to residential segregation. Second, the briefs attempted to show that racial restrictions had no rational basis in economic or social facts. By highlighting the negative impact of covenants while undermining white homeowners' standard rationalizations for their use, the attorneys sought to expose these agreements as nothing more than punitive instruments of bigotry grounded in a baseless fear of African Americans and other minority groups.

Both the *McGhee* and *Hurd* briefs dramatized the plight that housing discrimination forced upon black urban populations. The "nation-wide destruction of human and economic values which results" from housing segregation, the Detroit brief argued, "makes this form of discrimination peculiarly repugnant." An "unprecedented overcrowding and congestion" in black districts and the subsequent deterioration of existing homes was nothing short of devastating. The attorneys insisted that covenants were the "direct and major cause" of these overburdened conditions. Deprivation prevailed in many forms, they argued, throughout the nation's distended racial ghettos. It came with a tremendous cost.[100]

The social ills flowing from the constriction that covenants caused became a significant point of emphasis. Both briefs underscored the "increase in disease, death, crime, immorality, juvenile delinquency, racial tensions, and economic exploitation" along with vice and mob violence that accompanied the disadvantages forced upon black citizens. These costs, in turn, not only affected the communities in which they occurred, they also proved injurious to the successful functioning of America's cities and society as a whole. This was a strategy of argumentation that had its own risks, a line of reasoning that might evoke condemnation of "damaged" black urban populations rather than moral outrage. Here, however, the negative depictions of urban life for African Americans were not some misguided attempt to identify black residents as irrevocably broken by the strain of segregation—nor was this a plea simply on behalf of those with the means to escape the shadow of a distressed underclass. Instead, the NAACP's attorneys highlighted the disruptive aspects of life in the ghetto as much for legal reasons as for moral ones.[101]

The damage caused by racial restrictions formed a critical portion of the Association's public policy claims before the Court. If the proven consequences of residential discrimination through covenants were these degrees of misery and unrest, the attorneys argued, then the exercise of state power to promote these conditions could only be seen as unseemly, unconscionable, and unacceptable. Courts could not legitimately permit the state to exercise its power in furtherance of an end that was so clearly harmful to the continued health and function of the state itself. The attorneys painted black urban communities not as being so damaged that they needed the Supreme Court's special protection, but instead as populations suffering under a debilitating, but temporary, state of hardship with an acute, readily identified, and remediable cause.

With the costs of enforcing covenants thus displayed, the Brandeis briefs then attacked the irrationality of restrictive agreements from another angle. The NAACP's legal team believed it was critically important—whether for the benefit of the Court or a popular audience—to contest some of the key justifications that undergirded the use and maintenance of covenants. The Brandeis brief became a forum to rehabilitate the image of African Americans as good homeowners and to debunk claims that residential integration caused permanent damage to property values and the social harmony of white neighborhoods. In this line of argument, the attorneys took on two of the most insidious claims that covenants' advocates had employed to spread the use of racial restrictions over the previous decades.

The financial rationale for exclusion became the first target. There were, the brief stated plainly, absolutely "no economic justifications for restrictive covenants against Negroes." Black occupancy did not inevitably lead to the depreciation of values across a given neighborhood. Quoting at length from a study by Robert Weaver, the attorneys claimed that African American homeowners, "instead of displaying any 'natural' characteristics to destroy better property," showed a greater tendency to maintain and improve their residences than "any other groups of similar income." In fact, the argument held that numerous instances in cities like Washington, D.C., and New York had demonstrated an upward trend in home prices after black homebuyers entered a neighborhood. Concerns about plummeting values in the wake of integration and the instances when this did occur resulted only from the spread of unfounded fears and rumors that became self-actualizing during panic selling.[102]

The attorneys took on a second popular justification for covenants when they challenged the idea that "forced" integration of neighborhoods would lead to social unrest and violent conflict between the races. In a darkly comic moment, Charles Hamilton Houston insisted that "this Court's decision declaring racial restrictive covenants unenforceable will not cause revolutionary disturbances." Such fears amounted to nothing more than ignorance and a willful disregard for recent history—including the record in the case at hand. "The people who see the end of the white race in America if restrictive covenants are outlawed," Houston remarked, "have their minds already made up and closed." These individuals who predicted bloodshed and the destruction of American society were nothing more than fearmongers and their victims. They were the same people, the brief claimed, who "predicted that political revolution and election by bullet instead of by ballot would result" after the white primary case in 1944. They foretold "wholesale riots" after the Court invalidated a segregation law for interstate bus passengers. Dismissing the most dire warnings of procovenant forces as hysterical bombast, Houston and his team argued that there was "no cause for alarm here. . . . All that elimination of restrictive covenants will do is to remove an intolerable, artificial restrictive barrier and permit the functioning of the economic and social forces which affect and control city growth." Armageddon was not waiting in the wings.[103]

Though these arguments had more of a popular focus than a legal one, the briefs used these claims to insist that a decision against covenants would do no harm to white property owners. The attorneys posited that the only true motive behind restrictive agreements was a capricious and malicious racial hatred. Lest the Supreme Court find any ambiguity in their overarching message, the attorneys explained that "the sole reason for the enforcement of covenants are racial prejudice and the desire . . . to exploit financially the artificial barriers created by covenants." In the end, the Brandeis briefs attempted to show that for all of the harm these restrictions caused, the only tangible benefits fell to unscrupulous profiteers.[104]

IN PAGE AFTER PAGE, the NAACP's attorneys used extralegal arguments to hammer away at the injustice and irrationality of covenants. They did so with the force and authority that came from months of preparation and decades of antiracist scholarship. Through the work of Annette Peyser, Marian Wynn Perry, Charles Hamilton Houston, Louis Wirth, Robert Weaver, and a dedicated team of other social scientists committed to the NAACP's civil rights agenda, the legal team crafted its most expansive Brandeis brief ever. The social scientific data and extralegal claims in the Detroit and Washington suits gave voice to the networks of advocates and intellectuals who shared the strength of a desire for reform. In compelling fashion, the briefs had harnessed the power of a generation of scholarly efforts to undo the legacy of scientific racism.

With their forcefulness and urgency, the arguments in *McGhee* and *Hurd* displayed the NAACP's resolve in the fight to seize a fleeting moment of promise. The legal staff tapped the resources of a wide array of scholars, embraced a new boldness, and built a new strategic approach to their litigation. The Brandeis briefs in the covenant cases marked a crucial turning point in the NAACP's relationship with antiracist social science and the coalition of intellectuals who imagined a future without racial inequality. Now, the

Association would reach out to another group of allies and urge them to file briefs of their own.

Friends of the Court: A Coalition against Covenants

The NAACP found itself flush with offers of support and assistance as the date for arguing the cases in the Supreme Court approached. A wide range of organizations ultimately filed amicus briefs with the Court. What made the covenant cases unique was the number of groups that claimed a vested interest in the outcome. Driven by the impulse for reform in the wake of World War II and by the NAACP's deep connections to other advocacy groups, the *Shelley* cases yielded the largest collection of amicus briefs that had ever reached the Court. The development of this coalition offers insight into the interconnectedness of civil rights organizations and agendas in the 1940s as the events of the war buoyed the levels of activism on behalf of minority groups.[105]

In the end, nineteen of the twenty-three different amicus briefs supported the side of the black homeowners. The NAACP's combination of allies represented a broad spectrum of constituencies that spanned religious denominations, racial and ethnic groups, labor unions, legal advocacy organizations, and an assortment of other interests. They included long-standing stalwarts of political reform like the ACLU, the American Federation of Labor (AFL), the Congress of Industrial Organizations (CIO), and the Anti-Defamation League (ADL) alongside an amalgam of relatively recent causes including the American Association for the United Nations (AAUN), the American Veterans Committee (AVC), and the NLG. This coalition of supporters provided varied claims and arguments that revealed how deeply the issue of housing segregation cut in postwar America.[106]

Concern over the extent of housing discrimination alone, however, did not account for all of the motivations that brought this alliance together. The strong ties that existed between various civil rights organizations facilitated the NAACP's efforts to rally a broad backing for the test cases. Institutional interconnections permeated the still burgeoning field of minority advocacy where a host of organizations shared—to some degree—ideas, resources, and personnel in pursuit of postwar equality. Nearly half of the Association's amicus coalition evidenced these intertwined interests. The NBA, a professional society for African American lawyers, joined the case in part because *McGhee* attorney Loren Miller also served as the NBA's vice president. Miller's personal connections also undoubtedly influenced the filings of at least two other amici: a group of California anticovenant attorneys and the Japanese American Citizens League (JACL)—though the JACL had its members' own hardships with racial restrictions in mind as well. The NAACP's deep ties to the ACLU through its longtime counsel Arthur Garfield Hays and through active engagement with local branches helped bring about their participation. Indeed, Francis Dent, one of the Detroit attorneys who originally argued the *McGhee* case, served as a coauthor of the ACLU's brief and another of the authors had been active on the NAACP committee that prepared the sociological arguments for the Court. Among the other groups, Houston's cocounsel in the *Hurd* case, Phineas Indritz, also served as counsel for the AVC and prepared portions of their amicus brief. Marian Wynn Perry also had strong ties to the NLG, where she had worked before joining the legal team in the covenant cases. The connections ran long and deep.[107]

The amici filings also showed the strong ties between the NAACP and leading Jewish advocacy organizations. Thurgood Marshall and Charles Hamilton Houston both served on the board of the American Jewish Congress's Commission on Law and Social Action (CLSA) and helped spur the CLSA's filing in the covenant cases. Newman Levy, an attorney for the ADL and the American Jewish Committee (AJC), had been a stalwart supporter of the litigation and had worked closely with the NAACP attorneys throughout the summer of 1947. Finally, the relationship between NAACP executive secretary Walter White and the AJC's president Joseph Proskauer proved close enough that White actually lobbied the Association's legal team to allow Proskauer to deliver one of the oral arguments before the Supreme Court. The AJC also supplied the legal team with a $2,000 donation to help defray the litigation costs and give further evidence of their support and concern. The NAACP and Jewish activists' coalition proved especially productive on this issue.[108]

The Association's political ties in the 1940s further bolstered their combination of amici. Indeed, the decision of the nation's two major labor groups to file on behalf of the NAACP's cases stemmed in some measure from organized labor's growing receptiveness to the Association's workplace rights agenda. As the NAACP gained traction on workers' rights issues and continued to attempt building a healthy political alliance with labor groups, the Association found the AFL and CIO reciprocating that support in some valuable ways.[109]

Despite the personal and organizational ties that strengthened the amicus coalition, a genuine concern over the issue of restrictive covenants undoubtedly also brought these groups together. While the links between the

NAACP and many of these amici were far from trivial, each of these organizations might well have tried to join the fight regardless of their connections to the Association. As the legal team prepared their arguments in autumn, offers of assistance flooded in from a wide range of groups across the country. This support often came from organizations without the same close connections that helped rally other collaborators. At times, the NAACP actually felt compelled to turn potential allies away for fear of duplicating arguments or overwhelming the Supreme Court with supplementary materials. In the end, the Association only had to solicit the support of three out of the nineteen amici.[110]

Many of the amicus briefs that reached the Court represented a true partnership between the Association's attorneys and the filing groups. In several instances, NAACP lawyers and consultants commented on drafts of the briefs—exchanging thoughts on the details of the arguments and how they would fit into the overall presentation of the cases. One of the Association's key advisers on the covenant issue, housing expert Charles Abrams, also corresponded with some of the amici and offered some perspective on how they could best increase the NAACP's chances of victory. Rather than repeating the central legal logic in each brief, Abrams saw more value in emphasizing the nonlegal aspects of the cases' impact. He advised one interested group not to worry as much about the strength of their arguments on the law, because "if it creates a healthy doubt or insinuates even a slight justification for itself on moral grounds, it may bend the judge toward adopting the law advocated in the main brief." The role of these supporting briefs, he argued, "should be providing the arguments that will salvage the judges' consciences or square with their prepossessions should they lean toward holding for us." With such powerful moral arguments to be made about the evils of covenants in American society, it seemed foolish to "desert all these rich and adventurous passages to jam the safe waters that should be reserved for the main advocates." The deepening of residential segregation in the postwar period had touched a nerve rubbed raw by the events of World War II and the anxieties over worsening conditions in America's cities. For NAACP consultants like Abrams and for the lawyers in the covenant cases, the amici needed to tap into these reserves of moral outrage and show the Supreme Court how profoundly the issue affected many corners of American society.[111]

The legacy of the Second World War weighed particularly heavily on the minds of the amici. In the consolidated brief of the AJC, ADL, Jewish War Veterans, and Jewish Labor Committee, the authors claimed a particular awareness of the "dangers to democracy arising from racial or religious residential segregation." The experiences of Jews, they reminded the Court, "gave rise to the word 'ghetto,'" and it was the "threat of revival of that institution—implicit in the mushroom growth in almost every major American city of racial restrictive covenants" that sparked Jewish concern in the matter and demanded these groups' intervention in the cases at hand. Similar concerns drove the arguments of the Anti-Nazi League. For the AVC, their participation in the cases represented a continuation of the "basic aims for which they had fought" and an attempt to protect black veterans who suffered from housing discrimination. In another brief, the AAUN emphasized the relevance of the newly written United Nations Charter in the issue before the Court. The authors claimed that the covenant cases directly spoke to "the good faith of this country in observing the intent of the Charter" and the spirit of cooperation and tolerance that the United Nations hoped to foster in the postwar world. For each of these organizations, the outcome of these cases would have a lasting impact on the real meaning of the victory in war that the nation had sacrificed so much to secure.[112]

Other members of the amicus coalition interceded largely out of a concern for the impact of restrictive agreements on the quality of life in American cities. The three Christian groups that filed briefs in the cases grounded their claims in the moral costs of housing discrimination—both from the conditions it produced and the inherent "sin of racial segregation" embodied in the agreements themselves. From another angle, the AFL and CIO intervened on behalf of their growing black constituencies and made particularly detailed presentations on the disparities in both the quality and quantity of African Americans' housing supply. The physical, social, and economic tolls exacted upon black communities, their briefs argued, made the injustice of covenants indisputably clear and rendered them untenable.

The legal advocacy groups—the ACLU, NBA, and NLG—all attempted to bolster the NAACP's arguments about state action, international treaties, and property rights under the Fifth and Fourteenth Amendments. In addition, the black fraternal order called the Grand Lodge of Elks filed at the behest of longtime member George Vaughn and reiterated some of Vaughn's arguments about the Civil Rights Act of 1866. The attorneys clearly felt that some added support for the purely statutory and constitutional claims would benefit their case.

Regardless of their motivations in filing or the types of arguments they made, the amici organizations played an important role in highlighting the broad impact of the covenant issue across American society. The unprecedented cavalcade of interest groups that rallied behind the NAACP's cause made it clear to the Supreme Court that the cases at hand spoke to one of the central postwar concerns for advocates of many races, religions, and backgrounds. The Association had mobilized a remarkably diverse coalition of activists in support of their calls for equality in housing access and had fashioned a powerful consensus among some of the leading liberal groups of the day. That so many organizations united behind the cause revealed the strength of the desire for reform in postwar America and the lasting influence that the events of World War II had in 1940s civil rights struggles.

Legacies of War: Remaking the Fight against Discrimination

As the oral arguments steadily approached, the Association's legal team crafted two powerful Brandeis briefs and assembled an impressive array of supporters. In the final days of October 1947, however, the NAACP and its coalition of allies anxiously awaited word from one last potential amicus curiae—the U.S. Department of Justice. For two months, the Association and all of its collaborators had engaged in a full-scale struggle to persuade the attorney general to support their case. The federal government had proved extraordinarily reluctant to intercede in a civil rights case between two private parties, so the effort seemed from its inception to be something of a long shot. Still, the NAACP brought the full extent of its institutional influence and momentum to bear on Attorney General Tom C. Clark. Through sustained lobbying, the Association hoped to convince the most reluctant and most powerful potential ally in the nation to take a dramatic step in a case that kept defying precedents.

The fate of the NAACP's campaign to entice the Justice Department into the covenant cases rested in large part upon the enduring impact of World War II on the nation's collective conscience regarding racial matters. The country had only recently emerged from a violent and costly battle in defense of the ideal of freedom and was now poised to plunge into another and much longer conflict with the Soviet Union. As the Truman administration attempted to marshal international support for American democratic principles in yet another global contest, the contradictory legacies of the United States as both the greatest enemy of totalitarianism and one of the most ardent oppressors of racial minorities seized the nation's attention in new ways. The federal government would increasingly face the need to reconcile the promises of American ideals with the practices of a nation built upon segregated institutions.

For black activists and organizations like the NAACP, the attorney general's decision would signal a great deal about the prospects for reform in the postwar period. An intercession on behalf of the Association's case could indicate meaningful new possibilities through the addition of tremendous power and resources to the struggle for civil rights. Silence would likely mean that progress would have to come in spite of government action. Surely the Truman administration, with all of its recent calls for egalitarianism and its budding relationship with the NAACP, could not continue to ignore the desperate plight of urban black homeseekers. Surely the sacrifices and lessons of the war would yield something more than a future of crowded slums and dismal homes. The Justice Department's response would be a telling one. The attorneys and their allies looked toward Washington once again with growing anticipation.

FOUR

To Washington

The Department of Justice and the Supreme Court

As St. Louis attorney George Vaughn neared the end of his allotted time before the U.S. Supreme Court, something began to rise inside of him. The aging veteran had spoken for nearly thirty minutes, his address largely unbroken by questions from the justices who sat in a stony silence. Vaughn, whose booming oratory and flair for drama had made him one of the Gateway City's most prominent black public figures, had struggled through his arguments to this point—faltering on the biggest stage of his long and accomplished career. Suddenly, however, he lifted his voice to its peak. He shouted to the robed men before him, loosing a roar as though he wished to shake the marbled walls—and the decades of complacency toward racial restrictions—to their very foundation with the sheer force of his cry. His plea was simple, heartfelt, and tinged with a "spiritual rage" built upon nearly seventy years of segregation's humiliations and the pain of the communities that he spoke for. "I say to you today," he thundered, "the Negro stands on the porch and knocks. He holds in his hands the bill for nearly three centuries of unrequited toil. He knocks. 'Let me come in,' he says, 'Let me come in and sit by the fire. I helped to build this house!'" With that, he dropped to his chair and let the silence of the chamber linger. Nearly four decades later, one witness, though he had long forgotten Vaughn's name, vividly recalled his final remarks as "the most moving plea in the Court I've ever heard."[1]

Though Vaughn's closing stayed with many observers long after his day in court, it was the man who spoke before him that generated the biggest stir of the afternoon. Philip B. Perlman, the solicitor general of the United States, had risen on behalf of the black families in the cases and delivered an hour-long statement declaring that President Harry S. Truman's administration believed that "covenants are the product of racial antagonism, bigotry, ignorance and prejudice," and that they "should be relegated to the limbo of other things as dead as slavery."[2]

Perlman's unequivocal support for the rights of African American homeowners signified a powerful and transformative intervention of federal authority into the courts. The Truman administration's actions marked a crucial departure from standard practice. Before the *Shelley* cases, the Department of Justice had typically withheld its influence in civil rights litigation between private parties, thus giving silent sanction to racial injustice achieved under the guise of private action. The retreat from this permissiveness in 1948 represented an important shift for civil rights advocates.[3]

A powerful combination of pressures conspired to bring the Truman administration into the covenant cases. Domestic and international political turmoil focused new degrees of public scrutiny on the question of what President Truman intended to do to reform federal civil rights policies. By 1947, the conspicuous gap between the nation's promises of equality and its practices of racial subordination garnered increasing attention around the nation and across the globe. Persistent lobbying from civil rights advocates both inside and outside of the administration seized upon this opportunity to mobilize federal resources in support of the anticovenant litigation campaign.

This unexpected intervention offered one of the first glimpses into the transformations underway in the struggle for racial equality in the postwar years. When the Truman administration decided to throw its weight behind the *Shelley* cases, it forged anew what became a lasting relationship between the Justice Department and the NAACP that helped to energize civil rights litigation efforts. The actions of Solicitor General Perlman and Attorney General Tom C. Clark appeared to bring the federal government's growing commitment to egalitarianism out of the realm of rhetoric and into the everyday lives of millions of black homeseekers. Moving beyond symbolic gestures, Truman's administration advocated passionately for a sweeping and meaningful change. As the covenant cases made their way through the Supreme Court, black communities around the nation took the solicitor general's intervention as a promise of greater triumphs yet to come.

Joining Hands: The Federal Government as Amicus Curiae

Philip B. Perlman's journey to the Supreme Court on that cold January afternoon had begun even before most of the covenant cases went to trial. When Harry S. Truman assumed the presidency in April of 1945 following Franklin D. Roosevelt's death, he inherited leadership of a nation in the midst of profound political turmoil. The former senator from Missouri took control of a war nearing its endgame, a deteriorating relationship with the Soviet Union, an unwieldy and weakening Democratic constituency, and mounting tensions on the issue of civil rights. By 1947, as Truman guided the country from World War II into the Cold War and as a challenging reelection fight loomed on the horizon, demands for civil rights reform intensified. Consequently, the White House became increasingly susceptible to civil rights advocates' lobbying efforts. The NAACP had already enjoyed a banner year in 1947 as their influence within Truman's administration grew. Even before Perlman's intervention, the president's June address at the NAACP convention and the ongoing work of the PCCR had signaled that federal attitudes toward civil rights would have new contours in the years to come. The solicitor general's appearance in the covenant cases served as a concrete manifestation of the fact that federal support for black Americans' freedom struggles would expand even further.[4]

Several factors combined to make Truman's administration more receptive to the pleas of civil rights activists than any previous one. Together these elements created unprecedented opportunities for reform and for the translation of egalitarian oratory into specific actions on issues such as restrictive covenants. The first of these forces was the lingering legacy of World War II where federal officials had begun to confront the problem of vulnerabilities in America's global image. Anti-American propaganda highlighted the hypocrisy of a nation fighting under the banner of freedom while oppressing its own racial minorities and focused federal attention and energies on domestic racial policy in new ways. A second related factor was the heightened international scrutiny of human rights violations attendant with the establishment of the United Nations and America's leadership in the endeavor. The emergence of the United Nations Commission on Human Rights late in 1946 provided a global forum for African American activists to air their grievances and threatened to exacerbate critiques of America's democratic shortcomings.[5]

A third element sharpening Truman's focus on the pleas of civil rights advocates materialized as the Second World War gave way to a new sort of contest with the Soviet Union. By 1947, the Truman administration had begun significantly escalating its efforts to paint the nascent Cold War as a battle between the ideology of democracy and the specter of communist totalitarianism on a global scale. In a contest seemingly as much about ideas as military force and one that had explicit concerns regarding the alignment of non-Western and nonwhite populations, the administration remained apprehensive about the United States' international image. The Cold War soon became an overriding policy concern for the administration and continued to elevate the priority of civil rights reform.[6]

While various geopolitical factors played an important role in encouraging the president's receptiveness to lobbying efforts, other driving forces lay closer to home. The looming election of 1948 threatened to rend the New Deal coalition that had dominated the nation's electoral politics since 1932. Midterm voting in 1946 yielded the first Republican Congress since the Hoover administration and provided an ominous warning for Truman's upcoming campaign. A key concern became the possibility that African American voters would defect en masse from the Democratic ranks and seriously weaken the party's strength in the North and Midwest. The racially egalitarian platform of third party candidate and former vice president Henry Wallace intensified this threat.

Truman's advisers sensed a need to recapture the black electorate by taking a more aggressive position in favor of civil rights. One of the president's closest counselors wrote in 1947 that "unless there are new and real efforts . . . as distinguished from mere political gestures," Truman would lose a crucial bloc of voters and likely the election. Truman's own political future appeared inextricably linked to federal action against racial discrimination.[7]

The president also responded to an uptick in the viciousness of white supremacy at home. This fifth factor arose as Truman, like many Americans in the postwar era, confronted the brutality of racial violence and segregation's most pernicious effects with newfound discomfort. Instances like the vicious beating and blinding that black veteran Isaac Woodard suffered at the hands of a South Carolina police chief stirred the president's conscience. Though Truman's moral commitment to the cause of civil rights has remained a matter of dispute among historians, some measure of personal interest worked alongside the prevailing political forces.[8]

While these five factors gave the administration the will and rationale to act, civil rights advocates' protests and lobbying efforts forced those actions to take place. African Americans, particularly through the efforts of black veterans and the NAACP, increasingly applied pressure on Truman's White House. Indeed, rather than spontaneous acts of political opportunity, the administration's unprecedented civil rights efforts between 1946 and 1948 were to a large extent compelled by an effective and constant campaign of influence from minority advocacy groups. In many respects, insistent protest from African Americans played the most significant role in securing new forms of federal support for civil rights.[9]

The pressure that impelled Truman's White House to reevaluate its role in American race relations also came from within the administration itself.

A handful of individuals gave of their time and influence to mobilize federal resources. Anticovenant advocates found two particularly committed allies in the administration, an assistant attorney general named Philip Elman and a lawyer with the Department of the Interior named Phineas Indritz. Elman, a twenty-nine-year-old Harvard Law School graduate, was an assistant to the solicitor general and served as the Justice Department's point man on civil rights issues from the late 1940s through the mid-1950s. Elman became an outspoken advocate for greater federal intervention in civil rights litigation, urging his superiors to take a more proactive stance in pending Supreme Court cases such as *Shelley* and the various challenges to segregated education. Among civil rights supporters in the Truman administration, Elman was one of the best-equipped individuals to make direct use of his position. Throughout the late 1940s and early 1950s, Elman hounded the DOJ to do more with their authority.[10]

Other advocates in the federal ranks usually had to find more creative ways to lend their support to protests on behalf of minority rights. From his post in the Department of the Interior it seemed that Phineas Indritz could do relatively little, yet he played an even more intimate role on the covenant issue than Elman. Indritz was a thirty-one-year-old Illinois native who had earned a degree from the University of Chicago Law School in 1938 before taking a job at the Department of the Interior. After enlisting in the U.S. Army during World War II, Indritz resumed his work as a government attorney and began to privately lend his services to advocacy groups like the AVC and NAACP. In mid-1947, after following Charles Hamilton Houston's covenant cases through the Federal Circuit Court of Appeals in Washington, D.C., Indritz volunteered to moonlight as cocounsel while Houston prepared the suits for the Supreme Court.[11]

Like Elman, Indritz used his position to encourage administration officials to support the cases, but he also made federal resources available to the NAACP's attorneys however he could. Indritz began hosting strategy meetings in federal offices after hours with prominent local anticovenant lawyers, NAACP housing attorney Marian Wynn Perry, housing expert Robert Weaver, and a handful of federal lawyers from the Departments of Commerce, Labor, and Justice who assisted in the preparations. Through their protests and efforts to funnel resources to other advocates, civil rights allies like Indritz and his colleagues found ways to keep a steady groundswell of internal pressure on Truman's administration through the late-1940s. A furious group of Washington homeowners' associations tracked Indritz's attempts to help the NAACP and noted that he had secured "a general authority . . . to use the offices and the research and other facilities of the Department [of the Interior] for promotion of the anticovenant cases."[12]

ACTIVIST ATTORNEYS like Indritz sensed the susceptibility of the Truman administration to new demands from civil rights advocates. The formation of the PCCR late in 1946 and Truman's speech before the NAACP annual conference in the summer of 1947 had marked important symbolic gestures of support from the White House and reflected a deepening embrace of racial egalitarianism. Still, even the most inspired or nobly intentioned rhetoric would only advance the NAACP's agenda so far. When the covenant cases neared the U.S. Supreme Court hearing date late in 1947, then, the Association's legal and political leaders saw an important opportunity to solicit concrete actions from Truman's government. They sought to test whether the president's bold words could translate into meaningful policy changes by petitioning the DOJ for assistance in the covenant cases.

In determining the course of this new lobbying campaign, the Association made use of its connections to internal advocates for racial reform in the administration. Phineas Indritz had first spoken about the possibility of federal intervention in the Supreme Court at the NAACP's New York strategy conference in early September. There, he had insisted that the attorneys "should get the government behind [the] cases in filing [an] amicus brief." The conferees had eagerly welcomed the idea and agreed to establish delegations of prominent activists that would petition various heads of federal agencies for support. Indritz's assurances that the Association could expect the aid of the Department of the Interior and several other offices played an important role in emboldening the NAACP leadership to mount a fullfledged lobbying effort toward Truman's administration.[13]

Their strategy, hammered out by Houston, Thurgood Marshall, and Indritz, was a two-pronged plan designed to persuade Attorney General Clark that his department should join in the cases. First the NAACP's attorneys and allies would increase the pressure on the DOJ from internal sources in the administration. "There is IMMEDIATE URGENCY," Indritz wrote shortly after the September conference, "to get the government agencies to request [the Department of] Justice to participate." Houston, Marshall, Indritz, and Walter White all quickly began reaching out to various federal agencies that might prove sympathetic to their case. Within days, the Association had targeted the surgeon general, the Housing and Home Finance Agency, the

Veterans Affairs, the Department of the Interior, the Children's Bureau of the Social Service Administration, and the Department of Labor for support.[14]

In his direct appeals to these agency heads, Walter White spoke to the direness of the conditions that housing discrimination created. He wrote of the cases to Surgeon General Thomas Parran that "no more fundamental point concerning the future development of American democracy will be presented to the court." White asked these federal officials to convey to Attorney General Clark the challenges that covenants caused in the performance of their duties. Clark, a native Texan and the son of an ardent white supremacist, was a Democratic Party loyalist and a ten-year veteran of the Justice Department who had played a significant role in the forced relocation of Japanese Americans during World War II. Activists were thus unsure about where the attorney general stood on civil rights issues and believed that the more coercion they could offer, the better. White solicited remarks regarding the detrimental effects of racial restrictions on the "working conditions and employment opportunities of Negroes," the "health and welfare of Negroes," and black communities' "crying need for more and better housing." At least four of the NAACP's targeted agencies ultimately encouraged the DOJ to intervene and several offered assistance in the preparation of any materials to be submitted to the Court.[15]

The second aspect of the lobbying campaign was "the application of pressure directly to Tom Clark" from Association leaders and allied civil rights organizations. White composed a letter to the attorney general shortly after the September strategy conference officially requesting his participation in the cases. "The matter before the court," White wrote solemnly, "is of the highest public importance and concerns the most basic of human rights— the right to a home." White insisted that the Supreme Court's decision would "affect for many generations the welfare of all racial, national and religious minorities in America," and the import of the cases thus demanded that Clark intervene. White concluded his appeal with a declaration about the duties of the federal government with respect to the basic human rights of the nation's minorities. He asserted, "The Department of Justice owes to these minorities a deep responsibility to help the court to understand the issues involved and to arrive at a decision which will not set up in America legalized ghetto life for Negroes, Jews and any other group which may have the temporary disapproval of a dominant majority. I believe this is one of the most important requests for aid which Negroes have made to your Department, and I request an opportunity to discuss this with you in detail and to present to you the full import of your decision." Clark quickly replied that he had referred the entire matter to Philip Elman in the Justice Department's Civil Rights Section for a thorough review.[16]

Before the letter-writing campaign began, however, the attorney general was not particularly inclined to have his department join the fray of private battles over civil rights. White and his colleagues rightly sensed that they had an uphill climb on their hands. Clark's early correspondence with the PCCR in July of 1947, just two weeks after the Supreme Court had granted certiorari to the Detroit and St. Louis covenant cases, explained his belief that federal intervention in private matters had to be "resorted to rarely." Clark seemed especially concerned that such actions might leave the government "in danger of discriminating unfairly against one party or another," but conceded that further involvement could be necessary on a more frequent basis in the coming months. The mounting pressure that the NAACP and its allies applied made it all the more likely that Clark would tilt in their direction.[17]

Walter White kept the encouragement coming from all angles. He quickly began reaching out to other civil rights advocacy groups to urge that they join him in petitioning the administration for support. The NAACP legal team had already started to organize the largest amicus coalition in the Supreme Court's history and they used these partnerships to lobby Clark's office. At least six other groups joined the NAACP's effort in the days following the attorney general's decision to refer the cases to Elman. The AJC's appeal labeled the issue as one of "transcendent public importance," while the chief counsel for the CIO described covenants as "one of the gravest dangers to democracy in America." Letters from the ADL, the ACLU, NBA, and Negro Newspaper Publishers Association all followed shortly and were equally emphatic in expressing their concerns over residential segregation. The ACLU in particular stressed the international implications of covenants' continued enforcement. "At a time when democracy is on trial throughout the world," the group's appeal warned, "it behooves the United States Government to be particularly vigilant in stamping out all evidences of discrimination here." The fight against covenants presented an unparalleled opportunity for the Truman administration to disavow an especially pernicious form of racial subordination and reclaim the promise of freedom and equality for all.[18]

After a month of steady lobbying, the NAACP made significant inroads with the DOJ and, unbeknownst to them, had successfully swayed the attorney general to their camp. In October, the Civil Rights Section officially requested letters from ten federal agencies to obtain a clearer picture of the impact that covenants had on governmental policies and functions. By

October 22, Clark and Solicitor General Perlman had made the decision to join the cases and even urged President Truman to announce the department's intervention personally at a press conference later that week. Caution, however, would at least temporarily rule the day as the Justice Department withheld its announcement for eight additional days. In fact, when Clark agreed to a private meeting with Thurgood Marshall after making the decision he refused to confirm the department's official stance, but did leave Marshall with the impression that the administration was prepared to join the cases.[19]

For Marshall and his colleagues at the NAACP, the possibility was momentous. Not only would an intervention mark an unexpected break from the federal government's permissive attitude toward discrimination driven by private individuals, but more immediately it would significantly bolster the NAACP's chances of victory in the Shelley cases. The Association's legal and political leaders expected a deep division of the Court on the issues and believed that the DOJ's support might tip the balance in their favor. Walter White, in a letter to President Truman appealing for him to bring his influence to bear on the attorney general's decision, had suggested that federal intervention on the Association's behalf "would be of very material assistance . . . to secure a decision which will break this vicious practice." The vigorous attempts to coerce the Justice Department into action now stood poised to pay dividends. The attorney general simply waited for the opportune moment to make his announcement public.[20]

On October 29, four days after Marshall's promising meeting with Clark, that opportunity came at the hands of the PCCR. After months of gathering testimony and data, the committee issued its final report and set the stage perfectly for Clark to declare his intentions. That document, entitled *To Secure These Rights*, offered a sweeping assessment of the failures in the nation's civil rights record and a compelling statement of America's responsibilities in the protection of minority rights. Instantly hailed by many African American activists as a "blueprint for freedom," the report rapidly circulated around the nation and generated considerable excitement among civil rights advocates.[21]

The findings in *To Secure These Rights* proved particularly favorable and useful for the anticovenant campaign. This resulted in no small part from the fact that most of the information and recommendations regarding segregated housing came directly from the nation's leading anticovenant activists. Using written and oral testimony from individuals like Robert Weaver, Loren Miller, and several of the NAACP's amici, the PCCR discussed not only the nature and extent of restrictive agreements, but also turned its attention to the legal issues involved in covenant enforcement. Commenting directly on the pending Supreme Court cases, the report endorsed the central argument that NAACP attorneys had offered against residential restrictions in the suits, namely that courts' enforcement of covenants represented an unconstitutional exercise of state power to support racial discrimination. The PCCR declared that "there is eminent judicial and professional opinion in this country that our courts cannot constitutionally enforce racial restrictive covenants," and later expressed its fervent belief that, "every effort must be made to prevent this abuse" of juridical power. In pursuit of the latter goal, the PCCR had firmly recommended an "intervention by the Department of Justice" in the litigation against restrictive agreements. Attorney General Clark, who knew of the report's stance some two months before its official release, now had the president's implicit support behind him and the attention of the nation.[22]

Just one day after the PCCR released *To Secure These Rights* to the American public Clark and Solicitor General Perlman officially announced that they would join in the argument of the *Shelley* cases before the Supreme Court. The Justice Department's actions resulted directly from the web of pressures that faced the Truman administration, including advocacy from sympathetic federal officials, the NAACP's lobbying campaign, and the political realities of an upcoming election year. Members of the administration later reflected on what drove this expanded role for the government in the covenant cases and offered some insight into how the decision came about. The conversations and negotiations between Clark, Perlman, and even President Truman—whom they directly consulted as they prepared to make their final decision—reflected a responsiveness to the urgings of civil rights advocates that was altogether new.[23]

At the heart of the department's move was the fact that activists now spoke with greater degrees of power and authority than they had in the past. Philip Elman, the assistant attorney general who became a go-between for Clark and Perlman as they navigated what to do about *Shelley*, discussed the impact that the PCCR had on his bosses. *To Secure These Rights* "was taken very seriously in the Solicitor General's office," he remarked, and he believed that the combination of his own advocacy and that of the PCCR "was the main impetus" for the DOJ's decision. The PCCR in particular had provided a unique vehicle for the formulation and expression of civil rights demands that helped sway key figures in the administration.[24]

The NAACP's extensive lobbying efforts played an equally critical role. Perlman later recounted that the Justice Department "was being importuned by organizations throughout the country" and identified the "number of letters filed . . . by different religious, racial, welfare, and civil rights organizations" as one of the persuasive factors in obtaining his support for the case. Initially, neither Clark nor Perlman had been especially eager to lend their names and energies to an exercise of federal authority against such a widespread practice. By the end of 1947, however, the dedicated efforts of civil rights advocates both inside and outside of the Truman administration had coaxed the two men into cooperating with the NAACP.[25]

Electoral concerns also helped convince the politically savvy duo to break from their initial reticence. Perlman in particular appeared sensitive to the "political mileage" that could accrue from a strong stand in support of racial egalitarianism and both he and Clark were more receptive to the NAACP's pressure as a result. Additionally, Truman's campaign advisers, already looking ahead to the contest in 1948, had simultaneously begun discussing the importance of federal action on behalf of civil rights. As the DOJ weighed its decision in September of 1947, a memorandum from strategist James H. Rowe began circulating within the administration. Rowe's outline for a multipronged strategy that emphasized in part the significance of growing black voting blocs in Northern swing states was co-opted nearly verbatim by Truman adviser Clark Clifford in November and became the guiding policy document for the ensuing campaign. The memorandum pointed to the areas that would be most politically impactful for the Truman administration's civil rights activities stating, "Unless the Administration makes a determined campaign to help the Negro (and everybody else) on the problems of high prices and housing—and capitalizes politically on its efforts—the Negro vote is already lost." While it is unclear whether the memorandum had caught the attention of Justice Department officials during their deliberations over *Shelley,* the unfolding conversations about civil rights within the executive branch clearly saw efforts for African Americans' housing rights as a major political boon. The potential electoral benefits apparently factored into the department's calculations.[26]

Truman's role in the decision-making process, though, remains somewhat unclear. In light of the significant departure from previous practices and knowing that it would undoubtedly have some political ramifications, Attorney General Clark seems to have consulted the president before making his determination. Though Truman would later claim on at least one occasion that the DOJ's intervention in the cases came "at my request," it appears instead that Clark sought and received approval for a decision that he had already made. Philip Perlman reflected that in general the president "didn't interfere or give instructions" on matters involving civil rights litigation, "but he was very much pleased" with the Justice Department's undertakings. Whatever the combination of motivations and actors involved, it immediately became clear that the attorney general's decision to intercede would be of great consequence.[27]

Reactions came quickly. Black newspapers heralded the move as a remarkable development in the ongoing struggle for civil rights. An editorial in Detroit's *Michigan Chronicle* called Clark's decision "historic" and a "significant step" that signaled the dawn of "a new era of race relations in America." Not since the Emancipation Proclamation, the paper opined, had the federal government embarked upon such an important "offensive against the doctrine of 'white supremacy.'" With the Truman administration squarely behind anticovenant advocates in this powerful show of support, the possibility of even more sweeping changes seemed on the horizon. "The tide," the column remarked, "is turning so swiftly that many of us may not realize what a tremendous move toward full citizenship is taking place." While few other observers would match this level of public exuberance before the cases even reached their hearing date, many black activists also found hope in the attorney general's decision.[28]

Excitement surrounded the government's intervention as both a practical benefit in the fight against covenants and as a symbol of what was to come. Arriving as it did so closely on the heels of *To Secure These Rights*, the attorney general's action struck many individuals as a sign of the administration's willingness to enact the PCCR's wide-ranging prescriptions for the nation's racial ills. One account called it the "first step in an effort to implement recommendations" from the report. Another cited the intervention as evidence of the administration's sincere commitment to significant policy changes and described the attorney general's action as being "full of promise for the future." Numerous commentators wrote of the importance of Truman's officials "joining hands" with African Americans in pursuit of equality. It signaled to some that the nation's government was finally ready to "accept the responsibility for leadership in securing fundamental civil rights." The struggle for racial freedom felt a bold new wind at its back.[29]

The administration's lawyers quickly set to work assembling the written brief. They had only a few weeks to pull together all the necessary materials and labored feverishly under the leadership of Philip Elman. As the early December deadline loomed closer, "We had to move fast," Elman recalled. "I had to postpone my honeymoon to get the brief done in time." The difficulties they encountered in this task highlighted the inadequacies of the DOJ's

Civil Rights Section, which lacked both the manpower and the know-how to tackle the project. Elman ultimately cobbled together a team of attorneys from wherever he could within the department, pulling in allies from the Office of the Solicitor General, the Claims Division, and the Tax Division to share the burden. The four men most responsible for crafting the brief were all Jewish, motivated at least in part by the growing impact of residential restrictions on Jews in the postwar period. Their final product, however, bore none of their names for fear that it would look "as if a bunch of Jewish lawyers in the Department of Justice put this out." They understood that the prevalence of anti-Semitic public perceptions could diminish the force and impact of the brief especially if prosegregation constituencies erroneously saw the administration's intervention as the pet project of a handful of Jewish activists rather than a full-fledged federal commitment to defending African Americans' civil rights in court. Instead they substituted the attorney general's name for their own—a departure from the standard practice of only listing the solicitor general—in the hopes that Clark's inclusion would lend additional credibility and authority to their case. Elman later remarked of this decision that "if I could have, I'd have put Truman's name on it." He wanted there to be no mistake about the administration's sincere commitment to the cause.[30]

The Justice Department's brief offered a powerful and uncompromising statement of African Americans' right to equal access in housing. Filling more than 120 pages, the document laid out in both legal and moral terms the responsibilities of the courts to black homeseekers. Elman and his team had purposefully included "a lot of high-blown rhetoric about liberty and equality" as part of their effort both to justify the solicitor general's involvement and frame the issues at stake more broadly. They also extensively excerpted *To Secure These Rights* and quoted various letters and statements from government officials, having "scissors-and-pasted" the brief together to portray a broad federal consensus. Court enforcement of covenants, the Truman administration declared in the opening pages, "is incompatible with the spirit and letter of the Constitution and laws of the United States."[31]

While the brief would thoroughly elaborate on the legal questions and precedents associated with covenants, state action, and property rights claims, the Justice Department's argument gave particular attention to the issue of public policy. Elman offered a lengthy treatment of the ways in which racial restrictions interfered with the government's interests and objectives. At the lower appellate levels, anticovenant attorneys like Willis Graves and Francis Dent of Detroit had tried and failed to frame covenant enforcement as an act of discrimination that directly undermined postwar American domestic and foreign policy. With this brief, however, the federal government breathed new life into these claims.

The opening section focused on the challenges that federal agencies faced in the execution of their duties as a result of residential segregation. Though not explicitly part of the public policy section of the brief, Elman presented the "interest of the United States" in such a way that it served substantially the same purpose. Here he drew at length from the various letters that other agency heads had filed in support of anticovenant advocates. The administrator of the Housing and Home Finance Agency (HHFA), the surgeon general, the undersecretary of the interior, and the legal adviser to the secretary of state all lent their words to the brief. Raymond Foley at the HHFA described the extent of residential discrimination and dealt in detail with the agency's difficulties providing adequate public housing for minorities as a result of the barriers that covenants placed on many potential building sites. Surgeon General Thomas Parran explained that because restrictive agreements limited minorities' access to "a sanitary and healthful environment," he considered the agreements to be "prejudicial to the public health." Oscar Chapman—Phineas Indritz's boss at the Department of the Interior—emphasized the impact of covenants on Native Americans and Puerto Rican immigrants. He stressed that the limitations on adequate housing deterred the urbanization and assimilation of Native Americans and was destructive to morale. Calling restrictive covenants a "cancer," Chapman concluded that they were "entirely inconsistent with the future national and international welfare of the United States in its relations with the 'non-white' peoples." Elman's team hoped to showcase the breadth of the destructive swath that covenants were cutting through the nation's cities, society, and political future.[32]

On the heels of Chapman's appeal for America's "international welfare," Elman turned to the State Department and covenants' relationship to the "conduct of foreign affairs." This section differed noticeably from the others in its construction, though not in its message. In contrast to the preceding subsections, which excerpted entire paragraphs and pages from agency heads, Elman quoted only a single sentence from State Department legal adviser Ernest Gross's letter to the attorney general. In it, Gross asserted that the United States had been "embarrassed in the conduct of foreign relations by acts of discrimination taking place in this country." Had Gross offered a more expansive or detailed statement about the effects of residential segregation on foreign policy, Elman would likely have included it. Instead—in a bit of creative editing—Elman coupled this single statement with a lengthy citation from a State Department letter written eighteen months earlier for a Fair Employment Practices Committee hearing. That letter had addressed the international implications of the "gap between the things we stand for in principle" and the daily acts of racial subordination that comprised Jim Crow. While it stopped short of making specific policy recommendations for federal intervention, the statement encouraged an end to discrimination's various forms as an important step in the nation's global relationships.[33]

After turning to address the history and effects of racial restrictive covenants and discussing at length the state action argument, the brief returned to the issue of public policy once again. Covenant enforcement, it argued unequivocally, "is inconsistent with the public policy of the United States." The brief's authors insisted that the nation's laws had clearly established "that it is the policy of the United States to deny the sanction of law to racial discriminations, to ensure equality under the law to all persons . . . and, more particularly, to guarantee to Negroes rights, including the right to use, acquire, and dispose of property." They highlighted legislative efforts to prohibit discrimination in jury service, the administration of homestead laws, federal public works and relief programs, and defense industry employment during World War II as examples of this rejection of racial bias. The authors also pointed to statements from Presidents Truman and Roosevelt that identified the "right to a decent home" as a fundamental part of "a truly democratic society." Glossing over the complicity of federal agencies in maintaining housing segregation, the brief crafted a vision of public policy that cast the American government as a staunch opponent of racial injustice since Emancipation.[34]

Then the authors returned to the arena of international affairs. The contours of the nation's public policy on race had to be understood through not only a backward glance at legislative history, but also through America's future responsibilities in the global community. They pointed to recent international pronouncements as a signal of the federal government's desire and intent to limit racial discrimination. They excerpted sections of the United Nations Charter that committed members to promote "universal respect for, and observance of, human rights and fundamental freedoms for all without distinction as to race." The brief also cited the 1945 Economic Charter of the Americas, where U.S. delegates had included language affirming the principle of "equality of rights and opportunities for all men, regardless of race or religion." Certainly the unambiguous egalitarian language of these treaties—documents that were meant to help define the path toward peace and greater freedom in the postwar world—provided a clear indication of the government's policy regarding the rights of racial minorities.[35]

Both domestically and internationally, then, continued support for residential segregation would prove tremendously costly to the nation's progress. The brief's conclusion delivered a scathing denunciation of the practice of housing discrimination and condemned it as a product of "ignorance, bigotry and prejudice." Restrictive covenants were "injurious to our order and productive of growing antagonisms destructive of the integrity of our society." As such, they posed an imminent danger to America's "free institutions" and were "abhorrent to the law of the land." Bearing the signatures of the Truman administration's two most powerful legal officers, this brief gave the NAACP's case a new jolt of energy and left the attorneys more hopeful than ever before.[36]

ACCLAIM FOR THE SUBSTANCE of the brief came quickly. Private letters to the attorney general from black advocates in his home state of Texas heaped praise upon him. The president of the NAACP's Texas Conference of Branches remarked that Clark's "noble deed" had made him into one of the state's "truly great sons," and called the brief the "most far-reaching [act] of democracy by the present Administration." The leader of Texas's Negro Chamber of Commerce labeled Clark as "one of the most potent influences for the preservation of democracy that the nation affords" and offered his "thanks and appreciation." Both men also called on the attorney general to publish the government's brief for national distribution in the hopes of further rallying public opinion behind the anticovenant cause.[37]

The idea of publication for general consumption seemed to strike a nerve with the attorney general. Three months after the brief's release, the Public Affairs Press began printing revised copies of the document under the title *Prejudice and Property: An Historic Brief against Racial Covenants*. Truman's Justice Department reaffirmed their commitment to the arguments they put forward for the Court. They wanted to ensure that their effort to articulate the case for equal access to housing would not simply "be gathering dust in the files of a dozen lawyers and judges." Instead, they wished for it to become a tool for civil rights advocates to use in mobilizing support and educating the public about the costs of racial discrimination. They sought, at least in part, to bring more attention to the importance of civil rights litigation, refashion the public image of the federal government as a defender of egalitarianism, and make the arguments against housing segregation more accessible to the general population.[38]

While anticovenant advocates reveled in this promising moment, restrictive covenants' supporters vigorously protested the Truman administration's decision to back the NAACP. White homeowners associations in Washington met shortly after the announcement to voice their frustration. "Who gave him [Tom Clark] the right to set the policy of the Government?" they seethed. "Who has given the Administration the right to take sides?" Formal letters of protest followed. Elsewhere, the vitriolic columnist Westbrook Pegler sneered at the DOJ's "blasphemy," while the vice president of Atlanta's Real Estate Board took to the press to assure Truman's White House that they had just lost many votes in the Democrats' southern stronghold.[39]

The most vehement response came from the procovenant attorneys in the *Shelley* cases. Henry Gilligan and James Crooks from the Washington suits vented their outrage in a formal rejoinder. Their separate reply brief to the government's arguments harshly castigated the administration's interference as an effort to assert that "the Negro petitioners, and Negroes generally, have rights superior to and beyond white citizens." The lawyers took to task the attorney general and solicitor general for what they charged were deliberate misrepresentations of legal precedents and the intentions of procovenant advocates. Gilligan and Crooks insisted that the government's claims were "insidious and indefensible" and labeled the administration's arguments that the Court should be concerned with "the broader social and economic consequences" of covenants as "utterly ridiculous statements" that should "completely discredit" the government's case.[40]

Feeling the full weight of the Justice Department's efforts against them, the attorneys railed at what they saw as an utter lack of fairness. "The Government," they fumed, "presumably serves all citizens, yet it charges these respondents and others with ignorance, bigotry and prejudice." While they would expect and tolerate such behavior from the private parties involved in the cases, the decision to put the force of federal executive power behind such allegations went too far. The administration "must not only be criticized, but condemned, for such practice," they concluded. Their blistering anger at the DOJ's brief indicated just how concerned procovenant advocates had become about the possibility of losing the case. Henry Gilligan in particular—a man who held dearly to the orthodoxies of racial separatism and judicial deference to the desires of private citizens—no doubt felt the shock of such a striking change of course. He saw the traditions and customs of a life built in a segregated world being washed away by the changing tide of federal attitudes toward civil rights.[41]

AS THE ATTORNEYS NEARED the December hearing date, the tension was palpable. The attorney general's intervention had raised the stakes yet again. Nervous energy coursed through the NAACP offices and despite their newfound ally, the lawyers recognized the enormity of the task ahead of them. Thurgood Marshall's friend and former colleague William H. Hastie summed up the mood of many observers when he asked Marshall to pass along a message to his cocounsels: "Tell Charlie [Houston] and Loren [Miller] that I wish you as much luck as you need, which is plenty."[42]

The sudden illness of Justice Frank Murphy only days before the original court date of December 8 unexpectedly postponed the hearing until mid-January of 1948. Left with five extra weeks to prepare—and agonize—Marshall confided to Hastie that "I do not believe this is a breathing spell for us. . . . I am afraid that the other side will take advantage of the delay to consolidate their forces." Marshall had undoubtedly hoped to capitalize on the surprise and frustration that the vehemence of the Justice Department's brief had created for the opposing side. Now Gilligan and Crooks had an additional month to regroup and determine how best to counter the attorney general's arguments.[43]

In the final week leading up to the new hearing date of January 15, reporters and attorneys began flooding into the nation's capital in anticipation of what commentators were calling "the most important cases in the field of civil rights since the Civil War." To prepare, the anticovenant lawyers joined the faculty and students at Howard University Law School to rehearse their arguments and practice fielding questions from their audience. This collaboration had played an important role in fine-tuning the NAACP's previous presentations to the Court and this latest instance would be no exception.[44]

When they arrived at the Supreme Court on the cold January morning of the hearing, throngs of eager onlookers lined the marbled hallways, waiting hours for the chance at a seat in the gallery. The attorneys felt the gravity of the moment more strongly than ever. They knew the crowd that filled the room beyond capacity was lured not by the spectacle of the fight, but by the hope that this day might mark the beginning of a better life for themselves and their families in America's cities. The meticulous preparation of the previous months and years now boiled down to seven hours stretched over the next two days.

Final Words: The Covenant Cases in the Supreme Court

The first shock of the day came with the announcement of the cases. As the clerk called forward the attorneys for both sides, three of the justices rose from their seats and strode out of the chamber leaving behind the murmurs of a stunned crowd and a sense of how deeply the issue reached across American society. Justices Stanley Reed, Robert Jackson, and Wiley Rutledge all recused themselves from the case without explanation, though rampant speculation held that each of the men owned covenanted properties. The NAACP had likely expected Reed and Jackson's recusal since they had abstained from participating on certiorari petitions in previous covenant cases, but the legal team had been counting upon Rutledge's vote as they calculated their prospects for victory. The sight of him exiting the chamber left them with a hollow, sinking feeling. With only a bare quorum left to hear the oral arguments the stakes had suddenly gone even higher. As one observer noted, "the three empty chairs of . . . Justices Rutledge, Reed and Jackson are the only vacant seats in the room, ominously symbolic of the seriousness of the business before the Court." All those seated in the packed chamber recognized the significance of what they had just witnessed.[45]

Six justices remained, led by their rather lightly regarded Chief Justice Frederick Moore Vinson. Vinson, who Truman had appointed to replace Harlan Fisk Stone in 1946, was a Kentucky-born politician from a blue-collar background, an ardent supporter of the New Deal, and an expert on economic policy. After twelve years in Congress, Roosevelt had rewarded Vinson's loyalty with a seat on the Federal Circuit Court of Appeals in Washington, D.C., in 1938. As the nation went to war in the 1940s, Vinson returned to politics to serve first as the director of the Office of Economic Stabilization and then as the director of the Office of War Mobilization and Reconversion. In these roles, Vinson became renowned for his "outstanding qualities as [an] administrator, negotiator and conciliator," and his oddly insatiable penchant for tax policy work and anti-inflationary measures earned him a promotion under Truman to the post of secretary of the treasury in 1945. When the vacancy on the Supreme Court arose the following year, the fifty-six-year-old Vinson moved from the Cabinet to the chief justice's seat.[46]

Truman hoped that Vinson's administrative skills might help to heal a divided Supreme Court that was struggling under the tension of personal squabbles between several of the justices. By appointing an outsider known more for his managerial talent than for his legal ability, Truman felt that he had installed a trusted adviser to mediate an increasingly fractured judicial body. Truman's trust in Vinson as a political ally and a personal friend also helped spur the decision to appoint him. The president believed that Vinson's loyalty and like-mindedness on issues of federal authority would make him a valuable addition to the Court. Yet the other justices were not especially pleased with their new colleague. A handful of the men on the Court and Justice Felix Frankfurter in particular regarded Vinson as little more than the administration's crony and a man without the legal intellect to deserve his position. One clerk recalled that Vinson "was openly scorned by several of his fellow judges . . . who made no bones about regarding him . . . as their intellectual inferior." Though Vinson's affable personality made him likable enough, he proved largely unable to steer the Court toward greater consensus and congeniality.[47]

The Vinson Court in 1948 stood divided into roughly three camps, with the chief justice leaning toward the most conservative bloc. Justices Hugo Black, William O. Douglas, Frank Murphy, and Wiley Rutledge formed the Court's "liberal" wing—more willing than their colleagues to depart from precedents in pursuit of their understanding of justice. The Court's "conservative" bloc consisted of Vinson and Justices Stanley Reed—another Kentuckian who had once managed some of Vinson's congressional campaigns—and Harold Burton, a former senator and the only Republican on the Court. Though politically moderate, the trio won their reputation as conservatives due largely to their judicial records on civil liberties. The remaining two justices, Felix Frankfurter and Robert Jackson, comprised a third faction that leaned in the direction of the "conservative" wing, but retained enough independence that they were not easily lumped together with Vinson, Reed, and Burton. Like their conservative colleagues, Frankfurter and Jackson tended to observe a philosophy of "judicial restraint" in which the Court often deferred to the legislative and executive branches, taking an expansive interpretation of the powers that the Constitution accorded to Congress and the president.[48]

Stocked full of Roosevelt and Truman appointees and without any true political conservatives, the Vinson Court took a relatively accommodating stance toward governmental interests. With a staunch Truman ally as chief justice and relatively strong relationships between the administration and several of the other justices, the Court often proved responsive to the desires of the federal government in legal disputes. This made the intervention of the solicitor general and attorney general in the covenant cases all the more significant as it might potentially swing the Court's conservative-leaning members to the NAACP's side. As the Court readied itself for the oral arguments, the justices' focused intently on what the Truman administration's representatives had to say.

WHILE THE GOVERNMENT'S AMICUS brief had made the administration's position on the issue exceedingly clear, Solicitor General Perlman also felt it necessary to offer an oral argument before the Court in the cases. The Court granted him an opportunity to do so and on January 15, the first day of arguments, Perlman addressed the justices for an hour. His statement reinforced many of the key themes of the written brief, but also delved even deeper into the rhetoric of egalitarianism and racial equality. Assistant Attorney General Philip Elman described it as a "real Fourth of July speech" that bore the unmistakable message that the Truman administration saw new importance in assuring constitutional protections for the rights of African Americans.[49]

Perlman hammered away on the detrimental effects that residential discrimination had on America's image abroad. He used the language of global scrutiny and the nation's fast-developing international responsibilities to argue that the enforcement of covenants would violate federal public policy. Calling the issue of restrictive covenants a matter "of the greatest importance," Perlman declared on behalf of the U.S. government that "existing conditions in this nation, and elsewhere throughout the world, have made the continuation of such a discriminatory device . . . to be a menace to the privileges of citizenship and to our democratic institutions of government." He insisted that courts' continued enforcement of covenants had "become a source of serious embarrassment to agencies of the Federal Government in the performance of many essential functions." "World events," he reminded the justices, "have given us the leadership of true democratic forces everywhere, but efforts to teach universal respect for the dignity of man are hampered by the discriminations and inequalities which we as a nation have failed to correct." His meaning was clear. In the recent wartime and emerging Cold War contests between freedom and totalitarian rule, restrictive covenants and their consequences had incontrovertibly weakened America's standing in the eyes of the world.[50]

The solicitor general then went well beyond the issue of public policy to address the morality of Jim Crow's hold on American life. As he reached the end of his presentation to the Court he turned to a sweeping discussion of what the promise of racial justice meant for the nation. "The Caucasians are under a heavy debt to the Negroes," he began. Perlman elaborated,

We brought them here as slaves, as chattels devoid of human rights, privileges and immunities. We set them free, promising them, in our amended Constitution and new laws, equal rights and privileges with all other people. Yet after three-quarters of a century, attempts are made, by such devices as restrictive covenants, to hold them in bondage, to segregate them, to hem them in so that they cannot escape from the evil conditions under which so many of them are compelled to live. They have been told, time and again, by this Court that this is a government of laws and not of men, and that all men are equal before the law. . . . They wait—millions of them—outside this courtroom door, to learn whether these great maxims really apply to them.[51]

This eloquent portrayal on behalf of the Truman administration asserted the Supreme Court's—and the nation's—responsibility to defend African Americans' civil rights and served as a genuine call to action. Perlman's rousing conclusion that covenants "should be relegated to the limbo of other things as dead as slavery" hung in the air. He had made his case with such force that the *Baltimore Afro-American* declared later that week that Truman's government had now expanded Roosevelt's heralded "Four Freedoms" to include a fifth—the "freedom to buy property and to occupy it in any section of a city where the owner is willing to sell."[52]

Perhaps even more significantly, Perlman's discussion of the "debt" owed to the nation's African Americans did not limit its focus to the single issue of restrictive covenants, but gestured as well to the problems posed by the denial of "complete equality in this [housing] and other respects." With this, Perlman signaled to civil rights advocates that the federal government's work on behalf of black Americans' rights in the courts was by no means finished. His words offered a platform, however shaky, for civil rights litigation to come.[53]

The solicitor general's speech proved a hard act to follow, yet the remaining anticovenant attorneys fought vigorously to sway the Court. George Vaughn took the floor first among his colleagues. Though his remarks would be best remembered for his emotional closing, the bulk of his legal arguments focused on the intent of the Thirteenth Amendment. He asked the Court to consider the "dire conditions and sufferings" of black urban populations and the actions and collusion that helped to create those inequities. Vaughn spoke about the state of African American communities in St. Louis as akin to the exploitation and misery of involuntary servitude. He urged the justices "to redefine that term in light of these conditions." "My grandfather was an adult slave in Louisiana," he explained. "Today, I, his offspring, stand here pleading with this court to grant to the members of his race the full measures of liberty and freedom intended to be bestowed upon that race by the Civil War Amendments." Despite the earlier admonitions of his colleagues in the NAACP legal office, Vaughn stood resolute behind his contention that residential segregation amounted to nothing less than a twentieth-century form of enslavement.[54]

Vaughn also echoed the solicitor general's emphasis on the international impact of domestic discrimination. "We stand here today your Honors," he solemnly pronounced, "with our finger on the Achillies [sic] Heel of American Democracy." The nation's reputation and ability to lead a free world was at stake. "The eyes of the nations are upon us," he continued. "The yardstick by which our claim to democracy is being measured today all over the world is the treatment accorded to our minority groups." The realities of the Cold War conflict provided Vaughn a lever with which he attempted to shift the considerable weight of precedent off of his clients. He followed these remarks with his memorable closing appeal.[55]

Though Vaughn's impassioned final words appeared to be among the most impactful moments of the day, his tensions with the NAACP did not lessen as a result. While most observers would remark on the power and emotional weight—albeit not the legal skill—of Vaughn's argument, Thurgood Marshall's contempt for his renegade colleague lingered on for decades. Indeed, Marshall would unfairly recount Vaughn's performance to one of his biographers as that of a doddering and overmatched fool who slept through most of the Supreme Court presentation and sang lines from the spiritual "Go Down Moses" during his oral argument. Marshall's recollections differed sharply from all of the available contemporary evidence, but served as a reminder that Vaughn's stirring final appeal had done nothing to heal his fractured relationship with the NAACP legal team.[56]

Marshall and Loren Miller's arguments in the *McGhee* case came next before the Court. They hoped to steer the justices toward the Association's preferred lines of argument, focusing on judicial decrees as state action and pressing them to consider the practical results of covenant enforcement by the courts. Marshall and Miller each pointed to the socioeconomic material contained in the NAACP's briefs in an effort to ensure that the Court understood exactly what was at stake for black urban populations. Echoing their written claims, they insisted that covenants forced African Americans into overcrowded and deteriorating sections of cities and that these conditions wreaked havoc on the physical and psychological well-being of black communities while fomenting social tensions between the races. Justice Frankfurter—who asked the majority of the questions during the arguments—bluntly demanded to know the relevance of the material. "If you are right about the legal proposition," he insisted, "the sociological material merely shows how it works. If you're wrong, this material doesn't do any good." The Court, he seemed to say, could only follow the constitutional questions involved. Marshall defended the legal relevance of the data, but also maintained that the justices did not have to rely solely on this information to overturn the enforcement. Frankfurter's response that "of course the sociological material is relevant in the District of Columbia cases and on the questions of due process," however, gave the NAACP's attorneys some hope. The Court appeared to put some stock in the Association's nonlegal material, validating the effort and resources the litigation team had committed to fashioning a Brandeis brief.[57]

In the Washington cases, Charles Hamilton Houston and Phineas Indritz also focused considerable attention on the capriciousness and cruelty of residential restrictions. Houston lingered on the facts of the case record to demonstrate that resistance to neighborhood integration served no real purpose other than to diminish the quality of life and the rights of black citizens. Like Marshall, Houston also asserted the relevance of the sociological data in his brief, emphasizing the societal costs that judicial enforcement incurred. His cocounsel Indritz pointed to the injustice of covenants by highlighting cases in which the courts had used residential restrictions to evict nonwhite spouses and children from homes they occupied with a white partner or parent. "The Nazi 'Nuremberg' laws," Indritz admonished, "never went so far." A tool of exclusion that would deny even respected individuals like singer Marian Anderson, the late George Washington Carver, Jewish scientist Albert Einstein, or former vice president Charles Curtis—of Native American descent—the right to own or occupy a decent home in many areas of the nation's cities struck Indritz as offensive to the "elemental concepts of fairness and decency." These are not "covenants," he chided, "they are, in truth, 'compacts to sin'—conspiracies against our fellow men and their right to live." The nation and the courts could not countenance such vicious instruments of racial prejudice. Both attorneys fought hard to establish the moral high ground in the case and captivated the attention of at least one of the justices, who scrawled in his diary that the two performances were "excellent."[58]

THE RESPONDING WHITE ATTORNEYS, however, put up an equally vigorous fight. Gerald Seegers, Henry Gilligan, and James Crooks held close to the traditional arguments that had defended covenants against judicial scrutiny in previous cases. While they acknowledged the hardships that urban black communities faced because of housing problems, they insisted that the remedies for these struggles could not come from the courts. "This is a law suit," Seegers said flatly. "This is a court of law, and the problems before the Court are legal ones. The Court . . . must therefore look to the statutes and legal precedents rather than to the sociological data presented by opposing counsel." The consequences of residential discrimination were immaterial to the matter at hand, he argued, because the actions involved were those of private citizens. The only way that the Court could justify an intervention on behalf of the black homeowners would be through creating a radical reinterpretation of the Fourteenth Amendment or by unilaterally "rewrit[ing] Missouri's public policy." Seegers and his colleagues decried the possibility of what they saw as "judicial amendment of the Constitution," or the effort of "the judiciary to substitute its judgment for that of the legislature." Their argument was plain: precedent was all that mattered.[59]

Seegers and his colleagues stretched this line of reasoning as far as they could take it. Strictly speaking, Seegers claimed, "the Negroes here are asserting deprivations of rights which they never had." Since the contracts of sale were clearly invalid under the terms of the covenant, the logic held: the African American families in the cases technically had no ownership or property rights to dispute and thus could not have had their rights violated by the enforcement of the covenant or their eviction from the premises. The Court appeared roundly unmoved by this argument. James Crooks took a different approach when he later insisted that court enforcement of the restrictions was not a discriminatory act. African American purchasers were not excluded because of their race, he maintained, but because they had violated the terms of a contract. When Justice Frank Murphy pointed out the absurdity of suggesting that the breach of a covenant based upon race had nothing to do with the race of the violators, the courtroom broke out into muffled laughter.[60]

Henry Gilligan went even further. After lambasting the Truman administration's decision to intervene, he offered a vocal defense of discrimination as a natural right. "Discrimination," he pronounced, "is as much a law of nature as gravity." Insisting that there was "nothing disgraceful" about it, Gilligan called the right to discriminate "a precious privilege" that citizens exercised in "the food we eat . . . in the clothes we wear and everything that we do." Racial and ethnic discrimination, he insisted, was a moral and legal choice for individuals to make. In an effort to drive home this point to the justices he stressed ethnic affinity among Jews and insisted that throughout history Jewish communities "have discriminated so much that whole nations in which they had lived have disintegrated and disappeared while the Jews retained their racial unity." For Gilligan, the core issue at stake in the cases was whether or not white Americans could choose to spend their lives exclusively among those of their own race. Gerald Seegers offered similar sentiments, calling discrimination a right that came "from human nature" and that "covenants represent an exercise of these natural rights." To these attorneys—and the clients they spoke for—racial exclusion was an innate and fundamental human and social condition, one upon which the rule of law and the sanctity of society depended. They argued that discrimination was at the heart of human freedom. "Forced social equality," Gilligan warned, "is tyranny."[61]

When Gilligan and Crooks finished, the final words of the oral argument belonged to Charles Hamilton Houston. In his rebuttal, he sought to return the Court's focus to the broader meaning that their ruling would hold for the nation. Continued enforcement of covenants would only continue to divide the country, sow the seeds of discord, and tarnish America's international reputation. The courts' record of thoroughgoing support for residential segregation made "racial unity impossible" and was "endangering national security," as evidenced by the Truman administration's passionate arguments in the case. For Houston, the grizzled veteran of decades of injustice and a long career of advocacy, the message that the Court had to send was clear: "racism in the United States must stop." There was simply too much at stake for the nation's judiciary to ignore the rights and needs of African Americans desperately in search of decent homes. "It was," wrote the Baltimore Afro-American, "the day in court for all minority peoples in a free America."[62]

EVEN BEFORE THE PACKED courtroom had emptied, observers speculated about what the outcome would be. No one had a clear sense of how the Court would divide on the issue. The intervention of the federal government had no doubt helped the NAACP's case, but it was decidedly unclear whether that would be enough. The St. Louis Argus reported ominously that the attorneys for the black homeowners "appeared to be disconsolate as they left the court room. . . . Privately they expressed a belief that the cases were lost." Uncertainty prevailed. Common wisdom in the weeks after the oral arguments was that the Court would split either four to two in favor of the NAACP or break evenly, leaving the lower courts' enforcement in place. African American commentators held the likelihood of more favorable results as slight and the possibility of a loss loomed large. "Are we," worried one reporter, "to have another Dred Scott decision?"[63]

A surprisingly small number of questions from the Court during the seven hours of oral arguments contributed to the confusion of the attorneys. One lawyer remarked that even the questions the justices did ask left little indication of their attitudes on the case. A reporter opined wryly that "if books were made on the outcome . . . the odds on the four racial restrictive covenant cases probably would be 5 to 4—take your choice." Observers believed that the remaining "liberal" bloc comprised of Justices Black, Murphy, and Douglas seemed firmly in the NAACP's camp while Chief Justice Vinson and Justice Burton appeared reliably in favor of enforcement. Most expected that Justice Frankfurter would tip the balance.[64]

Because of the anticipated tightness of the vote, the attorneys on both sides braced themselves for a protracted wait for the decision. As weeks turned into months the tension mounted for all involved. Nearly four months passed while the fate of the six black families in the cases and the hopes of black urban communities across the country lingered unaddressed. When the Court finally delivered its opinion on Monday, May 3, of 1948, the result took nearly everyone by surprise.

"Live Anywhere!":
The Supreme Court's Decision and Public Response

As Chief Justice Vinson weighed his decision in the days following oral arguments, he seemed to recognize the enormity of the task ahead of him. He tried to disregard the passion of the appeals, scrawling in his notes regarding the DOJ's brief that his determination would need to *Put aside embarrassment*," and, "rest upon *the law*." He could not deny the "heart appeal" of the black homeowners' plight, but the case at hand, he remarked to himself, "is for the *head*." Perhaps the native Kentuckian also felt the countervailing pull of his roots in the Jim Crow South. While he was a relative moderate on racial issues, a quarter century earlier he had stood on the floor of the House of Representatives and railed about the superiority of Western European stock and declared that "water will not mix with oil, neither will peoples of diverse habits, traits and characteristics." Still, as he pored over the briefs arguing each side, he found himself ready to "compromise his own ideas" and decide in favor of the black families in the cases.[65]

One of Vinson's clerks would later confirm that the chief justice had in fact leaned toward the NAACP's arguments long before the attorneys appeared in the Court. A critical factor in Vinson's predisposition was the dissent in *Hurd v. Hodge* that his former colleague, Judge Henry Edgerton, had authored for the Federal Circuit Court of Appeals in Washington, D.C., in May of 1947. Vinson held Edgerton in tremendously high regard. In fact, just two weeks after the oral arguments for *Shelley* and *Hurd*, Vinson wrote a tribute to Edgerton's work in the court of appeals highlighting his "deep friendship and affection" for the man and the "respect for the law," "brilliance of analysis," and "cogency of reasoning" that defined his legal opinions. The chief justice's relationship with Edgerton undoubtedly helped shape the outcome in the covenant cases.[66]

In the end, Vinson saw court enforcement of covenants as a clear exercise of discriminatory state power. "This should be reversed on the letter of the Fourteenth Amendment," he stated flatly to the other justices. "There is state action. They [the black homebuyers] have been deprived of their constitutional rights." Vinson grasped the gravity of the issue before the Court and perhaps sensed that these cases might offer him his moment in judicial history. Whatever his reasons, the chief justice quickly set about building a consensus among his colleagues.[67]

If the opinions of the Court's clerks were any indication, however, Vinson's colleagues had not been nearly as favorable toward the NAACP's arguments from the outset. The clerks for Justices Stanley Reed and Harold Burton had both recommended that the Court decline to hear the cases in the first place. "While the [state action] argument could hardly be called frivolous," wrote one of the young men, "it is probably not sound." He reflected the Court's sharp awareness of the housing crisis, writing that "no one who has had any experience with urban housing conditions can doubt that the restrictive covenant has resulted in a great many substantial social evils." Yet—reflecting much of the prevailing legal sentiment at the time—Reed's clerk argued that the NAACP's state action argument seemed untenable constitutionally and that furthermore, "an abrupt and sweeping judicial invalidation of all restrictive covenants might well create about as many problems as it would solve." Burton's clerk similarly wrote that "this case troubles me. The covenant enforced is obviously undemocratic and contrary to the theory of the Constitution," but the restrictive agreements in question seemed to him squarely in the realm of private action. Though the justices had obviously elected to grant certiorari despite these objections, the sentiments expressed in these memoranda revealed a key tension at the heart of the Court's and the nation's assessment of the issue. Both men acknowledged that covenants were exceptionally destructive in practice and yet neither believed the Court had any standing to address the issue.[68]

Even those who had supported the granting of certiorari in the summer of 1947 had expressed their skepticism that the Court could depart in such a glaring way from its previous treatment of private contractual rights. "The precedent seems to be against [the] petitioner," wrote William O. Douglas's clerk. "I don't see any way around the difficulty as I am sure the Court is not now ready to reverse the historic policy." Though these three clerks' pessimism cannot definitively reveal how the justices themselves were predisposed to the central question of the cases, the opinions that they expressed indicated that Vinson could expect at least some resistance.[69]

Creating a unanimous Court, however, became a mission of particular importance and pride for Vinson. A man that anticovenant lawyers had always counted among their adversaries suddenly became a powerful advocate in support of their cause. Another clerk later described the chief justice's efforts to wrangle the rest of the justices into agreement and make the Court "speak . . . as an institution with but one voice" on the matter. By the time the justices met in early February for a preliminary conference on the cases, Vinson had begun to exercise the managerial skills that had won him the job. "He had cajoled prima donnas, had bullied the foot-dragging conservatives, had rallied a fellow institutionalist" demanding unity out of the contentious group. The private conference in February revealed the unanimity that Vinson had sought after. One by one, each of his colleagues declared himself in support of reversing the lower courts. The chief justice of the Supreme Court, it seemed, had helped to ensure a stunning victory for the NAACP's legal team.[70]

The task of writing the Court's opinions, however, could still fragment Vinson's consensus and undermine the impact of the decision. Vinson, using his prerogative as chief justice, assigned himself to craft the language for both the state cases and the District of Columbia cases. Rewriting decades of established legal custom regarding covenant enforcement would be no small burden, but Vinson eagerly took up the challenge. For ten weeks the chief justice fashioned an opinion that he hoped would satisfy his colleagues and withstand the inevitable scrutiny of critics. In mid-April, Vinson circulated his first draft for the *Shelley* and *McGhee* suits and won praise from the others on the Court for his work. Only two justices offered suggestions for revision and these changes were minor. The remaining group lauded Vinson's effort. William O. Douglas praised the opinion for the two state cases as "proud jobs." Hugo Black found the logic and length to be "just right," and Harold Burton assured Vinson that "this is an excellent bid for a unanimous court." Vinson had kept his consensus intact.[71]

Vinson's opinion in *Shelley* and *McGhee* firmly vindicated the NAACP's state action argument. After delineating the particulars of both cases and justifying the Court's intervention on the grounds that the question of judicial state action had never previously been adjudicated with respect to covenants, Vinson launched into a full-throated defense of black homebuyers' rights. Relying heavily at times on political scientist Horace Edgar Flack's 1908 treatise detailing the precursors, events, and debates surrounding the drafting and adoption of the Fourteenth Amendment, the chief justice argued that the amendment had always intended to protect property rights from discriminatory infringement. "Equality in the enjoyment of property rights was regarded by the framers of that Amendment," he wrote, "as an essential pre-condition to the realization of other basic civil rights and liberties which the Amendment was intended to guarantee." The substance of equal citizenship in America, he suggested, depended upon the right of individuals to own and enjoy property freely if their means allowed.[72]

There were limits, however, to the Court's ability to protect these rights. Vinson's opinion unequivocally maintained that private citizens could discriminate as they wished and that restrictive covenants themselves did not violate the Fourteenth Amendment's prohibitions on state action. Residential discrimination through "voluntary adherence" to the provisions of restrictions remained beyond the scope of the Court's authority to intervene and Vinson bluntly stated as much. For anticovenant advocates like George Vaughn who had hoped the Court might disallow their use entirely, Vinson's assurance that the Fourteenth Amendment provided "no shield against merely private conduct however discriminatory or wrongful" came as a blow—though not an unexpected one. While the chief justice confirmed the right of individuals to impose their private discriminations, he insisted that in the cases before him "there was more . . . the purposes of the agreements were secured only by judicial enforcement by state courts." The question that the Court now had to answer was whether or not that enforcement breached the proscriptions of the Fourteenth Amendment.[73]

Vinson first tackled the issue of judicial bodies as state actors. For him it seemed clear that the Supreme Court had long been willing to scrutinize the activities of the judiciary as actions of the state. "The short of the matter," he wrote, "is that from the time of the adoption of the Fourteenth Amendment until the present, it has been the consistent ruling of this Court that the action of the States to which the Amendment has reference includes action of state courts and state judicial officials." While the interpretations had varied as to whether those actions were therefore improper, the precedent was unmistakably in favor of recognizing judicial authority as synonymous with the authority of the state.[74]

Having dispensed with that concern, Vinson then turned to address the constitutionality of the state courts' enforcement of the covenants. Here again, the Court found the issue to be fairly obvious. "It is clear," Vinson insisted, "that but for the active intervention of the state courts, supported by the full panoply of state power, petitioners would have been free to occupy the properties in question without restraint." He continued, remarking that "the States have made available . . . the full coercive power of government to deny to petitioners, on the grounds of race or color, the enjoyment of property rights." Without this involvement of state actors, the African American families would have been free to occupy their properties and exercise their rights "on an equal footing" with their white neighbors. By prohibiting these families from doing so solely because of their race, the courts of Missouri and Michigan had "denied petitioners equal protection of the laws . . . therefore, the action of the state courts cannot stand." Vinson and the unanimous Court behind him ordered the reversal of the lower courts' judgments.[75]

The chief justice's parting words once again pointed to the "historical context" of the Fourteenth Amendment as a guide. "Whatever else the framers sought to achieve," he wrote, "it is clear that the matter of primary concern was the establishment of equality in the enjoyment of basic civil and political rights and the preservation of those rights from discriminatory action on the part of the States based on considerations of race or color." Vinson declared that the amendment's fundamental purpose had been to assure racial equality in the exercise of American citizenship, a powerful statement that he matched with an effort to expand the scope of what civil rights advocates could use that amendment to achieve. Vinson's colleague Harold Burton wrote privately in late April that the opinion "will be a major contribution to the vitality of the [Fourteenth] Amendment, . . . the general subject of interracial justice, and the strength of this Court as the 'living voice of the Constitution.'" The justices believed that their decision marked a moment of particular importance—one that might stimulate substantive improvements in the rights of the nation's racial minorities.[76]

Days before Vinson circulated this final draft to the Court, he also distributed his initial opinion in the District of Columbia cases. Following much the same pattern as his logic in *Shelley*, Vinson quickly addressed the details of the case and reaffirmed the fact that the Court had never before ruled on the propriety of federal court enforcement of covenants. He noted that Charles Hamilton Houston and Phineas Indritz had relied primarily on the Fifth Amendment's guarantee of due process in their arguments—which offered the same protections under federal jurisdiction that the Fourteenth Amendment did under that of the states. After reiterating the details of the petitioners' Fifth Amendment pleas, Vinson promptly dispensed with the issue as "unnecessary" given that other nonconstitutional grounds fully supported the reversal of the lower court.[77]

He turned first to the Civil Rights Act of 1866 that offered particularly strong language assuring the equality of property rights for individuals of all races. Expounding again upon the original intentions of the Reconstruction-era Congress, Vinson declared that the Act clearly prohibited the exercise of federal authority to impose racial restrictions on the access to and enjoyment of property rights. Given the circumstances of the cases at hand, Vinson wrote, "to suggest that the Negro petitioners have been accorded the same rights as white citizens to purchase, hold, and convey real property is to reject the plain meaning of language." The idea that equality could exist alongside the enforcement of covenants seemed almost laughable. As a result, he continued, "We hold that the action of the District Court directed against the Negro purchasers and the white sellers denies rights intended by Congress to be protected by the Civil Rights Act and that, consequently, the action cannot stand." Washington too would be forced to end its judicial support for restrictive covenants.[78]

Vinson, however, had not quite finished. The chief justice insisted that "even in the absence of the statute," sufficient grounds for reversal existed on the issue of public policy. Pointing to the Court's ruling in *Shelley*, Vinson argued that it would be inconsistent with public interests to allow federal courts to engage in discriminatory actions that had now been prohibited in state courts. "We cannot," Vinson contended, "presume that the public policy of the United States manifests a lesser concern for the protection of such basic rights" in the nation's capital than it did in the states. The chief justice's original draft of this opinion shed some additional light on his thinking with respect to the matter of public policy. Vinson remarked there in a footnote justifying the Court's intervention that covenants were not "matters of merely local interest and concern" that were thus immune from the Court's supervision of national policy. Instead, the covenant cases put at issue "fundamental rights . . . where the importance and implications of the matters adjudicated are not confined to the District of Columbia." While Vinson's final draft deleted this language in favor of a purely statutory justification of the Court's jurisdiction, it seemed clear that the chief justice believed the issue of residential restrictions had crucial implications for American society as a whole.[79]

The opinion in the *Hurd* cases, however, failed to keep slight fissures from developing in Vinson's consensus. While the Court remained unanimous as it would in *Shelley*, Felix Frankfurter felt compelled to write a brief concurrence rather than simply joining in Vinson's argument. Privately, Frankfurter expressed a deep skepticism about his colleague's foundational assumptions regarding the intentions of the Civil Rights Act and the Fourteenth Amendment. "The investigation which I made of the Civil Rights legislation . . . has made me very wary of arguments drawn from that legislation. . . . The scope and validity . . . have for me been left in confusion and doubt, and I prefer not to get involved . . . if a decision may clearly and cleanly be reached otherwise," he wrote. Frankfurter echoed Vinson's public policy arguments instead by asserting that it was both imprudent and inequitable for a federal court to take actions that—if performed by a state court—would be in clear violation of the Constitution. This was especially true, Frankfurter argued, because the issue involved "touch[ed] rights so basic to our society." While Vinson would not be the Court's only voice, his colleague did not stray far from the chief justice's opinion.[80]

Vinson announced the two opinions to the public on May 3 and even in his delivery he sought to convey the importance of the action that he and his colleagues had undertaken. Justices typically offered abbreviated readings of their written findings for public consumption—only summarizing their conclusions for the sake of expedience. For the *Shelley* and *Hurd* decisions, however, Vinson elected to recite the Court's opinions in full. In doing so, he signaled the magnitude of what the Court believed its action would mean for race relations and American society as a whole. From his seat in the gallery that day, NAACP executive secretary Walter White noted the chief justice's "face and voice filled with deep feeling" as he leaned forward to proclaim the black homeowners' victory. White telegrammed Vinson that afternoon to thank him "for not only that magnificent decision . . . but for the conviction with which you delivered the opinion." Perhaps the most gratifying praise, however, had come earlier that day when Vinson's colleague, Detroit native Frank Murphy, had passed him a handwritten note shortly before the reading. Murphy wrote that his words would be "as important as Dred Scott and other epoch making decisions," and encouraged him to "take his time" in the moment. Murphy insisted that whatever the initial reaction, in the future, "the cases will make you immortal."[81]

AFRICAN AMERICANS and anticovenant advocates from all quarters greeted the Court's ruling as a momentous event. For the six families at the heart of the cases, the sense of joy was palpable. After more than three years of fighting through the courts with the looming uncertainty of whether or not they would actually have a roof over their heads when the dust finally settled, they found vindication in the Supreme Court's decision. In Detroit, Orsel McGhee told the attorneys and the community that had supported his family's case that he could not say enough "in expressing how grateful we are to everybody for the great help that was given us in this fight. . . . My wife and my sons, who have served their country in the armed services, now feel that life is worth living and that eventually true democracy will be a reality in the United States." "We have a mighty nice little home here," he exhaled, "and we didn't want to lose it." Minnie McGhee expressed her own feelings of gratitude to the six justices "who put principles before cheap politics." For the McGhees, the triumph validated all the sacrifices and the indignities they had endured and justified the efforts of friends and strangers who had invested their own hopes in the case. As the mother and father of two servicemen, the victory also meant much more that the security of a home. It was a promise that their children might live in a more just society, a down payment on the freedom that should have been their birthright.[82]

In St. Louis, the Shelley household proved unable to sleep the night of the Court's ruling. Nearly three years after their purchase, they had yet to spend a day in their home without a lawsuit hanging over them. The combination of long-deferred excitement and the congratulatory phone calls that flooded in from across the country and even overseas made that first night of certainty a restless one. Ethel Lee Shelley, whose resolve and faith had sustained the family through the entire ordeal, remarked, "My little soul is overjoyed. Wait till I get by myself. I'll tell the lord of my thankfulness." The real estate brokers who had bankrolled her case celebrated with slightly more ostentation by arranging a mass meeting to acclaim their role in the victory.[83]

On Bryant Street in Washington the decision gave the victors a similar thrill. For Pauline Stewart the case meant that her eighty-seven-year-old father—a man born at the outset of the Civil War—would live out the rest of his life in comfort. "Thank God," he hollered upon hearing the outcome. The withered man contemplated the significance of the moment and informed a passing reporter that "it goes to show you. If you live a decent, honest, respectable life, what more can be expected of you?" Stewart had worked a lifetime to bring his family into Washington's black middle class and his daughter had fought to carve out a piece of progress, security, and dignity in the segregated city. The victory served as proof that Jim Crow's defenders could no longer deny the fruits of generations of striving and struggle. It was a vindication of America's promise of opportunity. One of Stewart's younger black neighbors encapsulated this postwar spirit of expectation succinctly. "I knew it couldn't stay that way," he said of the Court's repudiation. "This is America, brother." Further down the block, the Hurd family confessed the secret of their resolve, insisting that "we ha[d] too much invested in this house to give it up easily." Whether they meant their financial outlay or—like their neighbors—an investment of faith in the nation's principles, the Hurds found themselves undeniably relieved to have their investment intact at the end.[84]

Even those black homeseekers not immediately involved in the cases found a deeply personal meaning in the victory. A poignant column in the *Pittsburgh Courier* declared that beyond the broader social and political symbolism of the moment, "The Court has handed me a dream. . . . I may never have a house with a garden that slopes down into Rock Creek Park, but I don't have to dismiss the idea. This is my American heritage, which has been restored at long last. . . . We are all prepared to deal with the burning cross, the neighborhood gang, the tossed bomb, and above all with the cold shoulder. What has been unendurable was that the Courts lent their comfort and the long arm of the injunctive process to the enemy of American dreams for an unconscionable time." The decision put the law and the words of the U.S. Supreme Court and the Justice Department squarely behind black Americans who sought decent homes. True, individual prejudice would live on untrammeled by the high court's opinion, but the decision had stripped that bigotry of its cloak of legitimacy and the sanction of the law and left it naked. However dangerous it might still be, black homeseekers would no longer have to suffer the humiliation of being told by the courts that their exclusion from adequate housing was in keeping with the nation's ideals of justice. As the *Chicago Defender* put it, the Court had quite suddenly "given substance to the dream of democracy."[85]

Some exuberant observers interpreted the results as the most significant event in the pursuit of racial progress and equality since the Civil War. Columns in the *Pittsburgh Courier, Michigan Chronicle,* and *Washington Post* all hailed the decision as something akin to a "second emancipation." Responses from St. Louis, Los Angeles, Chicago, Kansas City and other hotbeds of covenant litigation elicited a similar response. Even those who stopped short of invoking Lincoln assigned tremendous importance to the victory. Banner headlines in black newspapers announcing the decision declared that African Americans could now "Live Anywhere!" and that residential discrimination had been "Outlawed." "The United States Supreme Court," one writer trumpeted, "has made perhaps the greatest contribution to American democracy that is within its power to make," by putting a stop to the growth of "the biggest ghettoes in history." Other observers also saw the decision as the "beginning of the end of the Negro ghetto," and a breach that would "eventually break down racial segregation in American community development." Black communities imagined a new horizon of possibilities opening in America's cities.[86]

The NAACP's leaders proved especially eager to proclaim the magnitude of the moment. Thurgood Marshall announced that the victory gave "thousands of prospective home buyers throughout the United States new courage and hope in the American form of government." "It is obvious," he continued, "that no greater blow to date has been made against the pattern of segregation existing within the United States." Beyond these public pronouncements, Marshall wrote privately of his conviction that as a result of the cases "ghettos will be broken." Executive Secretary Walter White, who had traveled to Washington to hear the decisions announced in person, insisted that the cases "may turn out to be the greatest single contribution of our time towards the preservation of democracy," while Assistant Secretary Roy Wilkins remarked that the occasion "made democracy mean something to millions of Negroes who had about given up hope." With their unabashed enthusiasm the Association's leaders sought to paint the covenant cases as their most important victory yet.[87]

The NAACP's reactions, however, also reflected a political purpose. The case offered an opportunity to shore up the national office's strength during a difficult moment of transition. Key officials believed that the victory might soften the blow of a doubled annual membership fee, a crackdown on political dissent within the organization, and an increasingly tense relationship between the national office and local branches as the Association worked to centralize control of its operations and agenda. Walter White visited the Detroit Branch in the days after the decision to herald the NAACP's role and kick off the annual membership drive. At the same time, national membership campaign chairwoman Daisy Lampkin put *Shelley* front and center when encouraging drive workers in the summer of 1948. "Certainly," she wrote, "no red-blooded American, black or white, could hesitate for a moment to support an organization that has made this victory possible. Now is the time to intensify our drive for members. Get out into the streets, in the churches, in your lodges, in your clubs. . . . Rally the people to the NAACP."[88]

For Roy Wilkins, the success of the cases simply provided evidence that centralized authority in civil rights activism was a necessary and proper step. Wilkins used the victory to argue for the importance of the NAACP's role as a clearinghouse in litigation efforts and to suggest that only a strong national leadership could direct and sustain the lengthy battles that would force lasting reform in American race relations. The inevitable conclusion, as he saw it, was that the Association "should have the financial and moral support not only of all Negroes, but of all who believe in America and its creed." Though membership would still drop considerably over the course of the year, NAACP officials believed that *Shelley* could mitigate some of the losses.[89]

Despite the general sense of enthusiasm the victory inspired, however, many observers in black communities greeted the decision with some skepticism and reservations. A handful were downright pessimistic about the meaning of the cases. An editorial from the *St. Louis Argus* dismissed the ebullience of those celebrating in the wake of *Shelley* as an "undue amount of excitement." The authors argued that a Supreme Court opinion that left racial restrictions intact and enforceable everywhere but the courtroom would never be enough to end the pervasive practices of residential discrimination. With the nation still mired in a housing crisis, they argued, black homeseekers faced the same basic problem that "we can only buy where [white] others will sell." Desegregation would proceed only with changing white attitudes and not by court decree.[90]

The authors had touched on the nagging fear that had dogged the campaign. Cautionary notes sounded among even the most ardent believers in the significance of the cases. "We will not witness any mass movement of Negroes into new neighborhoods as a result of this ruling," warned an otherwise celebratory column in Detroit's *Michigan Chronicle*. After all, offered another contributor, real estate brokers "for the most part have operated under a 'law' that they have created for themselves anyway." Black activists again and again signaled their awareness that the entrenched customs and practices of exclusion had deeper roots than covenants alone. Housing segregation would not simply vanish into the ether. This more cautious optimism anticipated some of the white backlash that would shortly ensue.[91]

As a whole, however, anticovenant activists and black communities felt an overwhelming sense of promise. *Shelley* might not be the decisive solution to the problem of America's racial ghettos, but it was at the very least a potent tool in an ongoing struggle. Victory served as a call to action and would help to point the way forward. Besides, success tasted far sweeter than the bitterness of indifference and rejection. While it remained to be seen if black Americans could now truly "live anywhere," the anticovenant campaign and the Supreme Court of the United States had finally told black homeseekers that they could try.

Turning Point: From the Courts to the Cities

Civil rights litigators now looked to the battles ahead. Though the covenant cases marked the triumphal culmination of the NAACP's more than thirty-year campaign against the legal instruments of housing discrimination, every participant knew that more remained to be done in the cities, communities, and courtrooms of America. The Supreme Court's decision undoubtedly lifted the spirits and aspirations of black activists and the Truman administration's intervention in the cases seemed to be just as significant a development. Still, a larger fight loomed in neighborhoods across the country and in Jim Crow's other arenas of oppression.

Covenants' defenders and detractors would each seek to shape the impact of *Shelley*'s outcome over the next several years, wrestling over how far the Court's decision might reach. The resulting contest had profound implications in the postwar era's resurgent struggle for black freedom. *Shelley* would ultimately change the tenor of that broader battle in lasting ways. As the coming years would reveal, victory in the covenant cases offered not an end, but a beginning.

FIVE

Failures and Foundations

The Covenant Cases and
Postwar Black Freedom Struggles

In October of 1949, just under eighteen months after the victory in *Shelley*, the eminent sociologist, activist, and anticovenant crusader Louis Wirth began drafting a painful note from his office at the University of Chicago. Wirth wrote to his colleagues at the ACRR and reflected on the results of the countless hours and considerable resources they had invested in restrictive covenant litigation over the previous years. Fund-raising had now slowed to dangerously low levels. "Indifference and apathy" appeared to displace the kind of public-spiritedness that had fueled a broader civil rights consciousness in the immediate wake of World War II. Perhaps most disconcerting of all, he lamented, "little remains of the initial wholesome impact of the President's Committee on Civil Rights or of the Supreme Court decision on restrictive covenants." So soon after the triumphal fanfare of victory, one of the important architects of the anticovenant campaign prepared to label the cases a failure.[1]

Public responses to the covenant cases that had unfolded over the previous year even led Wirth to question the soundness of litigation as a tactic to resolve the nation's racial inequities. "The fact that so many of the problems of racial and cultural relations have become defined in terms of . . . litigation," he wrote with disappointment, "has alienated a wide segment of public interest." Legal resolutions to community-level problems, he seemed to say, only served to exacerbate tensions over minority groups' civil rights claims. Among the disaffected were white Americans that previously "could be relied upon to support movements for improvement as long as they required only personal good will and called only for unofficial citizen organization and action." Progress and interracial harmony, Wirth implied, might only be possible if the solutions to racial injustice were voluntary and deferred to the comfort of white citizens. The tenacity of residential segregation that stood just outside his window in Chicago's neighborhoods provided all the evidence he needed to consign the legacy of the covenant cases to the margins of history.[2]

Indeed, the resistance that *Shelley* encountered when it returned from the Supreme Court to America's cities in the summer of 1948 became the central factor shaping the historical memory of the anticovenant campaign. Even the most optimistic of the covenant cases' supporters had acknowledged that housing discrimination would not suddenly disappear as a result of the decision. Decades of protest had imparted the lesson that wholesale change would rarely—if ever—come swiftly or easily. Yet the ferocity and effectiveness of white Americans' efforts to keep neighborhood segregation in place proved staggering. Residential color lines became perhaps the most indelible of those that white citizens drew and defended in the twentieth century. In the process, the reaction to *Shelley* helped seal the fate of the racial ghetto as one of the most intractable institutions in modern American life.

The enduring specter of America's segregated ghettos has subsequently cast a long shadow over the anticovenant campaign's victorious climax. Wirth's abandonment of *Shelley* presaged a sense of futility that many commentators would ascribe to the cases in the decades to come. Against the backdrop of unabated residential discrimination, the covenant cases have often served as a quintessential example of a "hollow hope" where litigation seems impossibly and tragically outmatched against the popular will of those who disagree with a court's ruling.[3]

From the 1950s onward, legal scholars would cast U.S. Supreme Court chief justice Frederick Moore Vinson's expansion of the state action doctrine as so untenably broad in its potential applications that it appeared to "leave little room for any private legal rights at all," and thus could never truly serve as a lasting influence in the realm of civil rights law. Conversely, historians of the civil rights movement and of urban segregation have pointed to the cases as largely obsolete from their inception and too narrowly targeted to assail the imposing boundaries of the ghetto. These historians have lent an air of inevitability to the covenant cases' shortcomings, depicting them as little more than a Pyrrhic victory over an outdated tool of exclusion. In many respects, *Shelley* has yet to escape the shadow of present conditions that obscure a different—and truer—narrative.[4]

The anticovenant campaign's consequences in the years following the Court's decision ultimately reveal the more complex, substantial, and enduring legacy that the cases rightfully deserve. As much as the fight against racial restrictions may have faltered in its highest objectives of providing black Americans with genuinely open access to housing, *Shelley* was able to accomplish a more limited set of aims in neighborhoods across the country that provided some immediate material benefits to black communities. Additionally and perhaps even more importantly, the successes of the campaign itself equipped legal activists with new experiences, tactics, and alliances to make even more substantive gains in other areas of advocacy. The covenant cases would soon play a critical role in fomenting civil rights litigators' intensive and far-reaching attacks on the legal foundations of Jim Crow. Assessing the consequences of both vehement white resistance to *Shelley* and black communities' efforts to seize whatever opportunities they could from the victory offers a compelling look at the role of law in social justice movements and the transformative influence of the anticovenant campaign on postwar American society.

"I Think We Can Keep It White": Defiance, Evasion, and the Ghetto's Stubborn Roots

Chief Justice Vinson's solemn and sonorous delivery of the Court's opinions in *Shelley* and *Hurd* had barely finished echoing before the cry of resistance arose in countless white communities. Residential segregation had sunk its roots deep into the soil of America's cities and clung tenaciously as the anticovenant campaign sought to tear loose its grip in the years following the decision. *Shelley* placed new pressures on the architects of housing's color lines and spurred a wave of defiance that simultaneously reified existing networks and strategies of resistance while stimulating creative energies that offered novel avenues of exclusion for white homeowners. Segregation's proponents not only voiced their displeasure at the decision, they quickly employed any means they could to prevent the fulfillment of its potential effects. From the moment that civil rights activists scored their victory, the movement for greater housing access confronted an invigorated backlash that helped ensure the persistence of the nation's ghettos.

Opposition to the Court's decision overflowed in neighborhoods and courtrooms across the country and resounded from the floor of Congress, exposing the fervor of many white Americans' commitment to the prerogative of residential exclusion. Though the responses of the mainstream press were generally favorable to the decision or at least tempered in their attitude, private letters and press reports of public meetings gave voice to a swelling outrage. The justices' offices fielded an assortment of vitriolic dispatches from America's anxious homeowners. One woman excoriated Vinson for his perceived "betrayal of the 'White Race' in this country," and lamented the idea that the Court had unfairly chosen to favor the rights of minorities over those of the white majority. An angry Los Angeles resident confronted with the prospect of impending residential integration venomously offered, "I'm sorry your office isn't elective—how quickly the people would put you all back on your front porch. . . . I am heart-broken and will sell my beautiful home."[5]

Chicago-based poet Oliver Allstorm flayed the justices in verses specially composed for the occasion, bringing the themes of his earlier antimiscegenation screeds to the topic of housing:

You say that White men in our State
Must never try to segregate;
That Negroes have the social right
To "*force*" themselves upon the White
And that henceforth each race reside
Close to each other, side by side;
And that the Blacks may dance and dine
Within the White man's Color-line.

Allstorm promised that he and likeminded citizens, would resist the Court's efforts at every turn. A more ominous commentator insisted that "American homeowners never will even recognize any such ruling, and if such races persisted in trying to move in next door, we—the people—would have to make our own laws." Violence, the author implicitly reminded the justices, had always been a ready tool to achieve exclusion and the Court's weakening of more respectable means simply invited a greater reliance on force.[6]

While this sort of individual resistance arose from the same long-standing fears regarding property values and prejudicial assumptions about the character of African American homeowners, the correspondence and public statements surrounding the covenant cases offered insight into some more complicated notions of race and home at stake in the housing battle. White property owners expressed their dismay at the prospect of integration in part because many of them understood their property claims as reaching well past their picket fences or the legal boundaries of their lots. "I believe a man's home," wrote one California woman, "extends beyond his own property line and includes the surrounding neighborhood." Another man offered similar thoughts, invoking the "right" of white neighbors to "collectively develop and enjoy the benefits and privacy of a combined home, whether it be a single building or group of buildings." These attitudes cast neighborhoods as more than a collection of properties linked by market value and instead reflected a more deep-seated vision of community and identity. Many individuals understood their home as a place of interaction and intimacy that encompassed both the physical space of their block and the relationships with their neighbors. Certainly not all homeowners felt such strong connections or shared equally broad definitions of home, but this sentiment helped fuel the bitterness and discomfort evident in the deluge of resistance.[7]

If a person's home included the neighborhood and one's neighbors, the logic seemed to hold, residential integration posed a fundamental challenge to the racial identity of homeowners. Perhaps the clearest evidence of this notion came from the Bryant Street block in Northwest Washington, D.C., where the Hurds, Stewarts, Savages, and Rowes had just won the right to keep their homes. The Purdue family at 146 Bryant, originally from Georgia, told reporters that the black families in the area were "fine neighbors . . . better than some white ones we had," but that their house would be on sale the next day. When the reporter asked Mrs. Purdue why she would abandon her home in spite of the congenial relationship she enjoyed with local black residents, the Georgia-born woman offered a curt, two-word response: "I'm white." Her choice was simple and deliberate. When popular conceptions of the home included one's neighbors, living with African Americans nearby could call into question her whiteness. Segregation and racial identities were defined and maintained by daily practices. Regardless of her experiences with these families, then, moving away and pursuing life in a segregated enclave elsewhere became the best way to preserve her claim to racial superiority.[8]

Elsewhere in Washington, local homeowners groups offered a communal space to air their members' grievances with the Court. The president of one association promised to organize his neighbors to combat the decision. "This area is strictly white," he told the gathered crowd, "and I think we can keep it white." For the leader of another association at the same meeting, even this declaration proved too "conciliatory." Calling white Americans the "victim[s] of partisan politics," he promised to take the issue back into the courts and left no doubt about his ultimate aims in the nation's capital. "There will once again be white supremacy," he thundered. Similar thoughts echoed from frantically assembled meetings in white neighborhoods around the nation.[9]

Rebukes of the Court came from more powerfully positioned Americans as well. Mississippi's congressional delegation was apoplectic after the decision's announcement. "There must have been a celebration in Moscow last night," bellowed Senator John Rankin, "for the Communists won their greatest victory in the Supreme Court . . . when that once august body proceeded to destroy the value of property owned by tens of thousands of loyal Americans in every State in the Union." He castigated the justices for attempting "to reverse the laws of nature by their own edict" and concluded by intimating that Vinson's Court had revived and revised the infamous Dred Scott decision. "White Christian Americans," Rankin seethed without any apparent hint of irony, "seem to have no rights left which the present Supreme Court feels bound to respect." His colleague, Representative John Bell Williams, suggested that *Shelley* would do more to reinvigorate the Ku Klux Klan than any event of the previous four decades. An Arkansas congressman took to the floor arguing that the cases were "forcing by law fundamental principles on the American people" and proposed a constitutional amendment to protect the sanctity of race restrictions.[10]

Resistance came from the ranks of the nation's judiciary as well. A federal district court judge from Kansas City denounced *Shelley* at the city's annual Bar Association meeting, telling the audience that "the time should never come when private citizens should not enjoy the right reasonably to say who their neighbors shall be." He urged a similar understanding on his colleagues. Perhaps the most telling moment came five months after the decision in the same Detroit courtroom that the McGhee family had been forced to visit in early 1945. Judge Guy Miller rendered a decision in a local case, *Bishop v. Kanfer*, that sought to enforce a covenant restricting whether property owners could take on boarders. Miller, the original jurist for the *McGhee* litigation, dispensed with the issues of the case quickly and instead devoted most of his ruling to the Supreme Court's reasoning in the recent covenant cases. Miller could hardly veil his contempt for the Court. "I disagree wholly with the conclusion," he fumed. "It is, of course, binding upon this Court as to matters contained within the four corners of that opinion; but it is of such a nature that it ought not to be extended one-thirty-second of an inch beyond that." Miller's opinion articulated the frustrations that many in the legal profession felt regarding the *Shelley* decision and represented the uncertainty and resistance that defined much of the white response to the Supreme Court's action. His determination to ensure that the covenant cases had the narrowest possible impact reflected a growing sense among white litigators and jurists that Vinson's Court had grossly overstepped its authority.[11]

Shelley marked an especially inflammatory example of the changing currents at work in the highest echelons of the American judiciary. The Supreme Court had overturned more than thirty precedents in the past decade and now offered a ruling that seemed to fly in the face of long-established contractual and property rights. Of equal concern was the sense that the Court had dramatically expanded the definition of state action and thereby poised itself to intervene in a wide assortment of other ostensibly private activities. Given the justices' correspondence with each other surrounding Vinson's opinion, the Court itself certainly believed for a time that it had broken new ground and sown the seeds of a judicial revolution. Vinson had, however, left considerable ambiguity as to how far-reaching this new understanding of state action would prove to be. Critics wondered aloud whether any private contracts or agreements could escape the Supreme Court's scrutiny under the principles that *Shelley* established. For Guy Miller, the *Bishop* case was a perfect example of the excesses the Court had invited. The Kanfer family used the *McGhee* case to argue that the restriction on their ability to rent rooms in their home violated the equal protection clause of the Fourteenth Amendment just as a restriction against race would. Miller found the idea patently ridiculous, but saw it as an inevitable product of the Supreme Court's misguided efforts in the covenant cases. Even for those individuals who were not primarily driven by the desire to ensure segregation's continued existence, the uncertainty surrounding the decision fostered an anxious defiance.[12]

Indeed, defiance remained the watchword for many white homeowners and real estate brokers as well. Though the inability to enforce covenants presented new difficulties, white neighborhoods continued to defend residential segregation vigorously and began closing off this avenue of progress as soon as it emerged. In response to the setback that *Shelley* created, real estate boards around the country dissuaded enterprising brokers from seizing the opportunity to ignore covenants. Within days of the Court's ruling, the Detroit Real Estate Board had gathered with local procovenant attorneys to discuss new strategies for "minimizing violations." From St. Louis, Gerald Seegers, the attorney for the Kraemer family and the MAIA, noted that within weeks the city's Real Estate Exchange had coordinated with white neighborhood associations to fix boundaries for racial "zones" in the city and threatened to revoke the membership of anyone who sold across the lines. While the threat of expulsion was nothing new for the exchange, *Shelley* spurred a feverish wave of organization and intimidation within the group's ranks. Other realty boards across the country followed suit.[13]

Homeowners and homebuilders also continued to establish covenants on new properties after 1948. The ACRR had noted that many white homeowners embarked on a concerted campaign to spread covenants in their communities after the cases had reached the Supreme Court. That momentum in cities like Detroit, Chicago, and Washington continued in spite of the Court's decision. A study of the Kansas City metropolitan area revealed that developers and property owners recorded hundreds of new restrictions in the years following *Shelley*. Between 1949 and 1951, an observer in the nation's capital noted that 10–15 percent of deeds in a random sample of new subdivisions contained covenants. Though this marked a substantial decrease in the rate of restrictions prior to 1948, white neighborhoods took advantage of the fact that covenants themselves were still legal and exerted considerable pressure to keep them intact.[14]

That coercion took a variety of forms, some new to the post-*Shelley* moment and some that were long-standing tools of intimidation and exclusion. When a Wayne County Court bailiff in Detroit sold his covenanted home to black purchasers late in 1948, his neighbors—now unable to sue for the enforcement of the covenant—turned to public protest tactics, establishing picket lines in front of the seller's new home and his workplace at the courthouse and "denouncing him for selling 'white' property to Negroes." The protests were disruptive and embarrassing enough for the bailiff to seek and successfully obtain an injunction against his former neighbors, who retreated when confronted with the court order. Extralegal pressures like these, however, witnessed a resurgence after *Shelley* and proved frighteningly effective in many cases.[15]

White homeowners in the weeks following the Court's decision also frantically devised new legal strategies to circumvent the loss of covenants' enforceability. Reports quickly percolated back to NAACP attorneys of various proposals formulating in communities across the country. Realtors in Los Angeles, confided a sympathetic financier, were creating "new neighborhood contracts wherein the parties agree not to sell to non-Caucasians on penalty of a large forfeiture." This tactic required homeowners to furnish a deposit that they would lose if they violated the covenant. Financial penalties, reasoned various subdividers and neighborhood associations, might keep existing restrictions from faltering. Some neighborhoods dabbled with the idea of insisting that all purchasers be members of a designated private social club since these groups were less readily subject to judicial scrutiny. Others arranged for each property sale to be subject to a vote of local residents or the developer's board of directors. New restrictions that avoided racialized language offered yet another potential option for those eager to hold the line. Though most of these methods proved too costly or unwieldy to take hold broadly, attorneys urged covenanted neighborhoods to keep testing tactics until they found one that could pass muster in the courts. Innovation suddenly abounded in America's segregated neighborhoods.[16]

The most promising of white homeowners' new lines of defense quickly became suits for financial damages. Neighbors targeted those who sold covenanted properties to minority purchasers, suing them for compensation as a result of the alleged destruction of property values that integration would cause. By the end of 1948, anticovenant attorneys in nearly every major city had begun fending off suits that sought penalties from willing white sellers. The litigation proved so extensive that Charles Hamilton Houston wrote urgently to the NAACP national office that "the second stage of the restrictive covenant fight . . . is here." Seeking thousands of dollars on behalf of each household covered by a restriction, white homeowners left the issue of enforcement aside and instead sought to make the process impossibly expensive for potential white covenant-breakers. By directing the litigation at white targets and playing on the Vinson Court's affirmation that covenants themselves constituted valid contracts, damage suits offered a potentially dangerous and seemingly race-neutral way around *Shelley*.[17]

Within five years, the Supreme Court felt compelled to address the matter head on. In *Barrows v. Jackson* (1953), a test case from Los Angeles under the direction of Loren Miller, the Vinson Court weighed the validity of compensatory claims. More than sixty neighborhood associations stretching from San Francisco to the nation's capital joined and filed amicus briefs with the Court defending this practice. Their efforts demonstrated some of the urgency and breadth of support that covenants enjoyed, a sign of the faith that homeowners continued to place in racial restrictions. Ultimately, though, the endeavor proved futile. The justices struck down the possibility of obtaining damages and blocked this avenue of evasion.[18]

Notably, however, the Court's lone dissenting voice came from the architect of the *Shelley* ruling, Chief Justice Vinson himself. Vinson offered a bitter response to his colleagues, who he felt had now stretched his logic from the covenant cases past its limits. Claims for damages involved no direct harm or discrimination against a nonwhite party, he insisted. The courts that awarded the penalties thus could not be engaged in a discriminatory act. Vinson's willingness to break with his colleagues and to endorse such a deliberate circumvention of his efforts in *Shelley* revealed both the limits of his constitutional vision on the question of racial egalitarianism and, perhaps, some of the anxieties he felt over popular reactions to the covenant cases. According to one of his earliest biographers, Vinson was notably attuned to the public's reception of the Court's decisions and the political climate in which he made his judicial interpretations. Part of his reluctance to bolster *Shelley* in *Barrows* may have stemmed from this sensitivity to popular opinion. Regardless of Vinson's motivations, the rest of the Court closed the damages loophole and further weakened the legal props supporting residential exclusion.[19]

Still, the desperate search for legal methods to prevent integration exposed the extent to which white homeowners viewed the law as a critical tool for the maintenance of housing discrimination. Exclusion could often be accomplished in fairly thoroughgoing fashion through less formal extralegal means. The return to legal devices again and again in the years after *Shelley* bespoke the significance and value that white communities had attached to covenants and to what they represented: a legal sanction to indulge their fears, prejudices, and desires. The comfort of legal approval, its attendant implication of moral rightness, and, just as importantly in many respects, the signal that racial restrictions conveyed about the collective commitment of white residents to the principles of exclusivity, were powerful enough that many neighborhoods sought to reinvent and re-create them as quickly as possible.[20]

Throughout the years following the decision in the covenant cases, white realtors and attorneys were abuzz with these efforts to engineer new loopholes. Maintaining racially homogenous neighborhoods had always required effort on the part of white communities, but had only rarely demanded much in the way of innovation in order to succeed. Now, however, creativity seemed the order of the day. Gerald Seegers and other procovenant lawyers began sharing suggestions and ideas across the country, establishing the kinds of networks that had proven so effective for civil rights litigators. Seegers promised one correspondent that "if anyone hits on a practicable plan I will hear of it. If and when I do I will disseminate it far and wide." Experimentation and cooperation of this sort stood as evidence of how jealously many white Americans guarded the prerogative of residential discrimination. The loss in *Shelley* had spurred local proponents of exclusion to link together what had typically been only loosely coordinated efforts up to that time.[21]

White homeowners unmistakably felt the anticovenant campaign's challenge to the sanctity of segregated communities. All those who denounced the Court's decision and all who drafted and deployed new tactics in its wake helped ensure the persistence of America's ghettos. They fed and nurtured the stubborn roots of residential segregation that held fast in the soil of urban neighborhoods from coast to coast. They did so with astounding effectiveness and disturbing consequence.

In subsequent decades, violence, intimidation, and institutional discrimination along with the flight of industry, white residents, and their capital to outlying areas would render integration exceedingly difficult. These processes simultaneously worsened the physical and economic conditions for many black communities. Housing segregation thus continued largely unabated after *Shelley* and even deepened in some respects. While the covenant cases were only a part of these larger transformations in America's cityscapes, they helped fuel white intransigence in the immediate postwar period. The enduring prominence of the nation's ghettos has made *Shelley* into the "noble failure" that many historians see it as today. Yet the obstinacy of segregationists' reactions cannot be the sum total of the covenant cases' legacy. Rendering the cases in this fashion denies the significance of the hopes and energies that civil rights advocates drew from the campaign. In the face of victory and a dramatic backlash, black communities understood that in more ways than one this was only the start of a much larger and longer fight toward justice.[22]

Making Movements: The Meanings of Victory

The fact of the matter was that most activists remained profoundly hopeful in the wake of *Shelley*. Indeed, black communities used the anticovenant campaign to seize new opportunities to expand their access to housing and to foment a broader and more successful assault on Jim Crow in the postwar era. The covenant cases opened a horizon of possibilities in the legal battle against segregation's legal foundations, convincing activists that if they could find the right combination of pressure and persuasion, the whole edifice of racialized inequality might come tumbling down. Even in the face of such intense white resistance, the real lesson that civil rights advocates took from *Shelley* was that resolve, cooperation, and creativity could break down even the most steadfast barriers to black progress. "The music is in the air," wrote the *Afro-American* in the weeks after the decision. "All that we need is a set to tune in the program."[23]

Reevaluating the covenant cases from the standpoint of what they made possible affords a unique perspective on the development of civil rights litigation in the years leading up to *Brown v. Board of Education* (1954). Black activists and communities found something more than symbolism or hollow triumph as they brought *Shelley* back from the Supreme Court to their neighborhoods and into their legal offices. While the extent of white opposition assured that the anticovenant campaign could never be an unqualified success, black Americans crafted their own meanings and improvements out of the covenant cases, forming a narrative of empowerment and uplift that has remained largely hidden.[24]

One of the most immediate consequences of *Shelley* was a tangible measure of relief that some black homeseekers found in the aftermath of the cases. African Americans enjoyed significantly increased access to properties that had previously been restricted. Though in many instances whites withdrew from transitioning neighborhoods, sowing the seeds of the suburban exodus that would span the next half century and thus keeping the levels of segregation high, black homeseekers nonetheless obtained the right to use a larger share of their cities' housing supply. Just days after the Court's ruling in 1948, black residents in St. Louis reported that "formerly restricted property is now being advertised in the daily papers as available to Negroes." Later in the summer, ACRR officials noted the "freer movement and fairer distribution of available housing" that black homeowners enjoyed. Other observers pointed to the potential financial benefits that could accrue from alleviating the artificial shortages that covenants had helped to maintain. Realtors estimated that black communities would save millions as a result of improved access and decreased litigation. Commentators, however, acknowledged that these gains could not fully solve the crippling shortage still confronting black communities, that most progress was limited to older housing stock instead of new subdivisions, and that financial exploitation of black purchasers seemed unlikely to abate significantly. These were, in the end, simply the "bigger and better ghettos" that Robert Weaver had warned of at the 1945 Chicago conference. Yet to many of the homeowners who now found some relief in this fashion it was cause for celebration.[25]

Less than three years after *Shelley*, the number of families who gained access to once-prohibited areas reached into the tens of thousands. By 1952, Chicago alone had witnessed some 21,000 relocations into covenanted areas according to local estimates. Phineas Indritz explained from Washington that "significant shifts in racial residential patterns are beginning to develop," while housing official Frank Horne described "maps of planning commissions in cities across the nation reveal[ing] an increasingly freer mobility of nonwhite families through the housing supply." Loren Miller, even as he lamented the lack of progress in residential integration, declared in 1955 that *Shelley* had afforded Los Angeles' minority populations the ability "to secure much better housing than was open to them before." Many families thus found new access to homes and obtained properties that were of a better quality. For these individuals, the anticovenant campaign had offered a chance for substantial improvements in their daily lives and they seized the opportunities whenever possible. Housing access gains proved so substantial that in a 1952 speech President Truman insisted that as a result of the covenant cases, "more Negroes are homeowners today than ever before in American history."[26]

Not all segments of America's black urban communities, however, enjoyed the advantages of this expansion. Middle-class African Americans benefited most directly from the changes underway while poorer black individuals remained largely trapped in identical—or worsening—circumstances. For the NAACP this was both an expected and acceptable outcome, at least for the short term. The attorneys had long understood that private housing, especially at shortage-induced prices, could only address part of the desperate need for adequate shelter in black neighborhoods. Because homeownership was intimately bound up with economic mobility and purchasing power, a significant portion of these communities would be consigned to stay in the slums. NAACP advocates hoped that the attack on covenants would have the ancillary benefits of opening previously restricted lands for public housing developments and that the potential outmigration of middle-class black Americans would alleviate overcrowding and price gouging, but few believed that the poorer segments of black society would derive the same advantages. This was in keeping with the overarching orientation of NAACP objectives that often privileged class-based advancement, viewing middle-class individuals as better ambassadors of respectability in the process of integration. While the immediate impact of *Shelley* would be fairly significant, then, the benefits of progress fell unequally along the lines of class and may well have exacerbated the concentration of poverty and flight of capital that deepened the disadvantages of those left behind. The vision of the anticovenant campaign was not without its costly limitations.

Still, the measures of improvement made as a result of *Shelley* went beyond the expansion of private housing opportunities. There was an incalculable benefit to the protection that nonwhite homeseekers now received from at least some of the vulnerabilities and harassments that covenants had made commonplace. As just one example, anticovenant activists celebrated a 1948 Texas court decision overturning a racial restriction that targeted people of Mexican descent. An unscrupulous individual had apparently sought to exploit a covenant provision that caused ownership of the home to revert to the original seller in the event of a violation. His scheme was to pocket the down payment of a Mexican American purchaser, reclaim title to the property, and then sell it again to a white buyer. Prior to *Shelley*, the local court would have been obligated to enforce the covenant's terms and implicitly support the practice. With the decision in hand, however, the Latino purchaser was rightfully able to win his ownership claim. The loss of down payments as a result of covenant litigation had been just one of the many financial and emotional hardships minority purchasers endured prior to 1948. Though exploitative practices and schemes would never disappear from America's urban housing markets, *Shelley* now provided more tangible protections from some of the humiliations and mistreatments that covenants had permitted.[27]

The limitations that remained were considerable, yet there was a distinct period of progress in the immediate aftermath of the decision. The gains were substantial enough that five years later at least a handful of observers believed that the trend was unmistakably "toward a gradual breakdown of enforced racial segregation in housing." Loren Miller and Frank Horne each saw the development of state "fair housing" laws as a result of the anticovenant campaign's lingering significance. For most anticovenant activists, then, the period after *Shelley* was a moment rich with possibility and some measure of success.[28]

Indeed it was telling that various individuals and organizations argued that the victory may well have slowed the worsening of conditions for black urban populations and prevented potentially more dire outcomes. Shortly before the Court rendered its decision, the National Association of Intergroup Relations Officials analyzed the various paths the justices could take in *Shelley* and tackled what failure to win would mean for black homeseekers. "Approval of racial covenants," they warned, "will serve to strengthen the efficacy and toleration of other devices over the long-run by reinforcing their moral and pseudo-legal sanction." An adverse decision would probably "accelerate [covenants'] use at a rapid rate" and "give the appearance of legality and respectability to any and all actions taken by residents in the areas entered by Negroes to drive them out." Given the rapid growth of covenanting in the postwar years leading up to *Shelley*, the disastrous predictions seemed entirely plausible and offer some insight into what might have transpired without the benefit of the Court's decision. Black homeseekers would have almost certainly suffered even greater hardships had restrictive covenants retained their full legal authority into the 1950s. Circumscribed as the effect of *Shelley* was, the alternative result could have been more destructive.[29]

THE COVENANT CASES' impact ultimately extended well beyond the neighborhoods of America's cities, stretching back into the offices of top civil rights litigators and the courtrooms where a resurgent battle against Jim Crow steadily blossomed. There, *Shelley's* success helped to shift the tenor and tactics of black legal protest in substantial ways that soon brought the NAACP to the brink of an assault on the "separate but equal" doctrine. As black activists absorbed and applied the lessons of the anticovenant campaign, their efforts revealed how that litigation encouraged a broader and more successful assault on segregation's legal legitimacy.

Three critical outgrowths of the victory helped yield an invigorated and newly equipped team of legal activists prepared to take on the greater challenges ahead. First, the resounding and unexpected triumph served as a call to action, mobilizing and emboldening civil rights litigators. The Court's embrace of innovative arguments and the unanimity of its opinion imparted a degree of hope and urgency that propelled the next wave of challenges forward. Second, *Shelley* yielded a newly strengthened and increasingly fruitful partnership between civil rights activists and the Department of Justice. By enlisting the Truman administration's support, the NAACP obtained the mantle of federal approval and additional resources from their most powerful ally yet. Finally, the experiences of the covenant campaign encouraged the Association and its collaborators to adapt the tactics they had tested in *Shelley* and deploy them in the mounting fight over segregated education. In the end, the covenant cases played a key role in putting the NAACP on an inevitable collision course with the lingering shadow of *Plessy v. Ferguson.* African Americans' redoubled battle for justice in the nation's courtrooms would be forever changed as a result.

Victory had quickly energized legal activists across the country. *Shelley* signaled to many that the Supreme Court was willing to give new force and meaning to the antidiscrimination provisions of the Fourteenth Amendment and that unfavorable precedents might not pose the same difficulties they had in the past. Hope and determination pervaded attorneys' reactions in the wake of the decision. From Chicago, anticovenant campaign leader Loring Moore rattled off a congratulatory note to Loren Miller insisting that now "we can move on to other battle fields." Miller whole-heartedly agreed. In his typically eloquent fashion, the ardent activist vowed that the recent triumph would serve as an instrument with which to press ahead in other areas of advocacy. Cautioning against "retir[ing] it to the trophy room of legal victories," he counseled that attorneys should instead immediately put the lessons of the case to use as a "potent weapon in our long quest for first class citizenship." Miller reasoned that "these are times when we should press every advantage we have and confront the Supreme Court as often as possible." The Court suddenly seemed a much more compelling ally in the march toward greater legal freedom.[30]

Anticovenant advocates also used the success of the covenant campaign to argue for more explicit connections between legal and social protest. Even as the NAACP used *Shelley* to justify consolidating power within the organization, individuals like Miller stressed the importance of mass activism and widespread education as critical partners in the courtroom fight against Jim Crow. Miller offered a blunt assessment of the role of litigation for black activists: "laws and court decisions do not solve social problems; they merely set limits within which those problems may be tackled and ultimately solved. It is up to us to give effect to the decision. . . . That job wouldn't be an easy one even if all Americans were inclined to accept the spirit of the Supreme Court's ruling. . . . The Supreme Court decision won't have the desired effect on residential segregation without sustained and vigorous effort." Here, Miller cut to the heart of a contentious debate over what purpose the law could serve in effecting social change. Legal activists faced a vocal contingent of their peers who maintained that looking for redress from an overwhelmingly white judiciary and a legal system steeped in white supremacy constrained the possibilities of protest and reform. Miller and many of his colleagues realized the strands of truth in these charges. He understood that court decisions could not singlehandedly undo long-standing traditions of racial subordination and urban discrimination, so he articulated a vision of how law and "social action" could intersect and how each expanded the capacities of the other. Litigation, he contended, represented a necessary tactic that could lay the groundwork for social change but required the use of extralegal activism to ensure the achievement of its objectives. Without protest, court decisions might amount to little more than symbolic "trophies." Yet the law provided a powerful tool for "organization and direction of the sentiment favoring change" when incorporated with other forms of pressure. Miller and like-minded anticovenant activists used the success of *Shelley* to call for more broad-based and far-reaching reform efforts.[31]

The hope and urgency that the covenant cases imparted to litigators manifested itself outside of the legal profession as well. Editorials in the black press exhorted readers to use the covenant cases to "inspire a greater fight against all forms of racial discrimination." "This is no time to rest upon our oars," insisted the *Afro-American*. "We must continue to press forward" on issues such as employment discrimination and Jim Crow in the military. NAACP executive secretary Walter White seemed particularly stirred by the moment. Addressing an enthusiastic crowd in Detroit, White vowed that "gradualism is a thing of the past" and that those engaged in the struggle for black progress had to "redouble our efforts to wipe out discrimination wherever it appears." Though White's uncompromising tone stood in contradiction to the Association's continued reliance on cautious planning and negotiation in its campaigns, his remarks exemplified a broader theme among the NAACP's leaders. The organization had begun its turn toward a full-blown assault on "separate but equal."[32]

ONE OF THE CRITICAL factors behind this shift in tone was the success of the lobbying campaign for the Justice Department's intervention. Tom C. Clark and Philip Perlman's roles in the cases offered new hope in the larger fight against Jim Crow and served as an especially exciting development for black activists. "It was said," wrote one columnist, "that there was no way for us legally to destroy residential segregation . . . but President Truman, Attorney General Tom Clark, and Solicitor General Philip Perlman, working with the best legal minds that we have, produced a way to do it." The executive branch's willingness to use its influence in unprecedented ways against racial injustice had helped secure a victory that had seemed improbable only two years earlier. With the Supreme Court and the Truman administration each showing signs of a more receptive attitude toward civil rights advocates' claims, for the first time in a long time the battle for racial equality looked like it might become a fair fight.[33]

That hope proved to be well founded. Perlman apparently relished the attention and acclaim that he won as a result of his oral argument and felt genuinely moved by the experience of fighting on behalf of the black homeowners in *Shelley*. Philip Elman, who had worked closely with the solicitor general throughout the process, mused that the moment "changed Perlman entirely" and transformed his attitudes toward civil rights litigation. "From then on," Elman reflected, "there was no holding him back, and he put us into everything we could possibly go into." Perlman "couldn't wait to go back to the Supreme Court again and again, arguing for equality, for liberty, for decency. He loved it." The restrictive covenant cases had fomented an enduring and powerful partnership between the DOJ and civil rights legal activists.[34]

The solicitor general himself acknowledged the transformation. He declared that *Shelley* "set a precedent" for his office and marked a "rejection of the notion that government should pursue a laissez-faire policy in the field of civil rights." Describing his efforts in a 1949 interview, he impressed upon the nation his sincerity. "We are waging no sham battle," Perlman insisted. "We are going to hit inequality wherever we can, at every opportunity." His success before the Court had also won the Justice Department a blanket approval from President Truman to intervene in any future civil rights cases they saw fit.[35]

The department's assistance came immediately and in various forms. Perlman's participation in civil rights litigation before the Supreme Court now became almost standard practice after *Shelley*. This marked a significant change from previous policies. Indeed, the DOJ had declined to join any of the Association's cases in the preceding decade—even when they directly involved discrimination by state actors. Now, however, the solicitor general brought his influence to bear through amicus filings in a number of subsequent suits. By 1950, he had joined the NAACP's attacks on segregation in professional education as part of *Sweatt v. Painter* and *McLaurin v. Oklahoma State Regents*. In these cases, Perlman began urging the Court to overrule *Plessy* and expunge "separate but equal" from the nation's legal lexicon as "an unwarranted deviation from the principle of equality under law."[36]

Perlman lent his energies and the voice of his office to legal activists outside of the NAACP as well. The experiences of *Shelley* spurred him into action on cases regarding segregation in railroad dining cars, the exclusion of African Americans from railroad firemen's unions, and the early stages of a suit dealing with public accommodations in the District of Columbia. He reveled in his newfound role as a champion of racial freedom and provided important symbolic and material assistance in an array of attacks on Jim Crow until he left the office in 1952.[37]

Perlman's precedent ultimately laid the groundwork for the DOJ's important contributions in the NAACP's *Brown* litigation. Though Perlman himself actually proved reluctant to attack segregation in primary school education and spent the early months of 1952 stymieing efforts to bring the department into *Brown*, the momentum established by his previous efforts helped to carry his successor inexorably into the landmark case. Even when Perlman had reached the limits of his commitment to racial equality, the partnership that black activists had forged with the Justice Department in *Shelley* continued to yield dividends.[38]

Nor did this relationship between activists and the Truman administration stop at the courtroom door. At the NAACP's urging, Perlman, Clark, and Truman adviser Philleo Nash inserted themselves into the process of once again amending the FHA's underwriting manual to prohibit it from insuring new residential developments that established restrictive covenants.

Throughout 1949, they worked closely on the issue with Raymond Foley, administrator of the HHFA, which oversaw the regulation and implementation of federal housing policy. Foley had remained unsure about how to incorporate the Supreme Court's ruling in *Shelley* into the HHFA's long-standing practices promoting and demanding covenants' usage. A week after the decision, Foley wrote privately that because it was still legal to establish restrictive agreements and "human reactions to mixed occupancy" were unlikely to change immediately, the FHA's responsibility was to continue using covenants as a key factor in their appraisal process.[39]

Over the course of the following year, however, Foley embraced a new policy that Perlman and Nash had constructed in direct consultation with Thurgood Marshall and Loren Miller. By December of 1949, Foley convinced the FHA and Veterans Affairs to amend their guidelines "so as to refuse to aid the financing of properties . . . restricted on the basis of race or creed or color." These changes, approved by the NAACP, brought federal home financing activities "into line with the policy underlying the recent decisions of the Supreme Court" and helped to further a somewhat more racially egalitarian tilt in the FHA's procedures. Though the implementation of federal housing policy would remain deeply discriminatory in the ensuing decades, anticovenant activists had at least secured the possibility of more equitable access to housing. These private negotiations, along with the public stances that the DOJ took in its amicus efforts, convinced civil rights advocates—and especially those in the NAACP—that *Shelley* had fostered a lasting and transformative change in federal attitudes toward racial discrimination.[40]

BUOYED WITH A MOUNTING enthusiasm and a blossoming partnership with the Justice Department, the NAACP's leading legal minds soon fixed their sights on a more thoroughgoing challenge to segregated education and Jim Crow's legal foundations. In his weekly column following the victory, Charles Hamilton Houston wrote matter-of-factly that "the next point of attack after restrictive covenants is the segregated school. In many ways the two discriminations are inseparably tied together." With African Americans gaining greater access to housing, neighborhood schools seemed more likely than ever to face pressure for desegregation and were thus ripe for new legal tests. Echoing these sentiments, Thurgood Marshall declared "this blow to racial segregation in the field of housing . . . opens up the pending fight against segregation in education which . . . must be carried on with renewed vigor." Jim Crow's schoolhouses stood as the Association's next targets. Indeed, the intensified struggle over education seemed to flow inevitably from the success of the covenant campaign.[41]

Even more than its mobilizing effects, though, *Shelley* equipped the NAACP's attorneys with new tactics for this next round of litigation. Among the tools now at the Association's disposal was a robust interracial coalition of organizations willing to lend their support as amici. Though the DOJ was by far the most influential of these new allies, the Association could soon count on regular assistance from a variety of other groups. Prior to the covenant cases, only the NLG and the ACLU had filed briefs in the NAACP's major education suits and no recent case had more than two amici. *Shelley* established alliances and networks that in turn provided a veritable cornucopia of collaborators for future campaigns. Though none of the subsequent cases approached nearly the same volume of supporting briefs, the Association now enjoyed reliable backing from the CIO, AVC, and Jewish advocacy groups like the CLSA and ADL in *Sweatt*, *McLaurin*, and *Brown*. Regardless of what the Court made of these filings in its deliberations, these coalitions facilitated the sharing of intellectual and financial resources that helped ease the burdens of litigation. They became a valuable source of support for the NAACP.[42]

Shelley also furnished the Association's legal staff with a more powerful language to articulate the ongoing social consequences of segregation. While NAACP attorneys like Robert Carter had urged the more extensive use of Brandeis briefs in school desegregation cases since 1946, a transformation took hold after *Shelley*. Voices within the legal division urged the attorneys to adapt the scientific antiracist claims they had employed in the covenant cases as their educational litigation moved forward. The Association's briefs in the covenant cases had marked a dramatic increase in the use of nonlegal citations and this practice carried into subsequent efforts. Apart from the *McGhee* and *Hurd* cases, the 1948 *Sipuel v. Board of Regents* case—conducted almost simultaneously with the covenant suits—had been the Association's most substantial use of social scientific data yet with just under twenty different source materials. *McGhee* alone had used more than four times as many citations in its main brief while *Hurd* had marked a sevenfold increase in that number. When the next round of educational desegregation suits reached the Supreme Court in 1950, however, the shift became evident. In *McLaurin* and *Sweatt*, the legal team used fifty-two and sixty nonlegal citations respectively, three times the number they had deployed just two years earlier arguing relatively similar issues in *Sipuel*. As Marian Wynn Perry later put it, after the Brandeis briefs in *McGhee* and *Hurd*, "Thurgood Marshall saw its worth at once [and] liked it a lot." Though constitutional claims would always remain the central feature of their litigation, the legal team's experiment in the covenant cases had quickly changed the way the attorneys argued against segregation.[43]

The covenant cases would also help shape how the NAACP used the social scientific data it now enthusiastically included in its briefs. Annette Peyser, the socioeconomic analyst the NAACP had hired to help prepare for the covenant cases, became an outspoken advocate for the further use of extralegal data in subsequent campaigns. In particular, she expressed her conviction that psychology held the key to building a successful case against Jim Crow. Peyser first articulated her thoughts about the potential importance of social psychology at a legal conference in 1948 following the victory in *Shelley*. Delivering a speech entitled "The Use of Sociological Data to Indicate the Unconstitutionality of Racial Segregation," the young activist urged the development of a "better and more productive relationship between the legal expert and the social scientist." She remarked on the NAACP's recent experience with the Brandeis brief as a valuable instrument of attack against discrimination before suggesting possible areas of improvement. Foremost among her recommendations was a call for "scientific research on the subject of the psychological effects of segregation." As the NAACP made sociological arguments a regular component of its presentations to the Supreme Court in the ensuing years, Peyser continued to press the issue of how best to mobilize these arguments.[44]

In the summer of 1950, just weeks after the NAACP had won the *McLaurin* and *Sweatt* cases in part on the strength of robust extralegal claims regarding the inherent inequalities that segregation imposed, Peyser returned to the lessons of *Shelley* in a memorandum that called for her colleagues to embrace an even more expansive attack. She argued that the groundwork laid in 1948 and extended in the most recent education cases offered an ideal foundation to tackle directly the legitimacy of "separate but equal" jurisprudence. The anticovenant campaign, Peyser noted, had gone to great lengths to highlight not only the physical inequalities that emerged as a result of discrimination, but also the fact that the disparities in physical conditions created profound psychological consequences. "There is no *real* distinction," she insisted, "between the 'inequality' of physical facilities, and the . . . psychologically harmful effects of being separated from the majority group." The power of these arguments, tested even more explicitly in *McLaurin* and *Sweatt* with continued success, afforded the Association a chance to build upon these recent triumphs. "We must for the first time hit segregation . . . head on," Peyser urged. She believed whole-heartedly that the combination of legal and social scientific arguments against Jim Crow that the NAACP had mobilized in *Shelley* could now deliver a death-blow to persistent racial inequality. Peyser was certainly not alone in advocating this strategy, but her early and explicit formulation offers insight into this evolving approach.[45]

Though these arguments regarding the psychological consequences of segregation were not unproblematic, they did prove to be increasingly effective before the Supreme Court. The framework for the NAACP's sociological claims against the legal propriety of discrimination had grown dramatically in *Shelley*, continued in the graduate education cases, and ultimately formed a critical part of the pleadings in *Brown* with the inclusion of—among other sources—Kenneth Clark's now famous doll studies. The Brandeis brief tactic thus helped the NAACP to reach further in its attacks on Jim Crow, providing a valuable tool in the burgeoning assault on racial inequality.[46]

Beyond offering a set of tactics and alliances that became hallmarks of the Association's litigation, though, *Shelley* also presented some important encouragements to legal activists from the standpoint of its judicial reasoning. For William Coleman Jr., who in 1949 became the Supreme Court's first African American clerk, the covenant cases clearly portended the end of *Plessy*. In a memorandum for Justice Felix Frankfurter about the pending *McLaurin* and *Sweatt* litigation, Coleman addressed the significance of *Shelley* directly. Arguing that "faced with the question of whether segregation is constitutional, this Court will have to overrule *Plessy v. Ferguson*," Coleman reasoned that the covenant cases had laid the groundwork for this eventual conclusion. *Shelley*, he wrote, had offered the first instance in which the Court explicitly stated that "classifications based upon race are illegal when they result in equal facilities." The Court's opinion in the covenant cases, Coleman seemed to suggest, never argued that restrictive agreements prevented black homeseekers from obtaining property in a general sense or from obtaining property of an equal quality to that covered by a given restriction. The quality of African Americans' alternative options was in fact a moot point to the Court because it was the denial of access itself that was an affront to the principle of equal protection. Even if black purchasers could have easily found better homes than those denied to them by a covenant, the Court's logic would have been the same. The relative equality of available facilities did not matter because the act of exclusion—at least when given the sanction of state power—was inherently unconstitutional. To Coleman's mind, the Court had already declared that separate was fundamentally unequal.[47]

While it would take the Court another five years to make that pronounce-
ment explicit, Coleman brought this sense of possibility to his later work
with the NAACP. Shortly after he left his clerkship, he became one of Thurgood Marshall's closest advisers as Marshall steered the Association's preparations for *Brown*. Coleman's insights proved instrumental throughout that
campaign. Though he advocated caution and restraint in the buildup to
Brown, the Court had convinced him in *Shelley* that the justices would ultimately strip Jim Crow of its most valuable legal armor. Coleman played a
critical role in bringing that process to fruition.[48]

WHATEVER THE POSTWAR anticovenant campaign failed to do with respect to its highest ideals and objectives, it seems apparent from closer
examination that in fact it succeeded in accomplishing quite a bit. Confronted with largely intransigent and staggeringly effective white resistance to residential integration, black activists and the communities they
represented made the most they could out of the victory in *Shelley*. The substance of what they made in the ensuing years transformed not only the
lives of thousands of black families who obtained easier access to at least
somewhat better housing, but also forever altered the trajectory of black
Americans' fight for racial justice under the law.

Victorious in their campaign, legal activists moved on from the covenant
cases invigorated and hopeful that their continued advocacy could further
revitalize the Fourteenth Amendment's protections in other areas of their
lives. An adviser to the NAACP's legal team and one of the architects of Chicago's anticovenant efforts remarked that "perhaps the whole range of issues
arising in connection with racial segregation may be encompassed by logical application of the constitutional theory adopted" in *Shelley*. The cases, it
appeared, could "open to federal judicial scrutiny much, if not all, of the area
of racial discrimination" and offer new avenues of relief for black populations
wrestling against the various constraints of Jim Crow. Although *Shelley*'s
constitutional theory never quite gained the traction that activists hoped it
would, the case nonetheless left its mark on black Americans' resurgent
movement for civil rights.[49]

Taken together, the experiences of *Shelley* not only set legal activists on
an inevitable collision course with "separate but equal" jurisprudence, but
also equipped them with essential alliances and tactics to succeed in that
fight. Attorneys across the country took the victory in the covenant cases as
a signal to press on faster and further than they ever had before in their pursuit of equality. The cases also bolstered these activists' faith in tactical in-

novation as a solution to the problem of entrenched juridical support for segregation. Just two years after the Supreme Court had denied certiorari in *Mays v. Burgess*, legal activists had developed a strategy for their campaign that persuaded the Court to abandon more than two decades of almost unbroken indifference toward restrictive agreements. *Shelley* also spurred forward a strain of social science-based legal advocacy that helped to galvanize some quarters of popular opinion and that quickly became a valuable mainstay of NAACP desegregation suits. Litigators now fought for racial justice differently than they had before. Finally, the covenant campaign fomented unprecedented partnerships and coalitions in the struggle for legal freedoms, establishing a new era of federal receptiveness to African Americans' civil rights claims. Each of these developments simultaneously pointed black legal activists toward a confrontation with the long shadow of *Plessy* that had constrained the possibilities of progress for black Americans over more than half a century.

In many respects, the covenant cases were uniquely situated to bring about these transformations. Urban conditions and the contours of the ghetto were one of the central preoccupations of social scientific scholarship in the immediate postwar era, making the issue of housing access ideal for the NAACP's growing reliance upon Brandeis briefs. The covenant issue also proved an exemplary cause for the development of multiracial alliances and the enlistment of federal support on the side of civil rights litigators. Residential restrictions targeted a broader array of Americans than any other practice of discrimination in use at the time while the growth of the urban ghetto raised the specter of American race relations' parallels with Nazism in singularly disturbing ways. The fight for access to a decent home also presented an issue fundamental to the enjoyment of American citizenship, the priorities of New Deal liberalism, and emerging global conceptions of human rights. No other matter could have evoked quite the same constellation of pressures that inspired the DOJ's initial intervention.

Black activists took conscious advantage of each of these peculiarities throughout the campaign. The unique dimensions of the covenant cases were thus not simply the products of coincidental timing or luck, but instead the result of intentional and significant effort, careful planning, rigorous innovation, and a deep determination on the part of activists. These were men and women who rightfully saw that without an appreciable change in housing conditions, black communities were destined to suffer disproportionate hardships and to see the fruits of other costly battles for racial freedom wither away beyond the reach of those locked into segregated slums. In this, the first national postwar battle over the future of the American ghetto, black activists understood the stakes to be impossibly high.

It was in part this realization that led civil rights litigators to seize whatever gains they could from the victory, to suck the marrow of the Court's decision and the energies of the campaign that had made it a reality. As their efforts foundered in the face of white Americans' intractable devotion to residential segregation, they channeled the lessons of *Shelley* into other arenas in search of new cracks in Jim Crow's bedrock. In the process, they remade the trajectory of the legal fight for civil rights and left a lasting legacy that has yet to receive the recognition it deserves. The story of the covenant cases in both their triumphs and their failures is in many ways a largely untold narrative about the making of a new civil rights movement in postwar America.

Afterword

A Lingering Debt

Shelley v. Kraemer marked a turning point in the course of black legal activism and the struggle against Jim Crow. It opened new possibilities through the creativity, collaboration, and resolve of civil rights attorneys and the communities they represented. This transformation was a product of anticovenant advocates' collective efforts as well as a unique moment in American political, social, and intellectual development. The persistent echoes of World War II and the threat of fascism, the rapid emergence of the Cold War, the maturation of scientific antiracism, and a crippling housing shortage all intersected with the unrelenting desires of African Americans to secure a measure of comfort and security in the postwar world and to claim their rightful share of opportunity.

The *Shelley* campaign tells the story of men and women who dared to imagine a future without ghettos, who challenged the injustice and indignity of America's segregated cities, and who believed that they might make racial inequality into nothing more than an affliction with a rapidly dwindling half-life. In their complexity, the covenant cases left a legacy that was both unwieldy and powerful. Historians of urban segregation and of the civil rights movement have often seemed unsure about whether to label *Shelley* as a milestone or a millstone, though prevailing opinion seems to trend toward the latter. In the face of the ghetto's tenacity, the anticovenant campaign has appeared to be an effort woefully unequal to the enormity of its goals. Yet, in many respects, that is the very essence of social change in America. It is an imagination whose reach must constantly outstrip its grasp. Telling its story can never be a hagiography of grand campaigns perfectly suited for their moment. It is more truthfully a patchwork of responses to false starts and failures that gradually proved meet for the task at hand.

Shelley aspired to be more than it became. But in the face of an opposition that proved stronger and more unforgiving than nearly anyone involved could have anticipated, perhaps the more compelling story is that it still became something at all. In fact, reclaiming the restrictive covenant cases from

the margins of history reveals that they became something quite significant indeed.

Though the narrative of what the anticovenant campaign achieved has remained largely untold, a more thorough examination of this struggle has
much to offer to the emerging scholarship on black protest in the twentieth
century. The events of *Shelley* provide insight into the dynamics of legal activism at both a local and national level and shed light on the interactions
between local actors and the NAACP's centrally coordinated campaigns. The
cases demonstrate the complexity of these exchanges and the ways in which
conflict, cooperation, and experimentation shaped the processes of reform.
Understanding the evolving contours of civil rights litigation in the immediate postwar period also furnishes an important perspective on the context
from which the larger challenge to "separate but equal" would emerge and
the forces that helped make possible the 1954 victory in *Brown v. Board*. That
landmark success owes a debt to the efforts that took shape in the fight over
the racial ghetto's postwar destiny.

Just as importantly, the covenant cases also highlight the value of rendering the legal history of the civil rights movement in conversation with African Americans' daily lives and struggles at the grassroots. Delving into the
imbrications of law within black communities provides a truer sense of legal
activism's significance on the ground in American cities. The intensely personal and human drama unfolding on the frontlines of the nation's segregated neighborhoods serves as a reminder that individual discontent, resolve,
and inspiration played a critical role in fomenting legal change.

Shelley's history also helps to tell a larger set of stories about the dramatic
transformations underway in American society in the wake of World War II.
The experiences of the litigants and their advocates, both black and white,
offer windows into the reshaping of the American metropolis, the expansion of federal power, the development of liberal coalitions, the domestic
consequences of international politics, and the growing urgency and effectiveness of black Americans' struggles against segregation. The cases played
a role in each of these narratives.

YET IT WOULD BE a disservice to those who championed the anticovenant
campaign to set aside the purpose left unfinished in its wake. Indeed, perhaps the greatest and most enduring debt of all is that still owed to the cities
and the communities that they fought for. Despite the good that the covenant cases accomplished, housing segregation remains a fact of American
life and the travails of the nation's racial ghettos have worsened in many

respects in the ensuing decades. *Shelley*'s history offers a powerful reminder of the ways that—at both an individual and an institutional level—racial prejudice built America's ghettos and foreclosed upon the energies that hoped to break them. Block by block, inequality became even more deeply inscribed into urban life.

A quarter century after *Shelley*, Thurgood Marshall would comment upon the growing disparities he saw from the seat that he now occupied on the Supreme Court. He reflected on the difficulties of urban desegregation efforts and on the role that expedience, prejudice, and discrimination had played in allowing "our great metropolitan areas to be divided up each into two cities—one white, the other black." This was a path, he wrote, that "our people will ultimately regret." No doubt he also thought back to the postwar campaign that he had helped to build in order to prevent such an outcome. He may have recalled the hope and urgency that had fueled those early efforts to remake the American city. Whatever his thoughts, the weight of what *Shelley* proved unable to achieve hung heavy on that day and it has continued to do so in the four decades since.[1]

Acknowledging these failures, however, has too often doomed the restrictive covenant cases to an undeserved irrelevance in histories of the civil rights movement. The rightful legacy of the anticovenant crusade ought to embrace the story of the struggle as being equally as important as the shortcomings. It is, after all, in the fight that took shape that the rich and complicated substance of black Americans' strivings for a more meaningful realization of freedom and justice can be found. The remembrance of the *Shelley* campaign must ultimately be one that speaks of hope alongside hardship, of determination and resilience alongside disappointment and frustration.

There are perhaps no better witnesses to just how much the restrictive covenant cases meant than the families whose dreams of the future were so intimately bound up in the struggle. At its heart, the campaign for the right to decent shelter was a profoundly personal one. The six families at the center of the cases—the Shelleys, McGhees, Hurds, Stewarts, Savages, and Rowes—could not have known the impact that their fight to keep their homes would have on the larger currents of American social and political change. Nor could they have foretold the depth of white resistance or the tenacity of the racial ghetto that would mitigate the larger objectives of this struggle. For them, the stakes had always been both simple and desperate. A loss would have meant terrifying uncertainty and a painful reaffirmation that, despite their best efforts and sacrifices, the nation's promise of equality might forever remain more rhetoric than reality. A victory meant the right to live in the homes they had chosen and held out at least the possibility that a greater and fuller freedom might one day come.

Through three years they waited, offered what help they could, and watched. They watched as the nation's foremost civil rights lawyers rallied around their cause and carried it all the way to the Supreme Court. They watched as the attorney general offered his support and President Truman's solicitor general pleaded their case to the Court and to the American people. They watched the face of civil rights litigation change as men and women from around the country worked alongside and within the NAACP to develop more powerful attacks on racial discrimination's various forms. They watched as victory came and their dreams of owning a decent home broke free of the weight of racial restrictions. It was in the end their resolve in the fight for housing access that began to make possible the end of the age of "separate but equal." Like the generation of activists and organizers that would follow in subsequent decades, these six families and their advocates quite simply would not be moved.

Notes

Abbreviations

AHPP   Annette H. Peyser Papers, 1945–51, Schomburg Center for Research in Black Culture, New York, N.Y.

BHP   Black History Project (1895–1983), Western Historical Manuscripts Collection, Microfilm, University of Missouri–St. Louis

BVBC   *Brown v. Board of Education* Collection, Manuscripts and Archives, Sterling Memorial Library, Yale University, New Haven, Conn.

CETRR Committee on Education, Training and Research in Race Relations Records, Special Collections Research Center, University of Chicago, Chicago, Ill.

CHHP   Charles Hamilton Houston Papers, Moorland-Spingarn Research Center, Howard University, Washington, D.C.

EGP   Elmer Gertz Papers, Manuscripts Division, Library of Congress, Washington, D.C.

FFP   Felix Frankfurter Papers, Manuscripts Division, Microfilm Collection, Library of Congress, Washington, D.C.

FMDC   Francis M. Dent Collection, Charles H. Wright Museum of African American History, Detroit, Mich.

FMDP   Francis Morse Dent Papers, Burton Historical Collection, Detroit Public Library, Detroit, Mich.

FMVP   Frederick Moore Vinson Papers, Wendell H. Ford Public Policy Research Center, University of Kentucky, Lexington, Ky.

HHBP   Harold Hitz Burton Papers, Manuscripts Division, Library of Congress, Washington, D.C.

JBP   John Blandford Papers, Harry S. Truman Presidential Library, Independence, Mo.

LMP   Loren Miller Papers, Huntington Library, San Marino, Calif.

LWP   Louis Wirth Papers, Special Collections Research Center, University of Chicago, Chicago, Ill.

NAACP Records National Association for the Advancement of Colored People Records, Manuscripts Division, Library of Congress, Washington, D.C.

NAACP, Part 1 Papers of the National Association for the Advancement of Colored People, Part 1 (1909–50): Meetings of the Board of Directors, Records of Annual Conferences, Major Speeches, and Special

	Reports, Sterling Memorial Library, Microfilm Collections, Yale University, New Haven, Conn.
NAACP, Part 5	Papers of the National Association for the Advancement of Colored People, Part 5 (1914–55): The Campaign against Residential Segregation, Sterling Memorial Library, Microfilm Collections, Yale University, New Haven, Conn.
NAACP, Part 17	Papers of the National Association for the Advancement of Colored People, Part 17 (1940–55): National Staff Files, Sterling Memorial Library, Microfilm Collections, Yale University, New Haven, Conn.
PCCR	Records of the President's Committee on Civil Rights, Harry S. Truman Presidential Library, Independence, Mo.
PIP	Phineas Indritz Papers, Howard University Law Library, Washington, D.C.
PNP	Phileo Nash Papers, Harry S. Truman Presidential Library, Independence, Mo.
PPF	Post-Presidential File, Harry S. Truman Papers, Harry S. Truman Presidential Library, Independence, Mo.
RFP	Raymond Foley Papers, Harry S. Truman Presidential Library, Independence, Mo.
RHJP	Robert Houghwout Jackson Papers, Manuscripts Division, Library of Congress, Washington, D.C.
TCCP	Tom C. Clark Papers, Harry S. Truman Presidential Library, Independence, Mo.
WHHP	William H. Hastie Papers, Harvard Law School Library, Microfilm Collections, Harvard University, Cambridge, Mass.
WIGP	Willis and Irene Graves Papers, Charles H. Wright Museum of African American History, Detroit, Mich.
WODP	William O. Douglas Papers, Manuscripts Division, Library of Congress, Washington, D.C.

Introduction

1. *Baltimore Afro-American*, January 24, 1948, 1; *Pittsburgh Courier*, January 24, 1948, 3; Ming, "Racial Restrictions," 204–5. Ming also noted the presence of two "official observers" from foreign embassies, though he declined to mention which nations sent representatives. In all likelihood one of the nations was China, given that the Chinese consul took a particular interest in the cases. See Constance Baker Motley to Chinese Consulate General, May 19, 1948, in NAACP, Part 5, Reel 22, Frame 768.

2. The four cases were *Shelley v. Kraemer* 334 U.S. 1 (1948), *McGhee v. Sipes* 334 U.S. 1 (1948), *Hurd v. Hodge* and *Urciolo v. Hodge* 334 U.S. 24 (1948). W. E. B. Du Bois, "Civil Rights Legislation," January 25, 1947, in FMDC, Box 10, Folder 3. For more on restrictive covenants see, for example, Brooks and Rose, *Saving the Neighborhood*; Jones-Correa,

"Origins and Diffusion"; Long and Johnson, *People vs. Property*; Plotkin, "Deeds of Mistrust."

3. See Carle, "Race, Class," 124–28. See also Carle, "From *Buchanan* to *Button*"; Rice, "Residential Segregation"; Power, "Apartheid Baltimore Style."

4. *Buchanan v. Warley* 245 U.S. 60 (1917). For more on racial zoning and the *Warley* case see, for example, the 1998 *Vanderbilt Law Review* colloquium including David E. Bernstein, "Philip Sober"; Ely, "Reflections on *Buchanan v. Warley*"; Fischel, "Judicial Reversal." On zoning's persistence after *Buchanan* see Brooks and Rose, *Saving the Neighborhood*, 45–46; *Harmon v. Tyler* 273 U.S. 668 (1927); *City of Richmond v. Deans* 37 F.2d 712 (1930). On the First Great Migration see, for example, Grossman, *Land of Hope*.

5. For an insightful discussion on the transition from zoning to covenanting see Jones-Correa, "Origins and Diffusion." For an intriguing reexamination of the legal theories behind residential segregation in this era see Godsil, "Race Nuisance." On the early growth of racial ghettos in the North see Spear, *Black Chicago*; Kusmer, *Ghetto Takes Shape*; Osofsky, *Harlem*.

6. *Corrigan v. Buckley* 271 U.S. 323, 329–30 (1926); Long and Johnson, *People vs. Property*, 12–13.

7. *Hansberry v. Lee* 311 U.S. 32 (1940); *Mays v. Burgess* 147 F. 2d 869 (D.C. Circuit, 1945). For a thorough discussion of the NAACP's early campaign against residential discrimination in the courts and some of the legal theories they advanced against covenants see Vose, *Caucasians Only*, 1–29 and 50–73.

8. On the Second Great Migration see, for example, Wilkerson, *Warmth*; Lemann, *Promised Land*; Boehm, *Making a Way*.

9. For population numbers see Capeci and Wilkerson, "Detroit Rioters," 51–52; Norman Humphrey, "Black Ghetto," *Christian Century* 64, no. 3 (January 1947): 78–79; Gibson and Jung, *Historical Census Statistics*. On race relations in the respective cities see, for Detroit: Sugrue, *Origins*; Freund, *Colored Property*; Boyle, *Arc of Justice*; Levine, *Internal Combustion*; Capeci, *Race Relations*; Thompson, *Whose Detroit?* For St. Louis: Lang, *Grassroots*; Gordon, *Mapping Decline*. For Washington: Green, *Secret City*; Pearlman, "Home Rules"; Moore, *Leading the Race*.

10. See Tom Sugrue's discussion of rights consciousness as a useful formulation. Sugrue, *Origins*, 10–12 and 59–60. See also Lovell, *Civil Rights*; Goluboff, "Thirteenth Amendment"; Kelley, *Race Rebels*. On rights-conscious rhetoric in housing see Freund, *Colored Property*.

11. For more on racial discrimination in New Deal housing programs see, for example, Gotham, "Racialization"; Hirsch, "Containment"; Kenneth T. Jackson, "Race, Ethnicity"; Abrams, *Forbidden Neighbors*. On New Deal housing policy more broadly see, for example, Radford, *Modern Housing*; Gelfand, *Nation of Cities*; Funigiello, *Challenge*. For Roosevelt's remarks see *New York Times*, January 12, 1944, 12.

12. On white homeowners' statements to this effect see, for example, Long and Johnson, *People vs. Property*, 49 and Sugrue, "Crabgrass-Roots Politics," 566. On rights

consciousness and the war era see, for example, Ward, *Defending White Democracy*; Jennifer Brooks, *Defining the Peace*; Gilmore, *Defying Dixie*; Shockley, *We, Too, Are Americans*; Kellogg, "Civil Rights Consciousness."

13. See Vose, *Caucasians Only*. For more recent treatments of the cases see the fall 1989 retrospective forum in the *Washington University Law Quarterly*, esp. Leland B. Ware, "Invisible Walls." See also Brooks and Rose, *Saving the Neighborhood*, esp. 129–67; Rose, "Property Stories"; Pritchett, "*Shelley v. Kraemer*"; Klarman, *From Jim Crow*, 212–17 and 261–64.

14. *Brown v. Board of Education* 347 U.S. 483 (1954). On the theoretical contours of the Long Civil Rights Era see Singh, *Black Is a Country*, 1–14; Hall, "Long Civil Rights Movement"; Terry, "Which Way to Memphis?" For earlier iterations of this call see Korstad and Lichtenstein, "Opportunities"; Dalfiume, "'Forgotten Years.'" For a critique see Cha-Jua and Lang, "'Long Movement.'"

15. For some excellent examples of the emphasis on labor organizing and interracial radicalism see Gilmore, *Defying Dixie*; Korstad, *Civil Rights Unionism*. For Long Civil Rights Era scholarship that addresses housing access efforts see, for example, Sugrue, *Sweet Land*; Rhonda Y. Williams, *Politics of Public Housing*.

16. Hirsch, *Making the Second Ghetto*, 16 and 30; Sugrue, *Sweet Land*, 209. Hirsch argues that by the late 1940s covenants were "a device that was already growing unequal to the task of preserving racial homogeneity," and that "throughout the 1940s, restrictive covenants in Chicago served as little more than a fairly coarse sieve." Sugrue's most recent work describes covenants as "in many respects the least effective tactic to enforce racial segregation."

17. See, for example, Goluboff, *Lost Promise*; Lau, *From the Grassroots*; Prifogle, "Law and Local Activism"; Brown-Nagin, *Courage to Dissent*; and some of the ensuing discussion surrounding her work including Gross, "From the Streets." For a debate over the "newness" of this shift toward community-level histories see Goluboff, "Lawyers, Law"; Mack, "Civil Rights History."

18. Political scientist Michael McCann has offered insight into the utility of a more bottom-up approach to understanding the impact of reform litigation. See, for example, McCann, "Reform Litigation on Trial." For policy-oriented accounts of civil rights reform see, for example, Dudziak, *Cold War Civil Rights*; McMahon, *Reconsidering Roosevelt*. For locally oriented studies see, for example, Dittmer, *Local People*; Theoharis and Woodard, *Groundwork*; Payne, *I've Got the Light*.

19. On the challenges of coordinating litigation campaigns see Wasby, "How Planned"; Rubenstein, "Divided We Litigate."

Chapter One

1. *Hurd and Urciolo v. Hodge*, Transcript of Record, 307–9.
2. Ibid., 309–14.

3. Blank, *Volume*, 11; "Trends in Housing during the War and Postwar Periods," *Monthly Labor Review* 64, no. 1 (January 1947), 12; Charles Abrams, "Homeless America, I," *Nation* 163, no. 25 (December 21, 1946), 723; Hauser and Jaffe, "Extent of the Housing Shortage," 9–10; "Probable Volume of Postwar Construction—Part 2: Demand for Private Construction," *Monthly Labor Review* 60, no. 3 (March 1945), 480; *Study and Investigation of Housing*, 80th Cong., 1st sess., October 24, 1947, Proceedings at St. Louis, Mo., 628.

4. Blank, *Volume*, 67.

5. "Trends in Housing," 12. Total urban construction stood at an average of 192,000 starts per year and 60.8 percent of the total from 1942–45 versus 175,000 starts per year and 64.0 percent of total building from 1930–39. See also "Housing Conditions," *Monthly Labor Review* 58, no. 3 (March 1943), 539; "Housing Conditions," *Monthly Labor Review* 60, no. 5 (May 1945), 1057; Capeci, *Race Relations*, 36; *Study and Investigation of Housing*, Proceedings at St. Louis, Mo., 685; Lester Velie, "Housing: The Chicago Racket," *Collier's* 118, no. 17 (October 26, 1946), 17.

6. Hauser and Jaffe, "Extent," 12; *Washington Post*, February 9, 1941, 13; *Washington Post*, July 15, 1947, 6; *St. Louis Post-Dispatch*, October 10, 1945, 7; *Study and Investigation of Housing*, Proceedings at St. Louis, Mo., 628; *New York Times*, September 6, 1944, 21; *Washington Post*, December 14, 1945, 6.

7. "Effects of Wartime Housing Shortages on Home Ownership," *Monthly Labor Review* 62, no. 4 (April 1946), 562–64.

8. Abrams, "Homeless America," 725 (italics in original).

9. Hauser and Jaffe, "Extent," 12–13; *Housing in America*, 80th Cong., 1st sess., 170–71; Wright, *Building the Dream*, 242; Blank, *Volume*, 67; John Blandford, "The Challenge of the Post-War Housing Job," February 5, 1945, in JBP, Box 20.

10. Wright, *Building the Dream*, 242; Memorandum for the President's Committee on Civil Rights from the American Veterans Committee, undated [c. 1947], in PCCR, Box 10; *Study and Investigation of Housing*, Proceedings at St. Louis, Mo., 686; *Washington Post*, December 6, 1945, 18; *Washington Post*, January 11, 1948, R1.

11. Wright, *Building the Dream*, 242; Frank Gervasi, "Housing: The Homeless Southwest," *Collier's* 118, no. 24 (December 14, 1946), 22; *Study and Investigation of Housing*, October 24, 1947, Proceedings at Detroit, Mich., 396 and 456; Sugrue, *Origins*, 42; Lester Velie, "Housing: Detroit's Time Bomb," *Collier's* 118, no. 21 (November 23, 1946), 75; *McGhee v. Sipes*, American Federation of Labor Amicus Brief, 29–30.

12. Gervasi, "Housing," 22; *St. Louis Argus*, November 9, 1945, 2; *Study and Investigation of Housing*, Proceedings at St. Louis, Mo., 669 and 697–702; Velie, "Housing: The Chicago Racket," 17 and 110. See a similar discussion of conditions in the East Bay Area of California in Kimble, "Restrictive Covenants," 51.

13. *Study and Investigation of Housing*, Proceedings at St. Louis, Mo., 629; Velie, "Housing: The Chicago Racket," 17; Velie, "Housing: Detroit's Time Bomb," 15; *New York Times*, June 26, 1947, 18.

14. Long and Johnson, *People vs. Property*, 63. See also Wiese, "Black Housing." For some general discussions of the real estate industry's racial standards see Helper, *Racial Policies*; Satter, *Family Properties*.

15. Hirsch, *Making the Second Ghetto*, 41; NAACP, *Appeal to the World*, 1947, 78 in PNP, Box 61; see also Jeannine Bell, *Hate Thy Neighbor*. For examples of pre-1940 housing violence in Detroit see also Boyle, *Arc of Justice*; Levine, *Internal Combustion*. For post–World War I violence see, for example, Grossman, *Land of Hope*; Tuttle, *Race Riot*. For a fascinating model explaining individual homeowners' motivations to maintain segregation see Schelling, "Models of Segregation."

16. Capeci, *Race Relations*, esp. chap. 5; Peterson, *Planning*, 118–21.

17. Capeci, *Race Relations*, chaps. 5–7; Meyer, *As Long*, 68–72; Sugrue, *Origins*, 73–75.

18. Peterson, *Planning*, 242–49; Capeci and Wilkerson, *Layered Violence*.

19. *Pittsburgh Courier*, October 9, 1943, 1; McKenzie, *Privatopia*, 60; Jones-Correa, "Origins and Diffusion," 543.

20. Mohl, "Second Ghetto." On the extent of segregation in local real estate boards see, for example, Lenerte Roberts to Harry S. Truman, August 9, 1949, in President's Personal File Box 604, describing that only the Real Estate Board of New York, out of the more than 1,000 local real estate boards in the nation, admitted black members in the 1940s; Memorandum on NAREB Semi-Annual Survey "Realtor Work for Negro Housing," undated, in LWP, Box 14, Folder 5.

21. See esp. Hirsch, *Making the Second Ghetto*; Hirsch, "Jim Crow."

22. Weaver, *Negro Ghetto*, 232; Abrams, "Homes for Aryans Only," 421–23; "Note to Key People regarding Decision of the U.S. Court of Appeals, District of Columbia, No. 8831," January 1945 (italics in original); NAACP, Part 5, Reel 21, Frames 103–4; President's Committee on Civil Rights, *To Secure These Rights*, 68. For some additional examples of this claim see Dean, "Only Caucasian," 428; Weaver, "Round Table," 38–41; Long and Johnson, *People vs. Property*, 8–9; William Ming to Robert K. Carr, June 2, 1947, in PCCR, Box 9; "Statement to the President's Committee Presented by the National Urban League," April 1, 1947, in PCCR, Box 18; Thurgood Marshall to Roger Baldwin, June 9, 1944, in NAACP Records Part II, Box B135; NAACP, *Appeal to the World*, 1947, 55, in PNP, Box 61.

23. Black, "Restrictive Covenants," 24; Gordon, *Mapping Decline*, 79; McKenzie, *Privatopia*, 69–72; Gotham, "Urban Space," 623–27. See also Brooks and Rose's discussion of developers and brokers as "norm entrepreneurs" in the field of racial discrimination and restrictive covenants in *Saving the Neighborhood*, 102–11. On the role of subdividers and NAREB on the practices of community planning and land use restrictions more generally and their influence on FHA policy see Marc A. Weiss, *Rise*.

24. Long and Johnson, *People vs. Property*, 40–43; McKenzie, *Privatopia*, 58.

25. Oscar Brown to Elmer Gertz, June 5, 1945, in EGP, Box 335, Folder 1; National Committee on Segregation in the Nation's Capitol, "Segregation in Washington," November 1948 in LWP, Box 15, Folder 1.

26. Memorandum of NAACP concerning the Present Discriminatory Policies of the FHA, October 28, 1944, in NAACP, Part 5, Reel 6, Frames 1038–50; Federal Housing Administration, *Underwriting Manual (1938)*, 973. For more on the FHA's role in supporting housing segregation during this period see, for example, Freund, *Colored Property*, esp. 155–62; Sugrue, *Origins*, esp. 62–67; Kimble, "Insuring Inequality."

27. Federal Housing Administration, *Underwriting Manual (1938)*, 902, and 932–37.

28. Tobey et al., "Moving Out and Settling In," 1414.

29. See Brooks and Rose, *Saving the Neighborhood*, esp. 160–67 on the signaling functions of covenants.

30. Velie, "Housing: Detroit's Time Bomb," 15; *Michigan Chronicle*, January 25, 1947, 6–7; *Michigan Chronicle*, May 3, 1947, 1; *Michigan Chronicle*, January 25, 1947, 6; Black, "Restrictive Covenants," 42.

31. Dean, "Only Caucasian," 428–29; Gotham, "Urban Space," 618–23; *Evening Star*, May 4, 1948, A-4.

32. Black, "Restrictive Covenants," 5–6; *Michigan Chronicle*, August 25, 1945, 3; Plotkin, "Deeds of Mistrust," 29 and 235; McIntyre, "Status of Racial Covenants," 16–18; Gordon, *Mapping Decline*, 86; Long and Johnson, *People vs. Property*, 86; Loren Miller, "Covenants for Exclusion," reprinted from the October 1947 edition of *Survey Graphic* in NAACP, Part 5, Reel 20, Frame 969; *U.S. News & World Report*, January 30, 1948. For similar sentiments see also *Evening Star*, May 4, 1948, A-4; Memorandum for the Sunday Morning Discussion Section of the 40th Annual Meeting of the American Jewish Committee, undated, in LWP, Box 16, Folder 2, noting the growing frequency of covenants targeting Jews in the years after World War II.

33. Miller, "Covenants for Exclusion," reprinted in NAACP, Part 5, Reel 20, Frame 971; B. T. McGraw and Frank S. Horne, "The House I Live In," *Opportunity* 24, no. 3 (Summer 1946): 125; *McGhee v. Sipes*, Brief Amicus Curiae from the American Federation of Labor, 29–30.

34. Long and Johnson, *People vs. Property*, 34–35; *McGhee v. Sipes*, Brief Amicus Curiae from the American Federation of Labor, 6 and 14–15; Reginald A. Johnson, "Housing—No New Problem for the Urban League," *Opportunity* 24, no. 3 (Summer 1946): 146.

35. *Monthly Summary of Events and Trends in Race Relations* 1, no. 4 (November 1943): 6; *McGhee v. Sipes*, Brief Amicus Curiae from the American Federation of Labor. See also "Statistics concerning Negro Population and Restrictive Covenants," undated, in EGP, Box 335, Folder 4.

36. *McGhee v. Sipes*, Brief Amicus Curiae from the American Federation of Labor, 7–22.

37. Ibid. The comparable central heating figures for whites were thirteen percent in Detroit and 25 percent in St. Louis. Comparable running water figures for whites stood at 3 percent for St. Louis and 1 percent for Washington. Thomas, *Redevelopment and Race*, 17; *Michigan Chronicle*, February 24, 1945, 7; Velie, "Housing: Detroit's Time Bomb," 77.

38. Reginald Johnson, "House to Rent for Negro Occupancy" *American City* 62, no. 5 (December 1947): 96.

39. *St. Louis Argus*, February 13, 1948, 15; *Shelley v. Kraemer*, Transcript of Record, 128.

40. One notable exception to this pattern of nonpolitical covenant-breaking was St. Louis attorney and Lincoln University Law School professor Scovel Richardson, who attempted to create his own test case in 1941 by purchasing a covenanted home in the city. Gordon, *Mapping Decline*, 80–81.

41. Irons, *Courage*, 73–74 (italics in original).

42. Irons, *Courage*, 74. On wartime conditions at the Small Arms Plant see Lucander, *Winning the War*, 115–28.

43. Irons, *Courage*, 74; *Shelley v. Kraemer*, Transcript of Record, 124; *Baltimore Afro-American*, May 15, 1948, 3.

44. *Shelley v. Kraemer*, Transcript of Record, 82, 109, and 116–18.

45. For a discussion of indirect methods of sale in Chicago neighborhoods see Plotkin, "Deeds of Mistrust," 106–7; *Shelley v. Kraemer*, Transcript of Record, 88 and 112. Prominent St. Louis realtor James T. Bush also relied in large part upon a cadre of straw-party purchasers to facilitate his business. See Wilson, *Twigs from the Bush*, 53–58.

46. *Shelley v. Kraemer*, Transcript of Record, 88; Long and Johnson, *People vs. Property*, 63. A broker with knowledge of conditions in St. Louis claimed that interest rates for blacks were "a standard six per cent" while whites often obtained loans as low as 4.5 percent. Similar interest rate gaps were present in other cities generally ranging "from one to two percent." See, for example, George Nesbitt to Elmer Gertz, September 5, 1946, in EGP, Box 335, Folder 3.

47. *Shelley v. Kraemer*, Transcript of Record, 102 and 117.

48. Ibid., 3–12 and 95–96.

49. Ibid., 125.

50. Ibid., 3.

51. *McGhee v. Sipes*, Transcript of Record, 49; Bureau of the Census, *Fifteenth Census, 1930*; *Los Angeles Times*, February 10, 1999, 12; Minnie McGhee Oral History, October 27, 1978.

52. Minnie McGhee Oral History, October 27, 1978.

53. Ibid.

54. *Baltimore Afro-American*, March 8, 1947, 11; *Michigan Chronicle*, May 3, 1947, 19; *Michigan Chronicle*, January 25, 1947, 6; Minnie McGhee Oral History, October 27, 1978.

55. Bureau of the Census, *Thirteenth Census, 1910*; *Hurd and Urciolo v. Hodge*, Transcript of Record, 169–70 and 238. The issue of Hurd's true racial identity remains unresolved. Questions of geography and the fact that Hurd's attorneys dropped all mention of his racial identity upon reaching the U.S. Supreme Court have led previous chroniclers of the covenant cases to dismiss his claims of being a Mohawk. Census records suggest that he was of mixed race, but leave no definitive answer about the specifics of his heritage.

56. *Hurd and Urciolo v. Hodge*, Transcript of Record, 244.

57. Ibid., 223.

58. Ibid., 75; *Baltimore Afro-American*, February 21, 1942, 24.

59. *Hurd and Urciolo v. Hodge*, Transcript of Record, 149–53; "Effects of Wartime Housing," 562.

60. *Baltimore Afro-American*, May 15, 1948, 4; *Hurd and Urciolo v. Hodge*, Transcript of Record, 154. Urciolo had also testified in at least one prior anticovenant case at the request of Charles Hamilton Houston, serving in his capacity as a high school teacher to provide testimony about the racial composition of a neighborhood on behalf of an African American family who sought to break the restrictions on Thirteenth Street in the Columbia Heights neighborhood of Washington. See *Hundley v. Gorewitz* 132 F.2d 23 (D.C. Circuit, 1942), Appendix to Brief for Appellants, 84–86, in Mary Gibson Hundley Papers, Box 2, Folder 17.

61. *Hurd and Urciolo v. Hodge*, Transcript of Record, 26.

62. Weaver, "Race Restrictive Housing Covenants," 183–93; see also Brooks and Rose, *Saving the Neighborhood*, 160–67.

63. Bureau of the Census, *Fifteenth Census, 1930*. In 1930, the Sipes' neighbors included electricians, a machinist at the Ford factory, a Wayne County clerk, and a handful of foremen and small business proprietors. A similar mix of blue- and white-collar workers populated the neighborhood in 1940. Bureau of the Census, *Sixteenth Census, 1940*. *McGhee v. Sipes*, Transcript of Record, 21–23.

64. *McGhee v. Sipes*, Transcript of Record, 22; Minnie McGhee Oral History, October 27, 1978.

65. Minnie McGhee Oral History, October 27, 1978; *McGhee v. Sipes*, Transcript of Record, 22.

66. Minnie McGhee Oral History, October 27, 1978; *McGhee v. Sipes*, Transcript of Record, 22.

67. Minnie McGhee Oral History, October 27, 1978.

68. Gordon, *Mapping Decline*, 79–81; *Shelley v. Kraemer*, Transcript of Record, 69–75.

69. *Shelley v. Kraemer*, Transcript of Record, 1, 76, and 114–15.

70. Bureau of the Census, *Thirteenth Census, 1910*; Bureau of the Census, *Fifteenth Census, 1930*. In 1930, before the arrival of a group of blue-collar Italian immigrants in the area, the Hodges' neighbors included a collection of bookkeepers, salesmen, government clerks, and teachers. *Hurd and Urciolo v. Hodge*, Transcript of Record, 18, 81–97, and 107–44.

71. *Hurd and Urciolo v. Hodge*, Transcript of Record, 31 and 296.

72. Ibid., 19–20.

73. Ibid., 68.

74. Ibid., 31 and 69; Vose, *Caucasians Only*, 174–75.

75. *Hurd and Urciolo v. Hodge*, Transcript of Record, 20–21.

76. Ibid., 244.

77. Ibid., 77–78.

78. Ibid., 64 and 69.

79. Ibid., 66 and 132–33.

80. *Shelley v. Kraemer*, Transcript of Record, 120–25.

81. *Hurd and Urciolo v. Hodge*, Transcript of Record, 245–48.

82. Ibid., 79. In his account of the *Shelley* cases, Clement Vose treated the letter as though it were from James Hurd himself, calling it a "model of restraint and agreeableness." Vose, *Caucasians Only*, 78–80.

83. *Hurd and Urciolo v. Hodge*, Transcript of Record, 248.

84. *St. Louis Argus*, January 3, 1947, 1.

85. *Hurd and Urciolo v. Hodge*, Transcript of Record, 153.

86. Chicago attorney Loring Moore, for example, had begun to win a series of covenant cases in the Windy City. Plotkin, "Deeds of Mistrust," 234.

87. *Hurd and Urciolo v. Hodge*, Transcript of Record, 248.

Chapter Two

1. *Los Angeles Tribune*, December 10, 1945, in LMP, Box 30, Folder 2; "Victory on Sugar Hill," *Time* 46, no. 25 (December 17, 1945): 24; *Los Angeles Sentinel*, August 20, 1936.

2. Nora Miller autobiography, undated, in LMP, Box 31, Folder 2; Reflection entitled "Let Tomorrow Come," undated, in LMP, Box 5, Folder 3. For more on Loren Miller see esp. Mack, *Representing the Race*, 181–206; Mack, "Law and Mass Politics."

3. Though Clarke's decision to examine personally the properties at stake was unusual, he had pursued a similar course of action in at least one other previous property dispute early in 1944. That matter, however, was not related to a racial restriction. *Los Angeles Times*, January 27, 1944, A2. See also Loren Miller Oral History, April 29, 1967, 20–25.

4. The term "collaborative legal activism" serves here to highlight some of the structural components of local civil rights litigation. It builds upon the observations and analysis of some of the most recent work exploring the contours and relevance of legal efforts in black freedom struggles. See Mack, *Representing the Race*; Mack, "Law and Mass Politics"; Brown-Nagin, *Courage to Dissent*. This lens captures more of the architecture of the process of litigation at midcentury rather than the law's relationship to daily battles against segregation in other walks of life and arenas of protest. Yet, by focusing on collaboration, it does address some of the connections that took shape between local legal advocates and the communities they served, as well as their links to a national community of civil rights lawyers. Litigation efforts, this model suggests, were both locally crafted and nationally influenced. For more on the structure and events of litigation campaigns see Tushnet, *NAACP's Legal Strategy*; Hine, *Black Victory*; Kluger, *Simple Justice*; Tushnet, *Making Civil Rights Law*. For more on the relationship of the law to broader black freedom struggles see Mack, "Bringing the Law Back"; Goluboff, *Lost Promise*; Klarman, *From Jim Crow*; Rosenberg, *Hollow Hope*; Randall L. Kennedy, "Martin Luther King's Constitution"; Glennon, "Role of Law"; Coleman et al., "Social Movements."

5. See Christopher W. Schmidt, "Freedom Comes"; and Mack, "Rethinking Civil Rights Lawyering" for a discussion of the complexities and evolving perceptions of the utility of law as an instrument of change.

6. See, for example, Green, "Stare Decisis."

7. Sullivan, *Lift Every Voice*, 295. For more on the impact of local activism in black freedom struggles see, for example, Brown-Nagin, *Courage to Dissent*; Payne, *I've Got the Light*; Dittmer, *Local People*; Theoharis and Woodard, *Groundwork*; Crosby, *Civil Rights History*.

8. Wilson, *Twigs from the Bush*, 65–66.

9. *Shelley v. Kraemer*, Transcript of Record, 105–13. Tomiko Brown-Nagin identifies a different response for black realtors and the Empire Real Estate Board in Atlanta where they endorsed the project of expanding the housing market for African Americans but not integration. The presumption, certainly true in some cases—though not, it would appear, in St. Louis—is that because black realtors effectively enjoyed a captive market within a segregated industry they risked a potential loss of business by opening up competition with white brokers for sales to black families. See Brown-Nagin, *Courage to Dissent*, 62–63.

10. See, for example, legal historian Kenneth Mack's discussion of the "race uplift" impulse in the African American legal tradition in Mack, "Rethinking Civil Rights Lawyering," 281–87.

11. Dreer, "Negro Leadership," 102; *St. Louis Argus*, September 12, 1947, 11; *St. Louis Argus*, September 2, 1949, 14; *St. Louis Argus*, August 19, 1949, 1 and 12; *St. Louis Argus*, August 26, 1949, 1 and 10; Herman Willer, "Notes on George L. Vaughn and Shelly [*sic*] v. Kraemer" in BHP, Box 6, Folder 106; Robert L. Gill, "Legacy of a Civil Rights Lawyer," reprinted from *Journal of Human Relations* 12, no. 1, in BHP, Box 7, Folder 120.

12. Gill, "Legacy of a Civil Rights Lawyer"; Kelleher, "History of the St. Louis NAACP," reproduced in BHP, Box 6, Folders 96–100.

13. *St. Louis Argus*, August 19, 1949, 1 and 12; Gill, "Legacy of a Civil Rights Lawyer"; Kelleher, "History of the St. Louis NAACP," reproduced in BHP, Box 6, Folders 96–100; Lieutenant George L. Vaughn, "The Negro in Labor and Industry," June 24, 1919, in NAACP, Part 1, Reel 8, Frames 543–47. For more on the impact of World War I on African American political activism see Lentz-Smith, *Freedom Struggles*; Chad L. Williams, *Torchbearers of Democracy*.

14. Lang, *Grassroots*, 23–24 and 46; Gill, "Legacy of a Civil Rights Lawyer." For more on the shifting political allegiances of African American voters see Nancy J. Weiss, *Farewell*; Sherman, *Republican Party*; Sitkoff, *New Deal for Blacks*.

15. Kelleher, "History of the St. Louis NAACP," reproduced in BHP, Box 6, Folders 96–100; Dreer, "Negro Leadership," 131–32.

16. Wilson, *Twigs from the Bush*, 54–58 and 73. Vaughn and Bush also appear to have shared a church for a period of time and both men were Masons, though it is unclear to what extent the two men actually knew each other before 1945. With respect to Vaughn's other covenant cases, Bush seems to have had an interest in at least one more

suit that came just weeks after the start of *Shelley*. See *St. Louis Argus*, October 18, 1946, 1 and 15.

17. Wilson, *Twigs from the Bush*, 36 and 53–58. It appears from his daughter's recounting of events that Bush had broken restrictive covenants before, but he evinced a particular interest in placing black families in white blocks during his return to business.

18. For a separate discussion of the conflicting objectives and allegiances of attorneys in civil rights litigation efforts see Derrick A. Bell, "Serving Two Masters."

19. Meeting Minutes/Transcript of Tuesday Afternoon Session, July 10, 1945, in NAACP, Part 5, Reel 20, Frame 629.

20. *Shelley v. Kraemer*, Transcript of Record, 12.

21. Ibid., 10–11 and Vose, *Caucasians Only*, 114–15.

22. *Shelley v. Kraemer*, Transcript of Record, 30–63.

23. Ibid., 14–15.

24. Ibid., 102–4.

25. Ibid., 116–18.

26. Ibid., 125 and 145.

27. Ibid., 141–44; Wilson, *Twigs from the Bush*, 67. The Kraemer family's attorney, in his motion for a new trial after this initial ruling, suggested that Koerner's decision reflected personal biases in favor of the Shelleys. The judge, he alleged, had apparently recognized one of the courtroom spectators who had come in support of the Shelleys' case and had invited the visitor up to the bench for a private conversation in the middle of the cross-examination of one of Vaughn's expert witnesses. Though Koerner was apparently appointed rather than elected under Missouri's nonpartisan court system, political or personal motivations may well have played a role in his willingness to strike down the covenant at hand. See *Shelley v. Kraemer*, Transcript of Record, 146.

28. *Shelley v. Kraemer*, Transcript of Record, 113 and 140.

29. "Potentialities of Change of Neighborhood Doctrine—Charles Hamilton Houston, Monday Afternoon Session," July 9, 1945, in NAACP, Part 5, Reel 20, Frames 582–83.

30. Ibid., Frames 583–84. See also Vose, *Caucasians Only*, 59–60.

31. Wilson, *Twigs from the Bush*, 67–68; Vose, *Caucasians Only*, 119–21.

32. *St. Louis Argus*, January 3, 1947, 1; *St. Louis Argus*, March 21, 1947, 8 and 11.

33. Wilson, *Twigs from the Bush*, 67–68; *St. Louis Argus*, January 3, 1947, 1.

34. Dreer, "Negro Leadership," 152–56; Pamphlet by St. Louis Citizens Steering Committee "An Effort to Improve American Democracy by Ending Residential Restrictive Covenants," undated, in NAACP, Part 5, Reel 22, Frames 350–52.

35. Pamphlet by St. Louis Citizens Steering Committee "An Effort to Improve American Democracy by Ending Residential Restrictive Covenants," undated, in NAACP, Part 5, Reel 22, Frames 350–52; Herman Dreer to NAACP National Office, November 23, 1947, in NAACP, Part 5, Reel 22, Frame 356.

36. Margaret Bush Wilson's account of the Citizens Committee's formation suggests that although prominent black civil rights advocates David Grant, the NAACP branch chairman, and Scovel Richardson, a noted anticovenant attorney, consulted with James T. Bush and Robert Bishop as the committee formed—and ultimately lent their names to its letterhead—they were only nominal participants in the group's activities. Wilson, *Twigs from the Bush*, 74–76; Pamphlet by St. Louis Citizens Steering Committee "An Effort to Improve American Democracy by Ending Residential Restrictive Covenants," undated, in NAACP, Part 5, Reel 22, Frames 350–52; Dreer, "Negro Leadership," 151–56.

37. For civil rights attorneys' work with black railway workers see, for example, Charles Houston's U.S. Supreme Court cases *Steele v. Louisville & Nashville Railroad Company* 323 U.S. 192 (1944) and *Tunstall v. Brotherhood of Locomotive Firemen and Enginemen, Ocean Lodge No. 76* 323 U.S. 210 (1944). On other labor litigation see Goluboff, "Economic Equality." Previous litigation by the NAACP was not without its own ethical dilemmas, however. On the complicated relationships between white NAACP attorneys, clients, and local bar associations see Carle, "Race, Class, and Legal Ethics."

38. Not all attorneys worked pro bono, however, even on cases that they took on behalf of—or in conjunction with—the local NAACP. Stalwart attorneys like Houston, Miller, and Loring Moore of Chicago often charged fees for their services in covenant suits.

39. *Corrigan v. Buckley* 271 U.S. 323 (1926) and *Hansberry v. Lee* 311 U.S. 32 (1940).

40. Rosemond, *Reflections*, 30; Vose, *Caucasians Only*, 122–24. For an enthralling account of the events surrounding the Sweet case see Boyle, *Arc of Justice*.

41. Rosemond, *Reflections*, 24 and 31–32; *Michigan Chronicle*, May 4, 1946, 5; *Michigan Chronicle*, February 23, 1946, 2.

42. Booker T. Washington Business Association 35th Annual Banquet Program, July 16, 1965 in WIGP, Box 2, Folder 24.

43. Unsigned handwritten note on Restrictive Covenant Cases, undated, in WIGP, Box 1, Folder 1; various correspondence and documents related to *Howard Flowers v. NHA, FPHA, and Sherwood Reeder* (1944) in WIGP, Box 2, Folder 38.

44. Bureau of the Census, *Fifteenth Census, 1930*; M Street High School Class of 1911 Roster, undated, in FMDP, Box 1; Obituary of Francis M. Dent, Esquire, undated [c. 1964], in FMDP, Box 1; Clotee Dent, "In Memorium [*sic*] to the Late Francis M. Dent, undated [c. 1964], in FMDP, Box 1.

45. Francis Dent to Mayor Frank Murphy, February 13, 1931 in FMDP, Box 10, Folder 6.

46. *McGhee v. Sipes*, Transcript of Record, 17–19; Vose, *Caucasians Only*, 127–28.

47. *McGhee v. Sipes*, Transcript of Record, 16–17.

48. See Kahen, "Validity"; McGovney, "Racial Residential Segregation."

49. McGovney, "Racial Residential Segregation," 6 and 15–18.

50. In December of 1944, Graves used a pretrial motion in another covenant case that denied the "defendant is a descendant of the African race as alleged by the petitioners." See Minutes of Detroit NAACP Legal Redress Committee, December 18, 1944, in FMDP, Box 31, Folder 12.

51. *McGhee v. Sipes*, Transcript of Record, 28. For more on the changing conceptions of race see Brattain, "Race, Racism, and Antiracism"; Barkan, *Retreat of Scientific Racism*; Baker, *From Savage to Negro*; John P. Jackson, *Social Scientists*, 17–59.

52. *McGhee v. Sipes*, Transcript of Record, 21–23 and 27–30. For more on the negotiation of racial identity see Pascoe, "Miscegenation Law"; Pascoe, *What Comes Naturally*; Brattain, "Miscegenation"; Gross, *What Blood Won't Tell*; Haney-Lopez, *White by Law*; Sharfstein, *Invisible Line*. For the U.S. Supreme Court's endorsement of the "common man's" interpretation of racial identity see *U.S. v. Bhagat Singh Thind* 261 U.S. 204 (1923).

53. *McGhee v. Sipes*, Transcript of Record, 52–53.

54. "Potentialities of Change of Neighborhood Doctrine—Charles Hamilton Houston, Monday Afternoon Session," July 9, 1945, in NAACP, Part 5, Reel 20, Frames 579–81. Graves and Dent may not have been the first attorneys in the nation to employ the racial classification attack on restrictive agreements. An anticovenant case from Berkeley, California, around the same time also challenged the ability to identify and define race, using the testimony of anthropologist Dr. Paul Radin. See Kimble, "Restrictive Covenants," 50–52.

55. "Potentialities of Change of Neighborhood Doctrine—Charles Hamilton Houston, Monday Afternoon Session," July 9, 1945, in NAACP, Part 5, Reel 20, Frame 580–81.

56. On the impact of black legal societies and the exchange of ideas see Smith, *Emancipation*, chap. 10. Though her work focuses primarily on black medical associations, see also Hine, "Black Professionals."

57. Spottswood Robinson, "No Tea for the Feeble," 3–4; McNeil, *Groundwork*, 30–56.

58. Mack, "Rethinking Civil Rights Lawyering," 287; McNeil, *Groundwork*, 59–138.

59. McNeil, *Groundwork*, 177.

60. Records of *Bishopp v. Chamberlain* in CHHP, Box 33, Folders 8–12, Memorandum from Charles Hamilton Houston, May 25, 1942, in CHHP, Box 33, Folders 20–21. See also Records of *Hundley v. Gorewitz* in CHHP, Box 34, Folders 5 and 17.

61. Memorandum by Charles Hamilton Houston in re: *Bishopp v. Broadway*, January 19, 1942, in CHHP, Box 33, Folder 12; Spottswood Robinson, "No Tea for the Feeble," 5–6.

62. Houston, though he respected Urciolo and appreciated his financial support of the cases, was initially displeased with having the cases tied. This may well have had to do with his admonitions about hiding the role of realtors in the covenant-breaking process. See *Hurd and Urciolo v. Hodge*, Transcript of Record, 13.

63. Potentialities of Change of Neighborhood Doctrine—Charles Hamilton Houston, Monday Afternoon Session," July 9, 1945, in NAACP, Part 5, Reel 20, Frame 579.

64. *Hurd and Urciolo v. Hodge*, Transcript of Record, 169–71 and 237–40.

65. Ibid., 305–7.

66. Ibid., 37–40. For a discussion of the centrality of the right of exclusion in the significance of race as both a social and legal construction see Harris, "Whiteness as Property."

67. *Hurd and Urciolo v. Hodge*, Transcript of Record, 101–5.

68. For previous discussions and omissions regarding Houston's racial identity arguments see Vose, *Caucasians Only*, 85–86; Leland B. Ware, "Invisible Walls," which makes no mention of Houston's racial claims; "Potentialities of Change of Neighborhood Doctrine—Charles Hamilton Houston, Monday Afternoon Session," July 9, 1945, in NAACP, Part 5, Reel 20, Frames 579–84. Houston's line of argument here, and particularly his insistence on the ambiguities of racial identity and race as a concept, helps to complicate the prevailing scholarly portraits regarding his ideologies of lawyering and professionalism. Mack and others have offered compelling depictions of Houston as an ardent proponent of race consciousness and racial loyalty in both his courtroom work and his professional advocacy (see, e.g., Mack's discussion of Houston's "pluralist" leanings in "Rethinking Civil Rights Lawyering," 290–92). Yet in *Hurd*, Houston made—and encouraged others to make—an argument rooted in social scientific testimony that race was simply too nebulous a concept to merit legal legitimacy.

69. *Hurd and Urciolo v. Hodge*, Transcript of Record, 6–7.

70. Ibid., 345–54.

71. Ibid., 154–57, 264–70, and 278–90.

72. Ibid., 83–84, 202–7, and 295–98.

73. Ibid., 8–9 and 251–56.

74. Ibid., 380–85.

75. Mack, "Law and Mass Politics," 52–62; Mack, "Rethinking Civil Rights Lawyering," 269; Loren Miller to Kathleen Sproul, August, 1947, in LMP, Box 7, Folder 2. The timing of Miller's rather abrupt transition from inveterate critic to invaluable ally may be explained by the Nazi-Soviet Pact of 1939, which received strong criticism from many African Americans aligned with the radical left politics in the 1930s. See Loren Miller Oral History, March 3, 1967, 6–7. For more on the links between radical organizing and civil rights struggles see Gilmore, *Defying Dixie*.

76. Loren Miller to Kathleen Sproul, August, 1947, in LMP, Box 7, Folder 2; Newspaper clipping, 1946, in LMP, Box 6, Folder 4, claiming that Miller was "reputed to have handled more covenant court cases than any lawyer in America." See also Loren Miller Oral History, April 29, 1967, 19–20.

77. Loren Miller to Robert C. Weaver, January 1, 1946, in LMP, Box 3, Folder 1; *Los Angeles Tribune*, December 10, 1945, in LMP, Box 30, Folder 2.

78. *Los Angeles Tribune*, December 10, 1945, in LMP, Box 30, Folder 2.

79. Ibid.

80. For Traynor's stance see *Fairchild v. Raines* 24 Cal.2d 818, 831–35 (Calif. Supreme Court, 1944, Traynor Concurrence); for Edgerton see *Mays v. Burgess*, 147 F.2d 869,

873–78 (D.C. Circuit, 1945, Edgerton Dissent); Crowe as quoted in *American Council on Race Relations Report* 2.7 (December 1947) in CETRR, Box 36, Folder 5. For examples of the appeal for legislative intervention see, for example, *Mays v. Burgess*, 147 F.2d 869, 878 (D.C. Circuit, 1945, Miller Concurrence). A contemporary of Edgerton's described his thinking as being "above all . . . shaped by a deep current of determination to effect justice and to announce principles and reach results that will best serve the interests of society." See Rosenzweig, "Opinions of Judge Edgerton," 149.

81. Pauli Murray to Loren Miller, December 8, 1945, in LMP, Box 5, Folder 2; A. L. Wirin to Loren Miller, December 10, 1945, in LMP, Box 5, Folder 2; Loren Miller to Lester Granger, December 18, 1945, in LMP, Box 3, Folder 1; Thurgood Marshall to Loren Miller, December 11, 1945, in LMP, Box 5, Folder 2. Though not an attorney, NAACP executive secretary Walter White added his praise to the litany of others in an editorial where he suggested that Sugar Hill might be "the most important single event of 1945 so far as the Negro and other minorities are concerned." See *Chicago Defender*, February 9, 1946, 15. On Murray's battle with restrictive covenants see *Baltimore Afro-American*, September 2, 1944, clipping; *Los Angeles Sentinel*, September 7, 1944, clipping in Pauli Murray Papers, Box 1, Folder 12.

82. See esp. "Letters—Loren Miller, 1935–1946" in LMP, Box 3, Folder 1; "Miller Correspondence, 1946" in LMP, Box 6, Folder 1; "Miller Correspondence, 1946" in LMP, Box 6, Folder 4; "Miller Correspondence, 1944/1945" in LMP, Box 5, Folder 2.

83. Loren Miller to William Henry Huff, December 21, 1945, in LMP, Box 5, Folder 2; Loren Miller to Maurice Weeks, January 1, 1946, in LMP, Box 3, Folder 1; Loren Miller to Robert C. Weaver, January 1, 1946, in LMP, Box 3, Folder 1; Loren Miller to William H. Hastie, January 1, 1946, in LMP, Box 3, Folder 1; Loren Miller to Andrew Weinberger, January 1, 1946, in LMP, Box 3, Folder 1. For correspondence from the other *Shelley* case attorneys see Raphael G. Urciolo to Loren Miller, February 25, 1946, in LMP, Box 6, Folder 4; "Miller Correspondence, 1946" in LMP, Box 6, Folder 4, for the exchange of briefs and comments with Charles Hamilton Houston; "Miller Correspondence, 1946" in LMP, Box 6, Folder 1, for the exchange of letters between Willis Graves and Miller as Graves prepared his appeal in *McGhee* and for communication with Vaughn after the *Shelley* decision. See also Pamphlet by St. Louis Citizens Steering Committee "An Effort to Improve American Democracy by Ending Residential Restrictive Covenants," undated, in NAACP, Part 5, Reel 22, Frames 350–52, for mention of the consulting fee.

84. See Freund, *Colored Property*, for a discussion of the interplay between the language of race and property rights in whites' exclusion efforts.

85. Wilson, *Twigs from the Bush*, 62–64; "Recent Additions to the Bench," *St. Louis Bar Journal* 17 (1970/71): 61; Bureau of the Census, *Thirteenth Census, 1910*; Vose, *Caucasians Only*, 105–6.

86. Bureau of the Census, *Thirteenth Census, 1910*; U.S. Selective Service System, *World War I Selective Service System Draft Registration Cards, 1917–1918* (Washington, D.C.: National Archives and Records Administration), for Marion Frank Chockley,

Lloyd Chockley's brother. Bureau of the Census, *Sixteenth Census, 1940*. Clement Vose, in his only mention of Chockley's involvement, incorrectly refers to him as "Charles Chockley."

87. *McGhee v. Sipes*, Transcript of Record, 79; Vose, *Caucasians Only*, 143–46.

88. *Washington Post*, April 4, 1937, 15; *Washington Post*, October 14, 1950, 11; Bureau of the Census, *Thirteenth Census, 1910*; Records of *Bishopp v. Chamberlain* in CHHP, Box 33, Folder 8.

89. *Washington Post*, February 20, 1932, 20; *Washington Post*, March 22, 1944, 10.

90. *Washington Post*, April 4, 1939, 9. For more on the intricate role of custom and civility in the negotiation of civil rights issues see the brilliant work by William Chafe. Chafe, *Civilities and Civil Rights*.

91. *Washington Post*, March 22, 1944, 10; Vose, *Caucasians Only*, 81.

92. *Washington Post*, November 29, 1942, R4; *Washington Post*, December 29, 1940; *Washington Post*, August 15, 1945. The imbrication of homeowners' groups with local governance was not limited to Washington, D.C. See, for example, *St. Louis Argus*, October 18, 1946, describing the participation of Elmer Ehler in a covenant case as president of the Chouteau-Lindell Improvement Association and a member of the mayor's Race Relations Committee.

93. *Hurd and Urciolo v. Hodge*, Transcript of Record, 4–5; *McGhee v. Sipes*, Transcript of Record, 8; *Shelley v. Kraemer*, Transcript of Record, 6–7.

94. See, for example, *Hurd and Urciolo v. Hodge*, Transcript of Record, 345–54; *McGhee v. Sipes*, Transcript of Record, 29–30.

95. Appellees' Consolidated Brief in *Hurd and Urciolo v. Hodge* (U.S. Circuit Court of Appeals) in CHHP, Box 41, Folder 4; Consolidated Joint Brief for Appellants in *Hurd and Urciolo v. Hodge* (U.S. Circuit Court of Appeals) in CHHP, Box 41, Folder 3; *Sipes v. McGhee* 316 Mich. 614, 25 N.W. 2d 638 (1947), Answering Brief for Appellees as quoted in Vose, *Caucasians Only*, 143–46.

96. *Kraemer v. Shelley* 355 Mo. 814, 198 S.W. 2d 679; *Sipes v. McGhee* 316 Mich. 614, 25 N.W. 2d 638; *Hurd v. Hodge, Urciolo v. Hodge* 162 Fed. 2d 233.

97. Consolidated Joint Brief for Appellants in *Hurd and Urciolo v. Hodge* (U.S. Circuit Court of Appeals) in CHHP, Box 41, Folder 3.

98. Vose, *Caucasians Only*, 137; *McGhee v. Sipes*, Transcript of Record, 67. For more on the impact of international law and the United Nations Charter on civil rights advocacy see Lockwood, "United Nations Charter," and Anderson, *Eyes off the Prize*.

99. Vose, *Caucasians Only*, 136–42; *Sipes v. McGhee* 316 Mich. 614, 25 N.W. 2d 638 (1947). For more on the relationship of Detroit's African American community and the United Automobile Workers union see Meier and Rudwick, *Black Detroit*.

100. *Shelley v. Kraemer*, Transcript of Record, 155–58; Vose, *Caucasians Only*, 117–19.

101. *Shelley v. Kraemer*, Transcript of Record, 159.

102. Wallentine, "Margaret Bush Wilson," 215; *St. Louis Argus*, January 10, 1947, 13; *St. Louis Argus*, January 17, 1947, 13.

103. Supreme Court of Michigan, "The People v. William Dean," *American Law Register (1852–1891)* 14, no. 12 (October 1866), 729; *McGhee v. Sipes*, Transcript of Record, 60–61.

104. *McGhee v. Sipes*, Transcript of Record, 63–65.

105. Ibid., 67–69.

106. *Michigan Chronicle*, January 11, 1947, 3; *Michigan Chronicle*, January 25, 1947, 1 and 19; *Michigan Chronicle*, January 25, 1947, 6; *Michigan Chronicle*, February 8, 1947, 4.

107. See *Hurd and Urciolo v. Hodge* 162 F.2d 233, 235–46 (D.C. Circuit, 1947, Edgerton Dissent); Vose, *Caucasians Only*, 92–99, McNeil, *Groundwork*, 179. For the dissents in *Mays* (argued first in November 1944 and then again in October 1945 on an appeal of a contempt finding after Mays refused to leave the premises) see *Mays v. Burgess*, 147 F.2d 869, 873–78 (D.C. Circuit, 1945, Edgerton Dissent) and *Mays v. Burgess* 152 F.2d 123, 125–28 (D.C. Circuit, 1945, Edgerton Dissent). For a discussion of Edgerton's judicial writing see Rosenzweig, "Opinions of Judge Edgerton."

108. *Hurd and Urciolo v. Hodge*, Transcript of Record, 420–22. Edgerton's understanding clearly mirrored that of D. O. McGovney in many ways. McGovney's article on state action was the first work that Edgerton cited in his dissent and undoubtedly had an influence throughout.

109. Ibid., 423–27. Procovenant attorney James Crooks called Edgerton's dissents in *Mays* and in *Hurd* the "first expressions in support of this view [of state action] from any Federal or State Court." See Crooks, "Racial Covenant Cases," 518n.

110. *Hurd and Urciolo v. Hodge*, Transcript of Record, 428–31; *McGhee v. Sipes*, Transcript of Record, 67.

111. *Hurd and Urciolo v. Hodge*, Transcript of Record, 431–32.

112. Loring Moore to Thurgood Marshall, November 8, 1947, in NAACP, Part 5, Reel 22, Frame 653; Loren Miller to Charles Hamilton Houston, June 5, 1947, in LMP, Box 7, Folder 3; McNeil, *Groundwork*, 180.

Chapter Three

1. "Notes on Monday Morning Session—Hastie," July 9, 1945, in NAACP, Part 5, Reel 20, Frames 568–69. For more on Hastie and his advocacy see Gilbert Ware, *William Hastie*; McGuire, *He, Too, Spoke*. Hastie proved particularly dedicated to the cause of housing desegregation, maintaining well into the 1950s that "patterns of urban housing and the factors which influence them represent the most serious problem underlying human relations in the American community." See Hastie to Robert C. Weaver, June 3, 1954, in WHHP, Reel 36. The Court also heard *Hansberry v. Lee* (1940) in the intervening years between *Corrigan* and *Mays*, but agreed to hear the case and made their decision primarily as an issue of class action procedure rather than as an examination of covenants' validity.

2. Memorandum to Members of the National Legal Committee, June 13, 1945, in NAACP, Part 5, Reel 20, Frame 506.

3. Thurgood Marshall to Oscar Brown, June 12, 1945, in NAACP, Part 5, Reel 20, Frame 504.

4. For more on the invigoration of black protest during World War II see Dalfiume, "'Forgotten Years'"; Sitkoff, "Racial Militancy"; Finkle, "Conservative Aims"; Klinkner and Smith, *Unsteady March*, chaps. 5 and 6; Gilmore, *Defying Dixie*, chap. 8.

5. Thurgood Marshall speech on "The Legal Attack to Secure Civil Rights," 1944, in NAACP, Part 1, Reel 11, Frame 402; Thurgood Marshall to Roger Baldwin, June 9, 1944, in NAACP Records, Part II, Box B135; Sullivan, *Lift Every Voice*, 299–301; Vose, *Caucasians Only*, 57–64. See also McNeil, *Groundwork*, 177–78.

6. Juan Williams, *Thurgood Marshall*, 149; James, *Root and Branch*, 191; *Smith v. Allwright* 321 U.S. 649 (1944); Letters from Thurgood Marshall to Oscar Brown and William H. Hastie, July 2, 1945, in NAACP, Part 5, Reel 20, Frames 549 and 550–51; "Tentative Agenda for Conference on Restrictive Covenants," undated, in NAACP, Part 5, Reel 20, Frame 556. For more on the relationship between Marshall and Houston see McNeil, *Groundwork*.

7. "Notes on Monday Morning Session—Hastie," July 9, 1945, in NAACP, Part 5, Reel 20, Frames 568–69.

8. "Notes on Monday Morning Session—Miller," July 9, 1945, in NAACP, Part 5, Reel 20, Frame 573; "Notes on Monday Morning Session—Graves," July 9, 1945, in NAACP, Part 5, Reel 20, Frame 575; "Notes on Monday Morning Session—Vaughn," July 9, 1945, in NAACP, Part 5, Reel 20, Frames 576–78.

9. "Potentialities of Change of Neighborhood Doctrine—Charles Hamilton Houston, Monday Afternoon Session," July 9, 1945, in NAACP, Part 5, Reel 20, Frames 579–84. For Houston's earlier victory see *Hundley v. Gorewitz* 132 F.2d 23 (D.C. Circuit, 1942). The "changed conditions" or "change of neighborhood" doctrine dated back to at least 1940. See "Negro Restrictions."

10. "Potentialities of Change of Neighborhood Doctrine—Charles Hamilton Houston, Monday Afternoon Session," July 9, 1945, in NAACP, Part 5, Reel 20, Frame 580; *Hurd and Urciolo v. Hodge*, Transcript of Record, 350–53; Nancy Wechsler, Housing and Civil Rights Memorandum, June 26, 1947, in PCCR, Box 17. For more on the limitations of the change of neighborhood argument and the idiosyncratic approach to covenant litigation see Delaney, *Race, Place*, 131–34.

11. *Hansberry v. Lee* 311 U.S. 32 (1940). See also Plotkin, "Deeds of Mistrust," 139–81; Kamp, "History Behind *Hansberry v. Lee*"; Richard R. W. Brooks and Rose, *Saving the Neighborhood*, 124–29. In *Hansberry*, the Court dealt exclusively with whether the white seller in the case, who had previously been party to a suit enforcing the same covenant, now had the right to challenge the covenant's legitimacy and implementation. The previous case had found the covenant to be properly executed in part because the anticovenant lawyers in that earlier suit had not thought to question the technical details of the agreement.

12. See, for example, "Choose Your Neighbors" Pamphlet from Cook County Property Owners Restrictive Association, undated, in NAACP, Part 5, Reel 21, Frames 42–44.

13. "Potentialities of Change of Neighborhood Doctrine—Charles Hamilton Houston, Monday Afternoon Session," July 9, 1945, in NAACP, Part 5, Reel 20, Frame 579; "Notes on Monday Morning Session—Hastie," July 9, 1945, in NAACP, Part 5, Reel 20, Frame 568.

14. "Potentialities of Change of Neighborhood Doctrine—Charles Hamilton Houston, Monday Afternoon Session," July 9, 1945, in NAACP, Part 5, Reel 20, Frame 579; Meeting Minutes of Tuesday Morning Session, July 10, 1945, in NAACP, Part 5, Reel 20, Frame 588; Meeting Minutes of Tuesday Afternoon Session, July 10, 1945, in NAACP, Part 5, Reel 20, Frame 633. For more on Weaver see Pritchett, *Robert Clifton Weaver.*

15. Meeting Minutes of Tuesday Morning Session, July 10, 1945, in NAACP, Part 5, Reel 20, Frames 589–97; "Potentialities of Change of Neighborhood Doctrine—Charles Hamilton Houston, Monday Afternoon Session," July 9, 1945, in NAACP, Part 5, Reel 20, Frame 579. The attendees undoubtedly knew the profound impact that propaganda on the issue of race could have in the arena of public opinion—both positive and negative. For more on the impact of wartime propaganda and educational campaigns see Hart, "Making Democracy Safe"; Koppes and Black, "Blacks, Loyalty, and Motion-Picture Propaganda"; Sklaroff, "Constructing G.I. Joe Louis"; Savage, *Broadcasting Freedom.*

16. Kahen, "Validity of Anti-Negro Restrictive Covenants," 211. Kahen here referenced in particular the *Smith v. Allwright* case from 1944 that expanded the definition of state actors to include political parties. See also McGovney, "Racial Residential Segregation." The question of state action had been particularly important in litigation against all-white political primaries. For further discussion see Klarman, *From Jim Crow,* 135–40 and 197–203. For more on the state action argument in civil rights litigation see Peretti, "Constructing the State Action Doctrine"; Tushnet, *Making Civil Rights Law,* 75–86. For more on the state action doctrine's history see, for example, Brandwein, "Judicial Abandonment of Blacks?"

17. Meeting Minutes of Tuesday Afternoon Session, July 10, 1945, in NAACP, Part 5, Reel 20, Frames 601–3.

18. Ibid., Frames 614–16.

19. Ibid., Frame 617; see Weaver, *Hemmed In*; "Report of the Secretary for the December 1945 Meeting of the Board" in NAACP, Part 1, Reel 7, Frame 117. Perry was also assigned to handle employment cases.

20. Tushnet, *Making Civil Rights Law,* 35 and 46; Clippings from "Yankauer, Marian Perry" in *Worcester Biography Clipping Files,* Worcester Public Library, Worcester, MA; Bureau of the Census, *Fifteenth Census, 1930*; Juan Williams, *Thurgood Marshall,* 149. After eventually leaving the NAACP in 1949, Perry would later go on to serve at the Housing and Home Finance Agency in Washington where she became deputy director for civil rights in the organization.

21. Interview notes from "Williams, Franklin" in BVBC, Box 6, Folder 110; Interview notes from "Perry, Marian Wynn" in BVBC, Box 4, Folder 79.

22. Interview notes from "Perry, Marian Wynn" in BVBC, Box 4, Folder 79; Tushnet, *NAACP's Legal Strategy,* 104.

23. See, for example, Dalfiume, "'Forgotten Years'"; Sitkoff, "Racial Militancy"; Finkle, "Conservative Aims"; Sullivan, *Lift Every Voice*, 287–383. See Francis, *Civil Rights*, for a discussion of some of the NAACP's earlier political inroads and influence in the antilynching crusade.

24. Sullivan, *Lift Every Voice*, 288–89; "Excerpts from Remarks of Walter White on Occasion of the 39th Annual Meeting of the NAACP, January 5, 1948" in NAACP, Part 1, Reel 7, Frames 536–37. On membership numbers see Dalfiume, "'Forgotten Years,'" 99–100. This growth undoubtedly occurred in part due to the tireless efforts and organizational brilliance of Ella Baker, who served as the NAACP's director of branches from 1943–46. For more on Baker and her impact within the Association see Ransby, *Ella Baker*, esp. chap. 4. In his recent study of the NAACP, Gilbert Jonas claims that the Association's membership had reached 200,000 at the end of the 1930s with close to 1,000 local branches. The more consistently cited and accepted figures, however, are those used by Dalfiume. Jonas does not identify where he obtained his numbers. Jonas, *Freedom's Sword*, 24. Membership rolls would start to decline significantly by the end of the decade partly as a result of economic retrenchment in black communities and increased annual membership fees. Berg, *"Ticket to Freedom,"* 111.

25. Tushnet, *NAACP's Legal Strategy*, 135; "Proposed Budget for Restrictive Covenant Cases," undated, in NAACP, Part 5, Reel 22, Frame 271; Interview Notes from "Marshall, Thurgood" in BVBC, Box 4, Folder 65; Berg, *"Ticket to Freedom,"* 111.

26. Dalfiume, "'Forgotten Years,'" 99. Dalfiume argues that this moment marked the first time that the Association had become truly "representative of the Negro masses" in its demographic makeup. For more on the NAACP's labor litigation see Goluboff, "Economic Equality"; Lee, "Hotspots in a Cold War." While Goluboff argues that these efforts tapered off in the late 1940s as the Association refocused on education cases, Lee has shown some of the significant ways in which this labor litigation continued.

27. *Morgan v. Virginia* 328 U.S. 373 (1946); Klarman, *From Jim Crow*, 220–24; see also Gilmore, *Defying Dixie*, 329. For the breadth of the NAACP's litigation activities see *Sipuel v. Board of Regents of University of Oklahoma* 332 U.S. 631 (1948); *Sweatt v. Painter* 339 U.S. 629 (1950); *McLaurin v. Oklahoma State Regents* 339 U.S. 637 (1950); Tushnet, *NAACP's Legal Strategy*, chap. 6; Tushnet, *Making Civil Rights Law*, chaps. 9 and 10; Kluger, *Simple Justice*, esp. chap. 12; Klarman, *From Jim Crow*, chap. 6. For additional treatments see Sullivan, *Lift Every Voice*, chaps. 7, 8, and 9; Tushnet, *Making Civil Rights Law*, chaps. 2–10. For a broader examination of civil rights litigation in this period, including the activities of the NAACP, see Klarman, *From Jim Crow*, chaps. 4, 5, and 6.

28. *Smith v. Allwright* 321 U.S. 649 (1944). For the best treatment of the case and the history of the white primary see Hine, *Black Victory*. See also Klarman, *From Jim Crow*, 236–48. Keyssar, *Right to Vote*, 248; Walter White, "Will the Negro Elect Our Next President?," *Collier's* 120, no. 21 (November 22, 1947): 26 and 70. On registration efforts see Berg, *"Ticket to Freedom,"* 141. The NAACP certainly did not single-handedly register all of the new voters, but they played a prominent role. Indeed, Berg claims that during this decade "no other organization had a greater part in increasing black

registration in the South" (254). See also Lawson, *Running for Freedom*, 26–28; David Kennedy, *Freedom from Fear*, 768; Jones, "Black Americans and the City," 271–72. Jones places the total net figure of Southern black outmigration at 1,597,000 between 1940 and 1950.

29. Benjamin Davis, "Face to Face," undated, in NAACP, Part 17, Reel 21, Frame 540. On black migration's impact on the political process in post–World War II America see, for example, Grant, "Relocation and Realignment."

30. See, for example, White, "Will the Negro Elect Our Next President?"; Moon, *Balance of Power*. At this time, Moon was serving as the NAACP's director of public relations; Topping, "'Supporting Our Friends,'" 17–35; Janken, *White*, 265. Clarence Lang's work on the class politics of civil rights protest in St. Louis argues that the NAACP's national leadership cared more about "being able to claim thousands of members" than "their actual mobilization." There is some evidence for this argument by the middle of 1948 as the national office tightened control over local branches as a means of clamping down on political dissent leading up to the 1948 election. While these changes had some detrimental effects on the membership and local effectiveness of the Association, it also served in the short-term to strengthen the political ties and influence the national office forged with Truman's administration. See Lang, *Grassroots*, 78–80.

31. White, *Man Called White*, 299; McCoy and Ruetten, *Quest and Response*, 20–21.

32. White, *Man Called White*, 330–32. The other two officers were Channing Tobias of the board of directors and Leslie Perry of the Washington, D.C., branch office. For more on the PCCR see Juhnke, "Creating a New Charter"; Dodd, "Presidential Leadership."

33. White, *Man Called White*, 333; McCoy and Ruetten, *Quest and Response*, 86. See also Lawson, *To Secure These Rights*, esp. 167–85.

34. Memorandum of NAACP concerning the Present Discriminatory Policies of the FHA, October 28, 1944, in NAACP, Part 5, Reel 6, Frames 1038–50. See Federal Housing Administration, *Underwriting Manual (1947)*, esp. 1320. For discussions of the changing language between 1938 and 1947 and the limitations of those changes see Groner and Helfeld, "Race Discrimination in Housing," 437; Lowe, "Racial Restrictive Covenants," 19. See also Freund, *Colored Property*, 207–9; Kimble, "Insuring Inequality," 399–434 and esp. 417.

35. Frank S. Horne to Loren Miller, May 28, 1947, in LMP, Box 7, Folder 3.

36. White, *Man Called White*, 347–48; Berman, *Politics of Civil Rights*, 61.

37. Berman, *Politics of Civil Rights*, 62; White, *Man Called White*, 348.

38. White, *Man Called White*, 348.

39. Thurgood Marshall as quoted in Dodd, "Presidential Leadership," 1641.

40. Some historians of NAACP litigation have noted that popular and historical memory of the Association's campaigns has often overemphasized the degree of planning and regimentation in the process. The works of Mark Tushnet, Kenneth Mack, and Risa Goluboff show the ways in which pre–*Brown v. Board* civil rights litigation

was often fluid, evolving, and convoluted. No doubt in many instances the NAACP desired a thoroughly planned and coordinated campaign, but the realities of litigation as a process frequently prevented such an organized procedure. See, for example, Tushnet, *NAACP's Legal Strategy*, esp. 144–66; Mack, "Rethinking Civil Rights Lawyering"; Goluboff, "Economic Equality," esp. 1473–83. For discussions of the difficulties between the national office and local attorneys in earlier cases see, for example, the experience of the NAACP with *McCabe v. Atchison, Topeka, and Santa Fe Railroad Co.* in Carle, "Race, Class, and Legal Ethics," 122–24. See also an extended discussion of *McCabe* and the unexpected victory that local lawyers scored in Benno C. Schmidt, "Principle and Prejudice," 485–94. For a discussion of the struggles of organization in post-*Brown* litigation see Wasby, "How Planned Is 'Planned Litigation'?" and *Race Relations Litigation*.

41. Juan Williams, *Thurgood Marshall*, 150–51. Williams's account of Vaughn's U.S. Supreme Court oral arguments as related by Thurgood Marshall goes so far as to suggest that Vaughn fell asleep during the hearing and that he concluded his argument by loudly singing a line from the spiritual "Go Down Moses." Though Vaughn did have a flair for the dramatic, Marshall's recollection differs sharply from all contemporary accounts.

42. Loren Miller to Marian Wynn Perry, December 20, 1946, in NAACP, Part 5, Reel 22, Frame 306.

43. Thurgood Marshall to George Vaughn, December 30, 1946, in NAACP, Part 5, Reel 22, Frame 307.

44. George Vaughn to Thurgood Marshall, January 16, 1947, in NAACP, Part 5, Reel 22, Frame 310. Vaughn's enthusiasm for being involved in the case was regularly on display throughout the year; see, for example, Vaughn, "Resisting the Enforcement," 400, in which he professed his excitement and gratitude at "having the opportunity to be an instrument in securing this end [a final determination on the future of covenants]."

45. Loring Moore to Thurgood Marshall, January 21, 1947, in NAACP, Part 5, Reel 22, Frames 440–42; Sidney Jones to Thurgood Marshall, January 23, 1947, in NAACP, Part 5, Reel 22, Frame 449; Loren Miller to Thurgood Marshall, February 3, 1947, in NAACP, Part 5, Reel 22, Frame 458; Andrew Weinberger to Thurgood Marshall, January 22, 1947, in NAACP, Part 5, Reel 22, Frame 448; William R. Ming to Thurgood Marshall in NAACP, Part 5, Reel 22, Frames 461–62.

46. Memorandum from Marian Perry regarding "Conference on Restrictive Covenants held at Howard University Sunday, January 26, 1947, 11:30 A.M. to 2 P.M." in NAACP, Part 5, Reel 22, Frame 118. For more on the NAACP's use of the United Nations in civil rights protest see Anderson, *Eyes off the Prize*. On the potential of the United Nations Charter as a tool for civil rights cases see Lockwood, "United Nations Charter."

47. Memorandum from Marian Perry regarding "Conference on Restrictive Covenants held at Howard University Sunday, January 26, 1947, 11:30 A.M. to 2 P.M." in

NAACP, Part 5, Reel 22, Frame 120; Willis M. Graves to Clement Vose, September 9, 1957, in FMDP, Box 10, Folder 6.

48. Memorandum from Marian Perry regarding "Conference on Restrictive Covenants held at Howard University Sunday, January 26, 1947, 11:30 A.M. to 2 P.M." in NAACP, Part 5, Reel 22, Frames 119–20.

49. *Anderson v. Auseth*, L.A. No. 19, 759; Loren Miller to William H. Hastie, January 1, 1946, in LMP, Box 3, Folder 1; Loren Miller to Charles Houston, June 5, 1947, in LMP, Box 7, Folder 3.

50. *Tovey v. Levy* Cook County Superior Court 45 S 947; Memorandum from Marian Perry to Thurgood Marshall, December 16, 1946, in NAACP, Part 5, Reel 21, Frame 29; *American Council on Race Relations Report* 2, no. 1 (June 1947): 2 in CETRR, Box 36, Folder 5; Byron S. Miller to Robert L. Carter, May 16, 1947, in NAACP Records, Part II, Box B132. Miller called *Tovey* "the best case of which I have heard" on the covenant question.

51. Loring Moore to Thurgood Marshall, February 7, 1947, in NAACP, Part 5, Reel 21, Frame 34; Loring Moore to Thurgood Marshall, January 21, 1947, in NAACP, Part 5, Reel 22, Frame 441. See also Plotkin, "Deeds of Mistrust."

52. Letter to Robert Bradby, March 1, 1947, in NAACP, Part 5, Reel 22, Frames 471–72.

53. Thurgood Marshall to George Vaughn, February 5, 1947, in NAACP, Part 5, Reel 22, Frame 312; *Shelley v. Kraemer*, Transcript of Record, 169.

54. *Shelley v. Kraemer*, Transcript of Record, 171; Memorandum to Files from Marian Perry about conversation with Clifford Forster, April 9, 1947, in NAACP, Part 5, Reel 22, Frame 317.

55. Memorandum to Files from Marian Perry, April 9, 1947, in NAACP, Part 5, Reel 22, Frame 317; Clifford Forster to Marian Perry, April 3, 1947, in NAACP, Part 5, Reel 22, Frame 316; Clifford Forster to Eugene Buder, April 10, 1947, in NAACP, Part 5, Reel 22, Frame 318.

56. Charles Elmore Cropley to Willis Graves, June 23, 1947, in NAACP, Part 5, Reel 22, Frame 512; Memorandum from Constance Baker Motley to Walter White, January 20, 1948, in NAACP, Part 5, Reel 20, Frame 995.

57. Thurgood Marshall to Francis Dent and Willis Graves, July 1, 1947, in NAACP, Part 5, Reel 22, Frames 518–19; Edward Swan to Thurgood Marshall, July 3, 1947, in NAACP, Part 5, Reel 22, Frame 521; Francis Dent to Clement Vose, November 9, 1959, in FMDP, Box 1, Folder 12.

58. Marian Perry to multiple recipients, July 9, 1947, in NAACP, Part 5, Reel 22, Frames 129–30.

59. *Baltimore Afro-American*, July 5, 1947, 14.

60. Minutes of Meeting of NAACP Lawyers and Consultants on Methods of Attacking Restrictive Covenants, September 6, 1947, in NAACP, Part 5, Reel 22, Frame 251; Vose, *Caucasians Only*, 157–60.

61. Vaughn gave a preview of his Supreme Court arguments in an article for the *National Bar Journal*. See Vaughn, "Resisting the Enforcement." Vaughn apparently did

not mention the Thirteenth Amendment directly in his arguments to the St. Louis City Circuit Court or the Missouri Supreme Court, but it had become a centerpiece of his strategy. He seems to have reverse-engineered the Thirteenth Amendment arguments from his initial claims before the circuit court that covenant enforcement violated sections 41 and 42 of Title 8 of the U.S. Code. As Vaughn explained, these provisions had been based upon Section 1 of the 1866 Civil Rights Act, which had itself been enacted "under the sole authority of the Thirteenth Amendment." This logic appeared to provide much of Vaughn's rationale for turning to the amendment in his arguments. See Vaughn, "Resisting the Enforcement," 385 and 389. Vaughn was also particularly enamored with Justice Stephen Field's lengthy dissent in the *Slaughterhouse Cases* 83 U.S. 36, 83–111 (1873, Field Dissent) and specifically highlighted Field's arguments that "a prohibition to him [the black American] . . . *to reside in places where others are permitted to live, would not be, in the strict sense of the term, in a condition of slavery, but probably none would deny that he would be in a condition of servitude. He certainly would not possess the liberties nor enjoy the privileges of a freeman*" (389; Vaughn's italics). The combination of these factors led Vaughn to readily proclaim covenants as instruments of involuntary servitude. Though roundly criticized by his contemporaries for this approach in *Shelley*, Vaughn was certainly not alone in experimenting with the Thirteenth Amendment as a tool for twentieth-century civil rights litigation. The Civil Rights Section of the Department of Justice had explored the use of the amendment in labor cases prior to Vaughn's efforts in 1947. For more on the Thirteenth Amendment as a potentially powerful vehicle for change in this moment see Goluboff, "Thirteenth Amendment."

62. REBA of St. Louis to NAACP St. Louis Branch Office, July 11, 1947, in NAACP, Part 5, Reel 22, Frame 322; Thurgood Marshall to David Grant, August 1, 1947, in NAACP, Part 5, Reel 22, Frame 324.

63. Minutes of Meeting of NAACP Lawyers and Consultants on Methods of Attacking Restrictive Covenants, September 6, 1947, in NAACP, Part 5, Reel 22, Frames 235–38 and 246. Hale was a strong proponent, and an early theorist, of the judicial enforcement as state action argument. See Hale, "Rights."

64. Minutes of Meeting of NAACP Lawyers and Consultants on Methods of Attacking Restrictive Covenants, September 6, 1947, in NAACP, Part 5, Reel 22, Frames 242 and 253.

65. Thurgood Marshall to David Grant, September 16, 1947, in NAACP, Part 5, Reel 22, Frames 330–31. In April of 1947, the NAACP national office had approved a $3,500 investment in their favored suit from Chicago. See Plotkin, "Deeds of Mistrust," 236.

66. Thurgood Marshall to James Bush, September 23, 1947, in NAACP, Part 5, Reel 22, Frames 337–39; Thurgood Marshall to David Grant, September 23, 1947, in NAACP, Part 5, Reel 22, Frames 342–43; Thurgood Marshall to David Grant, October 3, 1947, in NAACP, Part 5, Reel 22, Frame 347.

67. Herman Dreer to NAACP National Office, November 23, 1947, in NAACP, Part 5, Reel 22, Frame 356; Thurgood Marshall to Herman Dreer, December 5, 1947, in NAACP, Part 5, Reel 22, Frames 359–61.

68. Minutes of Meeting of NAACP Lawyers and Consultants on Methods of Attacking Restrictive Covenants, September 6, 1947, in NAACP, Part 5, Reel 22, Frames 243–44.

69. Ibid., Frames 243–47.

70. Ibid., Frames 253–54.

71. Francis, *Civil Rights*, details the NAACP's hybridized movement against mob violence that coupled public information campaigns about the causes and extent of lynching with lobbying efforts and litigation that culminated in *Moore v. Dempsey* 261 U.S. 86 (1923). Prominent social scientific practitioners in the early NAACP included Florence Kelley and W. E. B. Du Bois.

72. On the NAACP's ties to the American Legal Realist movement see Tushnet, *NAACP's Legal Strategy*, esp. chap. 7. Tushnet has labeled the NAACP's brief in the covenant cases "Realist to the core" (118). Roger Fairfax presents a more skeptical view of the realists' relationship to civil rights litigation in his examination of Houston's links to both sociological jurisprudence and legal realism. See Fairfax, "Wielding the Double-Edged Sword," esp. 28–33. See also "Legal Realism and the Race Question." On Wherry and Pillsbury see Carle, *Defining the Struggle*. On Llewellyn and Hale see Twining, *Karl Llewellyn*; Hull, *Roscoe Pound*; Fried, *Progressive Assault*. Hale proved to be a particularly active participant in the buildup to the covenant cases. On his involvement see, for example, Thurgood Marshall to Professor Robert Lee Hale, August, 1947, in NAACP, Part 5, Reel 22, Frame 195; Will Maslow to Robert Lee Hale, September 11, 1947, in Hale Papers, Box 7, Folder 95; Thurgood Marshall to Robert Lee Hale, November 5, 1947, in Hale Papers, Box 7, Folder 95; Program for Legal Conference on Federal Power to Protect Civil Rights, January 25, 1947, in FMDP, Box 10, Folder 3. On legal realism and its relationship to social science more generally see, for example, Schlegel, *American Legal Realism*; Paul L. Rosen, *Supreme Court*; Purcell, *Crisis of Democratic Theory*; Purcell, "American Jurisprudence"; Kalman, *Legal Realism*; John W. Johnson, *American Legal Culture*.

73. See *Buchanan v. Warley* 245 U.S. 60 (1917), Brief for Petitioners; *Corrigan v. Buckley* 271 U.S. 323 (1926), Brief for Petitioners; *Corrigan v. Buckley*, Brief for Respondents, 34–35. The attorneys cited eugenicist Madison Grant's vitriolic screed *The Passing of the Great Race* (1916), Charles W. Gould's *America: A Family Matter* (1920), and A. P. Schultz's, *Race or Mongrel* (1908). To provide a sense of the tone and scope of these works, a contemporary described Schultz's "study" as one that "advocates with hysterical fanaticism . . . the familiar view of the extreme anthropologists that racial impurity is the source of all evil." See "Review: *Race or Mongrel* by A. P. Schultz," *Journal of Political Economy* 17, no. 4 (1909): 238.

74. *Missouri ex rel. Gaines v. Canada* 305 U.S. 337 (1938), Brief for Petitioners, iii and 38–39. On Houston's urgings see Mack, "Rethinking Civil Rights Lawyering," 325–28. There were no nonlegal citations in briefs for either *Smith v. Allwright* or *Morgan v. Virginia*. Amicus briefs allowed organizations to voice their opinions on the issues at stake in a given case as a "friend of the court," without requiring them to be party to the suit itself. On the amicus filings' extralegal materials see *Steele v. Louisville &*

Nashville Railroad Company, Brief for the NAACP as Amicus Curiae and *Mendez v. Westminster* 161 F.2d 774 (9th Circuit, 1947), Brief for the NAACP as Amicus Curiae. The *Steele* brief contained seventeen unique nonlegal citations while the brief in *Westminster* contained nine such unique references. For the purposes of this study, nonlegal citations include all materials except statutes, previous court opinions, casebooks, law review articles, and a handful of miscellaneous sources that appear unrelated to social conditions and are generally cited apart from the rest of the nonlegal materials (e.g., Horace Flack's historical work on the adoption of the Fourteenth Amendment). There may be some margin of error on the exact numbers of sources that qualify as nonlegal citations in the spirit intended here, but that margin even under the most expansive of disagreements would still support the conclusions drawn in the remainder of the section.

75. See *Muller v. State of Oregon* 208 U.S. 412 (1908). On Goldmark and Brandeis's efforts in labor cases see in Vose, "National Consumers' League," 77–80. Despite their success in *Muller*, social scientific courtroom arguments remained relatively infrequent for several decades after this first use and only began experiencing a revival in the mid-1920s. Paul L. Rosen, *Supreme Court*, 102–17.

76. This discussion borrows the term "scientific antiracism" from Michelle Brattain and uses it as she does to denote a wide body of multidisciplinary scholarship that did not apply the term to itself but worked directly and indirectly to undo the harm done by scientific racism in preceding decades. Many of these social scientists did not necessarily see themselves as part of a movement, but taken collectively their efforts constituted an intellectual turn away from scientific racism. For an insightful discussion of the complexities of this movement in the postwar period and some its successes and failures see Brattain, "Race, Racism, and Antiracism."

77. Willis M. Graves to Clement Vose, September 9, 1957, in FMDP, Box 10, Folder 6. For examples of the concern that other lawyers showed see, for example, Memorandum from Marian Perry regarding "Conference on Restrictive Covenants held at Howard University Sunday, January 26, 1947, 11:30 A.M. to 2 P.M." in NAACP, Part 5, Reel 22, Frames 119–20; Sidney Jones to Thurgood Marshall, January 23, 1947, in NAACP, Part 5, Reel 22, Frame 449; Thurgood Marshall to Sidney Jones, January 31, 1947, in NAACP, Part 5, Reel 22, Frames 454–55.

78. Loren Miller, Speech for the National Bar Association, November 14, 1946, in FMDP, Box 32, Folder 3; Loren Miller to Thurgood Marshall, July, 1947, in NAACP, Part 5, Reel 22, Frames 141–42; Charles H. Houston to Marian Perry, August 22, 1947, in NAACP, Part 5, Reel 22, Frame 186.

79. Phineas Indritz to Ruth Benedict, August 22, 1947, in NAACP, Part 5, Reel 21, Frames 858–59. See also Phineas Indritz to Charles Abrams, July 23, 1947, and August 14, 1947, in NAACP, Part 5, Reel 22, Frames 155–56 and 182.

80. "Proposed Budget for Restrictive Covenant Cases," undated, in NAACP, Part 5, Reel 22, Frame 271. The allotment included $3,000 for the "printing of appendices for briefs containing sociological data necessary for an adequate appraisal of the

discriminatory practices in restrictive covenants" and $2,500 for "special research."
This amounted to 41 percent of the proposed $13,400 in combined expenses for the
cases pending before the Supreme Court. The same proposed budget from September
of 1947 listed an expenditure of $8,500 for a potential appeal of the Chicago case. What
is unclear about this amount is whether it includes the $3,500 that the national office
had supplied in April of that year (see Plotkin, "Deeds of Mistrust," 236). If this earlier
contribution is not included in the September proposal, the NAACP's investment in the
Levy case would have nearly equaled its total spending on all of the covenant suits that
reached the Supreme Court with *Shelley*.

81. Baker, *From Savage to Negro*, 26–53; Lyman, *Black American*, 15–25. Again, the
term "scientific antiracism" is an overarching construction that historians have begun
applying to a broad body of work rather than a contemporary term that these scientists
used to describe themselves. For discussions of this disciplinary shift see esp. Hovenkamp, "Social Science and Segregation"; John P. Jackson, *Social Scientists*; Barkan,
Retreat of Scientific Racism; Gleason, "Americans All"; Baker, *From Savage to Negro*.

82. Baker, *From Savage to Negro*, 99–126; John P. Jackson, *Social Scientists*, 17–42;
Pritchett, *Robert Clifton Weaver*, 116–34; Gilmore, *Defying Dixie*, 393–99.

83. See Purcell, *Crisis of Democratic Theory*, 15–46; John P. Jackson, *Social Scientists*,
43–59.

84. On reactions to Nazi racial ideologies see, for example, Kellogg, "Civil Rights
Consciousness," 30–35. On the impact in antiracist scholarship see Brattain, "Race,
Racism, and Antiracism." These antiracist scholars forged perhaps even stronger—and
certainly more formalized—bonds with the American Jewish Congress's Commission
on Law and Social Action during this same period. See John P. Jackson, *Social Scientists*,
63–78.

85. Michelle Brattain's work shows the complexities of this transition and the
enduring hold of scientific racism in areas of both popular and academic thought.
Though scientific antiracists certainly had the momentum, it by no means excised
racism from scientific discourse. Brattain, "Race, Racism, and Antiracism," 1386–413.
For more on the lingering legacy of scientific racism in postwar civil rights litigation
see John P. Jackson, *Science for Segregation*; Newby, *Challenge to the Court*.

86. Myrdal, *American Dilemma*; see also Walter A. Jackson, *Gunnar Myrdal*,
esp. 186–271. Myrdal's study was not unproblematic however. For a recent discussion of
the more troublesome aspects and some contemporary criticisms see Singh, *Black Is a
Country*, 142–54; Scott, *Contempt and Pity*, 166–67; Lyman, "Gunnar Myrdal's *An
American Dilemma*."

87. Examples of these studies include Horace Cayton's "Negro Housing in Chicago"
(1945), Horace Cayton and St. Clair Drake's *Black Metropolis* (1945), Myrdal's *American
Dilemma*, Mabel Walker's *Urban Blight and Slums* (1938), Richard Sterner's *The Negro's
Share* (1943), Charles S. Johnson's *Patterns of Negro Segregation* (1943), and various
works by Robert Weaver and Corienne Robinson.

88. Loren Miller to Thurgood Marshall, July, 1947, in NAACP, Part 5, Reel 22, Frames 141–42.

89. "Proposed Budget for Restrictive Covenant Cases," undated, in NAACP, Part 5, Reel 22, Frame 271.

90. Annette H. Peyser, "Description of My Work with the National Association for the Advancement of Colored People," undated, in AHPP, Box 1, Folder 3.

91. Jack Greenberg, *Crusaders*, 35; Peyser's older brother Seymour became a lawyer and worked for the International Military Tribunal at the Nuremberg Trials. Some detail about the family's upbringing can be found in an interview that he gave regarding his experiences there. Stave and Palmer, *Witnesses to Nuremberg*, 127–29; Bureau of the Census, *Fifteenth Census, 1930*.

92. Jack Greenberg, *Crusaders*, 35; Annette H. Peyser, "Description of My Work with the National Association for the Advancement of Colored People," undated, in AHPP, Box 1, Folder 1; Tushnet, *NAACP's Legal Strategy*, 119–20. *Mendez v. Westminster*, Brief for the NAACP as Amicus Curiae, 10–20, in Records of the U.S. Courts of Appeal (Ninth Circuit Court of Appeal, Appeal Case Files and Briefs), Record Group 276, Box 4468, Folder 11310, National Archives and Records Administration, San Bruno, Calif. See also the discussion in John P. Jackson, *Social Scientists*, 82–91. For more on the case see Strum, *Mendez v. Westminster*; Arriola, "Knocking on the Schoolhouse Door."

93. Thurgood Marshall, "Memorandum to the Executive Staff of the Legal Department," April 23, 1950, in AHPP, Box 1, Folder 3. When Peyser described the work that she actually performed on a day-to-day basis, however, the full extent of her role became clearer. In addition to handling correspondence and editing materials for the briefs, Peyser "worked as a liaison between the legal experts and social scientists," helped attorneys with "drafting the form that the testimony [of expert witnesses] would take," and corresponded with scholars about their testimony to ensure that they understood how the NAACP legal team wanted them to present their arguments in court. Peyser also provided information to help compose "pamphlets, papers, speeches, Congressional testimony," and other public communications for herself and other members of the legal team. See Annette H. Peyser, "Description of My Work with the National Association for the Advancement of Colored People," undated, in AHPP, Box 1, Folder 1.

94. Minutes of Meeting of NAACP Lawyers and Consultants on Methods of Attacking Restrictive Covenants, September 6, 1947, in NAACP, Part 5, Reel 22, Frames 230–31 and 248–49. The members of the committee were Annette Peyser, Loring Moore, Robert Weaver, William R. Ming, John P. Dean—a fellow at the Social Science Research Council, Louis Wirth of the University of Chicago, Byron Miller—the American Jewish Congress's Midwest Director of the Commission on Law and Social Action, Ruth Weyand of the National Labor Relations Board, Harold Kahen—a Chicago attorney who helped pioneer the state action argument against covenants, and James T. Bush of the St. Louis REBA. The inclusion of Bush on the committee likely

served the dual purposes of accommodating the fractious St. Louis contingent and attempting to steer Bush and Vaughn closer to the NAACP's preferred legal strategy.

95. Memorandum from Louis Wirth on the Program of the American Council on Race Relations, May 1, 1947, in LWP, Box 14, Folder 7; Memorandum from Louis Wirth "Progress Report on ACRR Activities," May 15, 1947, in CETRR, Box 28, Folder 2; Meeting Minutes for Chicago Members of the Executive Committee of ACRR, September 18, 1947, in CETRR, Box 28, Folder 2; Minutes of the Annual Meeting of the Board of Directors of ACRR, October 3, 1947, in CETRR, Box 28, Folder 2.

96. Minutes of Meeting of NAACP Lawyers and Consultants on Methods of Attacking Restrictive Covenants, September 6, 1947, in NAACP, Part 5, Reel 22, Frame 231; Memorandum from Louis Wirth on Proposed Coverage of Socio-Economic Brief on Restrictive Covenants, September 2, 1947, in NAACP Records, Part II, Box B132; "Social and Economic Aspects of Segregation and Their Relations to Residential Race Restrictive Covenants, Prepared by the Staff of the American Council on Race Relations (September, 1947)" in LMP, Box 26, Folder 15. Due to damage to the collection prior to its preservation, this copy of the study includes only the first thirty pages. No complete copies are known to exist.

97. Marian Perry to Charles Houston, October 16, 1947, in NAACP, Part 5, Reel 21, Frame 948; Marian Perry to Phineas Indritz, November 19, 1947, in NAACP, Part 5, Reel 21, Frame 1022.

98. *Sipuel v. Board of Regents* 332 U.S. 631 (1948), Brief for Petitioner, 37–51.

99. See *McGhee v. Sipes*, Brief for Petitioners; *Hurd and Urciolo v. Hodge*, Consolidated Brief for Petitioners; Interview notes from "Perry, Marian Wynn" in BVBC, Box 4, Folder 79.

100. *McGhee v. Sipes*, Brief for Petitioners, 47; *Hurd and Urciolo v. Hodge*, Consolidated Brief for Petitioners, 40. See also Scott, *Contempt and Pity*, on the problematic use of arguments about the "damaged psyche" of African Americans both in support of and in opposition to racially egalitarian policies.

101. *Hurd and Urciolo v. Hodge*, Consolidated Brief for Petitioners, 40 and 71–72; *McGhee v. Sipes*, Brief for Petitioners, 47 and 63–65.

102. *McGhee v. Sipes*, Brief for Petitioners, 71–75; *Hurd and Urciolo v. Hodge*, Consolidated Brief for Petitioners, 75–77.

103. *Hurd and Urciolo v. Hodge*, Consolidated Brief for Petitioners, 96–98.

104. *McGhee v. Sipes*, Brief for Petitioners, 71.

105. Filing an amicus brief required the written consent of both parties to the suit. There is no evidence that either side declined to give permission to any interested groups. The large array of amicus groups was what initially sparked the interest of the covenant cases' original chronicler, Clement Vose. See Vose, *Caucasians Only*, ix. See also McNeil, *Groundwork*, 181–82.

106. The complete list of amici is as follows: For the NAACP: Japanese American Citizens League (JACL), Anti-Nazi League, California Amici, Protestant Council of the City of New York, American Federation of Labor, American Civil Liberties Union,

American Association for the United Nations, American Indian Citizens League, American Jewish Congress, American Unitarian Association, American Veterans Committee, B'nai B'rith (Anti-Defamation League), Congress of Industrial Organizations, Independent, Benevolent, Protective Order of Elks of the World, Congregational Christian Churches of the United States, National Bar Association, National Lawyers Guild, St. Louis Civil Liberties Committee, and the government of the United States. For the white homeowners: National Association of Real Estate Boards, Arlington Heights Property Owners Association, Mount Royal Protective Association, and Federation of Citizens Associations of the District of Columbia. See also Vose, *Caucasians Only*, 163–67. For more on the JACL and housing discrimination against Asian Americans see Charlotte Brooks, *Alien Neighbors*; Kurashige, *Shifting Grounds of Race*; Hosokawa, *JACL*.

107. "Highlights of 21st Annual Convention," 116; Miller maintained a healthy correspondence with Los Angeles-based JACL attorney A. L. Wirin and Los Angeles covenant attorney Clore Warne, both of whom coauthored their respective amicus briefs. See, for example, Loren Miller to Clore Warne, November 2, 1947, in LMP, Box 7, Folder 1; A. L. Wirin to Loren Miller, December 10, 1945, in LMP, Box 5, Folder 2; Greg Robinson and Toni Robinson, "*Korematsu* and Beyond," 40–42. See also *Hurd and Urciolo v. Hodge*, Brief of the Japanese American Citizens League as Amicus Curiae and *McGhee v. Sipes*, Brief of California as Amici Curiae. *Shelley v. Kraemer*, Brief of American Civil Liberties Union as Amicus Curiae. Hays had served as cocounsel with legendary defense attorney Clarence Darrow in the case of Dr. Ossian Sweet, an African American physician prosecuted for murder after defending his home in Detroit from a violent mob of local whites. See Boyle, *Arc of Justice. Shelley v. Kraemer*, Brief of American Veterans Committee as Amicus Curiae.

108. See, for example, Memorandum from Walter White to Thurgood Marshall, July 1, 1947, in NAACP, Part 5, Reel 20, Frame 914; Newman Levy to Phineas Indritz, August 15, 1947, in NAACP, Part 5, Reel 22, Frame 183; Walter White to Charles Houston, December 19, 1947, in NAACP, Part 5, Reel 21, Frames 1072–74; Memorandum from Walter White to Thurgood Marshall, September 11, 1947, in NAACP, Part 5, Reel 22, Frame 270; Thurgood Marshall to Newman Levy, November 6, 1947, in NAACP, Part 5, Reel 21, Frame 1004.

109. For more on the connections between the NAACP and labor unions see Bates, "New Crowd"; Nelson, "Organized Labor"; Korstad and Lichtenstein, "Opportunities Found and Lost"; Meier and Rudwick, *Black Detroit*; Lee, *Workplace Constitution*, esp. chaps. 1 and 2. On the difficulties of the period after *Brown* see Jonas, *Freedom's Sword*, esp. chaps. 9, 10, and 11.

110. The three amici that required some prodding were the Congregation of Christian Churches, the American Association for the United Nations, and the U.S. Department of Justice. See Charles Houston to Reverend Douglas Horton, September 4, 1947, in NAACP, Part 5, Reel 21, Frames 867–68, Marian Perry to Clark Eichelberger, October 16, 1947, in NAACP, Part 5, Reel 21, Frames 946–47; Memorandum from Marian

Perry to the Subcommittee of the American Association for the United Nations, October 17, 1947, in NAACP, Part 5, Reel 21, Frames 950–52; Walter White to Tom C. Clark, September 12, 1947, in NAACP, Part 5, Reel 21, Frames 875–77.

111. Charles Abrams to Newman Levy, November 13, 1947, in NAACP, Part 5, Reel 21, Frames 1010–11.

112. *Shelley v. Kraemer*, Consolidated Brief in Behalf of American Jewish Committee, B'nai B'rith (Anti-Defamation League), Jewish War Veterans of the United States of America, Jewish Labor Committee as Amici Curiae, 5; *McGhee v. Sipes*, Brief of the Anti-Nazi League as Amicus Curiae, 4–5; *Shelley v. Kraemer*, Brief of American Veterans Committee, 1–2; *Shelley v. Kraemer*, Brief for the American Association for the United Nations as Amicus Curiae, 2.

Chapter Four

1. Copy of George Vaughn's Oral Argument before the Supreme Court in BHP, Box 7, Folder 120; Elman and Silber, "Solicitor General's Office," 820. Vaughn borrowed his closing words from a liberal white southern writer and editor named Thomas Sancton. For more on Sancton see Lawrence P. Jackson, *Indignant Generation*, esp. chap. 6. Though Vaughn appeared to redeem himself here with the effectiveness of his closing, the NAACP legal team never forgave his earlier defiance, nor did they especially value his contribution to the oral arguments.

2. "Argument Prepared by Philip B. Perlman, Solicitor General, before the Supreme Court against Enforcement of Racial Restrictive Covenants," January 15, 1948, in NAACP, Part 5, Reel 21, Frames 1127–40.

3. Vose, *Caucasians Only*, 172–73 and 200–201.

4. For more on the Truman presidency see, for example, McCullough, *Truman*; McCoy, *Presidency of Harry S. Truman*; Barton J. Bernstein, *Politics and Policies*. For more on the role of presidential influence in civil rights policy see, for example, McMahon, *Reconsidering Roosevelt*; Schull, *American Civil Rights Policy*.

5. See, for example, Hart, "Making Democracy Safe"; Gilmore, *Defying Dixie*; Kellogg, "Civil Rights Consciousness," 30–35; Borgwardt, "Race, Rights"; Lauren, "First Principles." Between 1946 and 1951, three black advocacy groups including the NAACP filed formal petitions with the United Nations to highlight grievances and request remedies. See Martin, "Internationalizing 'The American Dilemma'"; National Negro Congress, *Petition to the United Nations*; Anderson, *Eyes off the Prize*.

6. On the role of Cold War politics in civil rights reform see esp. Dudziak, *Cold War Civil Rights*; Borstelmann, "Jim Crow's Coming Out"; Borstelmann, *Cold War*; Gilmore, *Defying Dixie*; Layton, *International Politics*; Skrentny, "Effect of the Cold War."

7. Clark Clifford as quoted in Sitkoff, "Harry Truman," 597. There remains considerable debate over what role political calculation played in the scholarship on Truman's civil rights record. Three key texts have addressed the administration's policies on the issue. In 1970 William Berman adopted a skeptical view of Truman's motives, suggest-

ing that the civil rights program sprang only from the need to court black votes and Truman's desire to "obtain maximum political benefit for him and his party." Berman, *Politics of Civil Rights*, 237. Three years later, Donald McCoy and Richard Ruetten argued that Truman's receptiveness to civil rights policies came from his desire to do "the right thing," his reliance upon sympathetic advisers, and efforts to stop "communism's exploitation" of American segregation. McCoy and Ruetten, *Quest and Response*, 349. More recently, Michael Gardner claimed in 2002 that Truman's actions demonstrated "moral courage and political recklessness" and suggested that Truman faced no political incentive to support a civil rights program. Gardner, *Harry Truman*, 3. For additional discussion of the Truman administration's civil rights record see McCoy et al., *Conference of Scholars*; Barton J. Bernstein, "Ambiguous Legacy." For more on the 1948 election see, for example, Sullivan, *Days of Hope*; Donaldson, *Truman Defeats Dewey*; Karabell, *Last Campaign*; Ross, *Loneliest Campaign*; Gullan, *Upset That Wasn't*; Frederickson, *Dixiecrat Revolt*; Yarnell, *Democrats and Progressives*. See also Moon, *Balance of Power*.

8. For the most ardent articulation of the president's moral impetus for reform see Gardner, *Harry Truman*.

9. Gardner argues in *Harry Truman* that "in reality, Truman was subjected to little, if any, serious nationwide political pressure in 1946 to act on civil rights reform for black Americans" (19). While Gardner's overall argument is often compelling, this particular assertion only holds if one were to discount African Americans as part of the national political scene. In reality, black advocacy groups and the NAACP in particular mobilized considerable political pressure on the administration during this time. See also Sullivan, *Lift Every Voice*, esp. chap. 9.

10. For more on Elman see Silber, *With All Deliberate Speed*; Elman and Silber, "Solicitor General's Office."

11. Vose, *Caucasians Only*, 187–90 and 203–4; McNeil, *Groundwork*, 180. See also NeJaime, "Cause Lawyers," on the importance of social movement lawyers and lawyering within official state positions.

12. *District of Columbia Citizen*, December 1947, in PIP, Box B21, Folder 8.

13. Minutes of Meeting NAACP Lawyers and Consultants on Methods of Attacking Restrictive Covenants, September 6, 1947, in NAACP, Part 5, Reel 22, Frames 230–31. While this marked the first documented discussion of the idea, the notion of petitioning the attorney general appears to have been in circulation even before the conference. Indeed, the American Jewish Congress formally submitted a request for Attorney General Clark's involvement on September 4. American Jewish Congress Press Release, September 4, 1947, in NAACP, Part 5, Reel 21, Frames 869–70.

14. Phineas Indritz to Marian Wynn Perry, September 11, 1947, in NAACP, Part 5, Reel 22, Frame 267; Memorandum from Marian Wynn Perry to Walter White, September 12, 1947, in NAACP, Part 5, Reel 22, Frame 272. See also assorted letters from Walter White in NAACP, Part 5, Reel 21, Frames 885–94.

15. Assorted letters from Walter White in NAACP, Part 5, Reel 21, Frames 885–94. Surgeon General Thomas Parran, HHFA administrator Raymond Foley, Secretary of

the Interior Oscar Chapman, and Secretary of Labor Louis Schwellenbach all eventually offered written statements to Attorney General Clark. Schwellenbach, who continued to correspond periodically with White and Marshall throughout the winter of the cases' hearing, also wrote that he had informed Clark "that the facilities of the Department of Labor will be made freely available for assistance in this matter." See Louis Schwellenbach to Walter White, November 6, 1947, in NAACP, Part 5, Reel 21, Frame 1002. See also Kluger, *Simple Justice*, 250–52. Clark would go on to assume a seat on the Supreme Court after Justice Frank Murphy's passing in 1949. His son Ramsey would become attorney general in the 1960s. For more on Tom C. Clark see Gronlund, *Supreme Court Justice*.

16. Walter White to Tom C. Clark, September 12, 1947, in NAACP, Part 5, Reel 21, Frames 875–77; Memorandum from Marian Wynn Perry to Walter White, September 12, 1947, in NAACP, Part 5, Reel 22, Frame 272; Tom C. Clark to Walter White, September 17, 1947, in NAACP, Part 5, Reel 21, Frame 881.

17. Tom C. Clark to Robert K. Carr, July 10, 1947, in PCCR, Box 6.

18. Assorted letters to Tom C. Clark in NAACP, Part 5, Reel 21, Frames 882–84, 896, 899, 901, 914, 918, and 925. The Negro Newspaper Publishers Association wrote to Clark but never filed as an amicus group.

19. Elliff, *United States Department of Justice*, 256; Marian Wynn Perry to Willis Graves, October 25, 1947, in NAACP, Part 5, Reel 22, Frame 637; Memorandum from Philip Perlman to the President, October 22, 1947, in TCCP, Box 74.

20. Walter White to Harry S. Truman, September 17, 1947, in NAACP, Part 5, Reel 21, Frames 887–88.

21. On the PCCR see Juhnke, "Creating a New Charter"; Lawson, *To Secure These Rights*, 1–36.

22. Lawson, *To Secure These Rights*, 101–3 and 181–82.

23. See Vose, *Caucasians Only*, 168–73, for a discussion of the murky motivations behind the decision; Juhnke, "Creating a New Charter," 155. Copies of the report's third draft went to both the Department of Labor and the DOJ in late August, but Clark had also been in discussions with the PCCR for several months beforehand. See Elliff, *United States Department of Justice*, 256, for a brief discussion of Clark's consultations with Truman. It is also worth noting that the timing of the decision to intervene came on the heels of the release of a second important document, the NAACP's petition to the United Nations authored primarily by W. E. B. Du Bois and entitled *An Appeal to the World: A Statement on the Denial of Human Rights to Minorities in the Case of Citizens of Negro Descent in the United States of America and an Appeal to the United Nations for Redress*. The official release came on October 23, 1947, indicating that the timing was more coincidental than causative given that the petition enjoyed a rather frosty reception from the Truman administration. See Anderson, *Eyes off the Prize*, 78–112.

24. Interview Notes for Philip Elman, August 19, 1971, in BVBC, Box 2, Folder 27; Elman and Silber, "Solicitor General's Office," 817–18; Vose, *Caucasians Only*, 168–73.

Elman received substantial criticism from legal scholar Randall L. Kennedy regarding his portrayal of the events surrounding federal intervention in midcentury civil rights litigation. Kennedy strongly rebuked Elman for exalting his own importance and the role of the DOJ over that of the NAACP and black civil rights attorneys in the legal progress of the late 1940s and 1950s. See Randall L. Kennedy, "Reply to Philip Elman"; Elman, "[A Reply to Philip Elman]: Response."

25. Transcript of Interview with Philip Perlman, December 16, 1954, in PPF, Box 642; Elman and Silber, "Solicitor General's Office," 817–18; Vose, *Caucasians Only*, 168–73.

26. Interview Notes for Philip Elman, August 19, 1971, in BVBC Box 2, Folder 27; Appendix B to Transcript of Interview with James H. Rowe, September 30, 1969, in Truman Presidential Library. See also Donaldson, "Who Wrote the Clifford Memo?," 747–54.

27. Transcript of Interview with Philip Perlman, December 16, 1954, in PPF, Box 642; "Address in Harlem, NY, upon Receiving the Franklin Roosevelt Award," October 11, 1952, in *Public Papers of the Presidents of the United States: Harry S. Truman*, vol. 8, 797–802; Memorandum from Philip Perlman to the President, October 22, 1947, in TCCP, Box 74. Truman typically only addressed the DOJ's actions in the covenant cases before predominantly black audiences and in previous speeches had avoided directly taking credit for the intervention. See, for example, "Address in Harlem, NY, upon Receiving the Franklin Roosevelt Award," October 29, 1948, in *Public Papers of the Presidents of the United States: Harry S. Truman*, vol. 4, 923–25, and "Commencement Address at Howard University," June 13, 1952, in *Public Papers of the Presidents of the United States: Harry S. Truman*, vol. 8, 420–24. For a more nebulous claim of responsibility from Perlman see Address by Philip B. Perlman to the Camden County Insurance Agents Association, March 10, 1949, in TCCP, Box 74.

28. *Michigan Chronicle*, November 22, 1947, 6.

29. *Baltimore Afro-American*, November 15, 1947, 2; *Baltimore Afro-American*, November 22, 1947, 4; *Chicago Defender*, November 22, 1947, 14. See also, *Los Angeles Sentinel*, November 20, 1947, 7; *Chicago Defender*, November 22, 1947, 1.

30. Elman and Silber, "Solicitor General's Office," 818–19; Interview Notes for Philip Elman, August 19, 1971, in BVBC, Box 2, Folder 27. The other attorneys who helped write the brief were Oscar Hirsch Davis of the Claims Division, Hilbert Zarky from the Tax Division, Stanley Silverberg of the Office of the Solicitor General. For a discussion of the inadequacy of the Civil Rights Section's manpower at the time see Lawson, *To Secure These Rights*, 144–45.

31. Elman and Silber, "Solicitor General's Office," 818–19; Interview Notes for Philip Elman, August 19, 1971, in BVBC, Box 2, Folder 27.

32. *Shelley v. Kraemer*, Brief for the United States as Amicus Curiae, 5–19.

33. Ibid., 19–20.

34. Ibid., 92–97.

35. Ibid., 97–101.

36. Ibid., 121–23.

37. John J. Jones to Tom C. Clark, December 12, 1947, in NAACP, Part 5, Reel 21, Frame 1064; Calvin N. Walker to Tom C. Clark, December 12, 1947, in NAACP, Part 5, Reel 21, Frame 1065. See also Richard E. Westbrooks to Tom C. Clark, December 9, 1947, in TCCP, Box 80.

38. Clark and Perlman, *Prejudice and Property*. Indeed, the introduction to the book—written by reporter and future Truman administration member Wesley McCune—dealt primarily with why it mattered that the DOJ chose to make the brief available to the public. McCune argued passionately that the legal workings of the nation had remained unclear and inaccessible to the public for too long and that the intelligibility of this brief for nonlegal readers was an important step toward greater public comprehension of the law and its role in American society.

39. *District of Columbia Citizen*, December 1947, in PIP, Box B21, Folder 8; *Los Angeles Examiner*, January 21, 1948; *Chicago Defender*, November 29, 1947, 7.

40. *McGhee v. Sipes*, Brief for Respondents in Reply to Brief for United States as Amicus Curiae, 2–13.

41. Ibid., 13–14.

42. William H. Hastie to Thurgood Marshall, December 5, 1947, in NAACP, Part 5, Reel 22, Frame 706.

43. Thurgood Marshall to William Hastie, December 10, 1947, in NAACP, Part 5, Reel 21, Frame 1060.

44. *Atlanta Daily World*, November 23, 1947, 6; Vose, *Caucasians Only*, 199–200; McNeil, *Groundwork*, 181–82.

45. "While the Argument Progressed," David Grant's notes on George Vaughn's Oral Argument in BHP, Box 7, Folder 120. It is unclear whether the justices did, in fact, own covenanted properties. Given the extent of restrictions, however, this is entirely plausible. A handful of attorneys offered alternative explanations, however, including the argument that Jackson and Rutledge had attended the NBA's annual convention in Washington in November 1947 where the respondent to Justice Jackson's keynote address had mentioned the pending covenant cases. Willis Graves speculated that this discussion of the cases before their official presentation to the Court might have been enough to provoke their recusal. Though Reed and Jackson were unlikely to sit for the case given their prior abstentions on petitions for certiorari, the NBA convention issue may have possibly played a role in Rutledge's departure. Rutledge, unlike Reed and Jackson, had shown no prior need to recuse himself when hearing matters related to covenants. See Willis Graves to Thurgood Marshall and Marian Wynn Perry, January 19, 1948, in NAACP, Part 5, Reel 21, Frame 156.

46. Citation to Accompany the Award of the Medal of Merit to Fred M. Vinson, June 5, 1947, in TCCP, Box 79. On Vinson's life and background see St. Clair and Gugin, *Chief Justice*; Wiecek, *Birth of the Modern Constitution*; Bolner, "Mr. Chief Justice Vinson"; Belknap, *Vinson Court*. For more on the Vinson Court see Urofsky, *Division and Discord*; Lefberg, "Chief Justice Vinson"; Whittington B. Johnson, "Vinson Court"; Frank, "Fred Vinson."

47. Letter from William K. Bachelder, June, 1974, in BVBC, Box 5, Folder 99.

48. Urofsky, *Division and Discord*, 15–30; Belknap, *Vinson Court*, 35–79.

49. Interview Notes for Philip Elman, August 19, 1971, in BVBC, Box 2, Folder 27.

50. Argument Prepared by Philip B. Perlman, Solicitor General, before the Supreme Court against Enforcement of Racial Restrictive Covenants, January 15, 1948, in NAACP, Part 5, Reel 21, Frames 1118–23.

51. Ibid., Frames 1139–40.

52. Ibid., Frame 1140; *Baltimore Afro-American*, January 24, 1948, 1.

53. Argument Prepared by Philip B. Perlman, Solicitor General, before the Supreme Court against Enforcement of Racial Restrictive Covenants, January 15, 1948, in NAACP, Part 5, Reel 21, Frame 1140.

54. Copy of George Vaughn's Oral Argument before the Supreme Court in BHP, Box 7, Folder 120.

55. Ibid. Vaughn's cocounsel for the Supreme Court was a Jewish attorney named Herman Willer. Willer's arguments conformed much more closely to the NAACP's model for the "proper" litigation claims.

56. Juan Williams, *Thurgood Marshall*, 150–51. Mark Tushnet—another of Marshall's biographers and a former clerk of his—has noted that "Marshall is a great raconteur, and his reconstructions of what happened thirty or forty years before must be accepted with a skepticism born of the knowledge that he is at least as much concerned with telling a good story as with telling the true one." The story Marshall wanted to get across here, however, is a telling one. Tushnet, *NAACP's Legal Strategy*, 204.

57. "Arguments before the Court," 3221–22; Frankfurter as quoted in Memorandum from Herman Edelsberg, January 16, 1948, in PIP, Box B21, Folder 12.

58. Oral Presentation by Phineas Indritz to the Supreme Court of the United States, January 16, 1948, in PIP, Box B21, Folder 12; "Arguments before the Court," 3223; Harold H. Burton Diary, 1948, in HHBP, Microfilm Reel 2.

59. "Arguments before the Court," 3220–21 and 3224; Vose, *Caucasians Only*, 201–2. While each of the attorneys for the white homeowners expressed the concern that this issue was a matter for the legislature and not for the courts to decide, further questioning by the justices revealed the dubiousness of this as a solution. Indeed, when asked, James Crooks admitted that even a legislative solution should not affect existing covenants and since the restrictions he was defending ran in perpetuity he all but admitted that the legislature would be powerless to resolve the issue in Washington.

60. "Arguments before the Court," 3221–22; Memorandum from Herman Edelsberg, January 16, 1948, in PIP, Box B21, Folder 12.

61. Memorandum from Herman Edelsberg, January 16, 1948, in PIP, Box B21, Folder 12; "Arguments before the Court," 3221.

62. "Arguments before the Court," 3224; *Baltimore Afro-American*, January 24, 1948, 2.

63. *St. Louis Argus*, January 23, 1948, 1 and 8; *Baltimore Afro-American*, January 24, 1948, 1 and 2. The Dred Scott decision in 1857, perhaps the most infamous of the Supreme Court's nineteenth-century pronouncements on race, had seen Chief Justice

Roger Taney declare that no African American could "become a member of the political community formed and brought into existence by the Constitution . . . and as such become entitled to all the rights, and privileges, and immunities, guarantied by that instrument to the citizen." *Scott v. Sandford* 60 U.S. 393, 403.

64. *St. Louis Argus*, January 23, 1948, 1 and 8; *Baltimore Afro-American*, January 24, 1948, 1 and 2; *Evening Star*, January 17, 1948, A-12, in PIP, Box B21, Folder 8.

65. Notes regarding Brief for the United States Government [italics in original], undated in FMVP, Box 241, Folder 3; Letter from William K. Bachelder, June 1974, in BVBC, Box 5, Folder 99; Vinson as quoted in St. Clair and Gugin, *Chief Justice Fred M. Vinson*, 26–27.

66. Allen, "Remembering *Shelley v. Kraemer*," 719–20; "Statements Given—Edgerton," January 31, 1948, in FMVP, Box 399, Folder 6.

67. Dickson, *Supreme Court in Conference*, 698–99.

68. Notes on Certiorari Petition for *Shelley v. Kraemer*, undated [c. June 1947], in HHBP, Box 76, Folder 3. Reed, however, declined to hear the case. For a similar expression of frustration against covenants coupled with an unwillingness to support a judicial remedy see *American Council on Race Relations Report* 2.7 (December 1947): 2 in CETRR, Box 36, Folder 5.

69. Notes on Petition for Certiorari, undated [c. June 1947], in WODP, Box 161, Folder 8.

70. Letter from William K. Bachelder, June 1974, in BVBC, Box 5, Folder 99; Dickson, *Supreme Court in Conference*, 698–99; Allen, "Remembering *Shelley v. Kraemer*," 721–22; Conference Notes, February 1948, in WODP, Box 161, Folder 8.

71. Draft Opinion in *Shelley v. Kraemer* with Notes from Justice Black to Vinson, April 12, 1948, in FMVP Box 241, Folder 2; Draft Opinion in *Shelley v. Kraemer* with Notes from Justice Burton to Vinson, April 12, 1948, in FMVP, Box 241, Folder 2; Justice William O. Douglas to Vinson, April 13, 1948, in FMVP, Box 241, Folder 3.

72. *Shelley v. Kraemer* 334 U.S. 1, 7. See Flack, *Adoption*. For other analyses of the opinions see, for example, Vose, *Caucasians Only*, 205–10; Leland B. Ware, "Invisible Walls," 768–71; Rose, "Property Stories"; Pritchett, "*Shelley v. Kraemer*."

73. *Shelley v. Kraemer* 334 U.S. 1, 10.

74. Ibid., 15.

75. Ibid., 15–16.

76. Ibid., 20; Draft Opinion in *Hurd and Urciolo v. Hodge* with Notes from Justice Burton to Vinson, April 25, 1948, in FMVP, Box 241, Folder 3.

77. As the Court noted in its opinion, "It is a well-established principle that this Court will not decide constitutional questions where other grounds are available and dispositive of the issues of the case." *Hurd and Urciolo v. Hodge* 334 U.S. 24, 30.

78. Ibid., 34.

79. Ibid., 34–35; Original language in typewritten draft of Opinion of the Court for *Hurd and Urciolo v. Hodge*, undated in FMVP, Box 241, Folder 4.

80. *Hurd and Urciolo v. Hodge* 334 U.S. 24, 36 (Frankfurter concurrence); Felix Frankfurter to Vinson, April 27, 1948, in FMVP, Box 241, Folder 3.

81. Justice Murphy as quoted in St. Clair and Gugin, *Chief Justice Fred M. Vinson*, 301–4; Allen, "Remembering *Shelley v. Kraemer*," 734; Walter White to Vinson, May 3, 1948, in FMVP, Box 205, Folder 1.

82. *Michigan Chronicle*, May 8, 1948, 1 and 8; Newspaper Clipping, "They Have Faith: Neighbors of McGhee Take Decision Calmly," undated [c. May 1948], in FMDC, Box 4; *Pittsburgh Courier*, May 15, 1948, 1.

83. "A House with a Yard," *Time* 51, no. 20 (May 17, 1948): 27; Irons, *Courage*, 72 and 78; *St. Louis Argus*, May 7, 1948, 1 and 8.

84. *Washington Post*, May 4, 1948, 3.

85. *Pittsburgh Courier*, May 15, 1948, 6; *Chicago Defender*, May 15, 1948, 14.

86. See for example *Michigan Chronicle*, May 8, 1948, 1 and 8; *Washington Post*, May 6, 1948, 16; *Pittsburgh Courier*, May 22, 1948, 6; *Los Angeles Sentinel*, May 6, 1948, 9 and 16; "Comments on the Decision," undated, in BHP, Box 7, Folder 120; William Henry Huff to Loren Miller, May 8, 1948, in LMP, Box 8, Folder 3. See also *Baltimore Afro-American*, May 8, 1948, 1; *Pittsburgh Courier*, May 8, 1948, 1; *Pittsburgh Courier*, May 15, 1948, 6; *Chicago Defender*, May 15, 1948, 14; Norman Williams, "Racial Discrimination," 141 and 155.

87. Press Release, "Statement by Thurgood Marshall," May 1948, in NAACP, Part 5, Reel 22, Frames 2–3; Thurgood Marshall to James T. Bush, May 24, 1948, in NAACP, Part 5, Reel 22, Frames 70–72; *Chicago Defender*, May 22, 1948, 15; *Michigan Chronicle*, May 15, 1948, 7.

88. *Michigan Chronicle*, May 15, 1948, 3a; Press Release, "Covenant Decision Spurs NAACP Drive," May 13, 1948, in NAACP, Part 5, Reel 22, Frames 42–43; *Detroit Tribune*, May 12, 1948, 4. For more on the changes in the NAACP at this time see Berg, *"Ticket to Freedom"*; Sullivan, *Lift Every Voice*.

89. *Michigan Chronicle*, May 15, 1948, 7.

90. *St. Louis Argus*, May 14, 1948, 12.

91. *Michigan Chronicle*, May 15, 1948, 6a; *Michigan Chronicle*, May 15, 1948, 6b.

Chapter Five

1. Memorandum from Louis Wirth, "Progress Report, April-September 1949," October 20, 1949, in LWP, Box 14, Folder 7.

2. Ibid.

3. For one of the more enduring critiques of the role of litigation in fomenting social change see Rosenberg, *Hollow Hope*, esp. 67–70 on the issue of housing.

4. On legal scholars' treatment of *Shelley* see, for example, Wechsler, "Toward Neutral Principles"; Henkin, *"Shelley v. Kraemer"*; Wiecek, *Birth of the Modern Constitution*, 677–78; Brooks and Rose, *Saving the Neighborhood*, 144. For critiques of *Shelley* from two of the preeminent historians of urban segregation see Hirsch, *Making the Second Ghetto*; Sugrue, *Sweet Land of Liberty*.

5. Mrs. W. E. Rockey to Vinson, May 6, 1948, in FMVP, Box 205, Folder 1; Mrs. Myrtle A. Pascoe to Vinson, May 4, 1948, in FMVP, Box 205, Folder 1. For a sampling of

positive or moderate reactions from mainstream newspapers see quotations from the *New York Herald Tribune, St. Louis Star-Times, P.M., Baltimore Sun, Philadelphia Bulletin, Newark Evening News, Brooklyn Equal, St. Louis Post-Dispatch,* and *Baltimore Evening Sun* in Newspaper Clipping, "St. Louis, Scene of Conflict, Applauds Action: Few Newspapers Seek Ways to Avoid Fair Play," undated [c. May 1948], in FMDC, Box 4; see also Jack, "Racism and the Supreme Court," 572–73.

6. Oliver Allstorm to Harold H. Burton, June 8, 1948, in HHBP, Box 76, Folder 3 (italics in original); Mr. H. L. Alder to Vinson, May 4, 1948, in FMVP, Box 205, Folder 1.

7. Florence Price to Harold H. Burton, January 19, 1948, in HHBP, Box 76, Folder 3; Arthur J. Brown to Harold H. Burton, January 20, 1948, in HHBP, Box 76, Folder 3.

8. Newspaper Clipping, "Opinions on Ruling vary in Block Where Covenant Battle Began," undated [c. May 1948], in FMDC, Box 4.

9. Newspaper Clipping, untitled [c. May 1948], in FMDC, Box 4.

10. *Congressional Record* 86 (May 4, 1948): 5256–57; *Congressional Record* 86 (May 11, 1948): 5626. See *Scott v. Sandford* 60 U.S. 393 (1857).

11. *Kansas City Star,* January 7, 1949, 1 and 2; Opinion of the Court in *Bishop v. Kanfer* (Wayne County Circuit Court), October 25, 1948, in NAACP, Part 5, Reel 21, Frames 188–204.

12. Opinion of the Court in *Bishop v. Kanfer* (Wayne County Circuit Court), October 25, 1948, in NAACP, Part 5, Reel 21, Frames 188–204; Vose, *Caucasians Only,* 177. Even those who have supported the Court's findings have taken issue with the limitations of the opinion. See "State Action Reconsidered." For later scholarly analysis of *Shelley* see, for example, Mark D. Rosen, "*Shelley v. Kraemer*"; Tushnet, "*Shelley v. Kraemer*"; Henkin, "*Shelley v. Kraemer*"; Cahen, "Impact of *Shelley v. Kraemer*"; Saxer, "*Shelley v. Kraemer*"; Brophy and Ghosh, "Whistling Dixie."

13. *Detroit Tribune,* May 15, 1948, 1 and 2; Vose, *Caucasians Only,* 227–28; Brooks and Rose, *Saving the Neighborhood,* 170.

14. Memorandum on Current Litigation before the United States Supreme Court Involving Race Restrictive Housing Covenants, April 23, 1948, in LWP, Box 53, Folder 3; Gotham, "Urban Space," 624; McIntyre, "Status of Racial Covenants," 19–23.

15. Opinion of the Court in *Brock v. Murphy* (Wayne County Circuit Court), January 7, 1949, in NAACP, Part 5, Reel 21, Frames 218–22; Joint Memorandum of the American Jewish Committee and Anti-Defamation League, April 16, 1953, in NAACP Records, Part II, Box B132; "Real Estate: 'Exclusive . . . Restricted," *U.S. News & World Report,* May 14, 1948; Report of the Second National Conference on Intergroup Relations, November, 1948, in LWP, Box 14, Folder 5. Extralegal pressures had always been present and in at least some communities were arguably more instrumental to the maintenance of residential segregation than covenants even before *Shelley.* For an example of this argument see Frank, "United States Supreme Court," 24–26, which anecdotally discusses conditions in Indianapolis.

16. William C. Carr to Loren Miller, May 14, 1948, in LMP, Box 8, Folder 2; *Detroit Tribune,* May 15, 1948, 1 and 2; "Real Estate: 'Exclusive . . . Restricted." For the most

detailed overviews and analyses of white efforts to circumvent the decision see Owens, "*Shelley v. Kraemer*," 93–155; Brooks and Rose, *Saving the Neighborhood*, 169–85. See also Livermore, "Circumvention of the Rule"; Walcher, "Property Rights Emancipated," 268–72; Hoelscher, "Use of Option"; Greenberg and Franklin, "Discrimination"; Sylvester, "Is an Agreement," Ming, "Racial Restrictions," esp. 216–24. See also Vose, *Caucasians Only*, 227–32.

17. Memorandum from Charles Hamilton Houston, January 3, 1949, in NAACP Records, Part II, Box B134. See also Vose, *Caucasians Only*, 230–46.

18. *Barrows v. Jackson* 346 U.S 249 (1953); Vose, *Caucasians Only*, 243–46.

19. Brooks and Rose, *Saving the Neighborhood*, 173–75; Bolner, "Mr. Chief Justice Vinson," 344.

20. Brooks and Rose, *Saving the Neighborhood*, 193.

21. As quoted in Vose, *Caucasians Only*, 228.

22. See Wiecek, *Birth of the Modern Constitution*, 680. On the social, economic, and political contours of race, suburbanization, and capital flight throughout the twentieth century see, for example, Lassiter, *Silent Majority*; Kruse, *White Flight*; Nicolaides, *My Blue Heaven*; Freund, *Colored Property*; Wiese, *Places of Their Own*; Self, *American Babylon* (which offers a remarkable look at urban and suburban interactions along racial and class lines); Kenneth T. Jackson, *Crabgrass Frontier*; Chase, "Process of Suburbanization." On the enduring hold of residential discrimination see, for example, Massey and Denton, *American Apartheid*; Darden, "Black Residential Segregation," 680–91; Sander, "Housing Segregation."

23. *Baltimore Afro-American*, May 29, 1948, 4.

24. Recent surveys of the scholarship on the interplay between law and social change have pointed to analyses of the "preexisting and anticipated barriers to success" as a useful factor in reassessing the meaning of civil rights litigation. Understanding the scale of white resistance to *Shelley's* implementation can offer a way to view "less-than-full implementation much more favorably," and encourages a deeper assessment of what the covenant cases truly accomplished. See Cummings, "Empirical Studies," 190.

25. *St. Louis Argus*, May 14, 1948, 13; American Council on Race Relations, "*To Secure These Rights* in Your Community," June 1948, in LWP, Folder 14, Box 6; *Los Angeles Sentinel*, May 6, 1948, 9 and 16.

26. *New York Times*, January 22, 1951, 19; Joint Memorandum of the American Jewish Committee and Anti-Defamation League, April 16, 1953, in NAACP Records, Part II, Box B132; Kluger, *Simple Justice*, 254; Indritz, "Racial Ramparts," 300; Frank Horne, "What Now in the Housing of Minorities?," April 28, 1954, in WHHP, Reel 36; Loren Miller, "Democracy's Key Fits Any Door," October 22, 1955, in LMP, Box 32, Folder 6; Brooks and Rose, *Saving the Neighborhood*, 185–86; "Address in Harlem, NY, upon Receiving the Franklin Roosevelt Award," October 11, 1952, in *Public Papers of the Presidents of the United States: Harry S. Truman*, vol. 8, 797–802. African Americans had enjoyed an increasing homeownership rate in the pre-*Shelley* period as well due to the improving economic status attendant with wartime employment. One study concluded that at the

end of the period from 1940 and 1947, black Americans were 40 percent more likely to own a home. See the reprint of Oscar Stern, "The End of the Restrictive Covenant," from *Appraisal Journal*, October 1948, in NAACP Records, Part II, Box B132.

27. Joint Memorandum of the American Jewish Committee and Anti-Defamation League, April 16, 1953, in NAACP Records, Part II, Box B132.

28. Ibid.; Miller, *Petitioners*, 331–32; Frank Horne, "What Now in the Housing of Minorities?" April 28, 1954, in WHHP, Reel 36. See also McGraw and Nesbitt, "Aftermath of Shelley versus Kraemer," 280–87.

29. Memorandum on Current Litigation before the United States Supreme Court Involving Race Restrictive Housing Covenants, April 23, 1948, in LWP, Box 53, Folder 2. For others suggesting *Shelley* mitigated potentially worse outcomes see, for example, Allen, "Remembering *Shelley v. Kraemer*," 734–35. Though these sorts of speculative explorations are limited in their utility for historians, legal scholar Scott Cummings has pointed to counterfactual analyses as a potentially valuable consideration when assessing the impact of law on the outcomes for social movements. See Cummings, "Empirical Studies," 199–202.

30. Loring Moore to Loren Miller, May 21, 1948, in LMP, Box 8, Folder 3; Loren Miller to David Grant, June 4, 1948, in LMP, Box 8, Folder 2. See also *St. Louis Argus*, May 14, 1948, 12; David Grant to Loren Miller, May 10, 1948, in LMP, Box 8, Folder 2.

31. Loren Miller, "Untitled," May 26, 1948, in LMP, Box 8, Folder 2. For more on the faith of civil rights litigators in the law as a vehicle of change and skepticism from the general public see Christopher W. Schmidt, "Freedom Comes"; Mack, "Rethinking Civil Rights Lawyering."

32. *New York Amsterdam News*, May 8, 1948, 10; *Baltimore Afro-American*, May 15, 1948, 1 and 2; *Michigan Chronicle*, May 15, 1948, 3a. For similar sentiments see, for example, *Baltimore Afro-American*, May 15, 1948, 3; *Baltimore Afro-American*, May 29, 1948, 4.

33. *Baltimore Afro-American*, May 15, 1948, 3; *St. Louis Argus*, May 7, 1948, 12.

34. Interview Notes for Philip Elman, August 19, 1971, in BVBC, Box 2, Folder 27; Elman and Silber, "Solicitor General's Office," 819–20.

35. Transcript of Interview with Philip Perlman, December 16, 1954, in PPF, Box 642; Perlman, "Civil Rights," 6; *Baltimore Afro-American*, November 19, 1949, 1 and 2. Perlman stated in his 1954 interview that after *Shelley* "whenever it was decided to go into another one [civil rights case], we didn't have to see the President—we knew where the administration, where Truman, was on it."

36. Perlman, "Civil Rights," 10–13. See Kluger, *Simple Justice*, 232–33, on Thurgood Marshall's failed attempt to enlist the DOJ's support in *Smith v. Allwright* (1944). On *Sweatt* and *McLaurin* see also Tushnet, *NAACP's Legal Strategy*, 130–37; Kluger, *Simple Justice*, 255–283; Klarman, *From Jim Crow*, 204–12 and 253–61.

37. See *Henderson v. U.S.* 339 U.S. 816 (1950); *Graham v. Brotherhood of Firemen* 338 U.S. 232 (1949); *District of Columbia v. John R. Thompson Co. Inc.* 346 U.S. 100 (1953); *Chicago Defender*, July 14, 1951, 6. Perlman also took the opportunity to intervene in *Takahashi v. Fish and Game Commission* 334 U.S. 410 (1948).

38. Kluger, *Simple Justice*, 560.

39. Raymond Foley to B. T. Fitzpatrick, May 11, 1948, in RFP, Box 1. On the maneuvering among Truman officials over FHA covenant guidelines see Memorandum concerning the Use of Public Funds by the Federal Housing Administration, undated, in PNP, Box 57; Memorandum to the President from Phileo Nash, October 31, 1949, in PNP, Box 57; Frank S. Horne to Raymond Foley, February 9, 1949, in PNP, Box 57; Philip Perlman to Tom C. Clark, July 7, 1949, in TCCP, Box 74. On the shifts in FHA housing policy see also Lamb and Nye, "Fair Housing Policy," 27–28; Kimble, "Insuring Inequality."

40. Statement by Solicitor General Philip B. Perlman for the New York State Committee on Discrimination in Housing, December 2, 1949, in PNP, Box 57; Philip Perlman to Tom C. Clark, July 7, 1949, in TCCP, Box 74; Philip B. Perlman to Thurgood Marshall, July 6, 1949, in LMP, Box 26, Folder 10; Miller, *Petitioners*, 331–32.

41. *Baltimore Afro-American*, May 22, 1948, 4; Press Release, "Statement by Thurgood Marshall," May 6, 1948, in NAACP, Part 5, Reel 22, Frames 2–3 and 9–10.

42. The NAACP had no amici in the *Gaines* (1938) or *Allwright* (1944) cases. In *Morgan v. Virginia* (1946), the ACLU and Workers Defense League joined as amici. In *Sipuel* (1948), the NLG and ACLU both filed.

43. See *McLaurin v. Oklahoma State Regents* 339 U.S. 637 (1950), Brief for Petitioners; *Sweatt v. Painter* 339 U.S. 629 (1950), Brief for Petitioners. Interview notes from "Perry, Marian Wynn" in BVBC, Box 4, Folder 79. See also John P. Jackson, *Social Scientists*, 95–103; Tushnet, *NAACP's Legal Strategy*, 127–41.

44. Annette H. Peyser, "The Use of Sociological Data to Indicate the Unconstitutionality of Racial Segregation," undated [c. 1948], in AHPP, Box 1, Folder 2.

45. Annette H. Peyser, "Memorandum," June 28, 1950, in AHPP, Box 1, Folder 3 (italics in original); also available in NAACP, Part 5, Reel 22, Frames 777–78. On the sociological arguments in *Sweatt* and *McLaurin* see Tushnet, *NAACP's Legal Strategy*, 127–31, 140–41, and 161.

46. See *Brown v. Board of Education* 347 U.S. 483 (1954). On the use of social science in the *Brown* case see, for example, Kluger, *Simple Justice*, chaps. 14 and 18; Jack Greenberg, "Social Scientists"; John P. Jackson, *Social Scientists*, 109–96; John P. Jackson, "Creating a Consensus"; Klarman, *From Jim Crow*, 296–303. For a different view on the role of social science in the Supreme Court's *Brown* decision see Mody, "*Brown* Footnote Eleven."

47. Memorandum for Mr. Justice Frankfurter on Sweatt v. Texas and McLaurin v. Oklahoma State Regents, August 5, 1949, in FFP, Box 218. On Coleman see Kluger, *Simple Justice*, 292–93.

48. Kluger, *Simple Justice*, 292–93.

49. Ming, "Racial Restrictions," 229–31.

Afterword

1. See *Milliken v. Bradley* 418 U.S. 717, 814–15 (1974, Marshall Dissent).

Bibliography

Archives and Microfilms

Cambridge, Massachusetts
    Arthur and Elizabeth Schlesinger Library on the History of Women in America
        Mary Gibson Hundley Papers
        Pauli Murray Papers
    Harvard University Law Library, Microfilm Collections
        William H. Hastie Papers
Chicago, Illinois
    University of Chicago, Special Collections Research Center
        Committee on Education, Training and Research in Race Relations Records
        Louis Wirth Papers
Detroit, Michigan
    Charles H. Wright Museum of African American History
        Francis M. Dent Collection
        Willis and Irene Graves Papers
    Detroit Public Library, Burton Historical Collection
        Francis Morse Dent Papers
        Minnie McGhee Oral History
Fullerton, California
    Center for Oral and Public History, California State University, Fullerton
        Loren Miller Oral History
Independence, Missouri
    Harry S. Truman Presidential Library
        John Blandford Papers
        Phileo Nash Papers
        Post-Presidential File, Harry S. Truman Papers
        President's Personal File, Harry S. Truman Papers
        Raymond Foley Papers
        Records of President's Committee on Civil Rights
        Tom C. Clark Papers
Lexington, Kentucky
    University of Kentucky, Wendell H. Ford Public Policy Research Center
        Frederick Moore Vinson Papers
New Haven, Connecticut
    Yale University, Manuscripts and Archives
        Brown v. Board of Education Collection

Yale University, Sterling Memorial Library, Microfilm Collections
  Papers of the National Association for the Advancement of Colored People
  Records of President Truman's Committee on Civil Rights
New York, New York
  Columbia University, Rare Book and Manuscript Library
    Robert Lee Hale Papers
  Schomburg Center for Research in Black Culture
    Annette H. Peyser Papers, 1945–51
San Marino, California
  Huntington Library
    Loren Miller Papers
St. Louis, Missouri
  Western Historical Manuscripts Collection, Microfilm, UM–St. Louis
    Black History Project (1895–1983)
Washington, D.C.
  Howard University Law Library
    Phineas Indritz Papers
  Howard University, Moorland-Spingarn Research Center
    Charles Hamilton Houston Papers
  Library of Congress, Manuscripts Division
    Elmer Gertz Papers
    Felix Frankfurter Papers
    Harold Hitz Burton Papers
    National Association for the Advancement of Colored People Records
    Robert Houghwout Jackson Papers
    William O. Douglas Papers
Worcester, Massachusetts
  Worcester Public Library
    Worcester Biography Clipping File

Cases

Barrows v. Jackson 346 U.S. 249 (1953)
Brown v. Board of Education 347 U.S. 483 (1954)
Buchanan v. Warley 245 U.S. 60 (1917)
Corrigan v. Buckley 271 U.S. 323 (1926)
District of Columbia v. John R. Thompson Co. Inc. 346 U.S. 100 (1953)
Fairchild v. Raines 24 Cal.2d 818 (1944)
Gandolfo v. Hartman 49 Fed. 181 (1892)
Graham v. Brotherhood of Firemen 338 U.S. 232 (1949)
Hansberry v. Lee 311 U.S. 32 (1940)
Henderson v. U.S. 339 U.S. 816 (1950)

Hundley v. Gorewitz 132 F.2d 23 (D.C. Circuit, 1942)

Hurd and Urciolo v. Hodge 334 U.S. 24 (1948)

Marsh v. Alabama 326 U.S. 501 (1946)

Mays v. Burgess 147 F. 2d 869 (D.C. Circuit, 1945)

McGhee v. Sipes 334 U.S. 1 (1948)

McLaurin v. Oklahoma State Regents 339 U.S. 637 (1950)

Mendez v. Westminster 161 F.2d 774 (9th Circuit, 1947)

Milliken v. Bradley 418 U.S. 717 (1974)

Missouri ex rel. Gaines v. Canada 305 U.S. 337 (1938)

Morgan v. Virginia 328 U.S. 373 (1946)

Muller v. State of Oregon 208 U.S. 412 (1908)

Plessy v. Ferguson 163 U.S. 537 (1896)

Scott v. Sandford 60 U.S. 393 (1857)

Shelley v. Kraemer 334 U.S. 1 (1948)

Sipuel v. Board of Regents of University of Oklahoma 332 U.S. 631 (1948)

Smith v. Allwright 321 U.S. 649 (1944)

Steele v. Louisville & Nashville Railroad Company 323 U.S. 192 (1944)

Sweatt v. Painter 339 U.S. 629 (1950)

Tovey v. Levy Cook County Superior Court 45 S 947

Tunstall v. Brotherhood of Locomotive Firemen and Enginemen 323 U.S. 210 (1944)

U.S. v. Bhagat Singh Thind 261 U.S. 204 (1923)

Periodicals

American City

American Law Register

Atlanta Daily World

Baltimore Afro-American

Chicago Defender

Christian Century

Collier's

Congressional Record

Crisis

Detroit Free Press

Detroit Tribune

District of Columbia Citizen

Evening Star (Washington)

Kansas City Star

Los Angeles Daily News

Los Angeles Examiner

Los Angeles Sentinel

Los Angeles Times

Los Angeles Tribune
Michigan Chronicle
Monthly Labor Review
Monthly Summary of Events and Trends in Race Relations
Nation
New York Amsterdam News
New York Times
Opportunity
Pittsburgh Courier
St. Louis Argus
St. Louis Post-Dispatch
Time
U.S. News & World Report
Washington Post

Government Publications

Federal Housing Administration, *Underwriting Manual: Underwriting and Valuation Procedure under Title II of the National Housing Act*. Washington, D.C.: U.S. Government Printing Office, 1938.

Federal Housing Administration, *Underwriting Manual: Underwriting Analysis under Title II, Section 203 of the National Housing Act*. Washington, D.C.: National Housing Agency, 1947.

Housing in America: Its Present Status and Future Implications—A Factual Analysis of Testimony and Studies. Washington, D.C.: U.S. Government Printing Office, 1948.

Public Papers of the Presidents of the United States: Harry S. Truman. 8 vols. Washington, D.C.: U.S. Government Printing Office, 1961–66.

Study and Investigation of Housing: Hearings before the Joint Committee on Housing. Washington, D.C.: U.S. Government Printing Office, 1948.

U.S. Bureau of the Census. *Fifteenth Census of the United States, 1930*. Washington, D.C.: National Archives and Records Administration, 1930.

———. *Fourteenth Census of the United States, 1920*. Washington, D.C.: National Archives and Records Administration, 1920.

———. *Sixteenth Census of the United States, 1940*. Washington, D.C.: National Archives and Records Administration, 1940.

———. *Thirteenth Census of the United States, 1910*. Washington, D.C.: National Archives and Records Administration, 1910.

Published Primary Sources

Abrams, Charles. *Forbidden Neighbors: A Study of Prejudice in Housing*. New York: Harper and Brothers, 1955.

———. "Homes for Aryans Only: The Restrictive Covenant Spreads Legal Racism in America." *Commentary* 3 (May 1947): 421–27.

———. *Race Bias in Housing.* New York: ACLU, NAACP, and ACRR, 1947.

"Arguments before the Court: Enforceability of Restrictive Covenants." *United States Law Week* 16, no. 28 (January 1948): 3219–24.

Clark, Tom C., and Philip B. Perlman. *Prejudice and Property: An Historic Brief against Racial Covenants.* Washington, D.C.: Public Affairs Press, 1948.

Crooks, James A. "The Racial Covenant Cases." *Georgetown Law Journal* 37, no. 4 (May 1949): 514–25.

Dean, John P. "Only Caucasian: A Study of Land Use Covenants." *Journal of Land & Public Utility Economics* 23, no. 4 (November 1947): 428–32.

Frank, John P. "The United States Supreme Court: 1947–48." *University of Chicago Law Review* 16, no. 1 (Autumn 1948): 1–55.

Green, Wendell E. "Stare Decisis and the Supreme Court of the United States." *National Bar Journal* 4, no. 3 (September 1946): 191–207.

Greenberg, Arthur N., and Robert A. Franklin. "Discrimination in Ownership and Occupancy of Property since *Shelley v. Kraemer.*" *UCLA Intramural Law Review* 1, no. 1 (June 1952): 14–22.

Greenberg, Jack. "Social Scientists Take the Stand: A Review and Appraisal of Their Testimony in Litigation." *Michigan Law Review* 54, no. 7 (1955/56): 953–70.

Groner, Isaac N., and David M. Helfeld. "Race Discrimination in Housing." *Yale Law Journal* 57, no. 3 (January 1948): 426–58.

Hale, Robert L. "Rights under the Fourteenth and Fifteenth Amendments against Injuries Inflicted by Private Individuals." *Lawyers Guild Review* 6, no. 5 (December 1946): 627–39.

Hauser, P. M., and A. J. Jaffe. "The Extent of the Housing Shortage." *Law and Contemporary Problems* 12, no. 1 (Winter 1947): 3–15.

"Highlights of 21st Annual Convention." *National Bar Journal* 5, no. 1 (March 1947): 115–27.

Hoelscher, Robert O. "Use of Option to Purchase Land to Control Occupancy." *Missouri Law Review* 15, no. 1 (January 1950): 77–82.

Indritz, Phineas. "Racial Ramparts in the Nation's Capital." *Georgetown Law Journal* 41, no. 3 (March 1953): 297–329.

Jack, Homer A. "Racism and the Supreme Court." *Christian Century* 65, no. 23 (June 1948): 571–73.

Kahen, Harold I. "Validity of Anti-Negro Restrictive Covenants: A Reconsideration of the Problem." *University of Chicago Law Review* 12, no. 2 (February 1945): 198–213.

Kimble, G. Eleanor. "Restrictive Covenants." *Common Ground* 6, no. 1 (Autumn 1945): 45–52.

Livermore, H. P. "Circumvention of the Rule against Enforcement of Racially Restrictive Covenants." *California Law Review* 37, no. 3 (September 1949): 493–98.

Long, Herman, and Charles S. Johnson. *People vs. Property: Race Restrictive Covenants in Housing*. Nashville: Fisk University Press, 1947.

Lowe, R. Gordon. "Racial Restrictive Covenants." *Alabama Law Review* 1, no. 1 (Fall 1948): 15–39.

McGovney, D. O. "Racial Residential Segregation by State Court Enforcement of Restrictive Agreements, Covenants or Conditions in Deeds Is Unconstitutional." *California Law Review* 33, no. 1 (March 1945): 5–39.

McGraw, B. T., and George B. Nesbitt. "Aftermath of Shelley versus Kraemer on Residential Restriction by Race." *Land Economics* 29, no. 3 (August 1953): 280–87.

Ming, William R., Jr. "Racial Restrictions and the Fourteenth Amendment: The Restrictive Covenant Cases." *University of Chicago Law Review* 16, no. 2 (Winter 1949): 203–38.

Moon, Henry Lee. *Balance of Power: The Negro Vote*. New York: Doubleday, 1948.

Myrdal, Gunnar. *American Dilemma: The Negro Problem and Modern Democracy*. New York: Harper and Brothers, 1944.

National Negro Congress. *A Petition to the United Nations on Behalf of 13 Million Oppressed Negro Citizens of the United States of America*. New York: National Negro Congress, 1946.

"Negro Restrictions and the 'Changed Conditions' Doctrine." *University of Chicago Law Review* 7, no. 4 (June 1940): 710–16.

Perlman, Philip B. "Civil Rights at the Half Century Mark." Paper presented at the Conference on Civil Liberties, Washington, D.C., 1950.

———. *The Work of the Office of the Solicitor General of the United States*. Washington, D.C.: U.S. Government Printing Office, 1949.

President's Committee on Civil Rights. *To Secure These Rights*. Washington, D.C.: U.S. Government Printing Office, 1947.

"Recent Additions to the Bench." *St. Louis Bar Journal* 17 (1970/71): 55–62.

Rosemond, Irene. *Reflections: An Oral History of Detroit*. Detroit: Broadside Press, 1992.

Rosenzweig, Simon. "The Opinions of Judge Edgerton—A Study in the Judicial Process." *Cornell Law Quarterly* 37, no. 2 (Winter 1952): 149–205.

"State Action Reconsidered in Light of *Shelley v. Kraemer*." *Columbia Law Review* 48, no. 8 (December 1948): 1241–45.

Sylvester, Christopher U. "Is an Agreement to Convey to a Negro Property Subject to a Racial Restrictive Covenant Actionable as a Conspiracy?" *North Dakota Law Review* 29, no. 1 (January 1953): 81–84.

Tefft, Sheldon. "*Marsh v. Alabama*—A Suggestion Concerning Racial Restrictive Covenants." *National Bar Journal* 4, no. 2 (June 1946): 133–35.

Vaughn, George L. "Resisting the Enforcement by Courts of Restrictive Covenants Based on Race." *National Bar Journal* 5, no. 4 (December 1947): 381–400.

Walcher, Wilson P. "Property Rights Emancipated: The Restrictive Covenant Cases." *Dicta* 26, no. 10 (October 1949): 263–74.

Weaver, Robert C. *Hemmed In: The ABC's of Race Restrictive Housing Covenants.* Chicago: ACRR, 1945.

———. *The Negro Ghetto.* New York: Harcourt, Brace, 1948.

———. "Race Restrictive Housing Covenants." *Journal of Land & Public Utility Economics* 20, no. 3 (August 1944): 183–93.

———. "Round Table—Are Race Res Covenants Justifiable?: No." *Negro Digest* 4, no. 4 (February 1946): 38–41.

White, Walter. *A Man Called White: The Autobiography of Walter White.* New York: Viking Press, 1948.

Williams, Norman, Jr. "Racial Discrimination by Restrictive Covenants—Judicial Support Ended." *American City* 58, no. 9 (September 1948): 141 and 155.

Secondary Materials

Allen, Francis A. "Remembering *Shelley v. Kraemer*: Of Public and Private Worlds." *Washington University Law Quarterly* 67 (1989): 709–36.

Anderson, Carol. *Eyes off the Prize: African Americans, the United Nations, and the Struggle for Human Rights, 1944–1955.* New York: Cambridge University Press, 2003.

Arriola, Christopher. "Knocking on the Schoolhouse Door: *Mendez v. Westminster*, Equal Protection, Public Education, and Mexican Americans in the 1940s." *La Raza Law Journal* 8, no. 2 (1995): 166–207.

Baker, Lee D. *From Savage to Negro: Anthropology and the Construction of Race, 1896–1954.* Berkeley: University of California Press, 1998.

Barkan, Elazar. *The Retreat of Scientific Racism: Changing Concepts of Race in Britain and the United States between the World Wars.* New York: Cambridge University Press, 1992.

Bates, Beth Tompkins. "A New Crowd Challenges the Agenda of the Old Guard in the NAACP, 1933–1941." *American Historical Review* 102, no. 2 (April 1997): 340–77.

Belknap, Michal R. *The Vinson Court: Justices, Rulings, and Legacy.* Santa Barbara, Calif.: ABC-CLIO, 2004.

Bell, Derrick A., Jr. "Serving Two Masters: Integration Ideals and Client Interests in School Desegregation Litigation." *Yale Law Journal* 85, no. 4 (March 1976): 470–516.

Bell, Jeannine. *Hate Thy Neighbor: Move-In Violence and the Persistence of Racial Segregation in American Housing.* New York: New York University Press, 2013.

Berg, Manfred. *"The Ticket to Freedom": The NAACP and the Struggle for Black Political Integration.* Gainesville: University Press of Florida, 2005.

Berman, William. *The Politics of Civil Rights in the Truman Administration.* Columbus: Ohio State University Press, 1970.

Bernstein, Barton J. "The Ambiguous Legacy: The Truman Administration and Civil Rights." In *Politics and Policies of the Truman Administration*, edited by Barton J. Bernstein, 269–314. Chicago: Quadrangle Books, 1970.

————, ed. *Politics and Policies of the Truman Administration*. Chicago: Quadrangle Books, 1970.

Bernstein, David E. "Philip Sober Controlling Philip Drunk: *Buchanan v. Warley* in Historical Perspective." *Vanderbilt Law Review* 51, no. 4 (May 1998): 797–880.

Black, Harold. "Restrictive Covenants in Relation to Segregated Negro Housing in Detroit." M.A. thesis, Wayne University, 1947.

Blank, David M. *The Volume of Residential Construction, 1889–1950*. New York: National Bureau of Economic Research, 1954.

Boehm, Lisa Krissoff. *Making a Way Out of No Way: African American Women and the Second Great Migration*. Jackson: University Press of Mississippi, 2009.

Bolner, James. "Mr. Chief Justice Vinson: His Politics and His Constitutional Law." Ph.D. dissertation, University of Virginia, 1962.

Borgwardt, Elizabeth. "Race, Rights, and Nongovernmental Organizations at the UN San Francisco Conference: A Contested History of 'Human Rights . . . without Discrimination.'" In *Fog of War: The Second World War and the Civil Rights Movement*, edited by Kevin M. Kruse and Stephen Tuck, 188–207. New York: Oxford University Press, 2012.

Borstelmann, Thomas. *The Cold War and the Color Line: American Race Relations in the Global Arena*. Cambridge, Mass.: Harvard University Press, 2001.

————. "Jim Crow's Coming Out: Race Relations and American Foreign Policy in the Truman Years." *Presidential Studies Quarterly* 29, no. 3 (September 1999): 549–69.

Boyle, Kevin. *Arc of Justice: A Sage of Race, Civil Rights, and Murder in the Jazz Age*. New York: Henry Holt, 2004.

Brandwein, Pamela. "A Judicial Abandonment of Blacks? Rethinking the 'State Action' Cases of the Waite Court." *Law and Society Review* 41, no. 2 (June 2007): 343–86.

Brattain, Michelle. "Miscegenation and Competing Definitions of Race in Twentieth-Century Louisiana." *Journal of Southern History* 71, no. 3 (August 2005): 621–58.

————. "Race, Racism, and Antiracism: UNESCO and the Politics of Presenting Science to the Postwar Public." *American Historical Review* 112, no. 5 (December 2007): 1386–1413.

Brooks, Charlotte. *Alien Neighbors, Foreign Friends: Asian Americans, Housing, and the Transformation of Urban California*. Chicago: University of Chicago Press, 2009.

Brooks, Jennifer E. *Defining the Peace: World War II Veterans, Race, and the Remaking of Southern Political Tradition*. Chapel Hill: University of North Carolina Press, 2004.

Brooks, Richard R. W., and Carol M. Rose. *Saving the Neighborhood: Racially Restrictive Covenants, Law, and Social Norms*. Cambridge, Mass.: Harvard University Press, 2013.

Brophy, Alfred L., and Shubha Ghosh, "Whistling Dixie: The Invalidity and Unconstitutionality of Covenants against Yankees." *Villanova Environmental Law Journal* 10, no. 1 (1999): 57–89.

Brown-Nagin, Tomiko. *Courage to Dissent: Atlanta and the Long History of the Civil Rights Movement*. New York: Oxford University Press, 2011.

Cahen, Donald M. "The Impact of *Shelley v. Kraemer* on the State Action Concept." *California Law Review* 44, no. 4 (October 1956): 718–36.

Capeci, Dominic J., Jr. *Race Relations in Wartime Detroit: The Sojourner Truth Housing Controversy of 1942*. Philadelphia: Temple University Press, 1984.

Capeci, Dominic J., Jr., and Martha Wilkerson. "The Detroit Rioters of 1943: A Reinterpretation." *Michigan Historical Review* 16, no. 1 (Spring 1990): 49–72.

———. *Layered Violence: The Detroit Rioters of 1943*. Jackson: University of Mississippi Press, 1991.

Carle, Susan D. *Defining the Struggle: National Racial Justice Organizing, 1880–1915*. New York: Oxford University Press, 2013.

———. "From *Buchanan* to *Button*: Legal Ethics and the NAACP (Part II)." *University of Chicago Legal Forum* 8 (2001): 281–307.

———. "Race, Class, and Legal Ethics in the Early NAACP (1910–1920)." *Law and History Review* 20, no. 1 (2002): 97–146.

Chafe, William H. *Civilities and Civil Rights: Greensboro, North Carolina, and the Black Struggle for Freedom*. New York: Oxford University Press, 1980.

Cha-Jua, Sundiata Keita, and Clarence Lang. "The 'Long Movement' as Vampire: Temporal and Spatial Fallacies in Recent Black Freedom Studies." *Journal of African American History* 92, no. 2 (Spring 2007): 265–88.

Chase, Susan. "The Process of Suburbanization and the Use of Restrictive Deed Covenants as Private Zoning, Wilmington Delaware, 1900–1941." Ph.D. dissertation, University of Delaware, 1995.

Coleman, Christopher, Lawrence D. Nee, and Leonard S. Rabinowitz. "Social Movements and Social-Change Litigation: Synergy in the Montgomery Bus Protest." *Law and Social Inquiry* 30, no. 4 (Fall 2005): 663–736.

Crosby, Emilye, ed. *Civil Rights History from the Ground Up: Local Struggles, a National Movement*. Athens: University of Georgia Press, 2011.

Cummings, Scott. "Empirical Studies of Law and Social Change: What Is the Field? What Are the Questions?" *Wisconsin Law Review* (2013): 171–204.

Dalfiume, Richard. "The 'Forgotten Years' of the Negro Revolution." *Journal of American History* 55, no. 1 (June 1968): 90–106.

Darden, Joe T. "Black Residential Segregation since the 1948 *Shelley v. Kraemer* Decision." *Journal of Black Studies* 25, no. 6 (July 1995): 680–91.

Delaney, David. *Race, Place, and the Law, 1836–1948*. Austin: University of Texas Press, 1998.

Dickson, Del, ed. *The Supreme Court in Conference (1940–1985): The Private Discussions behind Nearly 300 Supreme Court Decisions*. New York: Oxford University Press, 2001.

Dittmer, John. *Local People: The Struggle for Civil Rights in Mississippi*. Urbana: University of Illinois Press, 1994.

Dodd, Lynda G. "Presidential Leadership and Civil Rights Lawyering in the Era before *Brown*." *Indiana Law Journal* 85, no. 4 (Fall 2010): 1599–657.

Donaldson, Gary. *Truman Defeats Dewey.* Lexington: University Press of Kentucky, 1999.

———. "Who Wrote the Clifford Memo? The Origins of Campaign Strategy in the Truman Administration." *Presidential Studies Quarterly* 23, no. 4 (Fall 1993): 747–54.

Dreer, Herman. "Negro Leadership in St. Louis: A Study in Race Relations." Ph.D. dissertation, University of Chicago, 1955.

Dudziak, Mary. *Cold War Civil Rights: Race and the Image of American Democracy.* Princeton: Princeton University Press, 2000.

Elliff, John T. *The United States Department of Justice and Individual Rights, 1937–1962.* New York: Garland Publishing, 1987.

Elman, Philip. "[A Reply to Philip Elman]: Response." *Harvard Law Review* 100, no. 8 (June 1987): 1949–57.

Elman, Philip, and Norman Silber. "The Solicitor General's Office, Justice Frankfurter, and Civil Rights Litigation, 1946–1960: An Oral History." *Harvard Law Review* 100, no. 4 (February 1987): 817–52.

Ely, James W., Jr. "Reflections on *Buchanan v. Warley*, Property Rights, and Race." *Vanderbilt Law Review* 51, no. 4 (May 1998): 953–74.

Fairfax, Roger A., Jr. "Wielding the Double-Edged Sword: Charles Hamilton Houston and Judicial Activism in the Age of Legal Realism." *Harvard Blackletter Law Journal* 14 (Spring 1998): 17–44.

Finkle, Lee. "The Conservative Aims of Militant Rhetoric: Black Protest during World War II." *Journal of American History* 60, no. 3 (December 1973): 692–713.

Fischel, William A. "Why Judicial Reversal of Apartheid Made a Difference." *Vanderbilt Law Review* 51, no. 4 (May 1998): 975–92.

Flack, Horace Edgar. *The Adoption of the Fourteenth Amendment.* Baltimore: Johns Hopkins University Press, 1908.

Francis, Megan Ming. *Civil Rights and the Making of the Modern American State.* New York: Cambridge University Press, 2014.

Frank, John P. "Fred Vinson and the Chief Justiceship." *University of Chicago Law Review* 21, no. 2 (Winter 1954): 212–46.

Frederickson, Kari. *The Dixiecrat Revolt and the End of the Solid South, 1932–1968.* Chapel Hill: University of North Carolina Press, 2001.

Freund, David. *Colored Property: State Policy and White Racial Politics in Suburban America.* Chicago: University of Chicago Press, 2007.

Fried, Barbara H. *The Progressive Assault on Laissez Faire: Robert Hale and the First Law and Economics Movement.* Cambridge, Mass.: Harvard University Press, 1998.

Funigiello, Philip. *The Challenge to Urban Liberalism: Federal-City Relations during World War II.* Knoxville: University of Tennessee Press, 1978.

Gardner, Michael. *Harry Truman and Civil Rights: Moral Courage and Political Risks.* Carbondale: Southern Illinois University Press, 2002.

Gelfand, Mark. *Nation of Cities: The Federal Government and Urban America, 1933–1965.* New York: Oxford University Press, 1975.

Gibson, Campbell, and Kay Jung. *Historical Census Statistics on Population Totals by Race, 1790 to 1990, and by Hispanic Origin 1970 to 1990, for Large Cities and Other Urban Places in the United States.* Washington, D.C.: Population Division, U.S. Census Bureau, 2005.

Gilmore, Glenda. *Defying Dixie: The Radical Roots of Civil Rights, 1919–1950.* New York: W. W. Norton, 2008.

Gleason, Philip. "Americans All: World War II and the Shaping of American Identity." *Review of Politics* 43, no. 4 (October 1981): 483–518.

Glennon, Robert Jerome. "The Role of Law in the Civil Rights Movement: The Montgomery Bus Boycott, 1955–1957." *Law and History Review* 9, no. 1 (Spring 1991): 59–112.

Godsil, Rachel D. "Race Nuisance: The Politics of Law in the Jim Crow Era." *Michigan Law Review* 105, no. 3 (December 2006): 505–58.

Goluboff, Risa. "Lawyers, Law, and the New Civil Rights History." *Harvard Law Review* 126, no. 8 (2013): 2312–35.

———. "'Let Economic Equality Take Care of Itself': The NAACP, Labor Litigation, and the Making of Civil Rights in the 1940s." *UCLA Law Review* 52 (June 2005): 1393–486.

———. *The Lost Promise of Civil Rights.* Cambridge, Mass.: Harvard University Press, 2007.

———. "The Thirteenth Amendment and the Lost Origins of Civil Rights." *Duke Law Journal* 50, no. 6 (April 2001): 1609–85.

Gonda, Jeffrey D. "Litigating Racial Justice at the Grassroots: The Shelley Family, Black Realtors, and *Shelley v. Kraemer* (1948)." *Journal of Supreme Court History* 39, no. 3 (November 2014): 329–46.

Gordon, Colin. *Mapping Decline: St. Louis and the Fate of the American City.* Philadelphia: University of Pennsylvania Press, 2008.

Gotham, Kevin Fox. "Racialization and the State: The Housing Act of 1934 and the Creation of the Federal Housing Administration." *Sociological Perspectives* 43, no. 2 (Summer 2000): 291–317.

———. "Urban Space, Restrictive Covenants and the Origins of Racial Residential Segregation in a US City, 1900–50." *International Journal of Urban and Regional Research* 24, no. 3 (September 2000): 616–33.

Grant, Keneshia N. "Relocation and Realignment: How the Great Migration Changed the Face of the Democratic Party." Ph.D. dissertation, Syracuse University, 2014.

Green, Constance McLaughlin. *The Secret City: A History of Race Relations in the Nation's Capital.* Princeton: Princeton University Press, 1967.

Greenberg, Jack. *Crusaders in the Courts: How a Dedicated Band of Lawyers Fought for the Civil Rights Revolution.* New York: Basic Books, 1994.

Gronlund, Mimi Clark. *Supreme Court Justice Tom C. Clark: A Life of Service*. Austin: University of Texas Press, 2010.

Gross, Ariela J. "From the Streets to the Courts: Doing Grassroots History of the Civil Rights Era." *Texas Law Review* 90, no. 5 (2012): 1233–57.

———. *What Blood Won't Tell: A History of Race on Trial in America*. Cambridge, Mass.: Harvard University Press, 2008.

Grossman, James. *Land of Hope: Chicago, Black Southerners, and the Great Migration*. Chicago: University of Chicago Press, 1989.

Gullan, Harold. *The Upset That Wasn't: Harry S Truman and the Crucial Election of 1948*. Chicago: Ivan R. Dee, 1998.

Hall, Jacquelyn Dowd. "The Long Civil Rights Movement and the Political Uses of the Past." *Journal of American History* 91, no. 4 (March 2005): 1233–63.

Haney-Lopez, Ian. *White by Law: The Legal Constructions of Race*. New York: New York University Press, 1996.

Harris, Cheryl I. "Whiteness as Property." *Harvard Law Review* 106 (June 1993): 1707–91.

Hart, Justin. "Making Democracy Safe for the World: Race, Propaganda, and the Transformation of U.S. Foreign Policy during World War II." *Pacific Historical Review* 73, no. 1 (February 2004): 49–84.

Helper, Rose. *Racial Policies and Practices of Real Estate Brokers*. Minneapolis: University of Minnesota Press, 1969.

Henkin, Louis. "*Shelley v. Kraemer*: Notes for a Revised Opinion." *University of Pennsylvania Law Review* 110, no. 4 (February 1962): 473–505.

Hine, Darlene Clark. "Black Professionals and Race Consciousness: Origins of the Civil Rights Movement, 1890–1950." *Journal of American History* 89, no. 4 (March 2003): 1279–94.

———. *Black Victory: The Rise and Fall of the White Primary in Texas*. Columbia, Mo.: University of Missouri Press, 2003. First published 1979.

Hirsch, Arnold. "Containment on the Home Front: Race and Federal Housing Policy from the New Deal to the Cold War." *Journal of Urban History* 26, no. 2 (January 2000): 158–89.

———. *Making the Second Ghetto: Race and Housing in Chicago, 1940–1960*. Chicago: University of Chicago Press, 1983.

———. "With or Without Jim Crow: Black Residential Segregation in the United States." In *Urban Policy in Twentieth-Century America*, edited by Arnold Hirsch and Raymond Mohl, 65–99. New Brunswick, N.J.: Rutgers University Press, 1993.

Hosokawa, Bill. *JACL: In Quest of Justice*. New York: William Morrow, 1982.

Hovenkamp, Herbert. "Social Science and Segregation before Brown." *Duke Law Journal* 1985, no. 3 (June–September 1985): 624–72.

Hull, N. E. H. *Roscoe Pound and Karl Llewellyn: Searching for an American Jurisprudence*. Chicago: University of Chicago Press, 1997.

Irons, Peter. *The Courage of Their Convictions: Sixteen Americans Who Fought Their Way to the Supreme Court.* New York: Penguin Books, 1988.

Jackson, John P., Jr. "Creating a Consensus: Psychologists, the Supreme Court, and School Desegregation, 1952–1955." *Journal of Social Issues* 54 (1998): 143–77.

———. *Science for Segregation: Race, Law, and the Case against Brown v. Board of Education.* New York: New York University Press, 2005.

———. *Social Scientists for Social Justice: Making the Case against Segregation.* New York: New York University Press, 2001.

Jackson, Kenneth T. *Crabgrass Frontier: The Suburbanization of the United States.* New York: Oxford University Press, 1985.

———. "Race, Ethnicity, and Real Estate Appraisal: The Home Owners Loan Corporation and the Federal Housing Administration." *Journal of Urban History* 6 (August 1980): 419–52.

Jackson, Lawrence P. *The Indignant Generation: A Narrative History of African American Writers and Critics, 1934–1960.* Princeton: Princeton University Press, 2011.

Jackson, Walter A. *Gunnar Myrdal and America's Conscience: Social Engineering and Racial Liberalism, 1938–1987.* Chapel Hill: University of North Carolina Press, 1990.

James, Rawn, Jr. *Root and Branch: Charles Hamilton Houston, Thurgood Marshall, and the Struggle to End Segregation.* New York: Bloomsbury Press, 2010.

Janken, Kenneth Robert. *White: The Biography of Walter White, Mr. NAACP.* New York: New Press, 2003.

Johnson, John W. *American Legal Culture, 1908–1940.* Westport, Conn.: Greenwood Press, 1981.

Johnson, Whittington B. "The Vinson Court and Racial Segregation, 1946–1953." *Journal of Negro History* 63, no. 3 (July 1978): 220–30.

Jonas, Gilbert. *Freedom's Sword: The NAACP and the Struggle against Racism in America.* New York: Routledge, 2007.

Jones, Faustine C. "Black Americans and the City: A Historical Survey." *Journal of Negro Education* 42, no. 3 (1973): 261–82.

Jones-Correa, Michael. "The Origins and Diffusion of Racial Restrictive Covenants." *Political Science Quarterly* 115, no. 4 (Winter 2000/2001): 541–68.

Juhnke, William E., Jr. "Creating a New Charter of Freedom: The Organization and Operation of the President's Committee on Civil Rights, 1946–1948." Ph.D. dissertation, University of Kansas, 1974.

Kalman, Laura. *Legal Realism at Yale, 1927–1960.* Chapel Hill: University of North Carolina Press, 1986.

Kamp, Allen R. "The History behind *Hansberry v. Lee.*" *U.C. Davis Law Review* 20 (1986/87): 481–99.

Karabell, Zachary. *The Last Campaign: How Harry Truman Won the 1948 Election.* New York: Knopf, 2000.

Kelleher, Daniel T. "The History of the St. Louis NAACP, 1914–1955." M.A. thesis, Southern Illinois University Edwardsville, 1969.

Kelley, Robin D. G. *Race Rebels: Culture, Politics, and the Black Working Class*. New York: Free Press, 1994.

Kellogg, Peter J. "Civil Rights Consciousness in the 1940s." *Historian* 42, no. 1 (November 1979): 18–41.

Kennedy, David. *Freedom from Fear: The American People in Depression and War, 1929–1945*. New York: Oxford University Press, 2005.

Kennedy, Randall L. "Martin Luther King's Constitution: A Legal History of the Montgomery Bus Boycott." *Yale Law Journal* 98 (1989): 999–1067.

———. "A Reply to Philip Elman." *Harvard Law Review* 100, no. 8 (June 1987): 1938–48.

Keyssar, Alexander. *The Right to Vote: The Contested History of Democracy in the United States*. New York: Basic Books, 2000.

Kimble, John. "Insuring Inequality: The Role of the Federal Housing Administration in the Urban Ghettoization of African Americans." *Law and Social Inquiry* 32, no. 2 (Spring 2007): 399–434.

Klarman, Michael. *From Jim Crow to Civil Rights: The Supreme Court and the Struggle for Racial Equality*. New York: Oxford University Press, 2004.

Klinkner, Philip A., and Rogers M. Smith. *The Unsteady March: The Rise and Decline of Racial Equality in America*. Chicago: University of Chicago Press, 1999.

Kluger, Richard. *Simple Justice: The History of* Brown v. Board of Education *and Black America's Struggle for Equality*. New York: Knopf, 1975.

Koppes, Clayton R., and Gregory D. Black. "Blacks, Loyalty, and Motion-Picture Propaganda in World War II." *Journal of American History* 73, no. 2 (September 1986): 383–406.

Korstad, Robert. *Civil Rights Unionism: Tobacco Workers and the Struggle for Democracy in the Mid-Twentieth Century South*. Chapel Hill: University of North Carolina Press, 2003.

Korstad, Robert, and Nelson Lichtenstein. "Opportunities Found and Lost: Labor, Radicals, and the Early Civil Rights Movement." *Journal of American History* 75 (December 1988): 786–811.

Kruse, Kevin. *White Flight: Atlanta and the Making of Modern Conservatism*. Princeton: Princeton University Press, 2005.

Kurashige, Scott. *The Shifting Grounds of Race: Black and Japanese Americans in the Making of Multiethnic Los Angeles*. Princeton: Princeton University Press, 2008.

Kusmer, Kenneth L. *A Ghetto Takes Shape: Black Cleveland, 1870–1930*. Urbana: University of Illinois Press, 1976.

Lamb, Charles M., and Adam W. Nye. "Fair Housing Policy and the Federal Housing Administration: Policy Responsiveness and Administrative Implementation." *Buffalo Legal Studies Research Paper No. 2009–11* (April 2009): 1–45.

Lang, Clarence. *Grassroots at the Gateway: Class Politics and Black Freedom Struggle in St. Louis, 1936–75*. Ann Arbor: University of Michigan Press, 2009.

Lassiter, Matt. *Silent Majority: Suburban Politics in the Sunbelt South*. Princeton: Princeton University Press, 2006.

Lau, Peter F., ed. *From the Grassroots to the Supreme Court: Brown v. Board of Education and American Democracy*. Durham, N.C.: Duke University Press, 2004.

Lauren, Paul Gordon. "First Principles of Racial Equality: History and the Politics and Diplomacy of Human Rights Provisions in the United Nations Charter." *Human Rights Quarterly* 5, no. 1 (February 1983): 1–26.

Lawson, Steven F. *Running for Freedom: Civil Rights and Black Politics in America since 1941*. New York: McGraw-Hill, 1991.

———, ed. *To Secure These Rights: The Report of Harry S Truman's Committee on Civil Rights*. Boston: Bedford/St. Martins, 2004.

Layton, Azza Salama. *International Politics and Civil Rights Policies in the United States, 1941–1960*. New York: Cambridge University Press, 2000.

Lee, Sophia Z. "Hotspots in a Cold War: The NAACP's Postwar Workplace Constitutionalism, 1948–1964." *Law and History Review* 26, no. 2 (Summer 2008): 327–77.

———. *The Workplace Constitution from the New Deal to the New Right*. New York: Cambridge University Press, 2014.

Lefberg, Irving F. "Chief Justice Vinson and the Politics of Desegregation." *Emory Law Journal* 24, no. 2 (Spring 1975): 243–312.

"Legal Realism and the Race Question: Some Realism about Realism on Race Relations." *Harvard Law Review* 108, no. 7 (May 1995): 1607–24.

Lemann, Nicholas. *Promised Land: The Great Black Migration and How It Changed America*. New York: A. A. Knopf, 1991.

Lentz-Smith, Adriane. *Freedom Struggles: African Americans and World War I*. Cambridge, Mass.: Harvard University Press, 2009.

Levine, David Allan. *Internal Combustion: The Races in Detroit, 1915–1926*. Westport, Conn.: Greenwood Press, 1976.

Lockwood, Bert B., Jr. "The United Nations Charter and United States Civil Rights Litigation: 1946–1955." *Iowa Law Review* 69 (1983/84): 901–56.

Lovell, George I. *This Is Not Civil Rights: Discovering Rights Talk in 1939 America*. Chicago: University of Chicago Press, 2012.

Lucander, David. *Winning the War for Democracy: The March on Washington Movement, 1941–1946*. Urbana: University of Illinois Press, 2014.

Lyman, Stanford M. *The Black American in Sociological Thought*. New York: G. P. Putnam's Sons, 1972.

———. "Gunnar Myrdal's *An American Dilemma* after a Half Century: Critics and Anticritics." *International Journal of Politics, Culture, and Society* 12, no. 2 (Winter 1998): 327–89.

Mack, Kenneth W. "Bringing the Law Back into the History of the Civil Rights Movement." *Law and History Review* 27, no. 3 (Fall 2009): 657–70.

———. "Civil Rights History: The Old and the New." *Harvard Law Review* 126, no.8 (2013): 258–61.

———. "Law and Mass Politics in the Making of the Civil Rights Lawyer, 1931–1941." *Journal of American History* 93, no. 1 (June 2006): 37–62.

———. "Racial Uplift, Professional Identity and the Transformation of Civil Rights Lawyering and Politics, 1920–1940." Ph.D. dissertation, Princeton University, 2005.

———. *Representing the Race: The Creation of the Civil Rights Lawyer.* Cambridge, Mass.: Harvard University Press, 2012.

———. "Rethinking Civil Rights Lawyering and Politics in the Era before Brown." *Yale Law Journal* 115 (2005): 256–354.

Martin, Charles H. "Internationalizing 'The American Dilemma': The Civil Rights Congress and the 1951 Genocide Petition to the United Nations." *Journal of American Ethnic History* 16, no. 4 (Summer 1997): 35–61.

Massey, Douglas, and Nancy Denton. *American Apartheid: Segregation and the Making of the Underclass.* Cambridge, Mass.: Harvard University Press, 1993.

McCann, Michael W. "Reform Litigation on Trial." *Law & Social Inquiry* 17, no. 4 (Autumn 1992): 715–43.

McCoy, Donald R. *The Presidency of Harry S Truman.* Lawrence: University Press of Kansas, 1984.

McCoy, Donald, and Richard Ruetten. *Quest and Response: Minority Rights and the Truman Administration.* Lawrence: University Press of Kansas, 1973.

McCoy, Donald, Richard Ruetten, and J. R. Fuchs, eds. *Conference of Scholars on the Truman Administration and Civil Rights.* Independence, Mo.: Harry S Truman Library Institute for National and International Affairs, 1968.

McCullough, David. *Truman.* New York: Simon and Schuster, 1992.

McGuire, Phillip. *He, Too, Spoke for Democracy: Judge Hastie, World War II, and the Black Soldier.* New York: Greenwood Press, 1988.

McIntyre, John F. "The Status of Racial Covenants and Restrictive Devices in Washington, D.C. in the Three Years Following the Supreme Court Decision of 1948." M.A. thesis, Catholic University of America, 1954.

McKenzie, Evan. *Privatopia: Homeowner Associations and the Rise of Residential Private Government.* New Haven: Yale University Press, 1994.

McMahon, Kevin J. *Reconsidering Roosevelt on Race: How the Presidency Paved the Road to Brown.* Chicago: University of Chicago Press, 2004.

McNeil, Genna Rae. *Groundwork: Charles Hamilton Houston and the Struggle for Civil Rights.* Philadelphia: University of Pennsylvania Press, 1983.

Meier, August, and Elliott Rudwick. *Black Detroit and the Rise of the UAW.* New York: Oxford University Press, 1979.

Meyer, Stephen Grant. *As Long as They Don't Move Next Door: Segregation and Racial Conflict in American Neighborhoods*. Lanham, MD: Rowman and Littlefield, 2000.

Miller, Loren. *The Petitioners: The Story of the Supreme Court of the United States and the Negro*. Cleveland: Meridian Books, 1966.

Mody, Sanjay. "*Brown* Footnote Eleven in Historical Context: Social Science and the Supreme Court's Quest for Legitimacy." *Stanford Law Review* 54, no. 4 (April 2002): 793–829.

Mohl, Raymond A. "The Second Ghetto and the 'Infiltration Theory' in Urban Real Estate, 1940–1960." In *Urban Planning and the African American Community: In the Shadows*, edited by June Manning Thomas and Marsha Ritzdorf, 58–74. Thousand Oaks, Calif.: Sage Publications, 1997.

Moore, Jacqueline M. *Leading the Race: The Transformation of the Black Elite in the Nation's Capital, 1880–1920*. Charlottesville: University Press of Virginia, 1999.

NeJaime, Douglas. "Cause Lawyers inside the State." *Fordham Law Review* 81, no. 2 (November 2012): 649–704.

Nelson, Bruce. "Organized Labor and the Struggle for Black Equality in Mobile during World War II." *Journal of American History* 80, no. 3 (December 1993): 952–88.

Newby, I. A. *Challenge to the Court: Social Scientists and the Defense of Segregation 1954–1966*. Baton Rouge: Louisiana State University Press, 1967.

Nicolaides, Becky. *My Blue Heaven: Life and Politics in the Working-Class Suburbs of Los Angeles, 1920–1965*. Chicago: University of Chicago Press, 2002.

Osofsky, Gilbert. *Harlem: The Making of a Ghetto, Negro New York, 1890–1930*. New York: Harper and Row, 1966.

Owens, Lee Edward. "*Shelley v. Kraemer* and Its Impact on Racial Residential Segregation." M.A. thesis, University of California, 1952.

Pascoe, Peggy. "Miscegenation Law, Court Cases, and Ideologies of 'Race' in Twentieth-Century America." *Journal of American History* 20 (June 1996): 44–69.

———. *What Comes Naturally: Miscegenation Law and the Making of Race in America*. New York: Oxford University Press, 2009.

Payne, Charles. *I've Got the Light of Freedom: The Organizing Tradition and the Mississippi Freedom Struggle*. Berkeley: University of California Press, 1995.

Pearlman, Lauren. "Home Rules: Local Activism, Federal Oversight, and the Struggle for Control of the Nation's Capital, 1960–1980." Ph.D. dissertation, Yale University, 2013.

Peretti, Terri. "Constructing the State Action Doctrine, 1940–1990." *Law and Social Inquiry* 35, no. 2 (Spring 2010): 273–310.

Peterson, Sarah Jo. *Planning the Home Front: Building Bombers and Communities at Willow Run*. Chicago: University of Chicago Press, 2013.

Plotkin, Wendy. "Deeds of Mistrust: Race, Housing, and Restrictive Covenants in Chicago, 1900–1953." Ph.D. dissertation, University of Illinois at Chicago, 1999.

Power, Garrett. "Apartheid Baltimore Style: The Residential Segregation Ordinances of 1910–1913." *Maryland Law Review* 42, no. 2 (1983): 289–328.

Prifogle, Emily A. "Law and Local Activism: Uncovering the Civil Rights History of *Chambers v. Mississippi*." *California Law Review* 101, no. 2 (2013): 445–520.

Pritchett, Wendell E. *Robert Clifton Weaver and the American City: The Life and Times of an Urban Reformer*. Chicago: University of Chicago Press, 2008.

———. "*Shelley v. Kraemer*: Racial Liberalism and the U.S. Supreme Court." In *Civil Rights Stories*, edited by Myriam Gilles and Risa L. Goluboff, 5–23. New York: Foundation Press, 2008.

Purcell, Edward A., Jr. "American Jurisprudence between the Wars: Legal Realism and the Crisis of Democratic Theory." *American Historical Review* 75, no. 2 (December 1969): 424–46.

———. *The Crisis of Democratic Theory: Scientific Naturalism and the Problem of Value*. Lexington: University Press of Kentucky, 1973.

Radford, Gail. *Modern Housing for America: Policy Struggles in the New Deal Era*. Chicago: University of Chicago Press, 1996.

Ransby, Barbara. *Ella Baker and the Black Freedom Movement*. Chapel Hill: University of North Carolina Press, 2003.

Rice, Roger L. "Residential Segregation by Law, 1910–1917." *Journal of Southern History* 34, no. 2 (May 1968): 179–99.

Robinson, Greg, and Toni Robinson. "*Korematsu* and Beyond: Japanese Americans and the Origins of Strict Scrutiny." *Law and Contemporary Problems* 68 (Spring 2005): 29–55.

Robinson III, Spottswood W. "No Tea for the Feeble: Two Perspectives on Charles Hamilton Houston." *Howard Law Journal* 20 (1977): 1–9.

Rose, Carol M. "Property Stories: *Shelley v. Kraemer*." In *Property Stories*, edited by Gerald Korngold and Andrew P. Morriss, 169–200. New York: Foundation Press, 2004.

Rosen, Mark D. "Was *Shelley v. Kraemer* Incorrectly Decided? Some New Answers." *California Law Review* 95, no. 2 (April 2007): 451–512.

Rosen, Paul L. *The Supreme Court and Social Science*. Urbana: University of Illinois Press, 1972.

Rosenberg, Gerald N. *The Hollow Hope: Can Courts Bring About Social Change?* Chicago: University of Chicago Press, 1991.

Ross, Irwin. *The Loneliest Campaign: The Truman Victory of 1948*. New York: New American Library, 1968.

Rubenstein, William B. "Divided We Litigate: Addressing Disputes among Group Members and Lawyers in Civil Rights Campaigns." *Yale Law Journal* 106, no. 6 (April 1997): 1623–81.

St. Clair, James E., and Linda C. Gugin. *Chief Justice Fred M. Vinson of Kentucky: A Political Biography*. Lexington: University Press of Kentucky, 2002.

Sander, Richard H. "Housing Segregation and Housing Integration: The Diverging Paths of Urban America." *University of Miami Law Review* 52, no. 4 (July 1998): 977–1010.

Satter, Beryl. *Family Properties: Race, Real Estate, and the Exploitation of Black Urban America*. New York: Metropolitan Books, 2009.

Savage, Barbara Dianne. *Broadcasting Freedom: Radio, War, and the Politics of Race, 1938–1948*. Chapel Hill: University of North Carolina Press, 1999.

Schelling, Thomas C. "Models of Segregation." *American Economic Review* 59, no. 2 (May 1969): 488–93.

Schlegel, John Henry. *American Legal Realism and Empirical Social Science*. Chapel Hill: University of North Carolina Press, 1995.

Schmidt, Benno C. "Principle and Prejudice: The Supreme Court and Race in the Progressive Era. Part 1: The Heyday of Jim Crow." *Columbia Law Review* 82, no. 3 (April 1982): 444–524.

Schmidt, Christopher W. "Freedom Comes Only from the Law: The Debate over Law's Capacity and the Making of *Brown v. Board of Education*." *Utah Law Review* 2008, no. 4 (2008): 1493–560.

Schull, Steven A. *American Civil Rights Policy from Truman to Clinton: The Role of Presidential Leadership*. Armonk, N.Y.: M. E. Sharpe, 1999.

Scott, Daryl Michael. *Contempt and Pity: Social Policy and the Image of the Damaged Black Psyche, 1880–1996*. Chapel Hill: University of North Carolina Press, 1997.

Self, Robert. *American Babylon: Race and the Struggle for Postwar Oakland*. Princeton: Princeton University Press, 2003.

Sharfstein, Daniel J. *The Invisible Line: Three American Families and the Secret Journey from Black to White*. New York: Penguin Press, 2011.

Sherman, Richard B. *The Republican Party and Black American from McKinley to Hoover, 1896–1933*. Charlottesville: University Press of Virginia, 1973.

Shockley, Megan Taylor. *We, Too, Are Americans: African American Women in Detroit and Richmond, 1940–54*. Urbana: University of Illinois Press, 2004.

Silber, Norman I. *With All Deliberate Speed: The Life of Philip Elman, an Oral History Memoir*. Ann Arbor: University of Michigan Press, 2004.

Singh, Nikhil Pal. *Black Is a Country: Race and the Unfinished Struggle for Democracy*. Cambridge, Mass.: Harvard University Press, 2004.

Sitkoff, Harvard. "Harry Truman and the Election of 1948: The Coming of Age of Civil Rights in American Politics." *Journal of Southern History* 37, no. 4 (November 1971): 597–616.

———. *A New Deal for Blacks: The Emergence of Civil Rights as a National Issue*. New York: Oxford University Press, 1978.

———. "Racial Militancy and Interracial Violence in the Second World War." *Journal of American History* 58, no. 3 (December 1971): 661–81.

Sklaroff, Lauren Rebecca. "Constructing G.I. Joe Louis: Cultural Solutions to the 'Negro Problem' during World War II." *Journal of American History* 89, no. 3 (December 2002): 958–82.

Skrentny, John David. "The Effect of the Cold War on African-American Civil Rights: America and the World Audience, 1945–1968." *Theory and Society* 27, no. 2 (April 1998): 237–85.

Smith, J. Clay. *Emancipation: The Making of the Black Lawyer, 1844–1944*. Philadelphia: University of Pennsylvania Press, 1993.

Spear, Allan H. *Black Chicago: The Making of a Negro Ghetto, 1890–1920*. Chicago: University of Chicago Press, 1967.

Stave, Bruce M., and Michele Palmer. *Witnesses to Nuremberg: An Oral History of American Participants at the War Crimes Trials*. New York: Twayne Publishers, 1998.

Strum, Philippa. *Mendez v. Westminster: School Desegregation and Mexican-American Rights*. Lawrence: University Press of Kansas, 2010.

Sugrue, Thomas. "Crabgrass-Roots Politics: Race, Rights, and the Reaction against Liberalism in the Urban North." *Journal of American History* 82, no. 2 (September 1995): 551–78.

———. *Origins of the Urban Crisis: Race and Inequality in Postwar Detroit*. Princeton: Princeton University Press, 1996.

———. *Sweet Land of Liberty: The Forgotten Struggle for Civil Rights in the North*. New York: Random House, 2008.

Sullivan, Patricia. *Days of Hope: Race and Democracy in the New Deal Era*. Chapel Hill: University of North Carolina Press, 1996.

———. *Lift Every Voice: The NAACP and the Making of the Civil Rights Movement*. New York: New Press, 2009.

Terry, Brandon Michael. "Which Way to Memphis? Civil Rights in Historiography and Political Theory." Ph.D. dissertation, Yale University, 2012.

Theoharis, Jeanne, and Komozi Woodard, eds. *Groundwork: Local Black Freedom Movements in America*. New York: New York University Press, 2005.

Thomas, June Manning. *Redevelopment and Race: Planning a Finer City in Postwar Detroit*. Baltimore: Johns Hopkins University Press, 1997.

Thompson, Heather Ann. *Whose Detroit? Politics, Labor, and Race in a Modern American City*. Ithaca: Cornell University Press, 2001.

Tobey, Ronald, Charles Wetherell, and Jay Brigham. "Moving Out and Settling In: Residential Mobility, Home Ownership, and the Public Enframing of Citizenship, 1921–1950." *American Historical Review* 95, no. 5 (December 1990): 1395–1422.

Topping, Simon. "'Supporting Our Friends and Defeating Our Enemies': Militancy and Nonpartisanship in the NAACP, 1936–1948." *Journal of African American History* 89, no. 1 (Winter 2004): 17–35.

Tushnet, Mark V. *Making Civil Rights Law: Thurgood Marshall and the Supreme Court, 1936–1961*. New York: Oxford University Press, 1994.

———. *The NAACP's Legal Strategy against Segregated Education, 1925–1950*. Chapel Hill: University of North Carolina Press, 1987.

———. "*Shelley v. Kraemer* and Theories of Equality." *New York Law School Law Review* 33, no. 3 (1988): 383–408.

Tuttle, William. *Race Riot: Chicago in the Red Summer of 1919*. New York: Athenaeum, 1970.

Twining, William. *Karl Llewellyn and the Realist Movement*. London: Willmer Brothers, 1973.

Urofsky, Melvin I. *Division and Discord: The Supreme Court under Stone and Vinson, 1941–1953*. Columbia: University of South Carolina Press, 1997.

Vose, Clement. *Caucasians Only: The Supreme Court, the NAACP, and the Restrictive Covenant Cases*. Berkeley: University of California Press, 1959.

———. "The National Consumers' League and the Brandeis Brief." *Midwest Journal of Political Science* 1, no. 3/4 (November 1957): 267–90.

Wallentine, Kenneth. "Margaret Bush Wilson: Advocate, Counselor, Friend." *BYU Journal of Public Law* 4, no. 2 (1990): 207–18.

Ward, Jason Morgan. *Defending White Democracy: The Making of a Segregationist Movement and the Remaking of Racial Politics, 1936–1965*. Chapel Hill: University of North Carolina Press, 2011.

Ware, Gilbert. *William Hastie: Grace under Pressure*. New York: Oxford University Press, 1984.

Ware, Leland B. "Invisible Walls: An Examination of the Legal Strategy of the Restrictive Covenant Cases." *Washington University Law Quarterly* 67 (1989): 737–72.

Wasby, Stephen L. "How Planned Is 'Planned Litigation'?" *American Bar Foundation Research Journal* 9, no. 1 (Winter 1984): 83–138.

———. *Race Relations Litigation in an Age of Complexity*. Charlottesville: University of Virginia Press, 1995.

Wechsler, Herbert. "Toward Neutral Principles of Constitutional Law." *Harvard Law Review* 73, no. 1 (November 1959): 1–35.

Weiss, Marc A. *The Rise of the Community Builders: The American Real Estate Industry and Urban Land Planning*. New York: Columbia University Press, 1987.

Weiss, Nancy J. *Farewell to the Party of Lincoln: Black Politics in the Age of FDR*. Princeton: Princeton University Press, 1983.

Wiecek, William M. *The Birth of the Modern Constitution: The United States Supreme Court, 1941–1953*. New York: Cambridge University Press, 2006.

Wiese, Andrew. "Black Housing, White Finance: African American Housing and Home Ownership in Evanston, Illinois, before 1940." *Journal of Social History* 33, no. 2 (Winter 1999): 429–60.

———. *Places of Their Own: African American Suburbanization in the Twentieth Century*. Chicago: University of Chicago Press, 2004.

Wilkerson, Isabel. *The Warmth of Other Suns: The Epic Story of America's Great Migration*. New York: Random House, 2010.

Williams, Chad L. *Torchbearers of Democracy: African American Soldiers in the World War I Era*. Chapel Hill: University of North Carolina Press, 2010.

Williams, Juan. *Thurgood Marshall: American Revolutionary*. New York: Times Books, 1998.

Williams, Rhonda Y. *Politics of Public Housing: Black Women's Struggles against Urban Inequality.* New York: Oxford University Press, 2004.

Wilson, Margaret Bush. *Twigs from the Bush.* Chicago: American Bar Association, 2009.

Wright, Gwendolyn. *Building the Dream: A Social History of Housing in America.* New York: Pantheon Books, 1981.

Index

Brown, Oscar, 30

Brown-Nagin, Tomiko, 233 (n. 9)

Brown v. Board of Education, 8–9, 204, 213, 215

Buchanan v. Warley, 4, 134, 136, 248 (n. 73)

Burton, Harold, 123, 175, 183–84

Bush, James T., 97, 234 (n. 17), 251 (n. 94); Citizens Committee and, 235 (n. 36); on housing discrimination, 33; Marshall and, 132–33; profit realized by, 66–67; Real Estate Brokers Association and, 67–68; in *Shelley,* 58–61; Vaughn and, 233 (n. 16); as witness, 63

Carter, Robert, 144, 213

Caucasians Only (Vose), 8

Cayton, Horace, 125

Certiorari, 129

"Change of neighborhood" claims, 107–10

Chapman, Oscar, 169

Chicago, 5; housing shortage in, 21; NAACP conference in, 103–4, 105–11; restrictive covenants in, 30; violence in, housing discrimination and, 23

Children's Bureau of Social Service Administration, 162

China, 224 (n. 1)

Chockley, Lloyd, 89–90, 93, 94

Chouteau-Lindell Improvement Association, 239 (n. 92)

CIO. *See* Congress of Industrial Organizations

Citizens Committee (St. Louis), 68, 133, 235 (n. 36)

Civil rights: Cold War and, 158; covenant cases in history of, 8–14; in electoral politics, 159; invigoration of, after *Shelley,* 208–9, 212–13; legal activism and, 56–57; lobby, 157, 158, 159, 161–63; World War II and, 158

Civil Rights Act of 1866, 62, 100, 130, 187, 188

Civil Rights Section (Justice Department), 163–64, 168

Clark, Kenneth, 215

Clark, Tom C., 154, 157, 162–67, 171, 210–11, 255 (n. 13)

Clarke, Thurmond, 55–56, 85–88

Clifford, Clark, 166

CLSA. *See* Commission on Law and Social Action

Cold War, 157–58

Coleman, William, Jr., 215

Collaborative legal activism, 56–58, 232 (n. 4)

Commission on Law and Social Action (CLSA), 151, 213, 250 (n. 84)

Communication networks, in litigation, 57–58

Conditions. *See* Housing conditions

Congregation of Christian Churches, 253 (n. 110)

Congress of Industrial Organizations (CIO), 150, 151, 213

Constitution, U.S., 62, 70, 74–75, 84–88, 100, 111, 130, 131, 260 (n. 77). *See also* Fourteenth Amendment

Construction, new: housing shortage and, 18; segregation and, 30–31

Contracts, 62, 70, 74–75, 107, 200

Cooper, John M., 81

Corrigan v. Buckley, 5–6; in appeal, 97, 99–100; constitutional challenges and, 103; contracts in, 70; effects of, 103; McGovney and, 74–75; social science and, 136–37; in strategy, 93–94

Creativity, in litigation, 57, 70–71

Crooks, James A., 91–92, 172, 180, 240 (n. 109), 259 (n. 59)

Cropley, Charles Elmore, 127

Crowe, Robert E., 86

Cummings, Scott, 264 (n. 29)

Damages, claims for, as alternative to covenants, 202–3

Dean, John P., 251 (n. 94)

Defense, of covenants, 88–95, 180–81

Democracy, 95–96, 105, 162–63, 171, 178, 190–91

Democratic Party, 60, 157, 162

Grand Lodge of Elks, 153

Grant, David, 66, 131, 132, 235 (n. 36)

Grant, Madison, 248 (n. 73)

Graves, Willis, 70–77, 87–88, 95–96, 98; Miller and, 238 (n. 83); NAACP and, 123; at NAACP Chicago conference, 107; racial classification and, 236 (n. 50); steps down, for Supreme Court appeal, 128

Great Depression, 17, 18

Griffith, D. W., 73

Gross, Ernest, 169

Habitability, housing shortage and, 17–18. *See also* Housing conditions

Hale, Robert Lee, 131, 136

Hansberry v. Lee, 6, 108–9, 240 (n. 1), 241 (n. 11)

Harvard Law Review, 78

Hastie, William H.: on constitutional approach, 111; in desegregation, 240 (n. 1); Marshall and, 173; in *Mays v. Burgess,* 6; on *Mays v. Burgess,* 103, 107, 109–10; *McGhee and,* 123; Miller and, 88; on Supreme Court, 134

Hayes, George E. C., 73

Hays, Arthur Garfield, 151

Heating, 32, 229 (n. 37)

Herriot, Charles T., 67

HHFA. *See* Housing and Home Finance Agency

Hirsch, Arnold, 23

Hirsch, Oscar, 257 (n. 30)

Hodge, Frederic, 46, 80

Hodge, Lena, 46–48, 50. See also *Hurd v. Hodge*

HOLC. *See* Home Owners' Loan Corporation

Home, concept of, 197–98

Homeowners' associations: after *Shelley,* 200, 201; as enforcers of covenants, 27; and federal advocacy, 160–61; Justice Department amicus brief and, 172; local government and, 239 (n. 92); in *McGhee v. Sipes,* 43–44; reactions of, to *Shelley* decision, 196–97, 198; in *Shelley,* 45–46;

and suits for damages to property values, 202

Home Owners' Loan Corporation (HOLC), 7, 8, 43

Home prices, 148, 202

Horne, Frank, 205

Housing and Home Finance Agency (HHFA), 161–62, 169, 212

Housing conditions: in appeals cases, 97, 100–101; housing shortage and, 17–18, 20–21; overcrowding and, 31–32; restrictive covenants as responsible for, 147

Housing discrimination: "blight" and, 21, 25; in Detroit, 23–24; effects of, 147; government agencies in, 22, 25; groups perpetuating, 21–22; methods of, 22–23; "objectionable use" doctrine and, 24–25; in public housing, 23–24; real estate industry in, 22, 24–25; social science and, 142–43; violence and, 23, 24. *See also* Discrimination; Segregation

Housing production, housing shortage and, 18

Housing shortage: African Americans and, 21–33; construction and, 18; in Detroit, 18; Great Depression and, 17; housing conditions and, 17–18, 20–21; numbers on, 19; overcrowding and, 31; renters and, 19, 20–21; restrictive covenants and, 25–31; in St. Louis, 18; urban expansion and, 18; vacancy rates and, 18–19; veterans and, 19–20; World War II and, 16

Houston, Charles Hamilton, 56, 70, 77–84, 88, 101; and advocates within federal government, 161–62; in appeal, 93, 95; background of, 73; certiorari petition by, 129; in collaborative legal activism, 57; on continuing civil rights struggle, 212; fees charged by, 235 (n. 38); on integration, 148; at NAACP Chicago conference, 107–8; racial classification and, 76–77; real estate brokers and, 66; selection of, for Supreme Court appeals, 128–29; social science and, 136, 137, 138; at Supreme Court, 179–80, 181; Urciolo and, 231 (n. 60), 236 (n. 62)

Howard University, 71, 78, 91, 122, 138, 173

Human rights, World War II and, 158

Humphrey, Norman, 75–76

Hundley v. Gorewitz, 108

Hurd, James, 39, 47, 50–51, 70, 230 (n. 55), 232 (n. 82)

Hurd, Mary, 39, 70

Hurd v. Hodge, 39–40, 46–51, 77–84; on appeal, 99–101; opposition in, 90–92; social science in, 137, 138, 146; at Supreme Court, 179–80, 187, 188; in Supreme Court decision-making, 183. *See also* Litigation; *Shelley v. Kraemer*

Identity: integration and, 198; neighborhood and, 198; racial categorization and, 40, 75, 237 (n. 68). *See also* Race

Indritz, Phineas, 130, 138, 151, 160–62, 179–80

Institutional fixity, 57

Insurance, mortgage, 28

Integration: as "blight," 25; effects of, 82–83; Federal Housing Administration and, 28; housing discrimination alongside, 37; in litigation, 82–84, 108, 109–10; loopholes against, 203–4; negative effects of, 148–49; neighborhood development and, 108; property values and, 148; racial identity and, 198; resistance to, 22, 43, 91–92, 195–204; in St. Louis, 58–69; *Shelley* decision and, 190–92; Urciolo and, 41; and validity of covenants, 62; violence and, 197. *See also* Segregation

Interest rates, 230 (n. 46)

Interior Department, 160–61, 162, 169

Jackson, Robert, 123, 174, 258 (n. 45)

Japanese American Citizens League (JACL), 151

Japanese Americans, internment of, 162

Jeffries, Edward J., Jr., 24

Jewish Labor Committee, 152

Jewish War Veterans, 152

Joachim, Walter, 44

Johnson, Reginald, 32

Jonas, Gilbert, 243 (n. 24)

Jones, D. Calhoun, 89

Jones, Fred, 33

Justice Department: advocates within, 160–61; as amicus curiae, 157–73; anticipation of response from, 155; Civil Rights Section of, 163–64, 168; Clark in, 162–67; criticism of, 172–73; Elman in, 160, 163, 167–70; involvement as precedent, 210–11; lobbying of, 157; NAACP and, 157, 160–62, 163–64; Perlman on behalf of, 156–58; *To Secure These Rights* document and, 164–66; Truman and, 166–67

Kahen, Harold, 74, 84, 111, 251 (n. 94)

Kansas City, 29, 199, 201

Kaufmann, Aloys, 18, 19

Kennedy, Randall L., 257 (n. 24)

Koerner, William K., 36, 61–65, 86, 96, 234 (n. 27)

Koob, Emil, 45

Kraemer, Fern, 46

Kraemer, Louis, 46

Ku Klux Klan, 199

Labor Department, 162, 256 (n. 15)

Lampkin, Daisy, 192

Lang, Clarence, 244 (n. 30)

Latinos, 206–7

Lawyers, 69–88

Legal Realism, 248 (n. 72)

Letts, F. Dickinson, 79, 83–84

Levy, Newman, 151

Litigation: appeal, 95–101; broadening of issues in, 79–80; communication networks in, 57–58; communities in, 58; constitutional considerations in, 62, 74–75, 84–88, 100, 111; creativity in, 57, 70–71; defense of covenants in, 88–95; discrimination argument in, 73–74; Fourteenth Amendment argument in, 74–75; institutional fixity in, 57; integration in, 82–83, 108, 109–10; law in, 57; lawyers in, 69–88; NAACP strategy for, 105–14;

narrowing of issues in, 79; neighborhood makeup in, 81–82; professional networks in, 69–88; public policy argument in, 73–74, 98, 100–101; racial classification in, 75–77, 79–81, 236 (n. 54); real estate agents in funding of, 65–66; segregation in, 91–92; strategic similarities across, 92–93; Supreme Court as ultimate goal of, 70, 86, 88, 95, 101–2; as tactic, criticism of, 194–95; themes in, 56–57; veterans in, 95; World War II in, 95–96; zoning in, 134–35. See also *Shelley v. Kraemer*

Llewellyn, Karl, 136

Lobby, civil rights: ACLU in, 163; Clark and, 162–63; federal government advocates in, 161; Justice Department and, 157; Truman and, 158, 159

"Long Civil Rights Era" paradigm, 8–9

Los Angeles: housing conditions in, 20; restrictive covenants in, 30–31; Sugar Hill neighborhood in, 55–56, 84–88, 124, 238 (n. 81)

Marcus Avenue Improvement Association (MAIA), 45–46, 50, 89

Marshall, Thurgood, 112–13; and advocates within federal government, 161–62; Bush and, 132–33; Chicago conference and, 103–6; Clark and, 164; on continuing civil rights struggle, 212; Graves and, 72; Houston and, 78; Justice Department and, 164; Miller and, 87, 128–29; on NAACP in 1947, 120; Perry on, 213–14; as raconteur, 259 (n. 56); realtors and, 66; in *Shelley* case, 173; on *Shelley* decision, 191; at Supreme Court, 178–79; on Supreme Court, 221; Tushnet on, 259 (n. 56); Vaughn and, 121, 126

Mays, Clara, 41

Mays v. Burgess, 103; analysis of, 107; in appeal, 99; criticism of, 109–10; Edgerton and, 100–101; Supreme Court denies hearing on, 6, 104

McCann, Michael, 226 (n. 18)

McCoy, Donald, 255 (n. 7)

McCune, Wesley, 258 (n. 38)

McDaniel, Hattie, 56

McGhee, Minnie, 37–39, 50, 51, 70, 189

McGhee, Orsel "Mac," 37–39, 50, 51, 56, 70, 189

McGhee v. Sipes, 37–39, 43–45, 71–77, 94, 95–96; on appeal, 97–99, 238 (n. 83); funding of, 132; lawyer selection for, 128–29; Miller in, 138; opposition in, 89–90; Peyser in, 144–45; as potential Supreme Court case, 122–24, 125–27, 130–31; race in, 79; social science in, 137, 138, 145–46; at Supreme Court, 178–79; Supreme Court agrees to hear, 127–28; team for, 144–45. *See also* Litigation; *Shelley v. Kraemer*

McGovney, D. O., 74–75, 84, 87, 94, 111, 240 (n. 108)

McLaurin v. Oklahoma State Regents, 211, 213, 214

Mendez v. Westminster, 143–44, 248 (n. 74)

Mexican Americans, 206–7

Michigan Chronicle (newspaper), 167, 192

Miller, Byron, 144, 145, 251 (n. 94)

Miller, Guy A., 73, 75, 76, 199, 200

Miller, Loren, 57, 70, 84–88; background of, 55; on continuing civil rights struggle, 208–9; on Edgerton, 101; fees received by, 235 (n. 38); Graves and, 238 (n. 83); Marshall and, 128–29; in *McGhee* case, 138; Moore and, 208; at NAACP Chicago conference, 107; National Bar Association and, 150–51; in *To Secure These Rights,* 164; selection of, for Supreme Court appeals, 128–29; at Supreme Court, 178–79; Vaughn and, 121; on veterans, 30–31

Ming, William R., 122, 251 (n. 94)

Mississippi, 198–99

Montgomery Bus Boycott, 9

Moore, Loring, 124–25, 208, 235 (n. 38), 251 (n. 94)

Morgan v. Virginia, 115, 248 (n. 74)

Morison Investment and Realty Company, 71

Perlman, Philip B., 156–58, 164, 165–66, 176–77, 210, 211

Perry, Marian Wynn: background of, 112; at Housing and Home Finance Agency, 242 (n. 20); Indritz and, 160; on Marshall, 213–14; National Lawyers Guild and, 151; New York conference and, 129; Peyser and, 144; social science and, 146, 149; and *Tovey v. Levy,* 124–25; Vaughn and, 126

Peyser, Annette, 143–45, 149, 214–15, 251 (nn. 93–94)

Pillsbury, Albert, 136

Plessy v. Ferguson, 12, 208, 211, 215

Prejudice and Property: An Historic Brief against Racial Covenants, 171–72, 258 (n. 38)

President's Committee on Civil Rights (PCCR), 117–18, 161, 163, 164–66

Pro bono work, 52, 235 (n. 38)

Professional associations, 22

Profit, 58–59, 63–64, 66–67

Property rights, 62–63, 200

Property values, 148, 202

Proskauer, Joseph, 151

Public housing: in Detroit, 23–24; housing discrimination in, 23–24

Publicity, 78

Public policy argument, 73–74, 98, 100–101, 168–70

Race: classification and determination of, 40, 75–77, 79–81, 98, 236 (n. 54); in underwriting guidelines, 28. *See also* Discrimination; Identity

Race or Mongrel (Schultz), 248 (n. 73)

Racial restrictive covenants. *See* Restrictive covenants

Racism, scientific antiracism and, 139–42, 145, 213, 249 (n. 74), 250 (nn. 81, 85). *See also* Discrimination; Segregation

Radin, Paul, 236 (n. 54)

Rankin, John, 198–99

"Rating of Location," 28

Real estate agents: African Americans in, 58–69, 63–64, 65–66, 233 (n. 9); as

exploitative, 66–67; funding of litigation by, 65–66; in housing discrimination, 22, 24–25, 228 (n. 20); profit by, 58–59, 63–64, 66–67; restrictive covenants authored by, 26; in *Shelley* case, 63–64, 67–68, 69

Real Estate Board of Atlanta, 172

Real Estate Board of New York, 228 (n. 20)

Real Estate Brokers' Association (REBA), 52, 67–68, 97, 133

REBA. *See* Real Estate Brokers' Association

Recusals, on Supreme Court, 174, 258 (n. 45)

Reed, Stanley, 123, 174, 175, 183, 258 (n. 45)

Renters: and deterioration of housing, 108; housing shortage and, 19, 20–21

Republican Party, 159, 175

Residents, as enforcers of restrictive covenants, 27, 42–51

Restrictive covenants, 1–8; breaking, 33–42, 65–66; cases on, history and, 8–14; consequences of, 110–11, 147–48; defense of, 88–95, 180–81; enforcement of, 42–52, 100; as flawed instruments, 62, 73, 82; growth in, 29–30; housing shortage and, 25–31; new, after *Shelley,* 200–202; origins of, 26; public policy argument against, 73–74, 98, 100–101, 168–70; zoning and, 4–5

Richardson, Scovel, 230 (n. 40)

"Rights consciousness," 7

Robinson, P. T., 67–68

Robinson, Spottswood, 62, 78, 130

Roosevelt, Franklin D., 7–8, 110, 117, 174

Rowe, Isabella, 15–16, 39, 40

Rowe, James H., 166

Rowe, Robert Harris, 15–16, 40

Ruetten, Richard, 255 (n. 7)

Rutledge, Wiley B., 123, 174, 175, 258 (n. 45)

St. Louis, 6–7; enforcement of covenants in, 45–46; housing conditions in, 20–21; housing shortage in, 18, 20–21; integration in, 58–69; new construction in, 31; restrictive covenants in, 30; *Shelley* case in, 34–37, 45–46; vacancy rates in, 19; veterans in, 20

Clarke and, 86; "conservative" bloc of, 175; in *Corrigan v. Buckley*, 70, 74, 103; covenant cases in, 174–82; defenses of covenants at, 180–81; final opinion of, 183–89; in *Hansberry v. Lee*, 109; hearings granted by, 127–28; Justice Department amicus brief and, 175–77; "liberal" wing of, 175; Miller and, 88; NAACP analysis of, 123, 134; preparations for, 120–35; recusals at, 174, 258 (n. 45); test cases for, 4, 50, 106–14, 122, 124, 126, 202, 230 (n. 40); Vaughn at, 177–78; as Vinson Court, 175–76; on zoning, 134–35

Surgeon General, 161, 162, 169

Swan, Edward, 125

Sweatt v. Painter, 211, 213, 214

Sweet, Ossian, 71

Taney, Roger, 259 (n. 63)

Test case, 4, 50, 106–14, 122, 124, 126, 202, 230 (n. 40)

Thirteenth Amendment, 70, 131, 177

To Secure These Rights (Presidential Committee on Civil Rights), 117–18, 164–66, 168, 256 (n. 23)

Tovey v. Levy, 124–25, 132, 139

Traynor, Roger, 86

Treaties, 170–71

Truman, Harry, 101, 117, 118, 155; African American electorate and, 159, 257 (n. 27); civil rights lobby and, 157–58; motivations of, 254 (n. 7); NAACP and, 119, 158, 161, 164, 166; role of, 166–67; Vinson appointment by, 174–75; White and, 164

Tushnet, Mark, 259 (n. 56)

Underwriting, FHA guidelines on, 27–28, 211–12

United Automobile Workers, 96

United Nations, 256 (n. 23)

United Nations Charter, 96, 101, 170–71

Urban expansion, housing shortage and, 18

Urban League, 30, 32

Urciolo, Raphael, 40–42, 52, 79, 130, 231 (n. 60), 236 (n. 62)

Vacancy rates, 18–19, 31

Vaughn, George L., 96, 97; background of, 59–60; Bush and, 61, 233 (n. 16); Miller and, 88; NAACP and, 120–22, 125–27, 131–32; in *Shelley*, 52, 59–65, 177–78, 246 (n. 61); at Supreme Court, 156

Velie, Lester, 21

Veterans: housing conditions of, 20; housing shortage and, 16, 19–20; in legal strategy, 95. *See also* World War II

Veterans Affairs, 8, 162, 212

Vinson, Frederick Moore, 174–75, 182–83, 184–89, 202–3

Vinson Court, 175–76

Violence: in Detroit, 24; as effect of integration, 148–49; housing discrimination and, 23, 24; reliance on, in segregation, 197

Vose, Clement, 8, 232 (n. 82)

Voting rights, 115–16

Wagner Housing Act, 7

Washington, D.C., 6; Adams Street cases in, 78–79; Bryant Street in, 38–42, 46–51; case in, 15–16; enforcement of covenants in, 46–51; homeowners' associations in, 27; housing conditions in, 32; housing shortage in, 20; *Hurd* case in, 39–40, 46–51, 77–84; M Street High School in, 73; North Capitol Citizens Association in, 90, 92; overcrowding in, 31; restrictive covenants in, 29, 30; vacancy rates in, 19; veterans in, 20

Washington Real Estate Board, 22

Water, 32, 229 (n. 37)

Waters, Ethel, 56

Weaver, Robert: Brandeis briefs and, 144, 148, 149, 251 (n. 94); at Chicago conference, 145; on covenants and discrimination, 26; Indritz and, 160; on integration, 110; in publicity campaign, 112; social science and, 125; in Sugar Hill cases, 87; in *To Secure These Rights*, 164

Weinberger, Andrew, 122

Weyand, Ruth, 144, 251 (n. 94)

White, Walter: and advocates within federal government, 161–62, 163; American Jewish Committee and, 151; on continuing civil rights movement, 209–10; on NAACP, 114; on *Shelley* decision, 191; on Sugar Hill cases, 238 (n. 81); Truman and, 116–17, 119, 164

Whites: as enforcers of restrictive covenants, 27, 42–51; reactions of, to *Shelley,* 196–98; in straw-party sales, 35–36

Wilkins, Roy, 192

Willer, Herman, 259 (n. 55)

Williams, Franklin, 113

Williams, John Bell, 199

Wirth, Louis, 144, 145, 149, 194–95, 251 (n. 94)

Wolverine Bar Association, 96

World War II, 9; American image after, 158; amicus briefs and legacy of, 152–53; housing shortage and, 16; in legal strategy, 95–96; NAACP after, 114–20; social science and, 140–41. *See also* Veterans

Zarky, Hilbert, 257 (n. 30)

Zoning regulations, 4–5, 134–35